ETHNIC CLEANSING IN
WESTERN ANATOLIA, 1912–1923

Edinburgh Studies on the Ottoman Empire
Series Editor: Kent F. Schull

Published and forthcoming titles

The Ottoman Canon and the Construction of Arabic and Turkish Literatures
C. Ceyhun Arslan

Migrating Texts: Circulating Translations around the Ottoman Mediterranean
Edited by Marilyn Booth

Ottoman Translations: Circulating Texts from Bombay to Paris
Edited by Marilyn Booth and Claire Savina

Death and Life in the Ottoman Palace: Revelations of the Sultan Abdülhamid I Tomb
Douglas Scott Brookes

Ottoman Sunnism: New Perspectives
Edited by Vefa Erginbaş

*Ethnic Cleansing in Western Anatolia, 1912–1923: Ottoman Officials and
the Local Christian Population*
Umit Eser

Jews and Palestinians in the Late Ottoman Era, 1908–1914: Claiming the Homeland
Louis A. Fishman

Governing Migration in the Late Ottoman Empire
Ella Fratantuono

Spiritual Vernacular of the Early Ottoman Frontier: The Yazıcıoğlu Family
Carlos Grenier

*The Politics of Armenian Migration to North America, 1885–1915: Sojourners, Smugglers and
Dubious Citizens*
David Gutman

The Kizilbash-Alevis in Ottoman Anatolia: Sufism, Politics and Community
Ayfer Karakaya-Stump

Çemberlitaş Hamami in Istanbul: The Biographical Memoir of a Turkish Bath
Nina Macaraig

Hagia Sophia in the Long Nineteenth Century
Edited by Emily Neumeier and Benjamin Anderson

The Kurdish Nobility in the Ottoman Empire: Loyalty, Autonomy and Privilege
Nilay Özok-Gündoğan

Nineteenth-Century Local Governance in Ottoman Bulgaria: Politics in Provincial Councils
Safa Saraçoğlu

Prisons in the Late Ottoman Empire: Microcosms of Modernity
Kent F. Schull

Ruler Visibility and Popular Belonging in the Ottoman Empire
Darin Stephanov

The North Caucasus Borderland: Between Muscovy and the Ottoman Empire, 1555–1605
Murat Yasar

Children and Childhood in the Ottoman Empire: From the 14th to the 20th Centuries
Edited by Gülay Yilmaz and Fruma Zachs

euppublishing.com/series/esoe

ETHNIC CLEANSING IN WESTERN ANATOLIA, 1912–1923

OTTOMAN OFFICIALS AND
THE LOCAL CHRISTIAN POPULATION

Umit Eser

EDINBURGH
University Press

Edinburgh University Press is one of the leading university presses in the UK.
We publish academic books and journals in our selected subject areas across the
humanities and social sciences, combining cutting-edge scholarship with high editorial
and production values to produce academic works of lasting importance. For more
information visit our website: edinburghuniversitypress.com

© Umit Eser, 2024

Edinburgh University Press Ltd
13 Infirmary Street
Edinburgh EH1 1LT

Typeset in Jaghbuni by
Cheshire Typesetting Ltd, Cuddington, Cheshire, and
printed and bound in Great Britain

A CIP record for this book is available from the British Library

ISBN 978 1 3995 3324 9 (hardback)
ISBN 978 1 3995 3326 3 (webready PDF)
ISBN 978 1 3995 3327 0 (epub)

The right of Umit Eser to be identified as author of this work has been asserted
in accordance with the Copyright, Designs and Patents Act 1988 and the Copyright and
Related Rights Regulations 2003 (SI No. 2498).

Contents

List of Figures, Maps and Tables	vi
Acknowledgements	vii
A Note on Place Names and Calendars	ix
Introduction: Encounter with Catastrophe	1
1. *Fin-de-Siècle*: Gradual Intimidation in Western Anatolia	38
2. *Ioniki Tragodia*: Greek Administration in Western Anatolia	81
3. *Zoi*: A Survey of Social Life under the Greek Administration	126
4. *Roses and Hyacinths*: Ottoman Provincial Officials under the Greek Administration	158
5. *Millî Hareket*: The Formation of a National Resistance	195
6. *Tartaros*: Destruction of the Ottoman Coexistence	238
Conclusion: Forging Catastrophe as a Solution	264
Bibliography	270
Index	290

Figures, Maps and Tables

Figures

2.1 Smyrna Quay, 15 May 1919	81
3.1 Karl Baedeker's map of urban Smyrna, 1905	127
3.2 Greek Red Cross vaccine campaign	129
3.3 Greek Red Cross and the refugees	129
6.1 A burned Anatolian town: Alaşehir	240
6.2 Smyrna after the Great Fire	243

Maps

I.1 Aydın Province, 1913	3
1.1 Conflict points after the resettlement of Balkan migrants	51
1.2 Forced migrations, expulsions and massacres in the summer of 1914	54
2.1 Territory under the direct control of the Greek High Commission in the Treaty of Sèvres, August 1920	96
2.2 Military Occupation Zone in the summer of 1921	99
5.1 Reworking of Henry Arnold Cumberbatch's sketch map of brigandage centres, July 1906	213

Tables

I.1 Statistics on the population of Aydın Province	22
1.1 List of the governors of Aydın Province	65
2.1 Numbers of pre-war and habitable houses in the coastal settlements of the Smyrna and Karesi *sanjak*s in February 1919	107

Acknowledgements

During the writing of this book over the years, I have benefited from the help of many individuals and institutions. First of all, I am most grateful to my supervisor Benjamin C. Fortna for his everlasting support. Throughout these long years, his name has stood for helpfulness, devotion and courtesy. His patience and trust in me never ceased. I would also like to acknowledge the contributions of the other two members of my supervisory committee, Nelida Fuccaro and Konrad Hirschler.

I also owe a deeply felt debt of gratitude to George Vassiadis, who played a critical role in the later stages of this project and whose comments as an external thesis examiner always led me to sharpen my arguments. A special thanks goes to Frederick F. Anscombe, who has provided crucial insights into the discussions about the nature and discourses of the Turkish nationalist movement in its early phases.

Rachel Bridgewater, senior commissioning editor for Middle Eastern Studies at Edinburgh University Press (EUP), and Kent F. Schull, editor of the Edinburgh Studies on the Ottoman Empire, meticulously sculpted this book. I am profoundly indebted to the Series Advisory Board who provided insightful feedback on certain chapters and to the two anonymous reviewers who read this manuscript at EUP.

The realisation of this book project would have been impossible without the contribution of archivists, librarians and collectors from different countries. I would like to express my appreciation for the staffs of the National Archives at Kew Gardens, London; to those of the Ottoman Archives of Directorate of State Archives in Istanbul; to those at Military History Archives in Ankara; and to those at Centre des Archives diplomatique de Nantes (CADN). My archival research at the CADN, and studies at Centre d'études turques, ottomanes, balkaniques et centrasiatiques (CETOBaC) were supported by the French Embassy scholarships

Ethnic Cleansing in Western Anatolia

in 2018 upon the invitation of Nathalie Clayer, to whom I must express my gratitude. Respectable French institutions have continued to support me in my recent endeavours as well: I paid two academic visits to CETOBaC in 2022 and 2023, thanks to Fondation Maison des sciences de l'homme (FMSH) and the French Embassy, respectively. Neither of these visits could have been possible without the generous help and support of Marc Aymes. For most of the images, I owe gratitude to The Archives de la Planete – Musée Albert Kahn in France and Hellenic Literary & Historical Archive (ELIA) in Greece.

In Athens, Estia Neas Smyrnis (Nea Smyrni Hearth) was always a very welcoming place for me. I should also express my particular appreciation for the directorate and staff of the Genika Archeia tou Kratous (General State Archives) for allowing me access to their extraordinarily rich collection.

In addition to these archives, it was a great relief when Esma Livia Dino Deyer quickly gave me permission to view Rahmî Bey's personal archive kept in her beautiful belle époque-style house at Buca, Izmir. Among librarians, I am indebted to the personnel of the British Library, Bibliothèque Nationale, Hoover Library Archives at Stanford University and the library of the American College in Greece.

Meetings with different people who are enthusiastic about the past of Smyrna and Western Anatolia contributed to this research immensely. Regular meetings held by The Levantine Heritage Study Group provided new dimensions for my research, and Craig Encer, George Poulimenos, Achilleas Chatziconstantinou and Joseph Murat from this group were courteous enough to share their photographs, ideas and relevant primary sources with me. My meetings with Takis Tsakiris both in Athens and in Izmir opened a new path for this research. I am grateful to Dimitris Stamatopoulos and John Mazis for answering during the Balkan Worlds conference in Thessaloniki some key questions about Ion Dragoumis and the variants of the Greek nationalist project. Hervé Georgelin's final comments about the destruction of Smyrna were truly inspiring.

All the chapters in this book benefited from the constructive criticisms and effective comments of a diverse group of people. I would also like to thank Ayça Baydar Reyhanoğulları, Lin Jiao, Chrysovalantis Stamelos, Thomas Richard Bruce and Craig Encer for their feedback on certain chapters. Finally, I must thank my family, who have profoundly supported me during this very long period.

A Note on Place Names and Calendars

The geographical concepts of Anatolia, meaning 'East' in Greek, and Asia Minor do not always overlap since the latter has usually denoted the western regions of the Anatolian peninsula. Following the Ottoman conquest of the region, the new rulers formed the Eyâlet-i Anatoli (Anatolia Province), one of the two main *eyâlet*s, the other being Rumelia, at the end of the fourteenth century. Anadolu Eyâleti never included the Konya region or the territory east of Ankara within its borders. During the reign of Mahmud II, this *eyâlet* was divided into four parts in 1827: the *eyâlet*s of Aydın, Hüdevandigâr, Ankara and Kastamonu. The reason why I have used the term Western Anatolia throughout this study is twofold: the alternative Asia Minor has not been in use in recent studies focusing on the modern period, and the term Western Anatolia denotes fully the geographical area treated in this study.

For major cities, I have used the names in use during the 1920s: for example, Constantinople rather than Istanbul, Smyrna rather than Izmir, Salonica rather than Thessaloniki. The first reason behind this choice is that throughout the analysed period, the apparent name of the province's capital in Western diplomats' documents was Smyrna or Smyrne. The name of Constantinople or Kostantiniyye can be noticed in European and Ottoman documents, respectively, in this period. The second reason is that both Constantinople and Smyrna were very different from republican Istanbul or Izmir in terms of the ethnic and religious constituents of their population. For minor settlements, I have employed their modern Turkish names, giving the Greek names in parentheses in order to facilitate the job of the reader.

Since there is no standard way of transliterating Greek, the transliteration of Greek names presents many problems. My approach for lesser-known Greek names is the use of the American Library Association – Library

ix

of Congress' standardisation method. Owing to this problem, I have not anglicised Greek first names, except where individuals are better known by the English form, as in the case of the names of the Greek kings. I have provided the surnames of prominent Turkish personalities in parentheses as the Law on Last Names (*Soyadı Kanunu*) institutionalised the use of surnames in Turkey only after June 1934.

Various calendar systems have been used in the dating of the sources referenced throughout this study. Greek official documents and newspapers for the pre-1923 period carry the dates written according to the old (Julian) and new (Gregorian) systems. The Julian calendar is thirteen days behind the Gregorian in the twentieth century. As Greek dailies in Smyrna used both calendars, Gregorian dates are given in endnotes throughout this study, whereas in references to newspapers such as the Greek government newspaper published in Athens, Julian dates are given in parentheses with the abbreviation J. C.

Ottoman provincial newspapers were usually only two or four pages in length. Most Ottoman Turkish newspapers used the *Rûmî* calendar, Ottoman solar calendar based on the Julian calendar starting with the year of *Hijra* in 622 AD. All the *Rûmî* dates have been converted to Gregorian dates throughout this study, but *Rûmî* dates have also been given in parentheses for the issue of periodicals.

The formal identity of individuals in the Ottoman Empire rested upon religious affiliations. The *millet*s or religious communities defined the limits of this formal identity. The notion of '*millet-i Rum*' in Ottoman Turkish did not only refer the Greek-speaking Orthodox Christians, but also the Slavic-, Rumanian-, Albanian-, Arabic- and even Turkish-speaking Orthodox Christian communities in the Empire. As such, starting from the establishment of the nation-states in the Balkan Peninsula and the ensuing rise of the nationalisms, the word 'Rum' continued to refer to the Orthodox Christians in the remaining Ottoman territories, including Anatolia, despite the existence of tiny Catholic and Protestant Rum communities. In order to differentiate between the citizens of the Kingdom of Greece and the Orthodox Christian subjects of the Ottoman Empire, while defining the latter, I have used the phrase 'Ottoman Greeks' mainly or 'Greek Orthodox' sometimes, which is the closest in designation in English of the Greek term 'Rōmioi' and the Turkish term 'Rumlar'.

The houses I had they took away from me. The times
happened to be unpropitious: war, destruction, exile;
sometimes the hunter hits the migratory birds,
sometimes he doesn't hit them. Hunting
was good in my time, many felt the pellet;
the rest circle aimlessly or go mad in the shelters.

...

Houses, you know, grow resentful easily when you strip
them bare.

Giorgos Seferis, 'Thrush'

Introduction: Encounter with Catastrophe

From a historical perspective, the quest for a national self, essence or character in the Balkans in the late nineteenth and early twentieth centuries resulted in the impassioned differentiation of all Balkan countries from one another, including the Ottoman Empire/Turkey.[1] In Turkey, universal aspects of identity formation were intensified by a very speedy catch-up-with-Europe modernisation from above, as well as by a traumatic form of nation-building in the form of expulsions, mass murders and massacres. In the late Ottoman period, isolation from neighbours, combined with war traumas (1897, 1912–13, 1914–18, 1919–22), created the image of an opaque, adversely deviant and actively hostile neighbour. The Greco-Turkish War of 1919–22, as part of post-World War I conflicts, was the final part of a state formation process in which the expulsion of non-Muslim elements, especially Greeks and Armenians, was carried out. After several wars, new nationalist elites preferred fostering their mutual non-communication and separating people from their neighbours. This differentiation, from the very beginning, was a complex process that had a deep impact on the components of social and administrative structures, including public administration.

Remembering the past is of key importance in the making and perpetuation of nations; nevertheless, forgetting, as Ernest Renan points out, is also a crucial factor in the creation of a nation.[2] Ivaylo Ditchev, a cultural anthropologist, also asserts that certain historical moments may be forgotten in order to remember since 'memory is necessarily a rearrangement of the past, an introduction of hierarchies, of repression and glorification.'[3] There are two significant facets of silence which were censored by the nationalist narratives of the Greco-Turkish War of 1919–22: the multi-ethnic character of the biggest port city in the Ottoman Empire and the political elites' positions during the war. Firstly, the so-called shameful multi-ethnic character of Smyrna (Izmir), the main port of Ottoman Anatolia, was troublesome for emerging nationalist elites. Two crucial reasons can be enumerated for these efforts to cause to forget the multi-ethnic and multi-religious past of the Empire. The new Republic denied a series of ethnic cleansings performed in the region. Moreover, the Turkish historiographical myth, formulated in the 1930s, did not recognise the previous existence of non-Turkish populations in Anatolia.[4] Secondly, the oblivion of the existence of collaborators and of the volatile line between collaborators and resisters in the Greco-Turkish War was instrumental in constructing a nation. Reticence still prevails regarding the experiences of these people, especially high-ranking Ottoman public officials (*rüesâ-yı me'mûrîn-i mülkiyye*), in contemporary Turkish historiography. In order to decipher this silence, this study conducts research in the various locales of a former Ottoman province, namely the province (*vilâyet*) of Aydın (see Map I.1).[5]

As Alexis Rappas indicated, the notion of community in the Ottoman context was often related, by Ottomanists, to the 'forms of governance based on a delegation of certain fiscal and administrative powers to the leaders of non-Muslim religious communities'.[6] At the onset of the twentieth century, there were not any clear-cut ethno-religious boundaries in Aydın Province, whose coastal regions had a compact Orthodox population. Nevertheless, these Orthodox communities did not include only Greek-speaking people. Some Karamanlides, Turkish-speaking Greek Orthodox people in the Cappadocia region of Anatolia, had previously migrated to this fertile area.[7] The Muslim communities of the province resembled Orthodox communities in terms of the diversity of their languages and ethnicity in that they did not consist of only Turkish-speakers.[8] Relatively small groups of Circassian migrants[9] had also been settled in the province in the second half of the nineteenth century. Many Albanian- and Slavic-speaking Muslims had moved there after the Balkan Wars of 1912–13. Moreover, crucial dialectical differences and different interpretations of Islam made Turkish-speaking Muslims, settled or nomad, a heterogenous population. Neither did these groups present a homogenous picture in terms of political allegiance. There were sharp conflicts between Venizelist and Royalist camps within the Orthodox populations of Anatolia, while the supporters of the Committee of Union and Progress (CUP) and those of the Entente Liberale (Liberal Union), later the Freedom and Accord Party (Hürriyet ve İtilâf Fırkası), competed for political dominance within the Muslim population.

Following the loss of the Balkan provinces, the inner circles of the CUP began to regard Anatolia as the heartland of Turks.[10] Thus, they launched a

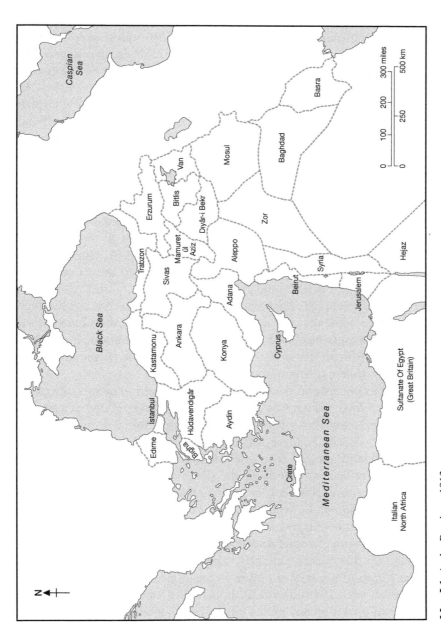

Map I.1 Aydın Province, 1913.

project of nation-building in multi-ethnic Ottoman territories. This project definitely led to a deterioration of relations with the Christian communities of Anatolia. As a result of its economic and commercial growth, particularly since the eighteenth century, Smyrna and its region were central to the expansionist policies of Greek nationalism, that is, the *Megali Idea* (the Great Idea); the irredentist ambitions of Italy; and the nationalisation attempts of the CUP in the mid-1910s. Prominent members of the CUP had already developed a national economy (*millî iktisât*) policy, inspired by the ideas of the German economist Friedrich List. Not only the officials but also local Muslim inhabitants of the region hoped to benefit from the implementation of this policy. Basically, the expulsion of each Christian family made possible the settlement of a Muslim migrant family on the property left behind. Furthermore, the unilateral annexation of Crete by Greece (1908) and the Balkan Wars (1912–13) triggered a commercial boycott of the products of the Greek Kingdom. Ottoman Greeks also continued to suffer from such activities in the years of World War I. With the outbreak of the war, a group of Greeks with British, French or Russian citizenship in Smyrna and in smaller ports on the western coast of Aydın Province chafed at the growing nationalism of the CUP leaders. The efforts to create a Turkish national economy exacerbated the antagonism between Muslims and non-Muslims, especially the Greeks. Even though these events made the coexistence of different ethnic elements in the province difficult, the economic boom continued since the inhabitants of the region shared a common interest.

In order to understand the Greek cause in Western Anatolia, the nature of the *Megali Idea*, somehow a pan-idea, must be investigated as a genuine national movement.[11] As can be grasped from the writings of Greek nationalist intellectuals, there was no unique or monolithic interpretation of this nationalist project. The less common variant of the *Megali Idea* premised a gradual infiltration of the Ottoman governance mechanisms and the emergence of Greek cultural and economic dominance in the Empire. Ion Dragoumis, who served as counsellor of the Greek embassies in Constantinople and various European capitals, and Athanasios Souliotis-Nikolaïdis, special counsellor of the Ministry of Foreign Affairs, had taken up this cause. Similarly, some Ottoman officers, co-opted by the Greek authorities, took positions in the Greek administration of Aydın Province between 1919 and 1922. In actuality, the Greek administration sought to co-opt Ottoman bureaucrats and civilians since Greek expansion in Western Anatolia would be resisted by the local population.

A study of collaboration and resistance[12] would be meaningless without the history of an occupying power since a history of collaboration and

Encounter with Catastrophe

resistance is always equated with a history of the occupying power. The Greek landing at Smyrna on 15 May 1919 is generally regarded as the catalyst of the Turkish National Struggle by the traditional interpreters of the modern history of Turkey. This event, which is historically depicted as the occupation of a city in the homeland, was seen as a milestone at the beginning of the National Struggle, though the city was famous for its crowded non-Muslim inhabitants, who formed the majority of its population. Similar to this classic assumption, the entrance of nationalist forces in Smyrna on 9 September 1922 is accepted as the traditional ending point of the war. However, this is an anachronistic interpretation since military conflict continued until 18 September with the Greek army evacuating the Thracian region at the end of November 1922. Contrary to this widely accepted view, this book argues that the Greek landing at Smyrna was neither a national disaster nor a catalyst for the Turkish nationalist movement.

The Greek administration offered a new political alternative for the local Turkish press as well, with some Turkish newspapers supporting the Greek cause. To illustrate, Sadık Bey, the owner of *Müsavat*, criticised the leaders of the CUP and emphasised their roles in the Armenian massacres. The same newspaper argued that the Defence of Rights (Müdâfaa-i Hukuk) associations would inevitably encourage former CUP members to reorganise in the provinces. *Âhenk*, another Turkish newspaper, claimed that the Greeks and Turks had to coexist for a long time and highlighted the soil brotherhood among Greek, Armenian, Turkish and Jewish elements, celebrating the state of belonging to Asia Minor (Asya-yı Suğrâlılık). *Köylü* and *Islahât*[13] followed this line as well. Especially in the last year of the Greek administration, this sentiment of supranationalist regional belonging was sought among both Christian and Muslim communities as an alternative to the centralising efforts of the nationalists in Ankara. In the context of this type of regionalism, the Greek administration intended to develop a local identity.

Throughout the occupied region, the Greek administration depended on local officials, security units and village guards (*korucu*s) from the local Muslim population to maintain order and overcome resistance movements. They were governors-general (*vâlî*s), district governors (*mutasarrıf*s), head officials (*kaymakam*s), legal experts on religious matters (muftis), prayer leaders (imams), teachers, officers and village guards. Hüsnü Bey, district governor of Manisa (Magnisia), is the most well-known representative, yet there were many other examples. Even in the Greek administration of Smyrna, Ottoman civil servants retained their posts. They were as real as the resisters, and probably just as numerous. In many cases, former

Ethnic Cleansing in Western Anatolia

Ottoman provincial officials became the new delegates of Greece generally without assimilation. Through co-optation policies, political and economic advantages were granted to individuals and social groups in return for their loyalty to the Greek administration. This proves that the co-optation of individuals was an interactive process subject to continuous renegotiations as circumstances altered.

It is usually taken for granted by contemporary nationalist historians that the extremes of resistance and collaboration were mutually contrasting patterns of behaviour. However, the imaginary line between them was, in fact, regularly crossed. My argument is that an intertwined dialectic of collaboration and resistance could be blended together in the same person, even within the boundaries of the same action. To illustrate, Çerkes Ethem, a militia leader of Circassian origin during the war of 1919–22, had to cope with both the Greek army and the centripetal tendencies of the Ankara government. That is to say, his case shows that being a resister did not mean he was the supporter or a pet of the Ankara government. In the moral grey line of in-betweenness, there were people who were compelled to make choices for the sake of survival.

Careful attention must be paid to the drives and motives behind the collaborations of those high-ranking Ottoman provincial officials who were classified by the national(ist) histories of the republican period as traitors or supporters of the enemy. To what extent were the acts of these people considered collaboration with the Greek forces? Were they perhaps a demand for regional stability, a form of power-sharing or an expression of personal hatred directed at the former Unionist cadres centred at Ankara? Did they arise from the constraints of the Ottoman authorities in Constantinople or the desires of these civil servants to be a part of the new governance mechanisms? Did these people plan to benefit from the Greek occupation that would pave the way for the redistribution of wealth in the region? Did they have a secret agenda for the restoration of Ottoman rule in the region through the feeding of inhabitants with hostility towards the Greek administration and attempting to exploit their posts to mislead the Greeks? If not, was it the inclusionary policies of the Greek administration that played a role in the formation of so-called collaborationist policies? Did the fluid and ambivalent character of the Greek administration offer the chance to the dissidents of Unionists to evade the nationalists in Ankara? At the same time, one should consider the functionality of certain modes of behaviour, especially their impact on the social system of an occupied region. Furthermore, a thorough assessment of the forms of this political behaviour is central to understanding the factional power struggles in the pre-republican period and the changing

Encounter with Catastrophe

politics of interests and solidarities. Addressing these questions will yield significant intellectual capacity to analyse the intertwined dialectic of collaboration and resistance.

In David Lowenthal's renowned maxim, for ordinary citizens, the past has now mostly turned into 'a foreign country'[14] conquered from within, and imaginations and myths of nationalism have kept dominating a remarkable portion of studies on history. Most of the nationalist canon in Turkey has been composed of the celebration of the heroic figures who were sacrificed for the glory of the nation and the continuance of the state. Of course, exaggerated stories and mythistories about local contributions to the cause of national liberation prevail in contemporary Turkish historiography. In some cases, national(ist) histories invented imaginary roles for the rural bandits and ex-guards who fought in the armed struggle. Even worse, glorified for their heroic deeds in official histories, many criminals and military deserters actually participated in the war in the absence of better-prepared soldiers. They were not, of course, influenced by nationalistic sentiments but by war profiteering. Official nationalist histories regard them as social bandits, though they in essence pursued their own interests. At this point, boundaries between self-interest and resistance get blurry. Even while evaluating the acts of ordinary peasants, a critical perspective is vital in order to reach a much more nuanced and detailed picture of the interactions between the Greek forces and the local populations. To illustrate, from this perspective, the act of withholding grain supplies from the Greek troops could be seen as an act of self-interest rather than resistance.

Whereas the nationalist canon celebrates the accounts of resistance,[15] the experiences of the Ottoman provincial officials and notables (*eşrâf*) favouring the Greek cause and the coexistence between different ethnic elements are overlooked since they are not compatible with the master-narratives of 'total war against the common enemy of the nation (*milletin müşterek düşmanına karşı topyekûn harb*)'. By means of a discourse of 'unity and solidarity (*birlik ve beraberlik*)', which was forged in the post-war period, the victory of nationalist forces was reconstructed as the backbone of the war against the common enemy.[16] Intensive post-war narrative production, which formed the reality of all realities, sought to transfix the memory of this period. On the one hand, little room was left for co-optation to the Greek administration in the retelling of the war years. On the other hand, nationalism as a collective movement of ethnic resistance served to regain the lost reality and unquestionable superiority of the Muslim community over other groups.

One governor-general (*vâlî*) and two out of three district governors (*mutasarrıfs*) in Aydın Province were accused of collaborating with the

Ethnic Cleansing in Western Anatolia

Greek administration by Kemalist historiography. According to this line, Ahmet İzzet Bey, the governor-general of the province, wanted to prevent any kind of resistance vis-à-vis the Greek army on 15 May 1919. Thus, he disclaimed the news of the Greek landing and blocked the organisation of a resistance movement. Hüsnü Bey, district governor of the Saruhan *sanjak*, also facilitated the Greek occupation of Manisa. Fuat Bey, deputy district governor of Aydın, who attempted to form militia out of Greek and Muslim bands, invited the Greek troops to the town on 24 June 1919.

The Greek administration was regarded as a lesser evil by some of the Muslim notables of Aydın Province, who were sickened by wars, due in part to the fear of the recrudescence of the CUP power represented by the nationalist movement in Ankara. Examples of officials that got along well with the Greek administration were not limited to Aydın Province. Indeed, the Greek administration employed different methods to co-opt Muslim populations in the inner provinces of Western Anatolia. It attempted to embrace Muslim clerics for the purpose of utilising them against the Ankara government. Some of the muftis and religious men had apparently been motivated by their own powerfully anti-nationalist and anti-CUP sentiments. The people who feared the radicalism of the nationalist government in Ankara and remained loyal to the imperial government in Constantinople, such as the Bandırma-based mufti Abdürrahim and mayor İsmail Hakkı, attended interviews with the High Commission (Ypatē Armosteia Smyrnēs). Even on 10 May 1922, the Muslim community of Bursa presented a notification to the Genoa Conference. This notification, which consisted of three main clauses, expressed the following views:

1. The administrators of Ankara, who robbed and seized the destiny of all nations (*bi'l-umûm millet mukadderâtını*), are nothing but the accomplice (*avânesinden*) of the Union and Progress, except that they only changed their name. These have gained the entire world's hatred since they have caused the destruction of several families without disregarding race (*cins*) and sect (*mezheb*) for fourteen years.
2. The Muslim people have fallen into dismay due to the rise of the Union (*ittihâd*), which has revolted against our great sultan and is nothing but a resurrected version of this cursed association (*melûn cemiyyet*), and thus express their wish to live freely by remaining under the rule of the caliph of the Muslims and taking refuge under the protection and help of great countries.
3. We feel obliged to thank the Greek administration, the lover of justice (*adâletperver*), which has ruled Bursa impartially by respecting the local people's national and religious customs.

Encounter with Catastrophe

This document had the signatures of the director of the pious endowments (*evkaf*) in Bursa, the president of the Party of Freedom and Accord in Bursa, the mufti of Bursa, and other notables of the city.[17]

The radical and inflexible nature of the Ankara government also limited the activities of civil servants. After the inauguration of the Grand National Assembly in Ankara on 23 April 1920, civil servants and bureaucrats who had reservations about the nationalist government were gradually exposed to a policy of constant alienation. Article 3 of the High Treason Law (*Hıyânet-i Vataniye Kanunu*), promulgated on 29 April 1920, stipulated temporary penal servitude for any person if there was a reasonable cause to believe that the alleged criminals had encouraged or instigated the crime of high treason through their writings or acts. If these acts led to the violation of public order, the alleged criminal was to be executed. From that point on, the nationalist government of Ankara could readily determine if any speeches or acts were for or against its *raison d'être*. Subsequently, the boundaries between the so-called collaborators and resisters became more blurred.

The Ankara government benefited from the existence of independent resistance groups as much as possible. Until 1921, the regular army of the Ankara government was very weak and the nationalists had to rely on Turkish and Circassian armed bands in Western Anatolia whose incursions had hindered the advancing Greek army. All the same, the strategy of the irregular resistance forces, in preparation for a temporary interception of the Greek army as the nationalists consolidated their power in Ankara, reflected their own divided priorities.

Paul Rexton Kan indicated that high levels of ethnic violence may cause individuals to join a militia as it provides 'more protection than remaining on the sidelines'.[18] During the conscription process, the Ankara government employed a rhetoric that encouraged Muslim men to fight in its own military units, implying that otherwise they would have to fight in Greek troops. This tactical move of the Ankara government left no room for ordinary people in the theatre of war. After the consolidation of the Ankara government, independent resistance groups had to either comply with its ordinances or face marginalisation.

Consequently, the Greco-Turkish War, which led to the expulsion of over a million people from Anatolia, resulted in a bloodbath. As such, this episode became an essential part of the proud national heritage of Turkey, while the catastrophic experiences of the people who established close connections with the Greek administration had to be relegated to oblivion. By 1920, the Ankara government had already charged most of these people with high treason (*hıyânet-i vatan*). When Turkish

Ethnic Cleansing in Western Anatolia

nationalists established control over Western Anatolia in September 1922, many civil servants were either unjustly punished or forced to migrate. After the war, a new regime institutionalised this crackdown by reproaching its political and social opponents who were stripped of their citizenship and exiled by being added to the notorious list of 'Hundred and fifties' (in Turkish, literally, *yüzellilikler*) for collaborating with the enemy.

This study is not a history of the Turkish War of Independence – a direct continuation of the Great War in Western Anatolia – or of what was known in the historiography of modern Turkey as *Kurtuluş Savaşı*, literally meaning the War of Liberation. There is no attempt here to evaluate the standard themes, such as the efforts of the Grand National Assembly to be recognised as a legitimate political body during the war years, or how the nationalist army defeated the Allied forces on various fronts.

Turkish, Greek, French, English and Armenian phrases in the chapter titles have been selected to highlight the cosmopolitanism of Smyrna. Having emphasised the ethno-religious diversity in Aydın Province in the introduction, the first chapter, '*Fin-de-Siècle*: Gradual Intimidation in Western Anatolia', will focus on the demographic engineering employed in Western Anatolia and the resulting ethnic violence on the eve of the Great War. The reasons behind the ethnic violence and the role of the CUP's national economy policy in this series of acts of violence during the World War I years are studied in detail. After presenting a brief account of the ideological tenets of the new elites in the Ottoman Empire, I discuss the roles of the provincial officials in the implementation of these demographic engineering policies. The second chapter, '*Ioniki Tragodia*: Greek Administration in Western Anatolia', intends to cast light upon the dynamics of the Greek administration in Western Anatolia between 1919 and 1922, and the conflicts between Aristides Stergiades, the Greek high commissioner and a very controversial figure in modern Greek historiography, and other interest groups and formations in the region. This chapter will explore the establishment of the High Commission and administrative–social reforms in Smyrna and its environs following a brief account of the Greek landing in May 1919. The third chapter, '*Zoi*: A Survey of Social Life under the Greek Administration', addresses different aspects of daily life during the Greek occupation period, and primarily aims to present the modernising efforts of the Greek administration in Smyrna and its reflections on social life. The practices of internal colonialism inherent in the Greek administration, which sought to introduce new methods and representations in Western Anatolia, were especially evident in daily life.

Encounter with Catastrophe

While analysing the ethnic violence directed against the Ottoman Christian communities in Western Anatolia, particularly in Aydın Province, during the Great War, the first three chapters also set the tone for the fourth chapter. In this chapter, '*Roses and Hyacinths*: Ottoman Provincial Officials under the Greek Administration', the roles of Ottoman civil servants in the Greek administration are discussed. This chapter deals particularly with four case studies exemplary of the so-called collaboration between a group of high-ranking Ottoman bureaucrats and the Greek administration in order to provide a holistic picture of politics at the time in the region. The fifth chapter, '*Millî Hareket*: The Formation of a National Resistance', investigates the relations between the Ottoman officers and paramilitary units, as well as their conflicts with the Greek administration. Instead of providing a virtually endless list of brutalities, exterminations and mass killings, this chapter aims at describing the motives of the several parties that participated in the Greco-Turkish War. The last chapter, '*Tartaros*: Destruction of the Ottoman Coexistence', explains in detail the making of a Turkish Anatolia through expulsions and mass violence orchestrated by the nationalist elites. The Great Fire of Smyrna in September 1922 and the subsequent population exchange had fatal consequences for the Ottoman Christian communities. Along with this homogenisation process, nationalist elites aimed to purge their local opponents in the province through the making of the list of traitors or *personae non gratae* (Hundred and fifties) in the Grand National Assembly of Turkey for the Lausanne Treaty of 1923 and the execution of the former Unionists in 1926. This chapter will demonstrate how these processes were linked.

Literature Review and Sources

Politics and history-writing are so interrelated in the case of the establishment of modern Turkey that political changes in the 1920s brought a new kind of historiography in the 1930s both in Turkey and abroad.[19] As the Kemalist elites of the young Republic were eager to construct a new national narrative that would be a meaningful summary of their collective experience, an official history thesis was formed in Turkey during the 1930s. A commission of historians wrote the textbook *The Fundamentals of Turkish History* (*Türk Tarihinin Ana Hatları*) in the framework of the Turkish History Thesis in 1930. The aim of this thesis was to 'recall the past of the Turkish nation, the roles of which in world history were consciously or unconsciously denied'.[20] History courses dictated by this thesis were taught in all schools, including the minority schools.[21] In 1931, the

Ethnic Cleansing in Western Anatolia

Turkish Historical Association (Türk Tarih Kurumu) was established. Two years later, the Institute of the History of the Turkish Revolution (Türk İnkılap Tarihi Enstitüsü) was established with the intention of researching 'the history of the Turkish Revolution' and disseminating Kemalist principles and reforms among the masses. The personality and ideas of Mustafa Kemal Atatürk have dominated Turkey's history since the early republican period. Even today, courses on Kemal Atatürk's Principles (*Atatürkçülük*) are mandatory classes in Turkish universities. Mustafa Kemal's *Nutuk* (*The Speech*),[22] a speech delivered at the Republican People's Party convention from 15 to 20 October 1927, is a principal source book for these courses.[23]

The textbooks taught in these classes are deeply influenced by *Nutuk* and share a common idealised narrative of the Republic of Turkey. According to this narrative, some soldiers and civilians did not accept the captivity of the Turkish nation at the hands of the Allied Powers, who – after the signing of the Mudros Armistice on 30 October 1918 – occupied some Ottoman provincial cities and anchored ships in Constantinople. Separatist tendencies increased in the provinces and the sultan acted like a puppet of the Allied forces. Notwithstanding this, in Anatolia, a patriot and a successful army officer named Mustafa Kemal took up arms in the name of the Turkish nation. Thus, the date of 19 May 1919, when he departed from Constantinople to Samsun, is traditionally accepted as the starting point of the Turkish War of Independence. In this mainstream narrative, Mustafa Kemal was portrayed as a *deus ex machina* person, a saviour, who was destined to reverse the decay and corruption persisting for centuries. His victory over the Greek army and proclamation of the republic, as well as the expulsion of the treacherous sultan, signified the awakening of the Turkish nation.

This narrative leaves many questions unanswered. Was the Turkish War of Independence a revolution or a civil or ethnic war? What were the roles of different elites in the struggle? Did this war really trigger radical changes in the administrative milieux? Furthermore, this narrative legitimises the imposition of Turkish national identity over all citizens. Thus, genuine ignorance of the experiences of the vast majority of the population (non-elites, ethnic and religious minorities, all kinds of political opponents, women and other subaltern groups) is the result of this Kemalist/ nationalist historiography.

The transition to multi-party politics in Turkey in 1946 stimulated Western academic interest towards Turkey. Furthermore, a tendency for social history appeared first in Europe and then in the United States in the 1960s and 1970s. This trend brought about a second generation of

Encounter with Catastrophe

publications in the form of canonical works about Turkey in the 1960s: *The Emergence of Modern Turkey* by Bernard Lewis in 1961, *The Development of Secularism in Turkey* by Niyazi Berkes in 1963, and *Atatürk: A Biography of Mustafa Kemal, Father of Modern Turkey* by Lord Kinross in 1964. Even though each of these three works constituted a meaningful contribution to the discussion, they did not displace the Kemalist narrative, but rather underlined the leadership of Mustafa Kemal in the National Struggle and his modernising vision.

Early critiques of the Kemalist narrative came from prominent leftist scholars, such as Mete Tunçay, Çağlar Keyder and Erik Jan Zürcher in the 1980s. These works constitute the third generation of academic publications. *Turkey: A Modern History* by Erik Jan Zürcher, which was built on his previous works, especially *The Unionist Factor*, objected to the orthodox Kemalist paradigm and provided a more critical reading of the history of modern Turkey, replacing the work of Bernard Lewis as a textbook. Zürcher pointed out that the early republican period cannot be understood in isolation from the late Ottoman period, and the CUP period in particular.

Zürcher's first book, *The Unionist Factor: The Role of the Committee of Union and Progress in the Turkish National Movement (1905–1926)*, is a major revision in the historiography of the nationalist movement. He argues that the networks of the CUP had a role in the organisation of the nationalist movement led by Mustafa Kemal starting in May 1919. Unlike previous Kemalist histories, one of the principal arguments in *The Unionist Factor* is that former members of the CUP organised the nationalist movement through the founding of a clandestine network, known as Karakol, in October 1918, and the smuggling of men and munitions to Anatolia. Zürcher emphasises that the CUP was effective in four distinct realms of activity: the political sphere, underground work, provincial bands and the military.[24] A second difference between this book and Kemalist histories is that Zürcher does not see a power struggle between Unionists and Kemalists. As such, he underlines the power struggle between those who claimed authority independent of Mustafa Kemal and those who were prepared to accept Mustafa Kemal's authority unreservedly.[25] A third challenge in Zürcher's book concerns the relationship between the Greek occupation of Smyrna and the emergence of the nationalist movement, which is presupposed by Kemalist histories. Zürcher objects to the view that this occupation triggered the nationalist movement and asserts that the idea of a nationalist resistance existed even in 1915 when the Allied forces tried to capture the Dardanelles.[26]

State and Class in Turkey by Çağlar Keyder is one of the earliest works to explore the disappearance of non-Muslims from the economy, formation of a national bourgeoisie and establishment of the new nation-state.[27] Keyder's work brought a Marxist revisionism to the literature and argues that bureaucracy, as a class that derives its power from its position in the state apparatus, both in the imperial and republican periods, is a part of the power structure. Even though social historians often research the history of those who live outside the power structure, Keyder gives a balanced account of these elites or mid-level elites in the state-formation process. He claims that bureaucracy played a pivotal role in the formation of a national bourgeoisie.

Mete Tunçay's book, *Türkiye Cumhuriyeti'nde Tek-Parti Yönetiminin Kurulması (1923–1931)*, explains the foundation of the single-party regime.[28] This book focuses on a nine-year period when many traces of Ottoman society were erased because of formal changes. Tunçay argues that the Sheikh Said Rebellion and the rise of the Free Republican Party (Serbest Cumhuriyet Fırkası) facilitated the emergence of a single-party regime. For example, with the outbreak of the Sheikh Said Rebellion (1925), the Progressive Republican Party (Terakkiperver Cumhuriyet Fırkası) was closed, and all the dissenters were silenced by the Law for the Maintenance of Order (*Takrîr-i Sükûn Kanunu*). Besides, the Izmir Assassination attempt (1926), a crucial event in the political liquidation of the former Unionists, and the Menemen Incident (1930), which resulted in the closure of the opposition Free Republican Party, played an important role in the emergence of a totalitarian single-party regime. Tunçay also addresses the issue of nation-building in the 1930s when non-Turkish-speaking Muslim minorities were provided with a pragmatic path for inclusion yet non-Muslims were not.

Political developments in Turkey continued to influence the historiography of the Turkish War of Independence. Following the *coup d'état* in September 1980, history textbooks were updated to reflect a more rigid, authoritarian and militarist Kemalism. However, in the 1990s, with the end of the Cold War, the Kurdish and Armenian questions, along with other minority problems, secularisation and anti-militarisation issues came to the fore. Since the 1990s, the integration of the histories of different ethno-religious groups into the social history of the Ottoman Empire has been a challenging task, closely related to the democratisation of former Ottoman territories, particularly Turkey, into civil and pluralistic societies. Thanks to the growing scholarship on nationalism and gender, the political structure of the late Ottoman and republican periods is being perceived very differently from how it was just a generation ago. Many academic works explore mass demographic transformations, such as the Muslim migrations to Anatolian provinces after the Balkan Wars of 1912–13 and the massacres and expulsions of Christians from the same region, starting in 1914, in the late Ottoman period.[29] This period is, doubtlessly, very important in the formation of the modern Turkish nation-state.

Reşat Kasaba contributes to the economic history of the region and criticises stereotypical views about non-Muslim merchants. In his article, 'Was There a Compradore Bourgeoisie in Mid-nineteenth-century Western Anatolia?', Kasaba challenges two generally accepted assumptions. The first assumption is that non-Muslim intermediaries constituted a comprador bourgeoisie whose wealth is the result of economic collaboration with foreign capitalists. Secondly, there was not a harmony of interests between foreign capitalists and non-Muslim intermediaries in the region. On the contrary, he contends that non-Muslim intermediaries were actually competing with European merchants. Although foreign merchants, especially the British, brought capital, expertise and means of production, they could not dislodge local intermediaries from commercial networks.[30]

Another of Kasaba's publications, *A Moveable Empire: Ottoman Nomads, Migrants and Refugees*, explores the migratory history of the Ottoman Empire from the perspective of displaced peoples. Kasaba argues that, starting in the nineteenth century, modernisation and centralisation efforts by the Sublime Porte increased across the provinces. In 1831, the first census was conducted, and tribes became the focus of centralisation and forced sedentarisation policies, especially in the Black Sea, Eastern Anatolia and Cilicia. He points out that the establishment of new settlements and decline in nomadism became more complicated due to the wave of Muslim refugees from the Caucasus beginning in the 1860s.[31] Kasaba also mentions mass population movements in the forms of exiles, deportations and massacres, which impacted the Ottoman Empire and the Balkan states in the twentieth century.

Ryan Gingeras's 2009 work, *Sorrowful Shores: Violence, Ethnicity, and End of the Ottoman Empire, 1912–1923*, refutes the Kemalist narrative of the National Struggle, focusing on the roles of Albanian and Circassian bandits and paramilitary leaders in the intercommunal violence between 1918 and 1922 in South Marmara region. Gingeras masterfully presents each paramilitary leader's role in the ethnic and ideological tensions in the region. Even though he emphasises the inclination of Circassian militias to collaboration in the southern Marmara region,[32] the Circassians were not the sole ethnic group that collaborated with the Greek occupying forces. In fact, there was no ethnic prerequisite for establishing close ties with the Greek administration, given that there were Circassian, Bosniak, Cretan, Turkish, Albanian, and perhaps other Muslim groups, whose interests were harmonious with the Greek administration.

Ethnic Cleansing in Western Anatolia

In the recent past, two noteworthy studies have been carried out to establish the history of the southern border of modern Turkey: *Imperial Resilience: The Great War's End, Ottoman Longevity and Incidental Nations* by Hasan Kayalı and *The Unsettled Plain: An Environmental History of the Late Ottoman Frontier* by Chris Gratien. Attempting to write an alternative history of the post-World War I period, Kayalı's study investigates the northern tier of the Ottoman Middle East and perfectly demonstrates that both Turkish and Arab nationalisms envisaged maintaining the Empire and the Caliphate at least in the earlier phases of the post-World War I period. Interpreting mostly from the vantage point of Turkish–Arab relations and examining the 'Ottoman longevity' in the Anatolian–Syrian–Mesopotamian frontier, this important book argues that nationalism did not become the defining political ideology for various Muslim groups in the Empire in this period, but actually an anti-colonial resistance was galvanised against the French and Greek occupying forces.[33] Although the author asserts that 'a reconceptualized Ottomanism, namely a Muslim civic ideal' contributed to the clusters of resistance in the Anatolia–Syria–Mesopotamia nexus, the book remains quite timid in its tone in explaining the difference between this reconceptualised Ottomanism and Muslim nationalism or Islamic solidarity. The crucial argument of this study is that both the Ottoman government and the nationalists centred in Ankara were not so reticent towards the idea of reforming a federated empire with Arabs. Nonetheless, the study does not explain why Arab provinces were not represented at the nationalist assembly in Ankara.

Pinpointing Çukurova and its mountainous hinterland as a frontier and focusing on the underrepresented groups in traditional histories, such as pastoralists, peasants and migrants in this corner of Ottoman countryside, Chris Gratien's *The Unsettled Plain* traces the history of an environmental and social transformation in a period spanning from the mid-nineteenth-century Ottoman project of Tanzimat to the mid-twentieth-century Turkey's technocrat development plans. Analysing Çukurova's regional dynamics of the 'frontier moment' in the remaking of Ottoman society, Gratien's use of the term frontier throughout the book is not the same as the conventional meaning of the term. According to the author, this frontier in Çukurova had three different characteristics: an internal frontier of the state, in which different forms of state existence were maintained; a settlement frontier, where millions of refugees had been poured out since the second half of the nineteenth century; and an ecological frontier, where plants, animals, humans and microbes emanated. He proves that malaria, which as a phenomenon has not been dealt with in detail by Ottomanists, actually had political repercussions over a century.

Encounter with Catastrophe

Apart from these sources, many scholars investigated different aspects of the Empire. Whereas Findley's works[34] aim to reveal the transformation of Ottoman bureaucratic institutions in the modernisation period, Fortna[35] provides a detailed scholarly analysis of changes in Ottoman educational institutions. In particular, Göçek[36] explores the bifurcation of the Ottoman bourgeoisie and its subsequent division into commercial and bureaucratic elements. In Göçek's view, the bureaucratic element of this bifurcated bourgeoisie gradually pioneered the formation of the new nation-state by liquidating the properties of the commercial bourgeoisie dominated by non-Muslims. *Turkey: A Past against History*, Christine Philliou's recent study based on the biography of dissident journalist Refik Halit Karay, shows how interconnected the fates of dissidents (*muhalifs*) such as Karay and non-Muslim communities were during the transition from the Empire to the Turkish nation-state, and reveals that they all partook in 'the same larger story'.[37]

Regarding the studies on Ottoman Smyrna, another volume, edited by Nikos Hatzigeorgiou,[38] presents the intercommunal social and economic relationships encountered in the lively port city of Smyrna, one of the centres of the Ottoman bourgeoisie. Although Hervé Georgelin's pioneering study[39] focuses only on Smyrna and lacks Ottoman archival sources, it does justice in its portrayal of the city as a bustling, cosmopolitan city. Nicholas Doumanis's meticulous research,[40] extensively based on British archival sources as well as refugees' post-catastrophe testimonies, sheds light on the intercommunal violence and ethnic cleansing during the final years of the Ottoman Empire.

Michael Llewellyn Smith's *Ionian Vision: Greece in Asia Minor, 1919–22* investigates the Greek dream of the restoration of a gigantic Hellenic Empire consisting of Ottoman territories such as Thrace, Constantinople, Smyrna and its environs, and the Pontus region. His book reveals the facets of British foreign policy towards the Middle East in the post-World War I period, and emphasises that Greece, supported by the British prime minister Lloyd George, launched her army into Smyrna on 15 May 1919. This moment is accepted as the starting point of the Greek campaign in Western Anatolia, which continued for three years. Although Smith is very skilful in using British and Greek archival materials, Turkish sources are absent in his book. Therefore, the Turkish side of this conflict emerges as a shadowy and ambiguous figure, whose internal conflicts and ruptures cannot be observed.[41]

Unfortunately, the writings of neither Turkish nor Greek scholars are exempt from nationalistic sentiments. While mainstream Turkish scholars overemphasise the disturbing events of the early days of the occupation

Ethnic Cleansing in Western Anatolia

and portray the Greek administration as an arbitrary rule,[42] mainstream Greek historians ignore the colonising vision of the Greek administration. Despite this, some scholars have achieved a number of outstanding works that overcome these problems. For example, Toynbee's somewhat Orientalistic narrative claimed that Western ideas and principles, especially nationalism, haunted Eastern societies.[43] In addition to these scholars, Solomonidis's doctoral study reassessed the deeds and the negative reputation of Aristides Stergiades, the Greek high commissioner for Smyrna.[44]

Despite the proliferation of works on the resistance to Greek rule, the issue of Ottoman civil bureaucrats incorporated into the Greek administration was probably the most problematic part of this research because of the lack of earlier work on this issue. A number of possible explanations for this lack of research come to mind. Firstly, the Kemalist regime made any meaningful discussion about the so-called collaboration very difficult; secondly, available documents on many aspects of the Greek occupation of Western Anatolia are scarce. Consequently, it is not particularly surprising that public discourse on the National Struggle of Turkey still remains emotional and irritable. Unravelling the threads of allegation and counter-allegation continues to be an important challenge for present-day historians.

Archives

The historical and theoretical frameworks of this study are drawn from extensive research on three main points: the political and social conditions in Aydın Province at the beginning of the twentieth century with particular examination of provincial governance, the Greek administration in the province and administrative–social reforms, and the relations of Ottoman civil servants and military officers with the Greek administration. The research presents the central debates and tries to pose challenges to the conventional knowledge on the above subject areas. Key sources include academic books, journal articles and conference papers, especially for the first and second points above. These sources were not chosen according to a particular timeline as chronological restrictions may require a holistic coverage.

This work required archival research both in Turkey and abroad. An archival study was conducted in the Ottoman Archives (in Istanbul), a branch of the State Archives of Turkey. Since the archives of the Special Organisation were expunged and the Central Committee archive of the CUP is missing, it is rather difficult to analyse the power relations between the ethnic cleansing policies and the Unionists between 1914 and 1922.

Encounter with Catastrophe

Nevertheless, useful materials on the socio-economic conditions in Aydın Province, intercommunal violence and nationalist organisations can still be found in the State Archives. Additionally, gendarmerie reports and bureaucratic directives to provincial officials, located in the Ottoman Archives, provide details about the internal situation of the Empire and the relations between the capital and the provinces during this interregnum, though the individuals writing these documents might have had implicit prejudices or value judgements.

The National Library (Millî Kütüphane) in Ankara offers a well-preserved collection of Ottoman census records and travellers' accounts. The provincial press presents information about the political elites and crime at the provincial level. An extensive newspaper collection can also be found in the National Library[45] in Izmir. The local press in Aydın Province deserves exceptional attention, particularly in Smyrna, prior to 1922.

The British National Archives in London also holds a must-see collection of historical documents. Intelligence reports written by ambassadors, consuls, intelligence officers and missionaries contribute to understanding the international dimensions of the conflict and the British policy towards the supporters of the sultan and the nationalists in Ankara. Besides, consular reports from the periods 1908–14 and 1919–22 assist our understanding of the reasons for intercommunal violence in the region. Furthermore, these reports provide information about the relations between the nationalist government in Ankara and the loyalist provincial officials during the early 1920s.

Whereas British documents shed only partial light on the Greek cause and co-optation, and documents from the Turkish archives do not draw a sufficient picture of the period due to self-censoring, the underutilised Greek archives yield new insights. Apart from my archival work in Turkey, I conducted research in the General State Archives of Greece. Since there is not one published monograph on the Ottoman provincial officials in the Greek occupation zone, a meticulous study in the archives was required as I had to rely entirely on original sources.

I used easily accessible sources, such as memoir accounts and interviews, to gain a multifaceted reading of the diverse representations of the so-called collaboration and resistance. In that respect, the governing cadre of the early republican period of Turkey is a generation of prolific memoirists, most of whom committed their memoirs to paper starting in the 1930s. An avalanche of retrospective and introspective memoirs came especially from resisters, each with their own distinct and authentic voice. After considering the cases of well-known and overshadowed collaborators and resisters, I will go on to investigate the relations and experiences of Ottoman civil servants with the Greek administration. Notwithstanding this, these accounts fail to be objective in terms of what they can tell because people often view the past through the filter of the present and so did the authors of these memoirs. It is often the case that the political issues of the time these memoirs were written obscured these recollections. Most autobiography writers unconsciously revise and consciously censor their lives through the lens of age. However, they help us hear the voices of the dissidents of the Kemalist regime, including those who collaboratored with the Greek administration as well as those who resisted it.

Panorama of a Multi-religious Province in the Ottoman Empire: Aydın Province

At the onset of the twentieth century, Aydın Province (*vilâyet*) was composed of four separate *sanjak*s (subdivisions of the province), namely Smyrna (Izmir), Manisa, Aydın and Denizli.[46] This Ottoman provincial unit possessed three major cities, that is, Smyrna, Manisa and Aydın, each with more than 90,000 inhabitants, as well as several smaller towns. With developing manufacturing sectors funded by foreign and domestic capital, Aydın Province was described as the 'richest and most productive province of Asiatic Turkey'.[47] Within its vast borders, the province was a tapestry of various population groups ranging from the urban bourgeois population in Smyrna and its suburbs to the landowners and peasants living in the peripheries of the Denizli and Saruhan *sanjak*s.

Starting in the seventeenth century, Smyrna gradually transformed from a small and quiet western Anatolian town at the foot of Mount Pagus into a rich and cosmopolitan port city of the Ottoman Empire.[48] In 1833, the capital of Aydın Province relocated from Aydın to Smyrna. The Anglo-Ottoman Commercial Treaty (1838), which marked the onset of free trade, played an important role in the development of this city. At the turn of the twentieth century, it was one of the busiest ports in the Levant. Having evolved into an important port for trade routes, Smyrna ceased to be an entrepôt providing agricultural products for Constantinople. It was undeniably the major port of the Ottoman province of Aydın, and its commercial influences extended beyond to the provinces of Hüdavendigâr, Konya and Ankara. Smyrna's population had already increased fivefold to become the second biggest city in the province by the end of the nineteenth century.[49] This port city was described as a modern city full of banks, insurance companies, all kinds of chambers of commerce and small-scale industries.[50] The fleet of both coastal and deep-sea ships waiting for their cargo was used to sail to the nearby ports of Constantinople, Salonica and

Encounter with Catastrophe

Alexandretta and to more far-flung entrepôts like Alexandria, Odessa, Leghorn, Trieste, Marseille and Antwerp. The expansion of the two railway lines connecting the port with the fertile plains in the interior augmented the integration of the province into the global economy.

According to the Ottoman census of 1914,[51] non-Muslims comprised slightly more than 20 per cent of the population of Aydın Province. The Smyrna *sanjak* was home to the most populous non-Muslim group within the province. In other words, the *kaza* (small administrative district governed by a *kaymakam*) of Smyrna, possessing Jewish, Armenian and Levantine communities, was the most cosmopolitan district in the province. Because of its compact non-Muslim population, Smyrna was known by a sobriquet: *Gâvur İzmir* (Infidel Smyrna).[52] While the Aydın and Saruhan *sanjak*s each had almost the same percentage of non-Muslims, 13.6 and 13 per cent respectively, the Denizli *sanjak* was heavily populated by Muslims, with non-Muslims in this administrative unit constituting only 1.7 per cent of the total population.

In the nineteenth and twentieth centuries, each census had its own political motivation to represent different sections of the population more favourably than others. These biases were seen in the dissolution period of the Empire, extending roughly from 1878 and 1922, since some Ottoman Christians did not want to be registered with Muslim civil authorities in order to avoid military service and to minimise their tax burdens.[53] In *Imagined Communities*, Benedict Anderson points out that the official censuses and maps are very important tools for constructing a homogenous space since both the census and the map yield figures for the embodiment of the nation as a real phenomenon.[54] When political incentives are involved, a census is never a pure statistical procedure of acquiring and recording information about a given population and usually tends to support a nationalist view. Therefore, it may be useful to compare data from the Ottoman census of 1914 with those of the Greek census of 1912 and the records of the Armenian Patriarchate from 1913[55] (see Table I.1).

THE MUSLIMS: TOWNSPEOPLE, NOMADS AND MIGRANTS

The Ottoman census of 1914 showed that Muslims constituted about 78 per cent of the total population in the province. Even though the inner towns had compact Muslim communities, the numbers of Muslims were not so high in the coastal towns.

Similar to the other communities, the Muslims did not create a picture of a homogenous group in this province due to the diversity of their languages and ethnicities. Continuous migrations of Muslims from the

Table I.1 Statistics on the population of Aydın Province

| | Ottoman Census, 1914 | | | | | | Greek Census, 1910–12 | Records of the Armenian Patriarchate |
	Muslims	Greeks	Armenians	Jews	Gypsies	Latins	Greeks	Armenians
Smyrna	378,883	217,686	13,207	27,967		1,785	360,792	
Manisa	378,336	47,326	4,637	3,883		8	50,820	
Aydın	237,449	30,399	934	3,151	2,796		22,101	
Denizli	254,399	3,685	617	617			4,613	
Total	1,249,067	299,096	19,395	19,395	2,796	1,793	471,326	25,000

Encounter with Catastrophe

Balkan provinces and the Caucasus were a major factor in the emergence of this non-homogenous structure. The first Muslim migrants were Crimean Tatars, who were settled in the province after the Russian annexation of Crimea in 1783. With the start of the Crimean War in 1853, a second wave of Muslim migrants from Russia came to Aydın Province.

The third wave of migrants dates to the Russo-Ottoman War of 1877–78. This wave consisted of an important part of the Turkish-speaking Muslim populations, and also Slavic-speaking Muslims and Caucasian migrants who had been resettled in the Balkan provinces of the Empire after the Crimean War but were poorly integrated. This third wave did not finish immediately after the war. Feelings of insecurity prompted by living under the rule of a Christian emperor after the Austro-Hungarian occupation of Bosnia Province and the Novi Pazar *sanjak* compelled the Bosnian Muslims to migrate to Ottoman territories in the 1880s.[56] In the last decade of the nineteenth century, there were almost 50,000 migrants who were recently resettled in Aydın Province.[57] Many Greek-speaking Muslim Cretans started to leave that island in 1908 after the unilateral declaration of union with Greece in 1908 and settled along the shores of the province.[58]

The outbreak of the Balkan Wars (1912–13) led to the settlement of the fourth wave of Muslim migrants in Aydın Province. This war deeply altered the characteristics of Muslim migrations from the Macedonian provinces of Salonica, Monastir and Kosovo (*vilâyât-ı selâse*) to Western Anatolia. The atrocities of Serbian, Bulgarian and Greek soldiers and bandits over Muslim civilians triggered the migration of hundreds of thousands of Muslims. Most of the Balkan migrants preferred to settle in either Adrianople (Edirne) Province or Aydın Province. The ethnic diversity of Muslims was based on these migrations. The Muslims in Aydın Province were Turks, Albanians, Bosniaks, Cretans, Caucasians and Tatars.

Due to the differing occupations and settlement patterns, there were discernible social differences within the Muslim groups. Doubtlessly, there was a nascent Muslim middle class in the province composed of army officers, bureaucrats, teachers, religious officials, lawyers and doctors, as well as a limited number of merchants engaged in export trade. Apart from these Muslim professionals, there was a class of landowners who possessed vast arable areas in the province and even inns, small factories and workshops in Smyrna. Although civil servants occupied an important position in society, they were also affected by the poor economic conditions of the Empire. Because of financial difficulties, the Empire could not regularly pay its civilian and military officials, and the wages were often paid late.[59]

Ethnic Cleansing in Western Anatolia

In contrast to the Muslims in Smyrna and some smaller coastal towns, most Muslims in the other settlements of the province were agriculturalists. Owing to the settlement of migrants, new lands were opened to cultivation and productivity increased. Furthermore, migrations brought about the transfer of capital and skills since a number of migrants belonged to wealthy classes, such as landowners, bureaucrats and officers.

Banditry menaced public order in the countryside during the second half of the nineteenth century. Especially after the heavy defeat of the Russo-Ottoman War in 1878, banditry emerged as a security problem in the province. Most of the bands which dominated the mountainous regions were composed of young Muslim military deserters. Moreover, banditry offered a path for young men to earn a living. They began to organise attacks on the trade caravans travelling to the inner regions of the province.[60] In case of emergency, the mountain villages, which were extremely poor and suffered from lack of communication, provided a safe haven for these bandits.

Although native Turkish speakers constituted the majority of the Muslim population in the province, even they never formed a homogenous whole. Varying dialects and different interpretations of Islam discerned Turkic nomads from the urban Turkish speakers. Various Turcoman nomads such as Manavs, Chepnis, Tahtacıs and Tatars lived in Aydın Province as dispersed groups.[61] Shortage of labour triggered seasonal migrations of nomadic groups to the province at harvest time. Apart from these local nomadic groups, migrant labourers from other tribes moved long distances to join in harvests in Aydın Province.[62] These nomadic groups were seen as a security threat by the authorities, and provincial newspapers launched campaigns aiming at their resettlement. In the province, the sedentarisation of nomadic groups, such as the Yörüks, was carried out at the dawn of the twentieth century.[63] The expansion of agricultural lands and production was targeted through the sedentarisation of the nomadic and semi-nomadic groups.

THE ORTHODOX GREEKS (RUMS): THE MOST NUMEROUS NON-MUSLIM COMMUNITY IN THE PROVINCE

In spite of the concentration of Greek Orthodox communities in coastal towns, most of them had migrated to Aydın Province in the eighteenth century.[64] The *kazas* of Urla (Vourla), Çeşme (Krēnē), Foça (Fōkaia), Karaburun (Karabourna) and Kuşadası (Kousadasi) in the Smyrna *sanjak* were overwhelmingly populated by Greeks. Exceptionally, there was a significant Greek community in Söke (Sokia), a district of the Aydın *sanjak*.

Encounter with Catastrophe

From the eighteenth century onwards, rapid population growth in the archipelago, where the land was limited and unproductive, spawned migration to Anatolian coastal towns, such as Çeşme and Urla, and also to the fertile alluvial plains of Menemen, Bergama (Pergamos) and Manisa, and the Menderes (Meander) river valley.[65] Although economic interests were the primary motive of that migration, Ottoman reforms, accelerating from the 1840s on, also encouraged migration. In addition to these insular migrants, some Karamanlides, Turkish-speaking Greek Orthodox people, migrated from the Cappadocian towns to Smyrna.[66]

These Greek Orthodox communities were socially diversified, ranging from peasants working in vineyards and orchards in the countryside, to urban salaried professionals, such as doctors, teachers, lawyers and prosperous merchants who had residences on the Quay. The poor Greeks in urban settlements were basically coffee shop owners, shopkeepers and fishermen.

Orthodox Christians could work in municipal offices and were represented in Ottoman provincial councils. Nonetheless, theoretically, non-Muslims could not be the heads of the provincial councils; therefore, the highest offices of the Ottoman local government were shut off to Christians.[67] The concessionaries and trading partners of industrial foundations were non-Muslims, particularly Ottoman Greeks. Moreover, growing trade between the Ottoman Empire and European states offered many opportunities to Greek merchants. Ottoman Greeks dominated commerce in the ports on the shores of Western Anatolia, and Greek was the lingua franca of commerce in Smyrna[68] and other coastal towns. Besides, Ottoman Greeks were particularly active in the light industry sectors where flour, alcoholic beverages and tobacco products were produced.

Non-Muslim dominance over the commerce and manufacturing activities in Aydın Province was based on the versatility of the non-Muslim merchants, who were engaged not only in commerce, finance and banking activities, but also in mining and agricultural production. Some Orthodox Christians from the Ionian Islands, Chios and Samos could obtain British, French or Russian citizenship in Smyrna and take advantage of the capitulations, that is, the protégé status and privileges given to the nationals of the European powers since the sixteenth century by the Ottoman Empire. These insular Orthodox Greeks established commercial networks stretching from London to Odessa and achieved a kind of capital accumulation. Thanks to their involvement in international trade, a number of Ottoman Greeks formed the backbone of the non-Muslim Ottoman bourgeoisie.[69]

The Orthodox Christian communities in the province experienced a rapid modernisation process in the nineteenth century. Greek schools and language education played an important role in the incorporation of the Greek Orthodox population of the Ottoman Empire into the value system of Greek nationalism. Even in inner districts such as Alaşehir (Philadelphia), by the early 1860s, younger generations of the Orthodox population had started to speak Greek instead of the local Turkish dialect.[70]

The new bourgeoisie represented a modernising force vis-à-vis traditional power-holders, such as the Orthodox clergy and the elders of the community. At the end of the nineteenth century, the nouveaux riches of the community, who earned their fortunes from commercial activities, began to challenge the old elites within the community and tried to be more active in the administration of their communities. Owing to the economic growth of the Smyrna bourgeoisie, the new regulation of the Greek Orthodox community of Smyrna was put into effect in 1910.[71]

SMALL BUT DYNAMIC COMMUNITIES: ARMENIANS, JEWS AND LEVANTINES

According to the 1914 Ottoman census, there were some 19,000 Armenians in the province, whereas Armenian sources claim that their number was approximately 25,000.[72] The Armenian population was concentrated in Basmane, the so-called Armenian quarter (Haynots) of Smyrna, and in suburbs such as Karatas, Bournabat (modern-day Bornova) and Cordelio. Also, there were significant Armenian communities, with their own churches and schools, in the provincial towns of Manisa, Ödemiş, Menemen, Kırkağaç and Nazilli.[73]

The origins of the Armenian communities in Western Anatolia date back to the thirteenth century. The Mongolian incursions of the 1230s had triggered the migration of Armenians to the western parts of Anatolia. Due to the disorder triggered by the Jelali revolts at the end of the seventeenth century, several hundred Armenian families left Eastern Anatolian provinces and settled in Aydın Province, mainly in Smyrna. At the end of the nineteenth century, there were important Armenian communities in the major towns of Aydın Province. The port of Smyrna accepted another wave of Armenian migrants from different Anatolian cities, such as Tokat, Erzurum, Muş and Diyarbekir, looking for security of property and livelihood at the end of the nineteenth century, especially after the Hamidian massacres of the 1890s.

Immediately after the announcement of the Reform Decree (*Islahât Hatt-ı Hümâyûnu*) in 1856, some Ottoman citizens attempted to change their *millet* affiliations without any relevant religious reasons. These alterations arose from a wish to escape from ecclesiastical taxes, a desire for individual political influence, or from the aim of benefiting from

Encounter with Catastrophe

the protégé status offered by the Great Powers.[74] With the official recognition of the Armenian Catholic *millet* in 1831 and that of the Protestant *millet* in 1850 due to the efforts of the missions, the Armenian *millet* fragmented.[75]

Sharp differences prevailed within the Armenian communities. They were mainly entrepreneurs and craftsmen dealing with sericulture, all kinds of weaving, tobacco production and copper-working. Some of the Armenian families who lent their land to the silk trade established commercial dynasties. Besides, there were small Armenian communities in the agricultural sector in the inner towns of this province.

The Ottoman Empire welcomed Sephardic Jews who were expelled from Spain in 1492 and from Portugal in 1497. Prominent Sephardic communities took root in major commercial centres, such as Constantinople, Salonica, Bursa and Adrianople, and continued to speak Ladino (Judaeo-Spanish, derived from Old Spanish). Indeed, there was already an indigenous Greek-speaking Jewish community in the Empire, known as the Romaniotes.[76] Apart from the numerous Jewish populations in Smyrna, where they constituted nearly 10 per cent of its population, smaller Jewish communities were formed in the provincial towns of Tire, Kasaba (present-day Turgutlu), Aydın and Manisa.

The Jewish communities of Aydın Province lost their prominent position to the Christians in the mid-eighteenth century and did not benefit from the economic boom. Their members were generally petty traders and craftsmen, such as greengrocers, tailors, peddlers and shoemakers.[77] In spite of prevailing poverty, small Jewish communities experienced a regional modernisation process thanks to the schooling activities of Alliance Israélite Universelle. At the turn of the nineteenth century, French began to spread as a second language among Jewish communities in the province because of the modernisation attempts within the community.

The Levantines are Latin Christians who were indexed to long-term or permanent settlement in the Ottoman Empire and who benefited from the capitulations. Although the Ottoman census of 1914 showed the number of the Latins (Catholics possessing Ottoman citizenship) to be less than 2,000 in Smyrna, the total number of residents (either Ottoman or European citizens) was more than 20,000 at the beginning of the twentieth century, which shows that the majority of the Levantines did not hold Ottoman citizenship.[78] Catholic Christians in Smyrna had nine parishes, many schools, hospitals and an orphanage. Apart from the old Frank quarter (Frankomachalas) in the city centre, they had settled in the emerging suburban areas of Boudjah and Bournabat, where many Levantine families constructed large mansions.

Ethnic Cleansing in Western Anatolia

By and large, Italian, French, Austrian and Ottoman Catholics constituted the Levantine community. The largest national group was the Italians. Other large groups were the French and Austrians. Due to the capitulations granted by Süleyman I to French merchants, an important number of French residents had been living in Smyrna since the 1550s. The French colony, which nearly monopolised the trade between France and the Ottoman port city of Smyrna, was under the strict control of the French Consulate and the Marseille Chamber of Commerce. The Austrian colony was composed of Venetian Italians, Dalmatian sailors and a tiny group of German-speakers.

Aside from European Levantines, there were Oriental Levantines descended from Genoese and Venetian sailors who had settled in the Aegean islands, particularly Chios, in the thirteenth and fourteenth centuries. These Greek-speaking Catholics, who were usually poor, earned their livings as sailors, small shopkeepers, farmers, and housemaids. Persans were Armenian Catholics who arrived in the seventeenth and eighteenth centuries from the Nakhichevan region near the Ottoman–Safavid border. Other Armenian Catholics, called Anguriotes, had migrated from Ankara Province. Along with the Persans, they are sometimes referred to as Uniates, a pejorative term used for the adherents of Eastern Catholic churches. Nonetheless, there was a very important difference between the Persans and the Anguriotes. The Persans, estimated to include approximately 200 families, were seen to be completely dissociated from the Armenian communities due to their marriages with local Catholics. Unlike the Persans, who were under Catholic Archdiocese of Smyrna, the Anguriotes remained under the jurisdiction of the Armenian Catholic Patriarchate.[79]

Notes

1. Alexander Kiossev, 'The Dark Intimacy: Maps, Identities, and Acts of Identifications', in *Balkan as Metaphor: Between Globalization and Fragmentation*, ed. Dušan Bjelić and Obrad Savić (Cambridge, MA: Massachusetts Institute of Technology Press, 2005), 165–91.
2. Ernest Renan, 'What is a Nation?', in *Becoming National: A Reader*, ed. Geoff Eley and Ronald Grigor Suny (New York: Oxford University Press, 1996), 42–55. Renan asserts that 'yet the essence of a nation is that all individuals have many things in common, and also that they have forgotten many things.' Marc Augé claims that since national memories are required for the rearrangement of the past, nation-states have to forget in order to remember, Marc Augé, *Les formes de l'oubli* (Paris: Editions Payot & Rivages, 1998), 9–37.

Encounter with Catastrophe

3. Ivaylo Ditchev, 'The Eros of Identity', in *Balkan as Metaphor: Between Globalization and Fragmentation*, ed. Dušan Bjelić and Obrad Savić (Cambridge, MA: Massachusetts Institute of Technology Press, 2005), 240–1.
4. Çağlar Keyder, 'A History and Geography of Turkish Nationalism', in *Citizenship and the Nation-State in Greece and Turkey*, ed. Thalia Dragonas and Faruk Birtek (London: Routledge, 2005), 3–17.
5. Despite the fact that the Greek occupation zone covered a wider area including Hüdavendigâr Province, the scope of this volume covers only Aydın Province. Since the south-eastern *sanjak* of Denizli (subdivision of the province) was not occupied by the Greek army, this region is not within the geographical confines of this study.
6. Alexis Rappas, 'Memorial Soliloquies in Post-colonial Rhodes and the Ghost of Mediterranean Cosmopolitanism', *Mediterranean Historical Review* 33, no. 1 (2018), 91–2.
7. Gerasimos Augustinos, *The Greeks of Asia Minor: Confession, Community, and Ethnicity in the Nineteenth Century* (Kent, OH: The Kent State University Press, 1992), 94.
8. See Fuat Dündar, *İttihat ve Terakkinin Müslümanları İskân Politikası (1913–1918)* (Istanbul: İletişim Yayınları, 2001). Dündar's pioneering work asserted that the Unionist leaders' demographic engineering policies for creating an ethnically homogenous homeland affected the lives of Muslim populations in the Ottoman Empire, as well.
9. Circassian is an umbrella term employed by the Ottoman bureaucracy for all the North Caucasians settled in the Empire. Georgians, Laz and Lezgins were among the other non-Turkic Muslims who had come from the Caucasus along with Circassians. These people had been militarised during their resistance against Russian expansionism in the second half of the nineteenth century.
10. Ronald Grigor Suny, *'They Can Live in the Desert but Nowhere Else': A History of the Armenian Genocide* (Princeton: Princeton University Press, 2015), 184–6.
11. See Richard Clogg, 'The Byzantine Legacy in the Modern Greek World: The Megali Idea', in *The Byzantine Legacy in Eastern Europe*, ed. Lowell Clucas (New York: Columbia University Press/East European Monographs, 1988), 253–81.
12. The words resistance and collaboration have an unfortunate fate. They are nationalistically loaded concepts that have lost their meanings. In particular, collaboration fell into such dishonour that it has been almost used in quotidian usage in the sense of crime. When nationalist anxieties became overriding in the writing of history, key words of historical literature took the shape of words loaded with subjective value judgements, such as oppression, heroism and treason.
13. The publisher and editor-in-chief of the newspaper *Islahât* was the attorney Sabitzâde Emin Süreyyâ, who was known by his affinity to Freedom and

Ethnic Cleansing in Western Anatolia

Accord Party. He was executed in September 1922 on the orders of Nureddin Pasha.

14. See David Lowenthal, *The Past Is a Foreign Country* (Cambridge: Cambridge University Press, 1985).

15. Almost all main avenues in the cities and towns in the Aegean littoral of Turkey carry the names of national heroes. Most of the schools and military barracks are dedicated to those heroes. Many marble monuments commemorating the national martyrs have been erected throughout the region.

16. The early examples of this rhetoric appeared firstly in *Nutuk* and in various writings by Unionist elites in the 1930s, and then it found its way into school textbooks and popular publications in the following decades. Beşikçi underlines the risk of the concept of total war turning into a master narrative, see Mehmet Beşikçi, 'Militarizm, Topyekun Savaş ve Gençliğin Seferber Edilmesi: Birinci Dünya Savaşı'nda Osmanlı İmparatorluğu'nda Paramiliter Dernekler', *Tarih ve Toplum: Yeni Yaklaşımlar* 8 (Spring 2009), 49–92.

17. 'Bursa Müslümânları Cenova Konferansına', *Islahât*, 9 June 1922 (R. 9 Haziran 1338).

18. Paul Rexton Kan, *The Global Challenge of Militias and Paramilitary Violence* (Cham: Palgrave Macmillan, 2019), 43.

19. In Europe and the United States, the first wave of written works published in the 1920s and 1930s drew a dichotomy between the old/backward empire and new/modern republic: *Modern Turkey* by Eliot Grinnell Mears (1924), *La nouvelle Turquie* by Berthe Georges-Gaulis (1924), *Petit manuel de la Turquie nouvelle* by Jean Deny (1933) and *Old Turkey and New* by Sir Harry Luke (1936).

20. *Türk Tarihin Ana Hatları* (Istanbul: Devlet Matbaası, 1930), 1–2.

21. Büşra Ersanlı Behar, *İktidar ve Tarih: Türkiye'de 'Resmi Tarih' Tezinin Oluşumu, 1929–37* (Istanbul: Afa Yayınları, 1992), 119–26.

22. This speech stresses the pivotal role of Mustafa Kemal in the defeat of the Allied forces in Anatolia and the foundation of the republic. In *Nutuk*, Mustafa Kemal describes the winter of 1918 as 'the gloomiest period in the history of the Turkish nation'. According to this narrative, Mehmed VI Vahdeddin, the Ottoman sultan, filled the vacuum of power through collaborating with the Allies. In accordance with the provisions of armistice, the Ottoman army was demobilised. Military deserters and demobilised soldiers contributed to the emergence of an internal turmoil. Whereas the Allies began to occupy Ottoman cities, the Greek and Armenian communities supported them. At this crucial moment, Mustafa Kemal decided to start the resistance in Anatolia.

23. In addition to *Nutuk*, publications of prominent mainstream Turkish authors, such as Tayyip Gökbilgin, Mahmut Gologlu, Enver Ziya Karal, Suna Kili and Şerafettin Turan, are also used. See Tayyip Gökbilgin, *Milli Mücadele Başlarken*, 2 vols (Ankara: Türkiye İş Bankası Yayınları, 1959–65); Mahmut Gologlu, *Türkiye Cumhuriyeti Tarihi, Birinci Kitap: Devrimler ve Tepkiler, 1924–1930* (Ankara: Başnur Matbaası, 1972); Enver Ziya Karal, *Modern*

Encounter with Catastrophe

Türkiye ve Atatürk (Ankara: Türk Tarih Kurumu, 1980); Suna Kili, *Türk Devrim Tarihi* (Istanbul: Tekin Yayınevi, 1982); and Şerafettin Turan, *Türk Devrim Tarihi 2: Ulusal Direnişten Türkiye Cumhuriyeti'ne* (Istanbul: Bilgi Yayınevi, 1995).

24. Erik Jan Zürcher, *The Unionist Factor: The Role of the Committee of Union and Progress in the Turkish National Movement (1905–1926)* (Leiden: Brill, 1984), 72. Despite the fact that Kemalist historiography emphasised the novelty of the republican regime, Unionist cadres continued to be active even in the early years of the republic. Moreover, the symbols of the *ancien régime* kept being used in the republican period. The Kemalist regime did not modify the Ottoman flag or Ottoman passports. Moreover, the Ottoman alphabet continued to be in use until 1928. Nevertheless, the human geography of Western Anatolia was completely changed during the war.

25. Ibid. 119.

26. Ibid. 105.

27. Çağlar Keyder, *State and Class in Turkey: A Study in Capitalist Development* (London: Verso, 1987).

28. Mete Tunçay, *Türkiye Cumhuriyeti'nde Tek-Parti Yönetimin Kurulması (1923–1931)* (Istanbul: Yurt Yayınları, 1981).

29. The end of the Cold War led to new waves of transnational movements. Mass immigration and floods of refugees have given rise to economic, social and cultural clashes, feeding into fresh problems of ethno-religious otherisation that have come to haunt the most stable democracies in the world. Simultaneously, Turkey's EU process brought into question a number of minority issues that stem from the legacy of the transition from the multi-ethnic Ottoman Empire into Balkan and Middle Eastern nation-states. This conjuncture contributed to a new interpretation of minority studies and state-formation process. See Martin van Bruinessen, *Agha, Sheikh, and the State* (London: Zed Books, 1992); Hervé Georgelin, *La fin de Smyrne: Du cosmpolitisme aux nationalismes* (Paris: CNRS, 2005); Bruce Clark, *Twice a Stranger: Greece, Turkey, and the Minorities They Expelled* (London: Granta Books, 2006); and Fuat Dündar, *Modern Türkiye'nin Şifresi: İttihat ve Terakki'nin Etnisite Mühendisliği (1913–1918)* (Istanbul: İletişim Yayınları, 2008). The number of collections of essays dealing with specific themes such as nationalism, minorities and forced migration cases also increased. Some examples are *Crossing the Aegean: An Appraisal of the 1923 Compulsory Population Exchange*, ed. Renée Hirschon (Oxford: Berghahn Books, 2003); *Yeniden Kurulan Yaşamlar: 80. Yılında Türk–Yunan Nüfus Mübadelesi*, ed. Müfide Pekin (Istanbul: Istanbul Bilgi Universitesi, 2005); *Türkiye'de Etnik Çatışma*, ed. Erik Jan Zürcher (Istanbul: Iletisim, 2005); *Smyrne, la ville oubliée? Mémoires d'un grand port ottoman*, ed. Marie-Carmen Smyrnelis (Paris: Editions Autrement, 2006); *A Question of Genocide: Armenians and Turks at the End of the Ottoman Empire*, ed. Norman Naimark, Ronald Grigor Suny and Fatma Müge Göçek (New York: Oxford University Press, 2011); *İmparatorluğun Çöküş Döneminde Osmanlı*

Ermenileri: Bilimsel Sorumluluk ve Demokrasi Sorunları, 24–25 Eylül 2005 (Istanbul: Istanbul Bilgi Universitesi, 2011); and *Untold Histories of the Middle East: Recovering voices from the 19th and 20th Centuries*, ed. Amy Singer, Christoph Neumann and Selçuk Akşin Somel (London: Routledge, 2011).

30. Kasaba's argument is backed up in the documents left by British trade circles, Reşat Kasaba, 'Was There a Compradore Bourgeoisie in Mid-nineteenth-century Western Anatolia?', *Review (Fernand Braudel Center)* 11, no. 2 (1988): 215–28. For instance, Aram Hamparzum, an Ottoman Armenian, managed to get into a rough rivalry with the Smyrna Fig Packers Ltd, a British company, between the years 1913 and 1919, first through Rahmî Bey's encouragement, then by forming a business partnership with Levantine H. Giraud, see TNA FO 626/27, 16 September 1919, Smyrna Representative of British High Commission to British High Commission in Constantinople.

31. Russian policy of the deportation of Circassians was a part of the modernisation policy. See Paul Henze, 'Circassian Resistance to Russia', in *The North Caucasus Barrier: The Russian Advance towards the Muslim World*, ed. Marie Bennigsen Broxup (London: Hurst, 1992), 62–111; and Austin Lee Jersild, 'From Savagery to Citizenship: Caucasian Mountaineers and Muslims in the Russian Empire', in *Russia's Orient: Imperial Borderlands and Peoples, 1700–1917*, ed. Daniel Brower and Edward Lazzerini (Bloomington: Indiana University Press, 1997), 101–14. Russia was not the only state which conducted such a brutal policy. There were modernisation policies in the western frontier of the United States as well as in British and French colonies in Africa. The Ottomans were also modernisers and Ottoman modernisation led to similar movements of resistance. Compulsory settlement of the Turcoman and Kurdish tribes is one of the episodes of the modernisation project of the Ottoman Empire. The targets of *Fırka-i Islahiye*, a centralist modernisation project conducted during the governorship of Ahmed Cevded Pasha in the province of Aleppo in 1866, were the chastening of the tribes and the extermination of nomadic societies. Çukurova was the most possible route for pilgrimage caravans; nevertheless, it was one of the most insecure parts of the Ottoman Empire as well because of nomadism and banditry that went hand in hand in this area, see Andrew Gould, 'The Burning of the Tents: The Forcible Settlements of Nomads in Southern Anatolia', in *Essays in Honor of Andreas Tietze*, ed. Heath Lowry and Donald Quataert (Istanbul: Isis, 1993), 71–86; and Selim Deringil, '"They live in a state of nomadism and savagery": The Late Ottoman Empire and the Post-colonial Debate', *Comparative Studies in Society and History*, 45 (2003), 311–42.

32. Ryan Gingeras, *Sorrowful Shores: Violence, Ethnicity, and the End of the Ottoman Empire, 1912–23* (Oxford: Oxford University Press, 2009), 118–23.

33. Hasan Kayalı, *Imperial Resilience: The Great War's End, Ottoman Longevity, and Incidental Nations* (Oakland, CA: University of California Press, 2021), 86–115.

Encounter with Catastrophe

34. Carter Vaughn Findley, *Bureaucratic Reform in the Ottoman Empire: The Sublime Porte, 1789–1922* (Princeton: Princeton University Press, 1980); and Carter Vaughn Findley, *Ottoman Civil Officialdom: A Social History* (Princeton: Princeton University Press, 1989).
35. Benjamin Fortna, *Imperial Classroom: Islam, the State, and Education in the Late Ottoman Empire* (New York: Oxford University Press, 2002).
36. Fatma Mümge Göçek, *Rise of the Bourgeoisie, Demise of the Empire: Ottoman Westernisation and Social Change* (New York: Oxford University Press, 1996).
37. Christine M. Philliou, *Turkey: A Past against History* (Oakland, CA: University of California Press, 2021).
38. *Smyrna: Metropolis of the Asia Minor Greeks*, ed. Nikos Hatzigeorgiou (Athens: Ephesus Publishing, 2001).
39. Georgelin, *La fin de Smyrne*.
40. Nicholas Doumanis, *Before the Nation: Muslim–Christian Coexistence and Its Destruction in Late-Ottoman Anatolia* (Oxford: Oxford University Press, 2012).
41. Aside from Smith's book, studies about the Greek occupation and administration of Western Anatolia are also numerous, including Pallis, Taçalan, Kitromilides, Berber and Erhan. See Alexandros Anastasios Pallis, *Greece's Anatolian Venture: A Survey of the Diplomatic and Political Aspects of the Greek Expedition to Asia Minor, 1915–22* (London: Methuen, 1937); Nurdoğan Taçalan, *Ege'de Kurtuluş Savaşı Başlarken* (Istanbul: Milliyet Yayınları, 1970); Paschalis Kitromilides, 'Greek Irredentism in Asia Minor and Cyprus', *Middle Eastern Studies* 26 (1990), 3–17; Engin Berber, *Sancılı Yıllar: İzmir, 1918–22: Mütareke ve İşgal Döneminde İzmir Sancağı* (Ankara: Ayraç Yayınevi, 1997); and Çağrı Erhan, *Greek Occupation of Izmir and Adjoining Territories* (Ankara: Stratejik Araştırmalar Merkezi, 1999).
42. For example, Berber's work, dealing with the *sanjak* of Smyrna between October 1918 and May 1919, reduces the return of the refugees to a colonisation process in which the High Commission acted in particular ways, especially by using coercion to acquire land for 'waves of Greek colonisers'. However, Berber seems to have forgotten to question to what extent these so-called colonisers were former refugees, expelled from their homelands in 1914.
43. Arnold J. Toynbee, *The Western Question in Greece and Turkey* (London: Constable, 1922).
44. Victoria Solomonidis, 'Greece in Asia Minor: The Greek Administration of the Vilayet of Aidin, 1919–1922', unpublished PhD thesis, King's College, University of London, 1984.
45. In spite of the fact that this library carries the same name with the National Library in Ankara, it belongs to an endowment.
46. As Alexandris pointed out, the *sanjak* borders are not in line with the metropolitan bishopric borders of the Greek Orthodox communities. According

to J. Lacombe, there were six different Orthodox metropolitanates in Aydın province in 1914: Ephesus, Smyrna, Heliopolis and Thyatira, Philadelphia, Krini and Anea, see J. Lacombe, 'Chronique des Eglises Orientales', in *Echos d'Orient* 24, no. 137 (January–March 1925), 90–1. Nonetheless, Demetrius Kiminas reveals that Anea was promoted to a metropolitan bishopric only at a later date, most probably in March 1917, cf. Demetrius Kiminas, *The Ecumenical Patriarchate: A History of Its Metropolitanates with Annotated Hierarch Catalogs* (San Bernardino, CA: The Borgo Press, 2009), 75–83. That these communities were divided in some cases into three *sanjak*s or between two provinces made it difficult for clerical leaders to represent people, see Alexis Alexandris, 'The Greek Census of Anatolia and Thrace (1910–1912): A Contribution to Ottoman Historical Demography', in *Ottoman Greeks in the Age of Nationalism*, ed. Dimitri Gondicas and Charles Issawi (Princeton: The Darwin Press, 1999), 46–69.

47. The wealth of Smyrna was one of the main themes in the accounts of the travellers who visited the province. After comparing the poor in Smyrna with those in London, Allen Upward admits that he did not see any 'signs of misery' in this port city, see Allen Upward, *The East End of Europe: The Report of an Unofficial Mission to the Provinces of Turkey on the Eve of the Revolution* (London: John Murray, 1908), 352.

48. Daniel Goffman, 'Izmir: From Village to Colonial Port City', in *The Ottoman City between East and West: Aleppo, Izmir, and Istanbul*, ed. Edhem Eldem, Daniel Goffman and Bruce Masters (Cambridge: Cambridge University Press, 2001), 87–95. Smyrna was a cosmopolitan city since all its inhabitants were united within a 'community of interests', sharing a common culture and benefits. For Levantine cosmopolitanism, see Robert Ilbert, 'Alexandrie, cosmopolite?', in *Villes ottomanes à la fin de l'empire*, ed. Paul Dumont and François Georgeon (Paris: Editions l'Harmattan, 1992), 171–85; and Philip Mansel, *Levant: Splendour and Catastrophe on the Mediterranean* (New Haven, CT: Yale University Press, 2011), 19–29.

49. Reşat Kasaba, 'İzmir', in *Doğu Akdeniz'de Liman Kentleri, 1800–1914*, ed. Eyüp Özveren, Çağlar Keyder and Donald Quataert (Istanbul: Tarih Vakfı Yurt Yayınları, 1994), 12–15.

50. Many European and American travellers started to visit the western coasts of Anatolia in the second half of the nineteenth century as western coasts of the province are home to ancient cities like Ephesus, Miletus and Clazomenae. While visiting the ruins, these travellers also took notes about the local population, cf. Petr Aleksandrovitch de Tchihatcheff, *Asie Mineure: Description physique, climatologie, zoologie, botanique, géologie, statistique, et archéologie de cette contrée*, 8 vols (Paris: Gide et J. Baudry, 1853–69); Charles Dudley Warner, *In the Levant* (Boston: Charles Osgood, 1877); Paul Eudel, *Constantinople, Smyrne et Athènes, Journal de Voyage* (Paris: E. Dentu, 1885); William Cochran, *Pen and Pencil in Asia Minor; or Notes from the Levant* (London: Law, Marston, Searle and Rivington, 1887); and Vital Cuinet, *La*

Encounter with Catastrophe

Turquie d'Asie, géographie administrative, statistique descriptive et raison-née de chaque province de l'Asie Mineure (Paris: E. Leroux, 1894).

51. The last Ottoman population data belong to the year of 1914. Indeed, this was not a real census but was obtained through the update of the results of the 1906–7 census. In this census, the Ottoman population was presented in twenty-two ethnic and religious categories such as Muslims, Greek Orthodox (Rum), Armenians, Jews, Catholics (Latin), Bulgarians, and so on. For this census, see Kemal Karpat, *Ottoman Population, 1830–1914: Demographic and Social Characteristics* (Madison: University of Wisconsin Press, 1985), 170–89.

52. Smyrna was an important centre of Christianity in the Ottoman lands. It was the seat of three archbishoprics, Orthodox, Roman Catholic and Armenian, and many foreign missions.

53. Alexandris, 'The Greek Census of Anatolia and Thrace', 46.

54. Benedict Anderson, *Imagined Communities: Reflections on the Origin and Spread of Nationalism* (London: Verso, 1991), 168–86.

55. See Malachia Ormanian, *The Church of Armenia: Her History, Doctrine, Rule, Discipline, Liturgy, Literature, and Existing Condition*, trans. Marcar Gregory (London: A. R. Mowbray, 1912), 239.

56. Alexandre Toumarkine, *Les Migrations des Populations Musulmanes Balkanique en Anatolie (1876–1913)* (Istanbul: The Isis Press, 1995), 61–2.

57. Cuinet, *La Turquie d'Asie*, 351.

58. For the migration of Cretan Muslims, see Emile Kolodny, 'Des musulmans dans une île grecque: Les "Turcocrétois"', *Mediterranean World* 14 (1995), 1–15. In Anatolia, Cretan resentment was channelled towards local Christians, who in turn described these Cretan Muslims as the 'most implacably hostile Turks', see Doumanis, *Before the Nation*, 136–42.

59. Donald Quataert, *Social Disintegration and Popular Resistance in the Ottoman Empire, 1881–1908: Reactions to European Economic Penetration* (New York: New York University Press, 1983), 23–5.

60. Reşat Kasaba, *The Ottoman Empire and the World Economy: The Nineteenth Century* (Albany: State University of New York Press, 1988), 52–6.

61. A relatively great number of semi-nomadic communities were living in Eastern Anatolia and Cilicia.

62. Reşat Kasaba, *A Moveable Empire: Ottoman Nomads, Migrants and Refugees* (Seattle: University of Washington Press, 2009), 32–3.

63. Cuinet, *La Turquie d'Asie*, 348.

64. Indeed, this century was a period of expansion for Greek Orthodox merchants in the Ottoman Empire, see Traian Stoianovich, 'The Conquering Balkan Orthodox Merchant', *The Journal of Economic History* 20, no. 2 (June 1960), 234.

65. In fact, the coastal towns of Aydın province had already attracted Greek Orthodox merchants from the Aegean islands since the seventeenth century. Similarly, the Veneto-Ottoman War of 1645–69, which shifted the control of

Ethnic Cleansing in Western Anatolia

Eastern Mediterranean trade from Salonica to Smyrna, triggered the migration of Chiot merchants to Smyrna and Çeşme.

66. Paschalis Kitromilides and Alexis Alexandris, 'Ethnic Survival, Nationalism, and Forced Migration: The Historical Demography of the Greek Community of Asia Minor at the Close of the Ottoman Era', *Deltio Kentrou Mikrasiatikon Spoudon*, 5 (1984–5), 13.

67. Ayşe Ozil, *Orthodox Christians in the Late Ottoman Empire: A Study of Relations in Anatolia* (London: SOAS/Routledge Studies on the Middle East, 2012), 46. In some exceptional cases, non-Muslims were able to get higher offices in the public administration, such as pashas and consuls in Europe. In 1919, a certain Anastas was appointed as the district governor (*mutasarrıf*) of Afyonkarahisar, see TNA FO 608/112, 25 August 1919, General Staff Intelligence report.

68. Except for a small number of Muslims, every dweller could speak Greek in the greatest port of Anatolia. A recollection from Bayrakli, a suburb of Smyrna, shows how the use of Greek was extensive even among the other communities: 'We spoke Greek, the dialect of Smyrna (Smyrneika). We did not know Turkish except one or two phrases. The strangers in Baïrakli also understood Greek. The Armenians, of course, the Jews, as well, used to speak Greek', see Hervé Georgelin, 'Armenian Inter-community Relations in Late Ottoman Smyrna', in *Armenian Smyrna/Izmir*, ed. Richard G. Hovannisian (Costa Mesa, CA: Mazda Publishers, 2012), 180–1.

69. Reşat Kasaba, 'Economic Foundations of a Civil Society: Greeks in the Trade of Western Anatolia, 1840–1876', in *Ottoman Greeks in the Age of Nationalism*, ed. Dimitris Gondicas and Charles Issawi (Princeton: Darwin Press, 1999), 77–88.

70. Paschalis Kitromilides, '"Imagined Communities" and the Origins of National Question in the Balkans', *European History Quarterly*, 19 (1989), 167–75.

71. Sia Anagnostopoulou, 'The Process of Defining Izmir's "Historical National Mission"', in *The Passages from the Ottoman Empire to the Nation-states: A Long and Difficult Process: The Greek Case* (Istanbul: The Isis Press, 2004), 77–86.

72. Ormanian, *The Church of Armenia*, 239.

73. Osman Köker, 'Tehcir Öncesinde Osmanlı Devleti'nde Ermeni Varlığı', in *İmparatorluğun Çöküş Döneminde Osmanlı Ermenileri: Bilimsel Sorumluluk ve Demokrasi Sorunları*, ed. Fahri Aral (Istanbul: Istanbul Bilgi University Press, 2011), 23.

74. Roderic Davison, *Reform in the Ottoman Empire, 1856–76* (New York: Gordion Press, 1973), 118–19.

75. Bruce Masters, *Christians and Jews in the Ottoman Arab World: The Roots of Secterianism* (Cambridge: Cambridge University Press, 2001), 108–9.

76. The Romaniote community chose a name from the Old Testament for their synagogues: Etz Hayyim (The Tree of Life). The extant Etz Hayyim

Encounter with Catastrophe

synagogue, along with other active synagogues in Smyrna, demonstrate the existence of a Romaniote Jewish community in Aydın Province.

77. Siren Bora, *İzmir Yahudileri Tarihi, 1908–1923* (Istanbul: Gözlem Basın ve Yayın, 1995), 117–21.

78. Oliver Jens Schmitt, 'Les Levantines, les Européens et le jeu d'identités', in *Smyrne, la ville oubliée?*, ed. Marie-Carmen Smyrnelis (Paris: Editions Autrement, 2006), 111–12.

79. Anahide Ter Minassian, 'Les Arméniens: Le dynamisme d'une petite communauté', in *Smyrne, la ville oubliée?*, ed. Marie-Carmen Smyrnelis (Paris: Editions Autrement, 2006), 70–91. At the beginning of the twentieth century, the Armenian Catholic Patriarchate appointed a simple priest as the patriarchal vicar in Smyrna in order to conduct services for the little Armenian Catholic community, cf. Raymond Janin, 'L'Eglise Arménienne', in *Echos d'Orient* 18, no. 110–11 (January–April 1916), 27.

Chapter 1

Fin-de-Siècle: Gradual Intimidation in Western Anatolia

European history in the nineteenth and twentieth centuries was marked by the mass deportations, resettlements, expulsions and forced migrations stemming from the emergence of nationalism and the resulting shift in people's sense of belonging and identity. With the dissolution of the great mainland empires in Eastern Europe in 1918, the concept of nation emerged as the most common source of belonging and loyalty. An ethnically homogenous nation-state paradigm with demographic engineering policies in the forms of resettlement, exile, forced migration and massacre became prevalent throughout Europe. Particularly in Eastern Europe and the Balkans, where complex cultural–ethnic amalgamation impeded purist expectations of the new nationalist elites, expansionism triggered migrations, exiles and massacres of undesired ethnic groups in the early twentieth century. New elites in the Ottoman Empire also contemplated the creation of a new nation through demographic engineering. The Christian, especially Greek Orthodox, communities in the Aydın Province, for one, were damaged by these policies due to the strategic importance of the province, the communities' compact presence in coastal towns and their prominent roles in the provincial economy.[1]

This chapter will focus on demographic engineering policies and the resulting ethnic violence in the region. After presenting a brief account of the ideological tenets of the new elites, I examine the roles of the provincial officials in these policies, and the radicalised implementation of these policies over time and their outcomes during World War I. The chapter concludes with an outline of the changing political atmosphere in the post-armistice period.

Ideological Tenets: Demographic Engineering on the Eve of World War I

The Tanzimat reforms and the failed attempt of Ottomanism (*Osmanlılık*) triggered the bifurcation of Ottoman society in the nineteenth century. As a result, young, middle-class Muslims who could not be employed in the business sector filled the ranks of the civil service and the military by way of state-run education and recruitment, while non-Muslim communities, especially Greeks and Armenians, constituted a nascent Ottoman bourgeoisie thanks to their multilingualism, business contacts and kinships abroad.[2]

Members of the Young Turk opposition movement, settled mainly in European capitals, especially Paris, demanded that the Hamidian regime restore the constitution. The core of this opposition movement was formed by disaffected intellectuals, but also included younger generations of Ottoman officers and high-ranking administrators, as well as civilian professions such as doctors and teachers. In its early years, the movement was not an explicitly Turkish nationalist organisation, having Muslim men from various ethnic backgrounds such as Turkish, Arab, Albanian, Circassian and Kurdish, and supported the idea of a union of ethnic elements (*ittihâd-ı anâsır*).[3]

Nearly two decades after the formation of this group, ideological disputes emerged at the First Congress of Ottoman Opposition in February 1902 in Paris that displayed the existence of two different factions within the movement. Representatives from almost all major ethnic groups participated in this congress, a forum for the negotiation of various opposition forces. The first faction, led by Prince Sabahaddin, argued that the provinces should have a decentralised administration in which all the ethno-religious communities were represented and that liberal economic policies should be conducted throughout the Empire. The second faction, led by Ahmet Rıza, championed the idea of a centralised constitutional monarchy.

The Committee of Union and Progress (CUP) descended directly from Ahmet Rıza's faction. Regarding the CUP's upper echelons, members from the Balkan provinces became increasingly prominent.[4] The young military officers who supported the movement were mostly Muslims from the Macedonian provinces. Since most of them had experienced urban life in the Balkan provinces, they were aware of the differences between the local Christian bourgeoisie and Muslim middle classes. These differences, being reproduced by *millet* and foreign schools, manifested themselves in the economic activities of these groups. Much to the dismay of the

Ethnic Cleansing in Western Anatolia

Muslims, railways, maritime activities, insurance companies, banks, hotels, department stores, and wineries were mainly controlled by non-Muslim and foreign entrepreneurs.

Starting with the restoration of the constitution in July 1908, the CUP was able to seize power in due course for three reasons. First of all, those who established the committee were acquainted with the rich tradition of secret societies and adopted the small-cell organisational structure of the Carbonari, a secret revolutionary society founded in nineteenth-century Italy, where a member was allowed to meet, at most, eight or ten other members. In this way, if one of the cells was discovered by the secret police, adjacent cells could immediately protect themselves.[5] Secondly, unlike the Christian armed groups in the Macedonian provinces, the CUP targeted the sultan rather than other communities in these provinces. Indeed, while spreading into the cities and towns in the region, the CUP appealed to Christian guerrilla bands for cooperation against the central authority in Constantinople. The third and the most important reason for the rapid growth of the CUP was its infiltration into the Third Army in Salonica. This army constituted the most intense focus of opposition against Abdülhamit II (r. 1876–1909) and the main bastion of the CUP in the Macedonian provinces.

The idea of mass mobilisation was combined with Social Darwinism, the growing importance of military assets and the centrality of Muslim nationalism in these demographic engineering campaigns of the Unionists. Having been educated in the most prestigious schools in the Ottoman Empire, Unionists could speak at least one European language and were highly familiar with the concepts of motherland, liberty and nation. Their materialist and elitist–authoritarian orientation originated from the positivist ideas of Auguste Comte, whose views resonated with the Unionists' aims of secularism and demand for centralisation. Moreover, most of them favoured Gustave Le Bon's cynical view of the masses as a purposeless mob that required guidance by a group of forceful elites, believing that a new nation may be built through social engineering.[6] In other words, in their mindset, a small group of elites must rule the country on behalf of the majority. During their education, these men had been deeply influenced by European-based nationalist and Social Darwinist ideas, which sought to apply biological concepts to politics. According to Social Darwinism, the principle of the 'survival of the fittest' is famously used to justify demographic engineering. As Frederick F. Anscombe points out, for Unionists, 'sultanic despotism was an affliction weakening the empire; as medical science showed, amputation of a diseased limb was sometimes necessary to save life, and squeamishness over such tasks

Gradual Intimidation in Western Anatolia

only hurt the patient in the long run.'[7] Thus, the Unionists made use of biological terms while identifying non-Muslim groups as outsiders. In his memoirs, Kuşçubaşı Eşref, a Unionist, depicted the non-Muslims as 'internal tumours' in the body of the Empire and hence they had to be 'excised'.[8]

The pan-Turkic movement, manifested in the written works of a group of Muslim intellectuals that migrated from Russia to Ottoman lands as a response to pan-Slavism, influenced the policies of the CUP.[9] These intellectuals underlined the linguistic affinities between the Turkish-speaking populations in the Ottoman Empire and the Turkic peoples in Russia. Furthermore, pan-Turkists were heavily inspired by the ideas of the populist and pre-socialist *narodniks*.[10] *Narodnik* ideas were introduced to the Ottoman Empire by Yusuf Akçura, a Tatar émigré, activist and ideologue of pan-Turkism, who was one of the founders and the editor of the periodical *Türk Yurdu* (Turkish Homeland).[11] He published his pioneering article 'Üç Tarz-ı Siyaset' (Three Types of Policy) in 1904 in the Cairo-based journal *Türk*. In that article, he did not give any credit to Ottomanism and stressed that Islamist and pan-Turkist ideas must be brought to the fore. He claimed that Islam should be one of the main features of the prospective pan-Turkic union among the different Turkic groups.[12]

The pan-Turkic movement, a brainchild of Russian Muslim émigrés, gained considerable influence within the CUP after 1908. The establishment of the first Turkish Hearth (Türk Ocağı) in Constantinople in 1912 aimed at awakening of nationalist feelings, and in itself was evidence of the influence of the pan-Turkic movement in the Turkish nationalism of the CUP. Turkish Hearth branches became the meeting places of CUP members, hosting nationalist lectures and theatrical performances to promote pan-Turkic identity among the new elites.

The largely peasant Muslim communities of Anatolia were considered suitable for assimilation into Turkish culture by Unionist intellectuals, particularly Mehmet Ziyâ Gökalp, a pioneer nationalist intellectual born in Çermik in Diyarbekir Province in 1876 to a Kurdish father and a Turcoman mother, daughter of a local landlord. The frontier environment of Diyarbekir Province had formed Gökalp's sense of national identity. After completing his high school education in Diyarbekir, he settled in Constantinople in 1896, where he built relationships with members of the Young Turk movement. He returned to Diyarbekir for a short time in order to establish the provincial branch of the CUP with the encouragement of his maternal uncle, Pirinççizâde Arif Efendi, the Unionist representative of Diyarbekir.[13] After participating in the Congress of Union and Progress in Salonica in September 1909, Gökalp was elected a member of the

Ethnic Cleansing in Western Anatolia

Central Committee of the CUP in 1910. He moved to Constantinople along with the Central Committee in 1912.

Inspired by the Durkheimian theory of the organic society, in which religion plays an important role, Ziyâ Gökalp emerged as a leading Unionist ideologue. His articles in the journal *Genç Kalemler* (Young Pens) implied a cultural–religious conception of Turkishness that could be inclusive of Kurds, Balkan Muslims and Caucasian migrants. In his writing, Islam constituted the most important bond among these communities for maintaining the Empire. Any Muslim individual who embraced Turkish culture (*hars*) had to be accepted as a Turk, regardless of their ethnic background. However, in his article 'Yeni Hayat ve Yeni Kıymetler' (New Life and New Values), published in Salonica in 1911, he argued that the Christian communities in the Empire, mainly Ottoman Greeks and Armenians, did not share the same culture with Ottoman Muslims. Thus, they constituted an unassimilable mass for his nation-building project.[14]

After the constitutional revolution of 1908 and the restoration of the constitutional monarchy, the Ottoman administration sought to form a national economy in accordance with the vision of the CUP. In one of his articles in *Türk Yurdu*, Turkish historian Fuad Köprülü described the Ottoman Empire as a circle, whose structure involved Turkishness (*Türklük*) at the centre, Islam (*İslâmlık*) around the centre, and Christian elements (*Hıristiyan unsurlar*) at the periphery.[15] Alexander Helphand, a Russian Jew from Berezino who moved to Constantinople in 1910 after having joined the Socialist Democratic Party in Germany, also penned his ideas in *Türk Yurdu* under the pen name Parvus Efendi. His main themes were the necessity of national economy policies and the formation of a so-called indigenous bourgeoisie. According to Helphand, the government must abolish capitulations and liquidate the properties of the non-Muslim bourgeoisie in order to follow the path of a national economy. Mehmet Câvit Bey, minister of finance (1909–11 and March–November 1914), was one of the first designers of national economy policies.[16]

While the nation-building project of the Unionists had a strong Islamic tone, the crucial term to define Unionist rule was '*millî*', which derived from the Arabic word '*al-milla*', meaning the true religion, that is, Islam. Inspired by the ideas of Ziyâ Gökalp, Unionist leaders regarded the Muslim population as part and parcel of the Empire, whereas the loyalty of the Christian communities remained questionable, leading to a hostile approach towards Ottoman Christians.[17] A set of *millî* associations, societies, banks, state-owned enterprises and cooperatives, all of which embraced the adjective *millî*, were established in order to support Muslim entrepreneurs in the social and economic lives of the provinces.

Gradual Intimidation in Western Anatolia

The regulations of these *millî* organisations did not limit the participation of the Ottoman Christians, yet *millî* was in practice synonymous with Ottoman Muslim.

After the Balkan Wars in 1912–13, the remaining territories of the Empire were overwhelmingly inhabited by the Muslim population. Unionist leaders implemented a policy based on the Muslim elements of the Empire, since the leading figures and intellectuals of the CUP were mainly of Turkish descent along with a significant number of Albanians, some Kurds and Circassians. Unionist intellectuals, such as Ziyâ Gökalp, claimed that all Muslim ethnic groups within the Empire could be integrated into a unified political body through voluntary assimilation. Therefore, the Unionist leaders appropriated Islamic themes in order to consolidate the support of the Muslim population. As a result, a Muslim collective identity was produced in opposition to the Ottoman Christians, who were purposely excluded from the committee.[18]

Restructuring the Population

Demographic engineering is a concept employed to explain the ethnic cleansing campaigns and forced migrations in many places of the world during modern times. Any state programme or project that aims to deliberately change the characteristics of a population in a specific region based on religious or ethnic discrimination, as well as ideological or political reasons, can be evaluated within the framework of demographic engineering. Demographic engineering methods (manipulations, economic boycotts, violent riots, compulsory population exchanges, expulsions and massacres) are a feature of the modern period when nationalism became one of the dominant ideologies.[19]

The Ottoman Empire had of course implemented forced resettlement to ensure political control in conquered lands. However, creating ethnic homogeneity was not the objective of these forced resettlements until the last quarter of the nineteenth century. During the decade following the Russo-Ottoman War in 1877–78, Abdülhamit II[20] planned to change the ethno-religious structure of the provinces.[21] Due to migrations from the Balkan provinces and the Caucasus, the number of Muslims continuously increased, reaching 80 per cent in the Anatolian provinces by the 1880s. Thus, Abdülhamit demanded a new policy geared to changing the demographic structure of certain regions. These migrations made him more determined to adopt an Islamist policy. As a result, a detailed resettlement policy was prepared for areas of strategic importance, such as the southern bank of the Danube, the Straits region and Cilicia.

Ethnic Cleansing in Western Anatolia

After the Berlin Congress in 1878, sociopolitical turmoil increased in the Macedonian provinces of the Empire. The Ilinden Uprising, an organised revolt against Ottoman rule in August 1903, and attacks by bands of the Internal Macedonian Revolutionary Organisation (IMRO), a Slavic nationalist movement, had devastating effects on the Greek Orthodox and Muslim populations in Monastir. As a reaction to the revolt, Muslim notables (*eşrâf*) assisted in the formation of Muslim paramilitary groups to support the Ottoman army. As the line between criminals and officers had already become blurred within the state apparatus since the rule of CUP, Ottoman officers would mimic politicised gang violence (*cheta* movements) in the Macedonian provinces.[22]

After the restoration of the constitution, there was an overly optimistic faith among the public in what this set of fundamental laws could achieve. Notwithstanding this, the CUP-dominated government was disposed to suppress civic liberties and limit the public participation of non-Muslim communities. With the Empire's territorial losses, frustrated attempts to create a common Ottoman identity and constant European interventions since the nineteenth century, Unionist leaders were persuaded that the survival of the Empire could be guaranteed only through leaning on the Turkish population. Since the Unionists regarded non-Turkish groups in border zones as a potential security risk and a pretext for foreign interventions, the CUP embarked on a secret campaign to weaken and destroy these so-called disloyal elements.

In May 1909, Mahmut Şevket Pasha, leader of the Mobile Expedition Army (Hareket Ordusu), was strongly in favour of recruiting non-Muslims. The imposition of compulsory military service for non-Muslims was considered burdensome for these communities, viewed, especially by the Greek Orthodox communities, as a step towards the Turkification of the Empire. Thus, the main opposition against the idea of universal conscription came from the Orthodox clergy. Owing to the insistence of the Orthodox clergy, Christian soldiers were allowed to take an oath on the Bible. Despite protests, the law for universal conscription was passed in July 1909.[23] The notables of the Greek, Bulgarian and Armenian communities declared that they approved of the changes to the conscription law, but with a prerequisite that members of their communities should serve under the command of Christian officers of the same ethnic origins. A circular announcing that no exemption tax (*bedel-i askerî*) would henceforth be exacted from non-Muslims was delivered to the provinces in August 1909. As a reaction to this decision, many Ottoman Greeks left the Empire or sought foreign passports.[24]

With the Associations Law (*Cemiyetler Kanunu*) issued on 16 August 1909, political associations carrying the names of ethnic groups were

Gradual Intimidation in Western Anatolia

banned; this was followed by the abolition of some Greek and Armenian associations.[25] The CUP pressed for the use of Ottoman Turkish in official correspondence as 'an effort to promote a far more rationalised and integrated state'.[26] The Law for the Prevention of Brigandage (*Men-i Şekavet ve Mütecâsirlerin Takîb ve Tedîbi Kanunu*) of 27 September 1909 provided measures for disarming armed groups of bandits. This law, which was designed for the Empire's Balkan provinces, was enforced in Aydın Province as well.[27]

Relations between the Unionists and local Christians deteriorated during the Italo-Ottoman War of 1911–12.[28] Immediately after the Bulgarian retreat during the Second Balkan War in 1913, the Ottoman army and paramilitary units began to destroy Ottoman Christian villages in Eastern Thrace, namely Adrianople Province.[29] Owing to these attacks, the non-Muslim population in this strategic region diminished. The Treaty of Constantinople, signed between Bulgaria and the Ottoman Empire in September 1913, stipulated the mutual exchange of populations in a specified zone along the borders. These policies gained new momentum in the summer of 1914, now mainly targeting Greek towns and villages on the Aegean coast.

After 1908, the CUP continued to hold the support of paramilitary formations and their prominent members, and also attempted to expand the ethnic base of paramilitary formations by including Circassians, Cretans and Bosniaks. Many young Albanian paramilitary troops joined the army under the direction of CUP magnates and participated in guerrilla warfare in the Macedonian provinces.[30] These gunmen were possibly chosen within a kind of patronage system in which smaller local bands came under the authority of a more important patron. Even though dispossessed men had been recruited into militias before the rise of the Macedonian question, new stress on the paramilitary struggle gradually instigated the transformation of formerly criminal groups into political alliances. For the formation of such paramilitary groups, Balkan refugees provided a significant source of recruits.

A number of officers attached to Enver Bey known as *fedâîs* were very active in the recapture of the old Ottoman capital of Adrianople from Bulgarian forces during the Second Balkan War in 1913. Enver's *fedâîs* were organised into secret operation units named Special Organisation (Teşkîlât-ı Mahsûsa). As Benjamin C. Fortna has noted, this organisation was a paramilitary force dedicated to intelligence gathering, warfare and propaganda.[31] Following the Bulgarian evacuation of Western Thrace, Special Organisation officers, including Kuşçubaşı Eşref, prompted local notables to establish the Provisional Government of Western Thrace

(Garbî Trakya Hükûmet-i Muvakkatası). According to Hüsamettin Ertürk's memoirs, apart from Kuşçubaşı, several members of the Special Organisation, such as Çerkes Ethem and his brothers, Sapancalı Hakkı and İskeçeli Mülâzım Arif, took part in paramilitary activities in this region.[32]

In conformity with the articles of the Treaty of Bucharest in August 1913, the Greek army broke the resistance of this organisation and then relinquished the control of the region to the Bulgarian army.[33] Nevertheless, the Special Organisation, whose cadres were based on Enver Pasha's personal networks, was enlarged as Kuşçubaşı Eşref was secretly recalled by the CUP leadership in late 1913.[34] This paramilitary group was reorganised as the protagonist of the dirty deeds of the CUP, such as assassinations, boycotts, liquidation of property and massacres directed at Ottoman Christians and the party's dissidents during the war years, carrying out conventional military operations as well. Although its core units were dominated by ethnic Turks, provincial gangs were recruited from Circassian, Cretan and Albanian migrants as well as local military deserters and prisoners in Aydın Province. The CUP spearheaded the formation of armed bands, killed Greek landholders and burned their properties. Although it was the Unionists who organised these attacks, the government tried to give the impression that it had nothing to do with these events.

The members of the Special Organisation exhibit the intertwined structure at the capital and provincial levels. According to the memoirs of Kuşçubaşı Eşref,[35] one of the leading men of the Special Organisation, a series of secret meetings were convened at the Ministry of War to lay out the framework of anti-Christian measures. Key positions were assigned to the most prominent Unionists in the province: Mustafa Rahmî (Arslan) Bey was responsible for the government,[36] Mahmut Celâl (Bayar) Bey for the committee and Cafer Tayyar (Eğilmez) Pasha for the army. Arif Bey, head official (*kaymakam*) of Bergama, was also an important figure in the organisation of boycotts. Kuşçubaşı aimed at the liquidation of Greek villages on the Aegean coast. Since he was a protégé of Enver Pasha, he benefited from privileged relations with the governor-general Rahmî Bey and emerged as a powerful leader in the boycott movements.[37]

One of the fomenters of the attacks was Celâl Bey, responsible secretary (*kâtib-i mesûl*) of the CUP branch in Smyrna. He was chosen for this duty by Midhat Şükrü (Bleda), general secretary (*kâtib-i umûmî*) of the committee. In his memoirs, Celâl ironically admits his role in the expulsions of Ottoman Greeks.[38] Mehmet Reşit Bey, Unionist governor of the Karesi *sanjak*, also emphasised that he played an important role in the expulsions

Gradual Intimidation in Western Anatolia

without resorting to violent methods in the northern towns of the Smyrna *sanjak*.[39] Later he would gain notoriety for organising the destruction of Armenian communities in Diyarbekir Province in 1915.

Not surprisingly, some of the provincial officials who played an important role in demographic engineering in the region had previously been employed in the Balkan provinces. A typical member of these cadres was Rahmî, governor-general of Aydın Province. Before being appointed as the governor-general of the province, he was a representative of Salonica in the Ottoman parliament as a key member of the CUP. Kuşçubaşı Eşref claims that Rahmî devoted himself to expelling the Greeks and establishing a band of Cretan migrants for this purpose. Heathcote Smith, the British consul at Smyrna, frequently met with Rahmî, and he reported on Rahmî's view about the Greeks in Aydın Province:

> In his conversations with me today, he definitely stated that he would from now on institute a campaign of expulsion against all well-to-do Hellenes and Greek rayahs who own real property. Hellenic subjects are to be the first victims. His plan is to expel them in groups and divide up the property thus 'abandoned' among Muslim refugees.
>
> He alleges that this plan will be a merely distinct imitation of the programme adopted by the Hellenic Authorities in Macedonia against the Turks.[40]

In another conversation with the British consul at Smyrna, Rahmî admitted his prominent role in the expulsion of Greek Orthodox communities: 'It was I whose policy it was to rid Turkey of the Greeks who have emigrated, and had the movement taken place as planned, the coast would now be clear.'[41]

BOYCOTTS

Boycott, fuelled by Ottoman territorial losses in the Balkans after 1908, was an important means of demographic engineering for the Unionist government. Following the annexation of Bosnia-Herzegovina, which had been under Austro-Hungarian occupation since 1878, the first boycott, targeting Austro-Hungarian products, commenced; this was the first example of boycotts that mobilised civilians in the Ottoman Empire. The disembarkation of Austro-Hungarian products was obstructed by dock workers in the ports of Aydın Province. Moreover, the masses were advised not to shop at enterprises where these products were sold. The provincial newspapers published articles claiming that foreign economic penetration should be limited. Some of the Greek newspapers, especially *Ergatis* and *Amaltheia*, ardently supported the boycott against Austro-Hungary products.[42]

The participation of Greek Orthodox communities in anti-Austrian boycotts is particularly noteworthy:

> In 1908 the Greeks of Smyrna declared a boycott on Austria. The circulating rumour had that people did not step in Orosdi-Back department store to do shopping for days. Thereupon, the manager of the store did not hesitate to inform the newspapers that the place in view had no relation to Austria but was rather related to a store of French origin and based in Paris. At the time he proved that this store definitely belonged to the French by putting forth signed papers confirmed by Pavlos Blan [Paul Blanc], the French consul of Smyrna, and Baluktzouoglou,[43] the head of the Smyrna Chamber of Commerce. Only then, that is, after all these actions, did the Greek customers silently end the boycott and the Greek people started to do shopping again.[44]

The second boycott wave targeted citizens of the Greek Kingdom. In October 1908, after the restoration of the constitution, the Greek government announced the unilateral annexation of Crete. In July 1909, four guarantor states (Britain, France, Italy and Russia) withdrew their troops from the island in favour of Greek troops. The Cretan question was continuously exploited by the CUP, with propaganda, protests and boycott campaigns against economically powerful Greeks in in Constantinople and Smyrna, spreading to Aegean coastal settlements with larger Orthodox populations who had better shipping connections with Greece. The most severe boycotts were conducted in Smyrna, where the Boycottage Association (Boykotaj Cemiyeti) was re-activated in August 1910.

The administrative board of the Smyrna stock exchange was one arena where the quarrel between Orthodox Christians and Muslims was played out. *Âhenk*, one of the Unionist provincial newspapers, objected to the membership of two Greek nationals, Kostas Palamidas and Anastasios Yorgakis, on its administrative board. In 1911, the Boycottage Association started to reveal the names of Ottoman Greek merchants possessing Greek citizenship. Although the Boycottage Association stated that this boycotting campaign was only being directed at Greek nationals,[45] it also inevitably targeted Ottoman Greeks because of the close contacts between, and fluidity of, Ottoman Greek and Hellene identities. *Köylü*, another provincial paper, embraced anti-Greek nationalism during the Cretan question, and made a call to the governor-general, Mahmut Muhtar Pasha, for the abolition of the Greek language in the stock market:

> A group of Greeks (*bir takım Yunanlılar*), who wanted to control all commerce in Smyrna, introduced the Greek language as a medium of communication to the Ottoman Stock Market of Foodstuffs. This situation was rooted in the unconcern of commissioners at the stock market. The Turkish language must

Gradual Intimidation in Western Anatolia

be the sole official language in this Ottoman institution. We expect the abolition of the use of Greek from your favour and patriotism now. That is one of the things that Smyrna awaits from you.[46]

Supported by the Turkish newspapers, the boycott of products made in Greece or advertising in Greek was one of the first action of the Unionist elites, whose agenda was the formation of a national economy, against Greek expansionism in Crete. In September 1910, Gerard Lowther, the British ambassador in Constantinople, reported to the Foreign Office that the boycott was organised by the CUP, and Talât and Câvit, two of the most important representatives of this committee, kept their dominant position in the Ottoman cabinet.[47]

Not only commerce but also individuals and their enterprises became the targets of the boycott. Several Catholic Greeks adopted French citizenship in order to protect their financial interests vis-à-vis the nationalist boycott. For instance, Petros Xenopoulos, who ran a shop of gramophone records in the rue Franque of Smyrna, took up the name Pierre along with French citizenship.[48] In another case, Nicholas C. Constantinides, a British subject who owned a shop in Smyrna, complained that his clients were obstructed in their attempt to enter the shop, and that the boycotters used foul expressions against the British flag. The boycotters continued to block the shop, and the shopfront was smeared with tar the following evening.[49]

Starting in late-March 1911, the boycott against Greek goods and firms grew more severe, and the Boycottage Association in Smyrna became much stronger than in previous years. In June, steamers of the Anglo-Hellenic Line flying the Greek flag were not allowed to enter the port of Smyrna and their cargoes were transshipped in Urla to boats under another flag.[50]

During the Balkan Wars, the Greek navy trapped the Ottoman navy in the Sea of Marmara by blocking the Dardanelles. A brochure entitled *Müslümanlara Mahsûs Kurtuluş Yolu* (Way of Independence Peculiar to Muslims), distributed free to the public, claimed that the Ottoman navy could not enter the Aegean Sea because of the Greek flagship *Averof*.[51] More importantly, this brochure asserted that Georgios Averof was indeed an Ottoman citizen and demanded the boycotting of shops belonging to Greek merchants. The boycott, secretly organised by the CUP,[52] spread to inland towns and was directed against all Christians in the province in 1914:

> In small towns such as Magnesia, and throughout the villages where the ubiquitous Greek petty trader is to be found, boycotting in a most severe form is being carried on. All Moslem or Greeks who are found entering raya shops are beaten and all semblance of free commerce or equality is at an end, while as

49

Ethnic Cleansing in Western Anatolia

things tend at present, the position of Greeks and Armenians in many districts is becoming more and more untenable.

The boycott is the direct result of Committee of Union and Progress influence, and Committee emissaries are everywhere investigating the people.[53]

The Balkan Wars had traumatic consequences in late Ottoman society and led to the radicalisation of the political scene. The comprehensive defeat suffered at the hands of small Balkan kingdoms and former subject peoples, and the advance of the Bulgarian armies towards the Ottoman capital made it all the more humiliating. After these wars, the Empire lost 80 per cent of its European domains and 20 per cent of its total population. In addition, these wars delivered the final blow to the last remnants of Ottomanism as a political project.

The traumatic effects of the defeat in the Balkan Wars and the influx of thousands of Muslims from the Balkan provinces to Constantinople and Western Anatolia nourished the CUP's suspicions about prospective conspiracies of Anatolian Christians, namely Greeks and Armenians. Despite the fact that only some extreme nationalists collaborated with the Balkan states[54] and that the war was a cause of anxiety for Ottoman Christians, they were perceived as an enemy within the nation by the Unionists. Widespread opinion among Unionists was that Christian Ottomans, especially the Greek Orthodox population, were the fifth column of the Balkan states.

RESETTLEMENT OF BALKAN MIGRANTS

The advance of the armies of the Balkan states through the Macedonian provinces and Thrace drove thousands of Muslim refugees into Anatolia, particularly Aydın Province. On 13 May 1913, the Directorate for Settlement of Tribes and Refugees (İskân-ı Aşâir ve Muhâcirîn Müdüriyeti)[55] was founded to address the resettlement of Balkan migrants, but also to inquire into the alleged disloyalty of non-Turkish groups. In response, a group of Unionist intellectuals were sent to Anatolia to conduct research.[56]

The CUP endorsed the settlement of Muslim refugees from the Balkans in Anatolia, especially Aydın Province, in order to increase the Muslim share of the population.[57] Some of these migrants received financial support from the Ottoman government, but most were compelled to settle in less desirable remote new rural settlements in rugged terrain or isolated peri-urban zones.[58] Inevitably, resettlement triggered competition for limited resources with the local elements, especially non-Muslim populations.

Moreover, masses of migrants who experienced tragic events in their former hometowns due to the atrocities of Bulgarian and Greek troops

Gradual Intimidation in Western Anatolia

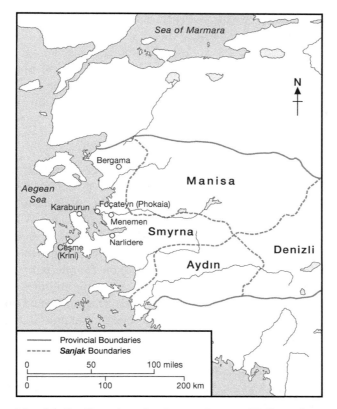

Map 1.1 Conflict points after the resettlement of Balkan migrants.

constituted an easy target to provoke against local Christians. The circulation of tragic stories brought by the Balkan Muslims raised tension in the cities and towns where Muslims and Christians from every walk of life coexisted. Despite threats by local authorities to resident Christians that their homes or property would be appropriated for use by Balkan migrants, in some places peaceful relations developed between Balkan migrants and Christians. Nevertheless, violent events in most of the coastal towns were reported by the British consular staff (see Map 1.1):

> The authorities of Smyrna had sent 5,000 or 6,000 Muslim refugees from Macedonia by 3 steamers from Smyrna to Katopanaya and the neighbourhood of Cheshmeh towards the end of May. Attacks on neighbouring Greek villages by bands of local Moslems, the arrival of these refugees, and the attitude of the local authorities had inspired the Greeks of Cheshmeh with such a feeling of panic that they had emigrated en masse to Gouni, Scio, Samos and elsewhere during the first days of June. We found that some 1,000 Muslim refugees had

Ethnic Cleansing in Western Anatolia

been installed in the town of Cheshmeh which had a deserted appearance, most of the houses being unoccupied.[59]

The resettlement of Balkan migrants was one of the most important triggers for the expulsion of Ottoman Greeks. These resettlements accelerated and became a general trend after the outbreak of the Balkan Wars.

FORCED MIGRATIONS, EXPULSIONS AND MASSACRES

The January 1913 *coup d'état* known as the *Bâb-ı Âlî* coup terminated pluralism in Ottoman political life and ensured sole power for the Unionists. When Talât Pasha was promoted from minister of posts to minister of the interior, Enver and Cemal acquired the rank of pasha. With the coup, Cemal became the commander of the capital and Enver, as architect of this sudden change, got the Ministry of War in January 1914. Until the end of World War I, the Ottoman Empire would remain a single-party dictatorship in spite of the existence of the parliament, since the military wing of the CUP would not allow a pluralistic system that accommodated opposition.

Despite the fact that the Unionists had been influential in the Ottoman government since 1908, they had to wait until 1914 in order to reform the ethnic structure of Anatolia. The first reason behind this decision was that the Great War offered a permissive theatre of operations for the Unionists. Secondly, the CUP had established full control over the government and eliminated all opposition since the coup of January 1913. Finally, the tragic stories of Muslim migrants from the Balkan provinces provided a basis for an anti-Christian sentiment.

The Unionists tried to constitute an epic culture through militarist discourse and war narratives. This attempt brought about a shift, which affected the culture of collective self, in the dominant cultural code of the Empire. Subsequent to the coup, Enver tried to create a cult around himself as a saviour and hero of the Balkan Wars. Not only Enver, but the Unionist officers were depicted as heroes, who struggled to maintain the unity of empire against external and internal enemies. The Turkish press was also militarised and newspapers bore names such as *Silâh* (Weapon), *Kurşun* (Bullet) and *Bıçak* (Knife).

Attacks on Greek Orthodox communities began in mid-June 1914, carried out by bands of Balkan migrants and local Muslims that had been supplied as reinforcements to the regular Ottoman gendarmerie. Provincial authorities secretly instigated these attacks, and tried to give the impression that the government did not go out of the legal framework. Concerning this wave of persecution, the British consul at Smyrna reported:

Gradual Intimidation in Western Anatolia

These methods consist of isolated attacks on Greeks who dared, despite the boycott, to continue their field work, and a few cases of pillaging, flogging, cattle-stealing, wounding and murder in each district suffice to convince the Greeks of the unwisdom of venturing forth. This cruel persecution has been carried out at the very gates of Smyrna, as at St Georges, which is near the Castle or Sanjak Kaleh on the Smyrna Gulf; or at Seudikeuy 9 miles from the Smyrna terminus of the British line; and naturally feeling has become deep-rooted in the terrified Orthodox that the Turkish Government wish for their undoing or even their destruction.[60]

The British consular reports showed that German officers in the Empire perceived the compact Greek Orthodox communities along the lengthy Aegean coastline to be a security threat in the event of military conflict with Greece.[61] However, the expulsions were not limited to the coastal towns (see Map 1.2). In some inland towns, local Muslim residents also participated in these attacks. As rumours of attacks increased, the British consul undertook a fact-finding tour in the rural parts of the Smyrna *sanjak*. He depicted the situation in Ulucak, a provincial town close to Smyrna, as follows:

> We found Ulujak, a Greek village of about the same size as Seiruk-Keui, also deserted. The church had been looted and desecrated. Villagers who accompanied us said that there had been little loss of life as no resistance had been offered. A Greek named Yorghi had been killed and another wounded. The 2 children of certain Yovann [*sic*] were missing. The attacking parties consisted of local Moslems, mostly from the neighbouring village of Harmandali.[62]

As Bruce Clark points out, Unionist leaders in the province sent armed bands, guided by intelligence officers and composed of irregulars, brigands, Balkan migrants, and even local Muslims in some cases, to intimidate and expel local Christian populations, though the Unionists denied 'all responsibility for the "excesses" which these supposedly uncontrolled elements have committed'.[63] By the end of June 1914, the Greek Orthodox inhabitants of the coastal towns of Çeşme, Foça and Karaburun had already been expelled.[64] Félix Sartiaux, an archaeologist excavating in Foça at that time, wrote that

> the plundering of this town was an organised plan aimed at the expulsion of the rayas from the seacoast. It is not possible that the invading brigands could have possessed so many firearms if they had not been distributed to them beforehand ... [65]

In Çeşme, the Russian church, erected in commemoration of the 1770 Russian victory against the Ottoman navy, and its guard house were set on fire.[66]

Ethnic Cleansing in Western Anatolia

Map 1.2 Forced migrations, expulsions and massacres in the summer of 1914.

World War I: Normalisation of Ethnic Violence

Having recently been defeated by Italy and the Balkan states in two separate wars, the Ottoman Empire was seen as a weak power in the lead-up to the Great War. Despite the recapture of Adrianople in July 1913 it had difficulties in finding an ally in the European alliance system. In May 1914, Talât Pasha, first Unionist minister of the interior, offered Ottoman friendship to Sergey Sazonov, the Russian foreign minister, in Livadia,

Gradual Intimidation in Western Anatolia

Crimea.[67] In early July, Cemal Pasha visited Paris to seek an alliance, but was met with a reply from the Allied statesmen that the neutrality of the Ottoman Empire was better than an alliance.[68]

It was Hans Freiherr von Wangenheim, German ambassador in Constantinople, who paved the way for the formation of the German–Ottoman alliance. He arranged secret meetings with Enver Pasha, the minister of war, and Talât Pasha, the minister of the interior. There were three main reasons for Germany to establish an alliance with the Ottoman Empire. Firstly, the entrance of the Ottoman Empire into the war could create new fronts against Russia and, in turn, Russia would be compelled to send some of its troops there. Secondly, the German policy-makers hoped that the call for holy war (jihad) by the chief religious official (*sheikh ul-Islam*) could lead to a revolt in the Muslim-inhabited colonies of the Allied Powers. Thirdly, the Ottoman Empire could be a springboard for German imperialist ambitions by, for example, the Berlin–Baghdad Railway used to transport raw materials for German industry.

CREATING THE NATIONAL ECONOMY AND MARGINALISING THE CHRISTIAN MERCHANTS

The entrance of the Ottoman Empire into World War I enabled the CUP government to create a vacuum where a Muslim bourgeois class might emerge. The first step towards this goal was the abolition of the capitulations, which would precipitate a sense of contentment among the Muslim populations of the Empire. When the war erupted in Europe, the Ottoman Empire declared immediately on 9 September 1914 that it unilaterally abrogated the long-resented system of capitulations, which facilitated favourable custom duties and tax exemptions for foreign nationals. Moreover, the consular courts and foreign schools also ceased to function because of the abrogation of the capitulations.

Following the abolition of the capitulations, the Ministry of Public Works expropriated the British and French railways, beginning in November 1914 with the Ottoman Railway from Smyrna to Aydın, a British property.[69] However, since there were no technical staff to manage the railways, Celâl Bey, responsible secretary of the CUP in Smyrna, initiated a railways management course for the Muslim youth. New customs tariffs were introduced to the parliament in December 1915, and approved in March 1916, to protect incipient domestic sectors in manufacturing industries. Similar to the abolition of the capitulations, national economy policies prompted protests by European states.[70]

55

Ethnic Cleansing in Western Anatolia

On the grounds that the port of Smyrna was under an Allied blockade in the course of the war, commercial products were being sent to Bandırma by railway and thence dispatched to Constantinople by sea. Considering that the port of Smyrna could be used as a base for German submarines, a British warship bombarded the port before the Gallipoli campaign. Over the course of time, the bombardments made commercial maritime traffic impossible along the Aegean coast, and eventually became routine in the provincial capital. Attacks by warships reached their climax between March and April 1915, coinciding with the most intense period of the Gallipoli campaign.

As the war began, the Levantines who were British and French citizens, the majority of whom had been settled there for generations and occupied a significant place in the financial life of the city, found themselves in a more delicate situation day by day. Their presence became a sore issue for the governor of Aydın when the Allied Powers declared war on the Ottoman Empire. Allied planes taking off from Makronisi (Uzunada) bombarded the Muslim neighbourhoods of Smyrna three times in the spring of 1916 (23 May, 29 May and 11 June), killing twenty-three people and leaving forty-nine wounded.[71] These attacks led to retaliations against Levantine residents possessing British or French citizenship.[72]

Nonetheless, the measures taken against Allied citizens were alleviated by Governor-General Rahmî. The outbreak of the war had given governors-general the opportunity to attain dictatorial powers and, in case of necessity, take preventive measures over the residents in their realms of authority. During this period, provincial administrators benefited from a certain measure of decentralisation. Rahmî was one of the forerunners of these governors who exercised considerable autonomy in the pursuit of his own political agenda and personal interests. In spite of the fact that he had close ties previously with the CUP triumvirate, Ottoman participation in the war on the German side prompted a disagreement between the Unionist leaders and the governor-general. In the meantime, he would maintain his pro-British position.[73] He acted as a semi-autonomous governor and ignored the decisions of the Central Office (*merkez-i umûmi*) of the CUP, which demanded from the governors the internment of the citizens of the Allied Powers. Allied citizens enjoyed Rahmî's liberal administration and could continue their everyday lives, thanks to him.

Even though the British and French Levantine families were officially regarded as enemies in the capital, Rahmî Bey had assured the American consul in Smyrna – who represented British and French interests – that the lives and property of British and French citizens would be protected by the local authorities.[74] Moreover, he maintained the habit of visiting his

Gradual Intimidation in Western Anatolia

Levantine friends at their homes in Bournabat and permitted them to stay in the province, appreciating the importance of maintaining good relations with the Levantine merchant families of one of the richest provinces in the Ottoman Empire.[75]

This consensus between the governor and the Levantine families was the result of a series of meetings and a correspondence process. Representatives of prominent Levantine families emphasised the delicacy of their situation in a letter to Rahmî dated 2 November 1914:

> As delegates from the English, French and Russian colonies of Smyrna, we have the honour to pay our respects on behalf of our citizens and us. We feel deeply grieved with the difficult circumstances in the country, where we have lived for so many years.[76]

Notwithstanding this, national economy policies continued at full speed in the province. The government's *étatist* control over the provincial economy and its attempts to facilitate the development of a national market through economic precautions, extraordinary taxes and confiscations devastated non-Muslim and foreign merchants, while benefiting their Muslim counterparts.

In the same period, the government invested capital for the formation of banks and corporations operated and staffed by Muslims. Local branches of the CUP, partnering with local credit agencies, provincial notables and local Muslim merchants, tried to mobilise Muslim tradesmen vis-à-vis foreign corporations and the non-Muslim bourgeoisie that controlled the market.[77] The envisioned Muslim bourgeoisie would be the chief rival of the Greek and Armenian merchants within a Muslim-dominated system. Special attention was given to this process in Aydın Province, where non-Muslim merchants controlled the commerce of the Smyrna *sanjak*. The most prominent Turkish corporations established in the province during the war years were the National Bank of Aydın (Millî Aydın Bankası), Manisa Agricultural Bank (Manisa Zirâât Bankası), Tobacco Farmers Bank (Tütün Zürrâ'ı Bankası) and Manisa Bank of Grape Farmers (Manisa Bağcılar Bankası).[78] These banks and corporations were founded under the patronage of Rahmî for the protection of the interests of Muslim producers and provided low interest loans to farmers.[79]

For Unionist notables, the Smyrna Chamber of Commerce was the most obvious economic institution in the province to be nationalised. Thanks to Rahmî Bey's interventions, Alaiyelizâde Mahmut Bey became the president of the chamber on 8 March 1915. Hadji Davud Farkoh, former president and an American-national Syriac Christian, was obliged to resign from the administrative board, though Mesrob Simonyan Efendi continued his duty as vice-president of the chamber.[80] In the same year, Rahmî took initiative for the publication of *İslâm Tüccâr ve Esnâflarına Mahsûs Rehber* (*The Guide Pertaining to Muslim Merchants and Artisans*), which was designed as a substitute for the renowned *Annuaire Oriental* commercial guides published in Constantinople. This pamphlet listed the names of Muslim-owned hotels, guesthouses, pharmacies, doctors, herbalists and merchants. Furthermore, it strongly recommended Muslim clients to shop at Muslim-owned shops.[81]

TEHCÎR: INTERNMENT OF THE OTTOMAN GREEKS TO THE INTERIOR

The Great War signalled a new phase for the national question of the Empire. The Unionists believed that the state of war gave them opportunities to limit the influences of European powers and pacify internal enemies. As such, the development of Turkish nationalism was being encouraged by provincial administrators as the support of the government increased for nationalist associations. In Aydın Province, Rahmî was the chief sponsor of nationalist associations such as the National Defence Committee (Millî Müdâfaa Cemiyeti) and Smyrna branch of the Turkish Hearth. Rahmî's name was always mentioned in the newspapers as one of the most important organisers of plays, lectures and cinema screenings for the benefit of the National Defence Committee.[82] Basically, these practices were useful attempts to guide cultural expression towards the ideology of the party and were directly related to demographic engineering. For example, the Turkish Hearths, which provided a vehicle for the promotion of CUP ideology, opened new branches in the provinces.[83] The Turkish Hearths provided venues for lectures and plays, and began to attract the attention of many young Muslim students.[84] The war years witnessed the creation of a whole set of national (*millî*) societies, institutions, clubs, firms and periodicals quickly following one another. When we look at their purposes and membership, it becomes clear that the word national/ *millî* referred only to Ottoman Muslim. Throughout the war years, the CUP emphasised Turkish national identity within the *millî* discourse. Courses on the Turkish language, Turkish history and geography were introduced in non-Muslim schools in March 1916.[85]

On the other hand, extreme forms of ethnic nationalism, such as deportations, expulsions and massacres, were conducted during the war years throughout the Empire. At the beginning of the war, the government had plans to relocate certain ethnic groups.[86] In order to shape a new homeland, the CUP needed a settlement policy concerned with unwanted elements, particularly the Greeks and Armenians. These communities were already marginalised by national security policies as antagonists, and demographic engineering policies were normalised in this particular region.

At the beginning of the war, Rahmî tried to establish his authority over the leaders of the religious communities through control of urban spaces. From the second half of the nineteenth century, distinct spaces for cemeteries were designated in urban areas for public health reasons.[87] Rahmî's decision to relocate the cemeteries in the suburbs of Smyrna shattered the relations between the governor and the Orthodox community. Rahmetullah Efendi, mufti of the province, had already objected to this decision. Chrysostomos, Orthodox metropolitan bishop of Smyrna, argued that these relocations meant desecration. Due to Rahmî's constant pressure, a ministerial decree that demanded the relocation of Chrysostomos to Constantinople was delivered to the Ecumenical Patriarchate of Constantinople in August 1914.[88] Since the Patriarchate remained silent on this issue, Ottoman gendarmes took the metropolitan bishop by force and sent him to Constantinople by an Italian ship in mid-August. His return to Smyrna was strictly prohibited.

Owing to large scale expulsions in 1914, the remaining Greek Orthodox communities were no longer an official threat to the security of the state until the launch of the Gallipoli campaign in the spring of 1915. In February 1915, the Allied headquarters decided to seize the Dardanelles in order to occupy Constantinople and re-establish maritime connections with Russia. In the spring of 1915, the Aegean islands of Mytilene, Chios and Samos were occupied by the Allied Powers whose influence began to increase in Greece. This occupation led to the intensification of anti-Greek policies in Aydın Province since there were rumours about an Allied conspiracy to involve a massive number of Greeks from across the province coming together. The Unionist officers suspected that the Allied navies would cut the route of the Ottoman army by bombarding and landing with the assistance of the local Christians on the Aegean coast.[89] Furthermore, Aydın Province emerged as more strategic for the survival of the Empire because it encircled several sea and rail centres linking the fertile Aegean valleys to the capital.

The Unionist authorities adopted a solution that directed the deportation of Christian communities from strategic regions to the areas in the interior. Therefore, the Orthodox villages in the *sanjak* of Kale-i Sultaniye (Çanakkale) and the northern coastal tip of Aydın Province were evacuated due to fears of supplying Allied submarines with provisions.[90] Besides, the Christian quarters in Gelibolu (Gallipoli), Erdek (Artakē), Ayvalık (Aïvali), Edremit (Adramyttio), Bergama and Dikili were forcefully abandoned and Christian communal buildings were ransacked.[91] Public hangings of potential traitors and other means of violence and intimidation increased, hastening the abandonment of the towns and villages.

In the summer of 1915, this forced migration campaign spread to the rural regions around Smyrna, such as Kilizman, Ayasuluk (present-day Selçuk) and Kuşadası.[92] European consuls monitored events in Smyrna more than in other parts of the province, so fewer organised internal displacements were observed there. However, the Ottoman Ministry of War required the evacuation of all the coastal villages made up of solely Greek Orthodox populations in Aydın Province.[93] This forced migration was handled by the commanders who were chosen for this process.[94] In the countryside, gendarmerie searches had become routine in Greek Orthodox villages.

Notwithstanding this, mass migration to Greece was prevented during the war years. As distinct from the pre-war period, Unionist authorities chose to intern Greek Orthodox communities in the inland regions.[95] The appeals of the Greek Orthodox deputies in the Ottoman parliament and the reactions of the Orthodox ecclesiastical leaders played an important role in this phenomenon.

The CUP demanded inventories of abandoned Greek properties from the provincial authorities.[96] The local Abandoned Property Commissions (Emvâl-i Metrûke Komisyonları) and the Liquidation Commissions (Tasfiye Komisyonları), which were authorised by both the Directorate for the Settlement of Tribes and Refugees and the Military High Command, monitored the protection and sale of unattended or abandoned property. On account of the internments and forced resettlements of the Ottoman Christians, many confiscated farms, businesses, workplaces and sections of industry passed into the hands of Muslim merchants.[97]

Compulsory military service also represented a serious risk for Ottoman Christians. Although many testimonies narrate that a limited number of non-Muslim soldiers continued to serve in the regular battalions (*nizâmiyye taburları*), they were kept behind the front and were assigned simple duties such as scribes or nursing staff. A government decree issued on 27 February 1915 ordered the surrender of all Ottoman Greek military deserters to the nearest recruitment office within ten days. The decree stated that unless these soldiers proved their presence in the Ottoman territories, their families would be exiled to the interior.[98] Labour battalions (*amele taburları*) were founded in order to isolate non-Muslim soldiers because of doubts concerning their loyalty. The main objective behind the labour battalions was to deter desertion by non-Muslim soldiers. Having to surrender their arms, Christian soldiers in these units were treated very badly, almost as prisoners of war. Compelled to work in miserable conditions in mines and road constructions, most of them were either killed or otherwise perished during their conscription.[99]

Contrary to general belief, members of the Armenian communities in Aydın Province also became subject to internment, though on a very limited scale. Towards the end of August 1915, Rahmî left Smyrna for Constantinople in order to discuss with prominent members of the CUP the drastic measures, which he refused to implement, against the Armenian communities. As soon as he left the city, police authorities immediately commenced arresting wealthy Armenians, sequestering their properties, placing troops in their homes and deporting them from Smyrna.[100] This first wave of detentions continued until December 1915.[101] The second wave of the deportations occurred in January 1916. At that time, another group was exiled from Aydın Province to Mosul.[102]

Rahmî's ultimate goal was the maintenance of his autonomous position as the governor-general against the Unionist triumvirate in Constantinople during the war years. In order to keep this position, he did not abstain from ignoring the orders of the Unionist government and embracing a pro-British stance. Since the existence of Orthodox Greeks was considered the main problem in the province, Rahmî could possibly have prevented the deportation of the Armenians. The main reason behind this thinking was that the deportation of a tiny Armenian community could potentially strengthen the position of the Greeks in the provincial economy. In other words, the business networks of the Armenian merchants would then be obtained by the Greek ones, which in turn would cause the main problem to worsen. As a result, there were still nearly 21,000 Armenians in the province in 1916 and 1917.[103]

Some authors have claimed that Rahmî, the long serving governor-general, strove to save the members of the Armenian communities and the citizens of the Allied states from the extremes of the war period.[104] Nevertheless, his harsh treatment of the members of the Greek Orthodox communities made him stand out as one of the representatives of the nationalist programme implemented by the CUP. In case of necessity, he did not refrain from applying systematic boycotts against Christian merchants and interning Greek Orthodox communities from strategic regions to the interior of the province. His pro-Allied position and mild attitude towards the Levantine merchants and Armenian communities were part of his double game.[105] On the one hand, he moderated the extremist policies of the Unionist centre in Constantinople in order to be favoured by the Allied Powers. On the other hand, he did not avoid implementing national economic policies in the province.

Ethnic Cleansing in Western Anatolia

False Peace: Post-armistice Period

The end of the Great War marked the beginning of a new period not only for Europe but also for the Ottoman Empire. Following a long cabinet crisis, the CUP government resigned on 8 October 1918, with Ahmet İzzet (Furgaç) Pasha, who was a clear nationalist but probably not a Unionist, succeeding in forming a new government. This new government would offer a ceasefire to Britain mediated by General Charles Townshend, who had been taken prisoner during the Siege of Kut in 1916.[106] On 27 October, the British government accepted the Ottoman proposal as a truce, with negotiations being planned on the Aegean island of Lemnos. The Ottoman delegation was presided over by Raûf (Orbay) Bey, minister of the navy, whereas Britain was represented by a committee under the leadership of Admiral Somerset Calthorpe, commander-in-chief of the British Mediterranean Fleet. The Armistice of Mudros, which signalled the unconditional surrender of the Ottoman Empire, was signed on 30 October.

With the signing of the armistice, a new period dawned on the Empire. The Empire had been decisively defeated and its statesmen were worried about the possible abuse of some articles in the armistice by the Allied Powers. To illustrate, Article 7 stipulated that the Allies 'have the right to occupy any strategic points in the event of any situation arising which threatens the security of the Allies'. Immediately after the armistice, British troops took over the Dardanelles and oil-rich Mosul, while French forces simultaneously landed in Cilicia. In November 1918, the Allies set up a collective administration in Constantinople. Also troubling was Article 24, which stipulated that 'In case of disorder in the six Armenian *vilâyet*s the Allies reserve to themselves the right to occupy any part of them.' Thus, the Unionist statesmen believed that Greek and Armenian nationalist activities would be facilitated through the support of the Allied Powers in the post-armistice period.

CRITICS OF THE WARTIME POLITICS

Muslim and Christian communities of the Empire reacted to the armistice treatyquite differently. The ethnic cleansing policies of the Unionist government, which had resulted in the slaughter of hundreds of thousands of Armenians, combined with the expulsion of thousands of Greeks to the Aegean islands or their internment in the interior regions, motivated both communities to regard the Allied Powers as saviours.

At the provincial level, the conflict between the Unionists and the Freedom and Accord Party intensified. This conflict was reflected in the

Gradual Intimidation in Western Anatolia

Turkish press of Smyrna, which had already been torn between the pro-Unionists and the supporters of the Freedom and Accord Party during World War I. The war crimes of the Unionist leaders were considered flagrant widely in the anti-Unionist press in the winter of 1918–19. *Müsavat*, one of the local newspapers supporting the Freedom and Accord Party, started to vehemently criticise the war time policies of the CUP:

> We are putting our hand on the Qur'an and asking you: Say for God's sake, what sort of *Haccac*[107] are they? One would come back to the world to persecute the people (*bu memleket halkına*) by way of mass executioners named Union and Progress (*İttihâd ve Terakki denilen cellâdlar kitlesinin*)? Which herd of ferocious beasts was seen to tear apart this many people and drink blood? ... Mercy on us (*El amân*) against the arduous and sharp-edged nails of cruelty, mercy on us.[108]

Although the Freedom and Accord Party and the Renovation Party (Teceddüt Fırkası), the political heir to the CUP, took part in the election process with a common list of deputies, the battle between the Unionist press and the supporters of the Freedom and Accord Party continued even after the municipal elections. Hasan Tahsin, working for the daily *Hukuk-ı Beşer*, published a rather harsh article addressing Haydar Rüştü, the main Unionist journalist in the province:

> Comprehensive delirium is addressed not only to me, but also to the newspapers *Müsavat* and *Islahât*, İbn Hazım Ferit, Emin Süreyya, the nation (*millete*), the country (*vatana*), the history, everyone, everything, the past, the current situation, every term, every moment ... They are recounting slanders and sluggish legends in the name of defence.
>
> They address the Greeks and Armenians with swear words (*Rum ve Ermeniler'e küfür ile*), the Arabs with insults, and pen insinuating articles for the view of the new governor. They protect profiteers, embrace Rahmî's servants and provoke bigotry. In brief, the Unionist spirit is the same as the rhetoric of bandits (*çeteci ağzı*), which aims to engage the nation in dangerous trends, make people hesitate, to confound them, and finally, to thrust themselves into God's playground (*meydân-ı Hudâ*) with a new mask and new tricks to get back to work as soon as the another opportunity to be chosen comes up (*intihâb takarrüb eder etmez*). This is their target ... This is their aim [...] Today we are talking about the organs of the murderer, his bloodshed; this miserable, bandit-souled, Satan-natured (*Şeytân tıynetli*) tyrant, thief and traitor, none other than the despicable Union and Progress, which is actually condemning itself to capital punishment (*kendi kendinin hükm-i idâmını vermektir*) ... These miserable souls deserve the gallows (*darağaçları*) rather than a court martial.[109]

The new cabinet formed by İzzet Pasha on 14 October 1918 planned to get rid all of the Unionist governors-general who had served during

Ethnic Cleansing in Western Anatolia

the war years. On 24 October, similar to the fates of other high-ranking Unionist provincial officials, Rahmî was removed from the post of governor-general because of his opposition to the new government. Due to accusations about the Armenian deportations and corruption in tobacco purchases, an inquiry was conducted against Rahmî immediately after his removal from office. Indeed, Christaki Athanasoula Efendi, a member of the administrative board in the chamber of commerce, had alleged that tobacco harvests were forcibly seized from non-Muslim merchants. Another accusation against Rahmî was made by Cevat Bey, former Muslim judge (*kadı*) of Bayındır, who argued that Rahmî was responsible for the forced deportations of Ottoman Greeks during the war years.[110] By reason of these allegations, Rahmî was arrested and taken to Bekirağa military prison in Constantinople where political convicts of the time were kept. He was later exiled to Malta with a group of nearly thirty key members of the CUP in 1920.[111]

After the Great War, the inhabitants of Aydın Province enjoyed a period of relative liberty for just over six months, at the beginning of which an armistice was signed, before the Greek troops landed in Smyrna. Undoubtedly, the Christian communities were more hopeful in this post-armistice period than the Muslim communities. However, the political atmosphere during this time signalled the uncertainty of Ottoman rule. Constant replacement of the governors-general (see Table 1.1), Christian–Muslim confrontations triggered by the continuous visits of Allied and Greek battleships to the Smyrna port, and the tough rule of Nureddin Pasha were the salient features of the political tensions of the province.

Nureddin Pasha, who supported the nationalist cause, was appointed governor-general on 20 January 1919, and posed a serious challenge to the intercommunal relations in the province.[112] A forty-nine-year-old officer coming from an exclusively military career with a history of suppressing local revolts against the Ottoman Empire in Macedonia and Yemen before World War I, and flattered by his victories against the British troops in Kut, Mesopotamia in 1916, Nureddin Pasha had a reputation for his brutal methods. As soon as he was appointed Ottoman commander of Smyrna and its environs on 11 February, he concentrated both civil and military power in his hands.[113] The simultaneous return of Chrysostomos, who had been exiled to Constantinople in 1914, and the rigid measures of Nureddin Pasha exacerbated the Christian–Muslim confrontation, polarising the masses. At first, Chrysostomos's return after a four-year-exile aroused enthusiasm among the Orthodox communities. On 1 January 1919, he complained to the representatives of the Allied Powers in Constantinople about Nureddin Pasha, who had served as vice-governor for a short period

Gradual Intimidation in Western Anatolia

Table 1.1 List of the governors of Aydın Province

Name	In office	Position	Previous office
WWI years and pre-Sèvres Treaty period			
Rahmî (Arslan) Bey	29 September 1913–24 October 1918	Governor-general	Deputy of Salonica
Nureddin İbrahim (Konyar) Pasha	25 October 1918–7 November 1918	Vice-governor	Commander of the Muğla and Antalya Regional Command
Tahsin (Uzer) Bey	9 November 1918–22 November 1918	Governor-general	Governor-general of Syria
Ethem Bey	25 November 1918–8 January 1919	Governor-general	Governor-general of Beirut
Nureddin İbrahim (Konyar) Pasha	20 January 1919–8 March 1919	Governor-general	Commander of the 25th Corps in Constantinople
Ahmet İzzet Bey	9 March 1919–5 January 1920	Governor-general	Minister of imperial foundations
Post-Sèvres period			
Ali Sâib Bey	8 January 1920–29 February 1920	Vice-governor	Chief secretary of Aydın Province
Ahmed Besim Bey	1 March 1920–12 August 1920	Vice-governor	Treasurer of Aydın Province
Câvîd Bey	5 May 1920–13 May 1920	Vice-governor	District governor of Aydın
Nâîbzâde Ali Bey	13 August 1920–24 September 1920	Vice-governor	Prefect of Drama and president of the Department of Muslim Affairs in the High Commission
Subhî Efendi	3 February 1921–September 1922	Vice-governor	*Kadı* of Smyrna
After the Entrance of the Nationalist Army			
Nureddin İbrahim (Konyar) Pasha	10 September 1922–19 September 1922	Military governor	Commander of the 1st Army
Abdülhalik (Renda) Bey	19 September 1922–8 August 1923	Governor (of Izmir)	Governor of Konya

Ethnic Cleansing in Western Anatolia

in October 1918. He accused Nureddin of establishing a secret society, distributing weapons to Muslim bandits, declaring martial law and levying high taxes on Ottoman Christians.[114]

Nureddin Pasha, on the other hand, kept track of Chrysostomos's every activity – even his sermons and speeches made in church – and shared this information with the representatives of the Allied states as well as with the Ministry of the Interior:

> Here is reported to the Blockade Command Headquarters of the Allied States that during the liturgy celebrated in the Church of Agios Ioannis in Smyrna (İzmir'in Aya Yani Kilisesinde) on 9 February in the presence of the Greek delegate Mavroudis [Greek military representative in Smyrna] and some Greek officers, Metropolitan Bishop Chrysostomos delivered a disquisition (*bir nutuk îrâdıyla*) to state that their every wish was granted and they would be successful. This would include the events on 8 February, where military uniforms and medical equipment were brought to the Smyrna port on the merchant ship *Adriatikos* and were transferred to the consulate and the Greek Orthodox hospital (*Rum hastanesine*), along with a doctor, three Greek officers (*üç Yunan zâbiti*), eleven marines and several Greek newspapers. Furthermore, he claimed that the Christian prisoners, whose names were being investigated by the metropolitan (*Metropolithânece bunların isimleri tahkik edilmekte olduğu*), would be released.[115]

Even though the Greek newspapers published in Smyrna started promoting conciliation, Nureddin Pasha was not persuaded. In a note he sent to the Ministry of the Interior on 9 February, he criticised what they had published earlier during the war.[116] On 22 February 1919, the Ottoman Ministry of the Interior launched an investigation into *Les Persécutions des Chrétiens*, a propaganda book compiled by Chrysostomos, on the grounds that the Greek high commissioner in Constantinople distributed its copies to foreigners and Ottoman Greek notables.[117] For all these reasons, the concerns of the Greek Orthodox communities increased under Nureddin's rule.

On 8 March, Nureddin Pasha was discharged from the office due to complaints from the Ottoman Christian communities, and Ahmet İzzet Bey, the former minister of imperial foundations (*evkaf-ı hümâyun nâzırı*), became the new governor in his place on 9 March.[118] Even though the members of the local Unionist branches did not want İzzet Bey as the governor-general, and had deliberately expressed their wishes in person to Prince Abdülmecid, cousin of Sultan Mehmed VI Vahdeddin (r. 1918–22) and heir to the Ottoman throne,[119] Abdülmecid chose not to interfere with this issue since İzzet Bey was most probably chosen by the imperial government, which aimed to diminish the complaints of the Ottoman Christians and the discontent of the Allied representatives. Immediately after the appointment of İzzet Bey and the end of Nureddin's hostile policies towards the Christian communities, tensions in the province abated.[120] This was soon realised through the actions of the new governor-general, as the French consul at Smyrna reported home on 12 April:

> The *Vali*, a newcomer, contributes to the calm by his desire to do well and by wise preventive measures: from the morning of 7 April, numerous police patrol the city in civilian attire; however, even this presence shows that any disorder would be quelled.
>
> I had another personal indication of this reasonable state of mind thanks to two conversations. On the one hand, Captain Mavroudis, who was charged with the protection of the Greek interests, told me İzzet Bey's appointment is good. A close friend of the *Vali*, on the other hand, expressed his satisfaction to me because of the willingness of the [Greek] civil and ecclesiastical authorities to cooperate. Thus, the main parties appreciate each other and one can foretell happy signs from it.[121]

It seems that the new governor was aware that the Unionists were still effective in the administration of the province along with the security forces.[122] Indeed, most of the military officers were pro-Unionist who had kept their offices during the governorship of Nureddin Pasha.[123] The new governor's first measure was the dismissal of these soldiers, who were considered a danger to provincial security. Furthermore, he ordered the arrest of the following prominent Unionist notables in the province: Cevdet Bey, ex-governor of Van and a prominent actor in the Armenian massacres; Mehmet Şükrü (Kaya) Bey, ex-director of the General Directorate for Refugees (Muhâcirîn Müdüriyet-i Umûmiyesi) and a close friend of Rahmî; Reşid Bey, Unionist delegate to Aydın; and Avni Bey, Unionist delegate to Manisa.[124]

Accordingly, the government in Constantinople had also asked Ahmet İzzet Bey about the presence of Bolshevik soldiers in the army; however, only fewer than a dozen pro-Bolshevik soldiers could be found. In the end, the governor demanded the dismissal of roughly 200 Unionist civil servants that could compromise provincial security. In addition, he closed down the Halka Doğru association, knowing that its responsible secretary Celâl Bey had left Smyrna to hide in the countryside,[125] and campaigned for the elimination of Ottoman Youth Unions (Osmanlı Genç Dernekleri), the quasi-military youth club of the Committee of Union and Progress. In terms of improving security, he raised to increase the salaries of the gendarmerie and enrol more gendarmes irrespective of religion and nationality.[126]

Ethnic Cleansing in Western Anatolia

These steps were generally appreciated by both Muslim and non-Muslim inhabitants of the province.[127]

The sultan appointed an advisory delegation (*heyet-i nâsıha*) under the leadership of Prince Abdürrahim to visit Western Anatolia to diminish the Unionist influence in the region, to show the harmony among the different elements, and to compensate for the Unionist mistreatment of non-Muslims during the war years. Seven people accompanied Prince Abdürrahim in the delegation: Ali Rıza Pasha, a deputy in the Ottoman Senate (Meclis-i Âyân); Ferit Mahmut Hayrettin Pasha, former chairman of the Ottoman court martial and a deputy in the Ottoman Senate; Ömer Fevzi Bey, the mufti of Bursa; Halil Fehmi Efendi, the former mufti of Pazarcık; Ohannes Ferit Efendi, chief secretary in the Ministry of the Interior; Yorgi Yuvanidis, former representative of Trabzon; and Süleyman Şefik Pasha, former general of Basra.[128] The Ottoman government approved the delegation since it would emphasise the power of the central authority.

It cannot be said that the Advisory Delegation was welcomed in every locality – although it tried to solve problems between Muslim and Christian communities. During the visit of the delegation, the attitude of the local Greeks towards the delegation was designated by the local authorities as impudent:

> In the days when the great Advisory Delegation came to Smyrna under the blessed presidency of the young prince Abdürrahim Efendi, not a single Ottoman flag was hoisted along the Quay, in Frankomachalas (*Frenk mahallesinde*) and particularly in the Greek quarters (*ve bilumum Rum mahallâtında*). This was the reality of the sentiment despite even having various Muslim trade institutions, stores and shops closed and the streets utterly decorated. Additionally, while the Great Delegation was walking around in Smyrna, no sign of respect was demonstrated by the Ottoman Greeks (*Rumlardan*), except for a few that were moved and cornered by the crowd and took their hats off. Only during the visit of the Great Delegation to Boudjah, and even then solely upon obligation stemming from an order given by the Metropolitan Bishop to the priest, did the Greek Orthodox school come out for reception (*Rum mektebi istikbâle çıktı*). The newspaper named *Vima*, which was published in Smyrna, took its insolence as far as attacking the members of the metropolitan bishop's office (*metropolithâne erkânına hücûm*), which had ordered the inhabitants of Boudjah, the majority being foreigners and Ottoman Greeks, to show respect. The newspaper also published an article that insulted the Advisory Delegation and His Excellency the Prince.[129]

The Ottoman government issued a decree for the return of exiled Ottoman Christians to their hometowns on 18 October 1918.[130] Following this

Gradual Intimidation in Western Anatolia

development, the Ottoman Greeks and Armenians, who had taken shelter in the territories occupied by the Allied states, began returning to their homelands. The Ottoman government established mixed commissions including Greek, Armenian and Muslim members with the aim of coping with the housing and property problems that could emerge from the return of the Greeks and Armenians.[131]

Following these events, the Armenian and Greek Section was established within the British High Commission in Constantinople. This section was divided into two sub-units as Armenian and Greek departments, and dealt with the issues of converted Christian orphans, the restitution of illegally requisitioned properties, and the removal of undesirable Ottoman officials who were active in the organisation of boycotts, expulsions and mass murders. Somerset Calthorpe, the British high commissioner in the Ottoman capital, warned the members of this department that they had to act cautiously as 'any excessive activity' could trigger the escape of Islamised Greeks and Armenians to the interior of Anatolia, where the Allied Powers were not able to exert their authority.[132] Besides his warning, he demanded the reparation of destroyed property and the cooperation of the Ottoman authorities with the members of the departments.

After the return of exiled Christians, the course of intercommunal relations differed from town to town. In the coastal districts of the Smyrna *sanjak* such as Çeşme, Karaburun and Foça, where the Greek Orthodox inhabitants had constituted the majority of the population prior to 1914, there was not a single Greek Orthodox citizen left by 1917.[133] Many of the most difficult problems emerged in these coastal towns where most of the migrants were concentrated. For example, the Greek Orthodox community protested against the misconduct of Emîn Fikrî Bey, commander of Gendarme Forces, in Urla. Intercommunal violence broke out in the town on 22 January. In early March, in the north of the Gulf of Smyrna, seven Orthodox Greeks were murdered by gendarme forces under the leadership of Refik Bey around the sacred spring (*agiasma*) of Agios Ilias Pavlos in Foça. The suburbs of Smyrna were not exempt from the violence directed at the returning Ottoman Christians. Ottoman Greeks celebrating the Greek New Year in Bayraklı on 14 January were fired on, with several people killed.[134] In Boudjah, a band composed of Cretan Muslims reportedly attacked Christian inhabitants there as well.[135]

Minor clashes that arose during the return of the refugees were likely to menace intercommunal relations and the security of the province. For instance, two Greek refugees, having landed from Samos in early March without official permission, insulted an official in the branch of the Ottoman Public Debt Administration (OPDA; Düyûn-i Umûmiye) in

Akköy (Ieronda), an exclusively Ottoman Greek village in the southwestern corner of the province. A gendarmerie officer accompanied by fifteen men was sent from Söke to investigate the incident. Upon arriving in Akköy, the officer called the head (*muhtar*) and elders of the village, and the whole affair was settled satisfactorily. Nevertheless, another group of Greek refugees ambushed the officer and his men on their return, broke into the military store and looted rifles and bombs. Since they began to attack the fortifications in Akköy, the 135th Regiment was sent from Ödemiş to Söke. Inasmuch as these incidents incurred great excitement in the neighbouring villages, Lieutenant Gooding went to meet with Governor Nureddin Pasha. Eventually, he persuaded the governor to banish the refugees who had lacked permission certificates instead of sending them to court.[136] Once Lieutenant Ben Hodder was posted to Akköy to monitor the situation, no further trouble occurred. Both Muslim and Orthodox communities were confident that in case of any disagreement, they could appeal to Hodder for an impartial decision.[137]

To sum up, the Unionist rule and the Great War brought about a political and social shift in the Empire. A series of political events such as the annexation of Crete by Greece in 1908 and the Balkan Wars in 1912–13 affected the practices of everyday life and played an important role in the polarisation of Christian–Muslim relations in the *fin-de-siècle* province. The trauma of the Balkan Wars raised Unionist doubts about the loyalty of the Christian communities. Talât Pasha, minister of the interior, estimated in a session in the Ottoman parliament that some 150,000 Ottoman Greeks 'abandoned' the Aegean coastal zone as a result of the expulsions of the Greeks organised by local branches of the Special Organisation in the summer of 1914.[138] According to statistics from the Ecumenical Patriarchate, 153,890 Ottoman Greeks were forced out of the Aegean littoral by the end of 1914.[139] In one of the earliest books on population transfers among the three post-Ottoman states, Ladas also confirmed these numbers.[140] The aim behind these expulsions was the liquidation of the property of Greek merchants living in the coastal towns of Aydın Province, and repopulating those towns with Muslim migrants from Salonica, Kavala and Kosovo.[141] The existence of large Greek Orthodox communities could not be tolerated by a political party whose interests lay in the expulsion of the non-Muslim commercial bourgeoisie. Prominent members of the CUP, therefore, adhered to the idea that the Ottoman Greeks in the coastal settlements of Aydın Province had close ties with the Kingdom of Greece and could serve as a fifth column.[142] Moreover, thanks to their expulsion, confiscated properties could be given to Muslim migrants who had arrived in the Ottoman territories in large numbers.

Gradual Intimidation in Western Anatolia

Ethnic cleansing in the region during World War I was conducted on two different trajectories; the one perpetrated in the urban settlements of Smyrna, Manisa and Aydın, and those carried out in the coastal towns, such as Urla, Çeşme and Foça. Perpetrators of ethnic cleansing deliberately created a wave of hatred directed against the Christians in locations such as Smyrna, Manisa and Aydın. However, their ultimate goal was not the utter annihilation of the Ottoman Christian population, but rather to intimidate these people into leaving. In coastal towns such as Urla, Çeşme and Foça, however, permanent banishment of the Ottoman Greek population for a purported threat to national security, justifying the intensive acts of intimidation and murder practised without hesitation in these smaller coastal towns. The next chapter traces the consequences of the refugee crisis on both sides of the Aegean and analyses to what extent these shaped the policies of the post-war High Commission.

Notes

1. Cemal Pasha, a member of the dictatorial triumvirate, states that 'the most important ethnic problem (*en mühim unsur meselesi*) was the question of the Ottoman Greeks (*Rumlar meselesi*) who constituted the majority of the population in the coastal part of Aydın province', see Cemal Paşa, *Hatıralar* (Istanbul: İş Bankası Yayınları, 2006), 88.
2. See Göçek, *Rise of the Bourgeoisie.*
3. Erik Jan Zürcher, 'The Young Turks – Children of the Borderlands?', *International Journal of Turkish Studies*, 9 (2003), 279–82.
4. Ibid. 281–3.
5. The committee's initiation process was similar to a ritual. In this ceremony, the prospective member had to take an oath on the Qur'an and a pistol, see George Gawrych, 'The Culture and Politics of Violence in Turkish Society, 1903–14', *Middle Eastern Studies* 22, no. 3 (1986), 312.
6. Le Bon explained that 'what most differentiates Europeans from Orientals is that only the former possess an élite of superior men', see Timothy Mitchell, *Colonising Egypt* (New York: Cambridge University Press 1988), 124.
7. Frederick F. Anscombe, *State, Faith, and Nation in Ottoman and Post-Ottoman Lands* (New York: Cambridge University Press, 2014), 123–4.
8. Celal Bayar, *Ben de Yazdım*, vol. 5 (Istanbul: Baha Matbassı, 1967), 1578.
9. For a specific case study, see François Georgeon, *Aux origines du nationalisme turc: Yusuf Akçura, 1876–1935* (Paris: Editions ADPF, 1980).
10. The *narodnik*s, which was an intellectual and populist movement, believed that *narod* (*Volk*) was a naive and simple people. According to this romantic idea, good-natured peasants were endangered by city life.
11. Masami Arai, 'Between State and Nation: A New Light on the Journal *Türk Yurdu*', *Turcica* 24 (1992), 279.

Ethnic Cleansing in Western Anatolia

12. Yusuf Akçura, *Üç Tarz-ı Siyaset* (Ankara: Lotus, 2005), 58–62.
13. Dündar, *Modern Türkiye'nin Şifresi*, 79–83.
14. Niyazi Berkes, *Turkish Nationalism and Western Civilization: Selected Essays of Ziya Gökalp* (New York: Columbia University Press, 1959), 58–9.
15. Arai, 'Between State and Nation', 289.
16. Cemal Pasha described Câvit Bey as 'the organiser and soul of the economic policies of the CUP', Cemal Paşa, *Hatıralar*, 80. As Zürcher points out Câvit Bey being a Sabbataist or *dönme* was the only exception among the Unionists who were Muslim males of different ethnic origins, see Zürcher, 'The Young Turks – Children of the Borderlands?', 279–82.
17. Erik Jan Zürcher, 'The Vocabulary of Muslim Nationalism', *International Journal of the Sociology of Language* 137 (1999), 89.
18. Erik J. Zürcher, 'The Young Turk Mindset', in Zürcher, *The Young Turk Legacy and Nation Building: From the Ottoman Empire to Atatürk's Turkey* (London: I. B. Tauris, 2010), 111.
19. For the concept of demographic engineering, see Milica Zarkovic Bookman, *The Demographic Struggle for Power: The Political Economy of Demographic Engineering in the Modern World* (London: Routledge, 1997); and Myron Weiner and Michael Teitelbaum, *Political Demography, Demographic Engineering* (New York: Berghahn Books, 2001).
20. Abdülhamit II, who established tribal schools (*aşiret mektepleri*) and Hamidiye regiments (*Hamidiye alayları*) and followed a pan-Islamist policy, benefited from the influx of Muslim migrants from the Balkan provinces and Caucasia. This migration would continue during the second half of the nineteenth century. During his reign, the idea that Christian elements cooperated with their nationalist counterparts gained popularity and hopes for an Ottoman union were disappointed. With the arrival of thousands of migrants, some strategic points in Western Anatolia were deliberately populated by loyal elements, that is, Circassians and Balkan Muslims. After the resettlement of the migrants, intercommunal relations became tense between migrant Muslims and local Christians. Some Ottoman documents mentioned that the migrants from North Caucasus were charged with theft, robbery and brigandage in the provinces, see BOA HR. MKT 898/66, BOA DH. TMIK. M 232/27 and BOA HSD. AFT 3/76.
21. Fikret Adanır, 'Bulgaristan, Yunanistan ve Türkiye Üçgeninde Ulus İnşası ve Nüfus Değişimi', in *Türkiye'de Etnik Çatışma*, ed. Erik Jan Zürcher (Istanbul: İletişim Yayınları, 2005), 21.
22. Gingeras, *Sorrowful Shores*, 55–6.
23. Therefore, the exemptions previously given to some groups were abolished as the law of universal conscription was ratified, as a result of which both the students of Muslim religious schools and non-Muslims were obliged to do military service.

Gradual Intimidation in Western Anatolia

24. Erik Jan Zürcher, 'Ottoman Labour Battalions in World War I', in *Der Völkermold an den Armeniern und die Shoah*, ed. Hans-Lukas Kieser and Dominik J. Schaller (Zurich: Chronos, 2002), 191–2.

25. See *Düstur*, 2. Tertib, vol. 1, no. 121, H. 29 Recep 1327 (16 August 1909) (Dersaadet: Matbaa-i Osmaniye, H. 1329), 604–8.

26. Ryan Gingeras, *Fall of the Sultanate: The Great War and the End of the Ottoman Empire, 1908–1922* (Oxford: Oxford University Press, 2016), 40.

27. Sabri Yetkin, *Ege'de Eşkıyalar* (Istanbul: Tarih Vakfı Yurt Yayınları, 1997), 133.

28. TNA FO 195/2396, 15 May 1912, Alfred Biliotti, Acting Vice Consul in Rhodes, to Henry D. Barnham, Consul General in Smyrna. Some Ottoman Greeks had welcomed Italian occupying forces in Rhodes. Actually, the Italo-Ottoman War of 1911–12, in a sense, became the first event that triggered these hostile policies targeting the Christian communities. Moreover, Fortna underlines that the Italo-Ottoman War was a critical point in the education of Muslim children and triggered the 'militarisation of learning'. Following this war, themes of militant nationalism prevailed over children's literature, see Benjamin C. Fortna, *Learning to Read in the Late Ottoman Empire and the Early Turkish Republic* (Basingstoke: Palgrave Macmillan, 2011), 27. In particular, Unionist statesmen suspected that the Christian communities on the Aegean islands contributed to the Italian navy. The CUP considered the existence of the non-Turkish and non-Muslim groups in the border regions of the Empire dangerous since these groups could be used by the Great Powers or their kin states as a pretext for the seizure of the Ottoman lands.

29. The plundering activities were so violent in the districts of Malkara and Tekfurdağı (Rodosto/Tekirdağ) that the consuls of European Powers (Britain, France, Germany, Austro-Hungary, Italy and Russia) protested against the attacks, see TNA FO 195/2453, 28 July 1913.

30. M. Şükrü Hanioğlu, *Preparation for a Revolution: The Young Turks, 1902–1908* (Oxford: Oxford University Press, 2001), 242–4.

31. Benjamin C. Fortna, *The Circassian: A Life of Eşref Bey, Late Ottoman Insurgent and Special Agent* (London: Hurst, 2016), 5.

32. Hüsamettin Ertürk, *İki Devrin Perde Arkası*, ed. Samih Nafiz Tansu (Istanbul: Sebil Yayınevi, 1996), 98. Hüsamettin Ertürk was a military officer and an important figure in the Special Organisation.

33. According to Cemal Pasha's memoirs, many members of the Special Organisation favoured the continuation of the provisional government. In spite of the Ottoman guarantee in the Treaty of Constantinople in September 1913 for the consolidation of the Bulgarian rule in Western Thrace, they planned to resist against the Bulgarian troops. See Cemal Paşa, *Hatıralar*, 63.

34. Fortna, *The Circassian*, 121.

35. Çerkes Mustafa Nuri Bey, Eşref's father, belonged to the retinue of Abdülhamit II. Hacı Selim Sami Bey, Eşref's brother, was sent to the

Ethnic Cleansing in Western Anatolia

province for the purpose of killing Çakırcalı Mehmet Efe, a well-known Turcoman bandit in September 1911. Later, Eşref also joined him with his Circassian bands, see Yetkin, *Ege'de Eşkıyalar*, 142–3. The arrival of Sami Bey and his early activities to kill Çakırcalı Mehmet triggered the hostilities between the Circassian and Turcoman bandit groups, BOA DH. H 14-2/27.

36. Rahmî was regarded as 'one of the leaders of the extremist section of the Committee of Union and Progress' by the British consul in Smyrna, see TNA FO 195/2458, 21 July 1914. He was born into a wealthy family that claimed ties with Evrenos, a fourteenth-century legendary Ottoman commander, in Salonica, another cosmopolitan port city of the Empire, in 1873. For a short biography of Rahmî Bey, see Mehmet Ali Keskin, *İzmir Valileri, 1300–1989* (Izmir: Karınca Matbaacılık, 1989), 81–2. He was one of the first members of the Ottoman Liberty Society (Osmanlı Hürriyet Cemiyeti), established in Salonica in the summer of 1906 and which was the predecessor of the Committee of Union and Progress. For the Ottoman Liberty Society, see Tarık Zafer Tunaya, *Türkiye'de Siyasal Partiler, vol. 1: İkinci Meşrutiyet Dönemi* (Istanbul: Hürriyet Vakfı Yayınları, 1984), 21–2. When the CUP movement emerged as one of the important political groups in 1908, Rahmî appeared as one of its prominent figures. He was elected as a representative of Salonica province in November 1908. In spite of the fact that he was not appointed to a cabinet-level position after the 1908 restoration, he was appointed governor of Aydın Province on 29 September 1913, following the Balkan Wars.

37. TNA FO 195/ 2458, 27 July 1914, Heathcote-Smith to H. D. Beaumont, Chargé d'Affaires in Constantinople.

38. Bayar, *Ben de Yazdım*, vol. 5, 1567–70.

39. Mehmet Reşit Şahingiray, *Hayatı ve Hatıraları: İttihad ve Terakki Dönemi ve Ermeni Meselesi*, ed. Nejdet Bilgi (Izmir: Akademi Kitabevi, 1997), 65–75.

40. TNA FO 195/ 2458, 22 September 1914, Heathcote-Smith to Louis Mallet in Constantinople.

41. TNA FO 195/ 2458, 8 July 1914, Heathcote-Smith to Louis Mallet in Constantinople.

42. Y. Doğan Çetinkaya, *1908 Osmanlı Boykotu: Bir Toplumsal Hareketin Analizi* (Istanbul: İletişim Yayınları, 2004), 135–66.

43. Here, Falmpos's account contradicts with the historical facts about the name of the head of the chamber. At that time, the head of the chamber was Hadji Davud Farkoh, a Syriac Christian possessing American citizenship.

44. Aristomenēs Kalyviōtēs, *Smyrnē, Ē Mousikē Zōē* (Athens: Music Corner & Tinella, 2002), 56, citing Filippos K. Falmpos, *Smyrnaïka Meletēmata* (Athens: n.p., 1980).

45. 'Belediyenin Taksîmi Mes'elesi', *Âhenk*, 17 August 1910.

46. 'Vilâyete ait Küçük Haberler', *Köylü*, 25 June 1910 (R. 12 Haziran 1326).

47. TNA FO 371/1015, 21 September 1910, Sir Gerard Lowther, the British Ambassador in Constantinople, to Foreign Office.

Gradual Intimidation in Western Anatolia

48. Aristomenēs Kalyviōtēs, *Smyrnē, Ē Mousikē Zōē* (Athens: Music Corner & Tinella, 2002), 52–4.
49. TNA FO 195/2360, 20 September 1910, Consul General Barnham to Sir Gerard Lowther.
50. TNA FO 195/2383, 7 June 1911, Barnham to Sir Gerard Lowther.
51. Since this battleship carried the name of Georgios Averof, Ottoman journalists presumed that this ship was donated by Averof. In fact, one-third of the money required to get this ship was donated by the foundation established by Georgios Averof, a Greek businessman in Alexandria. The remaining portion was met completely by the Greek state budget, Ayhan Aktar, 'Osmanlı Meclisi Ermeni Meselesini Tartışıyor: Kasım-Aralık 1918', in *İmparatorluğun Çöküş Döneminde Osmanlı Ermenileri: Bilimsel Sorumluluk ve Demokrasi Sorunları*, ed. Fahri Aral (Istanbul: Bilgi University Press, 2011), 357. Another piece of misinformation in this brochure was Averof's hometown. He was actually from Metsovo, not Korytsa (Görice).
52. According to Y. Doğan Çetinkaya, the boycott movements became a crucial weapon in the elimination of the Christian bourgeoisie from the Ottoman economy after the Cretan question, see Çetinkaya, *The Young Turks and the Boycott Movement* (London: I. B. Tauris, 2014), 120. However, it should be borne in mind that boycotts intensified at a later date, probably in the summer of 1914, and even the boycotts could not completely liquidate property of non-Muslim merchants. These boycotts were coordinated by prominent Unionists such as Rahmî Bey, governor-general, and Nazmi Bey, secretary general, cf. TNA FO 195/2458, 4 July 1914, Report of Investigation by W. Matthews to Louis Mallet. Rahmî Bey reported that it was difficult to control Muslim Cretans, the most conspicuous enforcers of the boycotts, TNA FO 195/2458, 8 July 1914, Heathcote-Smith to Louis Mallet.
53. TNA FO 195/2458, 18 February 1914, Consul-General Barnham to Sir Louis Mallet in Constantinople.
54. There are very rare examples of Ottoman Christians' collaboration with Greek forces during the First Balkan Wars of 1912–13. For example, a certain Nicholas and his four comrades, Ottoman citizens by birth, supported the Greek navy during the occupation of Mytilene. However, following the war, they were condemned to death by the military tribunal at Smyrna, see Fikret Adanır, 'Non-Muslims in the Ottoman Army and the Ottoman Defeat in the Balkan War of 1912–1913', in *A Question of Genocide*, ed. Ronald Grigor Suny et al. (Oxford: Oxford University Press, 2011), 124.
55. This directorate was renamed and restructured as the General Directorate for Refugees (Muhâcirîn Müdüriyet-i Umûmiyesi) in 1916.
56. Dündar, *İttihat ve Terakkinin*, 58–62.
57. Elçin Macar, 'The Muslim Emigration in Western Anatolia', *Cahiers balkaniques* 40 (2012), 227–34.

Ethnic Cleansing in Western Anatolia

58. Toumarkine, *Les Migrations*, 87–8.
59. TNA FO 195/2458, 21 July 1914, Report on tour in the Brusa and Smyrna districts by W. Matthews to H. D. Beaumont.
60. TNA FO 195/ 2458, 8 July 1914, Heathcote-Smith to Louis Mallet.
61. TNA FO 195/2458, 21 July 1914, Confidential memorandum.
62. TNA FO 195/ 2458, 21 July 1914, Report on tour in the Brusa and Smyrna districts by W. Matthews to H. D. Beaumont.
63. Clark, *Twice a Stranger*, 38.
64. TNA FO 195/ 2458, 27 July 1914, Heathcote-Smith to H. D. Beaumont.
65. See Félix Sartiaux, *Le sac de Phocée et l'expulsion des Grecs Ottomans d'Asie Mineure en juin 1914* (Paris: Typographie Philippe Renouard, 1914).
66. TNA FO 383/95, 7 May 1915, G. Anamissaki, British vice-consul in Chios, to F. Elliot, British Ambassador in Athens.
67. Mustafa Aksakal, *The Ottoman Road to War in 1914: The Ottoman Empire and the First World War* (Cambridge: Cambridge University Press, 2010), 85–8.
68. Cemal Paşa, *Hatıralar*, 124–30.
69. TNA FO 608/102, 5 June 1919, Memorandum by the Ottoman Railway Company.
70. Feroz Ahmad, 'Vanguard of a Nascent Bourgeoisie: The Social and Economic Policy of the Young Turks, 1908–1918', in *Social and Economic History of Turkey (1071–1920)*, ed. Osman Okyar and Halil İnalcık (Ankara: Meteksan Limited Şirketi, 1980), 336–7.
71. TNA FO 383/234, 21 June 1916, American Ambassador in Constantinople to Foreign Office. During the war, Smyrna was bombarded three times by the Allied planes. The second wave of bombing took place in July 1916 and the last wave in January 1918.
72. Donald H. Simpson, *Anglican Church Life in Smyrna and Its Neighbourhood 1636–1952*, manuscript, Diocese of Gibraltar, 1952, held by Guildhall Library, 95. See also 'Muhasım Devletler Tebaası', *Âhenk*, 9 March 1915 (R. 24 Şubat 1330). The newspaper mentions the imprisonment of the members of Whittall, Giraud and Guiffray families in Eşrefpaşa neighbourhood. Additionally, some properties of the Allied subjects, as in the case of Rees mansion in Boudjah, were forcibly requisitioned by the Ottoman authorities, cf. TNA FO 383/ 95, 22 January 1915, A. E. C. Bird to Foreign Office.
73. Mansel, *Levant*, 197–8.
74. TNA FO 383/91, 6 November 1914, George Horton, American Consul-General to the Secretary of State.
75. Simpson, 95.
76. Letter written by Levantine residents to Rahmî Bey, my thanks to Ms Esma Dino Deyer for allowing me access to this important source.
77. Zafer Toprak, *Türkiye'de Milli İktisat, 1908–1918* (Istanbul: Doğan Kitap, 2012), 62.

Gradual Intimidation in Western Anatolia

78. Manisa Bank of Vinedressers was founded under the leadership of the Unionists in order to restrict the market activities of non-Muslim and foreign merchants who dealt with the grape trade. Thirty-five of its fifty-eight founding members were actively affiliated with the CUP. Ibid. 278. National Bank of Aydın, which continued its activities in the building of the Turkish Hearth, was also established by Unionist merchants.
79. Ibid. 277.
80. *Âhenk*, 8 March 1915 (R. 23 Şubat 1330).
81. See *İslâm Tüccâr ve Esnâflarına Mahsûs Rehber* (Izmir: Donanma-yi Osmaniye, 1914).
82. Rahmî founded several commissions aiming to reduce the impact of emerging problems due to the outbreak of World War I. Nadir Özbek presents that first National Defence Committee was established in Constantinople on 1 February 1913 in order to serve the national cause during the critical days of the First Balkan War, see Nadir Özbek, 'Defining the Public Sphere during the Late Ottoman Empire: War, Mass Mobilization, and the Young Turk Regime (1908–18)', *Middle Eastern Studies* 43, no. 5 (September 2007), 800–1.
83. Kemal Karpat, 'The People's Houses in Turkey, Establishment and Growth', *The Middle East Journal* 17 (1963), 55–6. There are clues that Enver Pasha financially supported the activities of the Turkish Hearths. By 1918, the Turkish Hearts had twenty-eight branches in the provinces, see Günver Güneş, 'İzmir Türk Ocağı (1912–1918)', *Kebikeç* 4 (1996), 149.
84. Füsun Üstel, *İmparatorluktan Ulus-Devlete Türk Milliyetçiliği: Türk Ocakları, 1912–1931* (Istanbul: İletişim Yayınları, 1997), 51–69.
85. Alan Kramer, *Dynamic of Destruction: Culture and Mass Killing in the First World War* (Oxford: Oxford University Press, 2009), 150.
86. Erik Jan Zürcher, 'The Late Ottoman Empire as a Laboratory of Social Engineering', *Il Mestiere di Storico* 10, no. 1 (2009), 10–14. For the resettlement of Muslim migrants, see Dündar, *İttihat ve Terakkinin*.
87. Mark Mazower, *Salonica, City of Ghosts: Christians, Muslims, and Jews, 1430–1950* (New York: Alfred A. Knopf, 2005), 430.
88. Taçalan, *Ege'de Kurtuluş Savaşı Başlarken*, 40–1.
89. BOA DH. ŞFR 50/187.
90. BOA DH. ŞFR 53/75.
91. Llewellyn Smith, *Ionian Vision: Greece in Asia Minor, 1919–22* (New York: Columbia University Press, 1998), 34.
92. BOA DH. ŞFR 50/ 236, BOA DH. ŞFR 67/185, BOA DH. ŞFR 92/175 and BOA DH. EUM. 3ŞB 12/59-1.
93. BOA DH. ŞFR 54/118.
94. BOA DH. ŞFR 53/253.
95. Although Criss claimed that the Ottoman Greeks were sent to Greece as a deterrent against political uprising and suffered only from material losses, they were deported from the coastal regions with loss of life.

Ethnic Cleansing in Western Anatolia

For Criss's argument, see Nur Bilge Criss, *Istanbul under Allied Occupation, 1918–1923* (Leiden: Brill, 1999), 40.

96. BOA DH. ŞFR 71/111.
97. BOA DH. ŞFR 71/56.
98. BOA DH. ŞFR 102/56 and BOA DH. EUM. 3ŞB 12/51.
99. TNA WO 157/695, 15 September 1915, Intelligence Summary, Military Intelligence Office in Cairo. The Christian labour battalions were compelled to build the road from Kuşadası to Ayasuluk.
100. TNA WO 157/695, 27 September 1915, Intelligence Summary, Military Intelligence Office in Cairo.
101. BOA DH. ŞFR 58/191.
102. BOA DH. ŞFR 59/20.
103. See *1333 Senesi Tevellüdat ve Vefeyat İstatistiği: İzmir ve Çevresi Nüfus İstatistiği*, ed. Erkan Serçe (Izmir: Akademi Kitabevi, 1998).
104. Taçalan, *Ege'de Kurtuluş Savaşı Başlarken*, 30.
105. Giles Milton, *Paradise Lost: Smyrna 1922, The Destruction of Islam's City of Tolerance* (New York: Basic Books, 2008), 69–89.
106. Ali Fuat Türkgeldi, *Görüp İşittiklerim* (Ankara: Türk Tarih Kurumu, 2010), 153. General Townshend was kept as a war captive in Prinkopo (Büyükada).
107. *Haccac* is a specific term inspired by the personality of al-Hajjaj ibn Yusuf and given to a tyrannical ruler in Islamic history.
108. Irâkî, 'El-Âmân!', *Müsavat*, 17 January 1919 (R. 17 Kânûn-i Sânî 1335).
109. Hasan Tahsîn, 'Arama Bulmayasın!', *Hukuk-ı Beşer*, 29 March 1919 (R. 29 Mart 1335).
110. Hilmi Uran, *Hatıralarım* (Ankara: Ayyıldız Matbaası, 1959), 122.
111. Hüseyin Cahit Yalçın, *Siyasal Anılar* (Istanbul: Türkiye İş Bankası Yayınları, 1979), 259. He was set free in October 1921 due to efforts of Charlton Whittall, a prominent British Levantine from Bournabat. Despite his participation in the nationalist movement in the later phase, Rahmî would have a minor role in the movement.
112. BOA BEO 4552/ 341332.
113. BOA BEO 4555/ 341590.
114. Spyridon Loverdos, *O Mētropolitēs Smyrnēs: Chrysostomos* (Athens: P. D. Sakellarios, 1929), 179–80.
115. BOA DH. EUM. 3ŞB 27/47.
116. BOA DH. KMS 50/4.
117. BOA DH. EUM. AYŞ 9/20. This 270-page book narrated the attacks of the Unionist bands on the Greek settlements in the Aegean littoral on the eve of World War I and listed the names of the victims, see Loverdos, *O Mētropolitēs Smyrnēs*, 172–3.
118. BOA BEO 4559/ 341861.
119. Nail Moralı, *Mütarekede İzmir Olayları* (Ankara: Türk Tarih Kurumu Basımevi, 1973), 58–9.

Gradual Intimidation in Western Anatolia

120. TNA FO 371/ 4157, 7 April 1919, Ian M. Smith, Area Control Officer at Smyrna to General Staff Intelligence at Constantinople.

121. CADN, Izmir 643 PO/1, 26, 12 April 1919, Situation politique. Another document shows that İzzet Bey informed the Ministry of the Interior about peaceful Easter celebrations by the Greek Orthodox communities 'without unfurling the Greek flag' ('Yunan bayrağı ile eylemeksizin') in Smyrna, cf. BOA DH. ŞFR 624/147.

122. Even though the CUP was not the governing political party, it still formed a majority in the Ottoman parliament. The Unionists continued to be effective in the ranks of civil service, army, and provincial administration, see Zürcher, *The Unionist Factor*, 75–8. The CUP still possessed funds and a strong support within the army, cf. TNA FO 608/ 103, 12 May 1919, James Morgan, Smyrna representative of the British High Commissioner, to the British High Commission in Constantinople.

123. TNA FO 371/ 4157, 7 April 1919, Ian M. Smith, Area Control Officer at Smyrna to General Staff Intelligence at Constantinople.

124. TNA FO 608/103, 7 April 1919, W. Lewis Bailey, British Consul in Mytilini, to Lord Granville. Since Mehmet Reşit committed suicide in January 1919, it is more likely that it was rather Çerkes Reşit, Çerkes Ethem's brother, who was mentioned here. As Fortna indicated, the fact that the kidnapping of Rahmî's son, Alparslan, on 12 February 1919, by a group of bandits led by Çerkes Reşit proves that the Ottoman provincial authorities and Çerkes Reşit were clearly in a conflict at the time, see Fortna, *The Circassian*, 225–7.

125. It seems that Celâl continued working for the Unionist movement in the countryside of the province and was elected as the Saruhan *sanjak* representative in the Ottoman Parliament in October 1919 with Çerkes Reşit and Hamdullah Subhi, former chair of the Turkish Hearths, cf. BOA DH. ŞFR 651/73 and BOA DH. İ-UM. EK 117/60.

126. TNA FO 371/ 4157, 7 April 1919, Ian M. Smith, Area Control Officer at Smyrna to General Staff Intelligence at Constantinople.

127. TNA FO 608/103, 12 May 1919, James Morgan, Smyrna representative of the British High Commission, to the British High Commission in Constantinople. The members of the Ottoman Peace and Welfare Party (Sulh ve Selâmet-i Osmâniyye Fırkası) and Freedom and Accord Party were supporting the new governor-general, though they had little influence in the province, TNA FO 371/ 4157, 7 April 1919, Ian M. Smith, Area Control Officer at Smyrna to General Staff Intelligence at Constantinople.

128. TNA FO 608/108, 17 March 1919, Mehmed Ali, Minister of the Interior, to British Embassy.

129. BOA DH. EUM. AYŞ 8/105.

130. BOA DH. ŞFR 92/187 and BOA DH. ŞFR 92/199.

131. Stanford J. Shaw, 'Resettlement of Refugees in Anatolia, 1918–1923', *The Turkish Studies Association Bulletin* 22, no. 1 (1998), 62–6.

Ethnic Cleansing in Western Anatolia

132. TNA FO 608/111, 30 March 1919, Note of the British High Commission.
133. *1333 Senesi Tevellüdat ve Vefeyat.*
134. TNA FO 371/ 4157, 15 January 1919, Dixon, Resident Senior Naval Officer at Smyrna to British High Commissioner.
135. TNA FO 371/ 4157, 7 April 1919, Ian M. Smith, Area Control Officer at Smyrna to General Staff Intelligence at Constantinople.
136. TNA FO 608/113, 5 March 1919, Lieutenant Gooding to James Morgan.
137. TNA FO 608/103, 20 April 1919, Ian M. Smith, British Control Officer in Smyrna, to the British High Commission in Constantinople. According to Şefik Aker, Ben Hodder was an official of the Söke plant of the MacAndrews & Forbes company, a liquorice manufacturing and exporting company based in Smyrna, Şefik Aker, *İstiklâl Harbinde 57. Tümen ve Aydın Milli Cidali* (Istanbul: Askeri Matbaa, 1937), vol. 1, 14.
138. Gingeras, *Fall of the Sultanate*, 97.
139. Efē Allamanē and Krista Panagiōtopoulou, 'O ellēnismos tēs Mikras Asias se diōgmo', in *Istoria tou Ellēnikou Ethnous, vol. 15: Neōteros Ellēnismos apo to 1913 ōs to 1941* (Athens: Ekdotikē Athēnōn, 1978), 100.
140. Stephen Pericles Ladas, *The Exchange of Minorities: Bulgaria, Greece, and Turkey* (New York: Macmillan, 1932), 15–16.
141. Nesim Şeker, 'Osmanlı İmparatorluğunun Son Döneminde 'Demografi Mühendisliği' ve Ermeniler', in *İmparatorluğun Çöküş Döneminde Osmanlı Ermenileri: Bilimsel Sorumluluk ve Demokrasi Sorunları*, ed. Fahri Aral (Istanbul: Bilgi University Press, 2011), 169.
142. Matthias Bjornlund, 'The 1914 Cleansing of Aegean Greeks as a Case of Violent Turkification', in *Late Ottoman Genocides: The Dissolution of the Ottoman Empire and Young Turk Population and Extermination Policies*, ed. Dominik Schaller and Jürgen Zimmerer (London: Routledge, 2009), 36.

Chapter 2

Ioniki Tragodia: Greek Administration in Western Anatolia

At dawn on 15 May 1919, thousands of people were waiting at the pier of Smyrna in excitement. The entire city had been adorned with the flags of the Allied Powers (see Figure 2.1). While the liner *Patris* was entering the port, the sailors waved at the people on the shore. The 1/38 Regiment of Evzones landed in the middle of the Quay, and marched southwards along the port to Konak Square, where the Government House was located.

Pandemonium broke out half an hour later as the Evzones troops marched by the Sarı Kışla (Yellow Barracks), the main headquarters of the Ottoman army in the province. Somewhere close to Konak Square, a gun was fired. This was to become the catalyst for armed conflict.

Figure 2.1 Smyrna Quay, 15 May 1919. ELIA/MIET Photographic Archive – Photos Zographos, unnumbered.

Ethnic Cleansing in Western Anatolia

Firing on the Greek troops continued from the prison, military barracks and the gendarmerie school. Greek soldiers rushed into the barracks, where there was a small Ottoman battalion, and battled for twenty minutes. Ottoman military and administrative authorities, including Ahmet İzzet, the governor-general, were arrested and, according to Donald Whittall, an English Levantine merchant who witnessed the incident, 'were made to go through no end of humiliation and received a good deal of knocking about'.[1]

Ethnic fighting broke out in the streets. Civilian gangs, not all of them Greek, plundered Muslim-owned shops. Beyond downtown Smyrna, in Bournabat, fifteen Muslims were killed and farmhouses around the town were looted. In Paradiso, where the International College was located, a mob plundered an arms depot and killed three Muslims.[2] The Greek landing would change power relations in Western Anatolia.

Tracing the consequences of the refugee crisis on both sides of the Aegean, and analysing to what extent this shaped the policies of the High Commission of Smyrna in the post-World War I period, this chapter focuses on the administration of the areas occupied by Greece in Western Anatolia as a result of post-war considerations. Moreover, this chapter will cast light upon the dynamics of the Greek administration in Western Anatolia between 1919 and 1922, and the conflicts between the controversial Aristides Stergiades, Greek high commissioner, and other interest groups in the region.

I argue that these tensions were the main reasons behind the eventual inadequacy of the High Commission, beginning with its ambiguous character and a short assessment of the peaceful variant of the Greek nationalist project inspired by the ideas of Rigas Velestinlis. By the beginning of the twentieth century, gathering knowledge about Anatolia in the genre of *I Kath'imas Anatoli* (Our Anatolia) had become an area of expertise institutionalised in the Greek capital, especially in government ministries and the university. This expertise was reflected in popular writing, newspapers, consular reports, travellers' accounts and memoirs. On the eve of the Balkan Wars, this conception was elaborated in the works of Greek diplomat Ion Dragoumis in Constantinople. The chapter then explores the establishment of the High Commission, its organisational structure, and the challenges directed at it. Administrative and social reforms in the region are also investigated with a special focus on changes in administrative affairs, the judicial system, the regional economy and commercial regulations, and the resettlement of refugees. Finally, the chapter will deal with the movement of Asia Minorism (*Asya-yı Suğrâlılık*) as a supranational solution for the question of ethnic elements (*anâsır meselesi*)

Greek Administration in Western Anatolia

in the region, which became popular subsequent to the Conference of London in 1921, culminating in the creation of an autonomous zone around Smyrna.

A *Variant of the* Megali Idea

The *Megali Idea* (Great Idea), a dream incorporating Greek communities outside Greece into the Kingdom of Greece, permeated all segments of society in the late nineteenth century as the sole ideology in the Kingdom.[3] The classic definition of Greek expansionist ideology and its formulation were declared in the course of a debate in the Greek National Assembly in January 1844 by Ioannis Kolettis, the leader of the French Party.[4] By the turn of the twentieth century, many Greek nationalists had been inspired by the images of the glorious Byzantine Empire and had dreamed to liberate Constantinople one day from 'infidel Turks'.

A vein within the Greek nationalist project, *Megali Idea*, had an imperial conception.[5] Rigas Velestinlis (1757–98),[6] a political thinker and early proponent of Greek Orthodox/Rum nationalism, had proposed a Balkan Orthodox Empire. Born in Velestino, a small town in Thessaly, Rigas studied foreign languages in Constantinople and entered the orbit of the Phanariots, prominent Orthodox families residing in Constantinople and the Danubian Principalities. Later on, he established himself in Bucharest, the capital of autonomous Wallachia,[7] where he became acquainted with the works of the French *philosophes* thanks to Bucharest's proximity to the European capitals.

While the *Megali Idea* was not yet conceived as a nationalist project in Velestinlis's time, he adumbrated one of its archetypical versions in his writings. Velestinlis had served under the Phanariots in the Danubian Principalities and suggested the idea of a Balkan union for the future of the peninsula. He called this political structure the Greek Democracy (*Elliniki Dimokratia*), although it was a kind of restored Byzantine Empire with republican rather than monarchical institutions.[8] He defined the Greek people (O Ellinikē Laos) as the inhabitants of this country 'regardless of religion and language' ('chōris exairesin thrēskeias kai glōssēs').[9] He elaborated a very detailed draft for the administration of this restored Eastern Empire in one of his works, *Nea Politikē Dioikēsē tōn Katoikōn tēs Roumelēs, tēs Mikras Asias, tōn Mesogeiōn Nēsōn kai tēs Vlachobogdanias* (The New Political Administration of the Inhabitants of the Rumelia, Asia Minor, the Mediterranean Islands and the Danubian Principalities). In this text, he argued that freedom of religion should be guaranteed and that all religions (Christianity (*Christianismou*),

Islam (*Tourkismou*), Judaism (*Ioudaïsmou*) and others (*kai ta loipa*)) should not be restricted in this administration (Article 7).[10]

One of the most striking peculiarities of his works was that it anticipated that the new empire, which would stretch to Western Anatolia, would guarantee the rights of Orthodox Christians, as well as other religious groups, namely Muslims and Jews. Another important point was that these works embraced the trajectory of the Ottoman *millet* system to categorise the inhabitants of this new political structure. To exemplify, the word 'Greek' or 'Hellene' was not mentioned in *Thoureios* (Rousing Song), an epic poem written by Velestinlis; instead, Greek-speaking Orthodox Christians were referred to as 'Rōmioi' (Rums).

The Treaty of Adrianople, signed in September 1829 to end the Russo-Ottoman War, assured the establishment of an autonomous Greek state in the Peloponnese. In February 1830, plenipotentiaries of Britain, France and Russia signed the London Protocol which declared Greek independence. This protocol implied the establishment of an independent Greek state in the lands south of the bays of Arta and Volos. Othon of Bavaria, who became the first King of Greece in 1832 under the Convention of London, aimed to create a modern state and employed many scholars, civil servants and officers to begin a period of nation-building, which would continue until the second quarter of the twentieth century. The official historians of the state played a central role in the formation of the *Megali Idea* during this period. For instance, in 1843, Konstantinos Paparrigopoulos, an official in the Ministry of Justice, published his first survey, *Peri tēs epoikēseōs slavikōn tinōn fylōn eis tēn Peloponnēson* (On the Colonisation of the Peloponnese by Certain Slavic Tribes), which formed the intellectual basis of the *Megali Idea*. Emphasising the importance of Byzantium, Paparrigopoulos interpreted Greek history as a single continuum embodying ancient, medieval, and modern periods. Contrary to the views of Jakob Fallmerayer, a Bavarian historian who asserted that modern Hellenes were the descendants of Slavs and Albanians, Paparrigopoulos, who became a professor of history at the University of Athens, claimed in his works that present-day Greeks are the descendants of ancient Greeks, and Hellenic continuity was a linguistic and cultural one.[11] In order to establish this cultural continuity, he underlined the importance of Byzantium in his works.[12]

The ideal of Greco-Ottomanism, however, inspired by the ideas of Velestinlis, was to create a condominium of Orthodox Christians and Muslims in a reformed Ottoman Empire. This movement began to take shape during the relatively peaceful period following the Crimean War. This relatively peaceful variant of the *Megali Idea* developed within Greek nationalism throughout the nineteenth century and emerged in the twentieth century as an alternative to the tangible military variant. Since the messianic character of *Megali Idea* underwent several changes throughout the nineteenth century, modern Hellenic civilisation evolved into a cultural, rather than ethnic, concept. This cultural concept of Hellenic civilisation was accompanied by the idea of a multinational but Hellenised Eastern Empire. It seems that the Greek Kingdom attempted to co-opt the Muslim notables into the provincial notables in certain regions. When Prince George was appointed as the high commissioner of the autonomous Cretan state in December 1898, a proposal to adopt Eastern Orthodox Christianity as the official religion of Crete was rejected. In 1907, Article 7 of the Cretan constitution declared that 'Cretans of all religions are equal before the law and enjoy the same rights.'[13] Again, in April 1899, Hussein Yanitsarakis was appointed as the minister of gendarmerie and police in the first cabinet of Prince George.[14]

A faction within the Greek intelligentsia endorsed the idea of a coalition of the peoples in the Balkan Peninsula and Western Anatolia so as to halt encroachment of the Great Powers on the Empire. Rather than imagining Ottoman Greeks as part of the Kingdom of Greece, this faction sought to maintain Hellenism within a multinational Ottoman Empire. On the eve of the Balkan Wars, Ion Dragoumis,[15] an influential Greek diplomat posted in Constantinople, dreamed of the gradual Greek infiltration into the Ottoman state apparatus as a peaceful fulfilment of the *Megali Idea*. Dragoumis, a prolific nationalist author, served as vice-consul to the Greek consulates in Balkan towns of the Ottoman Empire, such as Monastir and Dede-Agatch, and in several Bulgarian cities between 1902 and 1907, during the critical years of the Macedonian question, before his appointment to Constantinople. As Kechriotis pointed out, Dragoumis's concept of Hellenism did not correspond to a modern European nation.[16] He envisioned a new Eastern Orthodox Empire dominating the Balkans and Western Anatolia:

> As in the case of the Roman state, when equality of rights was accorded to all peoples, the Greeks had succeeded gradually in turning the eastern part of the Empire into a Greek state ... so with the Turkish state ... now that equality of rights is granted to all peoples, the Greeks will take over the political power ... This is the only way to save ourselves. The ideal was an Eastern Empire encompassing all nations ...[17]

Dragoumis's main collaborator was Athanasios Souliotis-Nikolaïdis, who was very active in the establishment of clandestine nationalist organisations during the years of the Macedonian question while he was based in Constantinople. The Organisation of Constantinople (Organōsis

Kōnstantinoupoleōs), a sub-branch of the Panhellenic Organisation, founded through the efforts of Dragoumis and Souliotis, pursued this infiltration by winning the confidence and sympathy of the Muslim population. The main aims of the Organisation of Constantinople were the formation of an alliance with the Armenian and Albanian political parties against the pan-Slavic threat, adoption of Greek as the second official language by the Porte, and getting elected as many Greek representatives as possible to the Ottoman parliament.[18] This organisation was especially strong among the elites of the Greek Orthodox community in the Ottoman capital. In 1908, fifteen out of twenty-three Greek deputies in the Chamber of Deputies (Meclis-i Mebusan) had become members of the organisation.[19] In his works, Dragoumis argued that the fate of the Hellenes was tied to that of other nationalities within the Empire and to the coexistence between them. He envisioned a new Eastern Empire dominating the Near East and mediating between West and East.[20] The prospective Eastern Empire, as Dragoumis envisioned in his 1911 novel *Osoi Zōntanoi* (Those who are Alive), would be 'comprised of all the nations and controlled by the hands of the Greeks'.[21]

The Balkan Wars of 1912–13 dramatically altered the demographic composition of Greece and its relations with its Muslim minorities. After the acquisition of Aegean Macedonia and Epirus in 1913, Greece had to deal with substantial Muslim communities in its northern districts, such as Vodena, Kaïlaria (Ptolemaida), Kavala, Drama and Ioannina.[22] After the Balkan Wars, according to Greek state statistics, nearly 400,000 Muslims continued to live in Aegean Macedonia. Apart from this large community, there were smaller Muslim groups in Epirus, Crete, the Aegean islands and Thessaly. In spite of some atrocities during the Balkan Wars, the relations between Christians and Muslims were normalised in the so-called New Lands after the Balkan Wars.[23] The Treaty of Athens not only guaranteed the lives, property and religious autonomy of Muslim communities, but also protected their educational rights in Macedonia and Epirus.[24] Despite the fact that the application of sharia law was allowed regarding property and religious matters, the sharia courts were abolished and their duties were conveyed to muftis as religious authorities. Incorporation into Greece of these new territories, whose ethnic and religious structures were not homogenous, and the sociopolitical reforms instituted in these territories constituted a great experience for the Greek authorities since the *Megali Idea* project anticipated the establishment of the Greek administration in the ethnically heterogeneous Western Anatolia.

During his prime ministry from 1910 to 1915, Eleftherios Venizelos, a representative of the new political elite which tried to combine institutional

Greek Administration in Western Anatolia

modernisation with expansionist foreign policies, started to surpass the monarchy. Following the end of the Great War, Venizelos, who emerged victorious from a power struggle with King Constantine known as the National Schism (*Dichasmos*), officially dedicated himself to renew the *Megali Idea* project. Moreover, the self-determination and autonomous development principles of Wilson's Fourteen Points, which were the hallmarks of the armistice period, had serious repercussions in diplomatic circles.

Through this context, at the initial meetings of the Committee on Greek Affairs, an Allied committee, at the Paris Peace Conference to study the territorial questions relating to Greece, Venizelos presented the outline of the plan for 'Greece of two continents and five seas' which claimed northern Epirus, all of Thrace up to the gates of Constantinople, the region around Smyrna, and the Aegean islands of Imbros and Tenedos. He expressed hope that Italy would take the initiative in conferring the Dodecanese islands to Greece. He did not claim Constantinople, which the Powers had coveted for a long time. His opinion was that the city had to be transformed into a protectorate of the League of Nations. The region he demanded around Smyrna stretched from Bandırma in the north to the Dodecanese under Italian rule in the south.[25] This area was bigger than Aydın Province and contained the most fertile areas of the Ottoman Empire.

Between Local Opponents and Foreign Restrictions: Establishment of the High Commission of Smyrna

As Victoria Solomonidis has described, the Greek landing on 15 May 1919 was followed by the establishment of the High Commission of Smyrna (Ypatē Armosteia Smyrnēs), whose task was to supervise the Ottoman administration in the Greek-occupied zone. Until the summer of 1920, when the Greek military advance towards Anatolia started, the High Commission had de facto sovereignty in a zone that had almost the same borders as the Ottoman *sanjak* of Smyrna. Since the Greek administration purposely did not abolish the former administration in the region, both the Ottoman institutions and those associated with the High Commission continued to function together in the same areas.

The temporal boundaries of the High Commission can be examined as two distinct periods. The first of these two periods is from 15 May 1919, when the Greek landing took place, to 10 August 1920, when the Treaty of Sèvres was signed. The latter period stretches from the time the treaty was signed until September 1922, when the Kemalist army entered the region. The most important feature distinguishing the former period from

Ethnic Cleansing in Western Anatolia

the latter was that the Ottoman administrative mechanisms in the region continued to function and thus by this time the Greek authorities had not yet taken over the provincial administration. In this first period, the High Commission was to exercise control over the Ottoman administrative authorities, provincial officials and civil servants whose posts were to be preserved intact until the Sèvres Peace Treaty was signed.[26] Basically, the Greek and Ottoman systems of administration worked in conjunction in Smyrna until the treaty was signed.

In the latter period, the Ottoman provincial administration was reshaped in the *sanjak* of Smyrna through bureaucratic and juridical reforms. After the signature of the Treaty of Sèvres, the Greek government divided the Greek occupation zone into two regions, with the Greek Administration of Smyrna in the core and the Military Occupation Zone in the periphery, with different policies implemented for each. Upon signing the treaty, Greece, which occupied a vast area in Western Anatolia, resorted to a mode of institutionalisation only in the Smyrna *sanjak*. The Greek Administration of Smyrna was considered legitimate by the Ottoman government[27] and relations between the two went on in this respect, although the nationalists in Ankara thought otherwise.

As Harris Mylonas indicates, Venizelos 'had a very inclusive understanding of Hellenism'.[28] Indeed, Aristides Stergiades was finally persuaded by Venizelos to represent the Greek government in Western Anatolia and was seen to alight on the quayside of Smyrna six days after the Greek troops had landed. It is important to remember that Stergiades, just like Venizelos, was born in Crete in 1861. After studying law at Athens University, he continued his studies in Germany and France. He returned to Heraklion where he served as president of the municipal council between 1906 and 1910. Following the unification of Crete with Greece, he worked closely with Venizelos, as a renowned liberal and personal friend of Venizelos in the island, to contribute to the extensive legislative work underway. As an expert in Islamic law, he assisted the Liberal government in drafting the clauses concerning Muslim issues in the Treaty of Athens in 1913. In 1917, he was appointed governor-general of Epirus, where considerable numbers of Muslims still lived.

Venizelos strongly believed that Stergiades would be able to exert his authority over both the Greek army and the Ottoman provincial administrators, and deal successfully with the problems of the various ethno-religious communities in the province. As a person who had an inclusive understanding of Hellenism, Venizelos was sure that Stergiades had the merit to be the highest representative of the Greek government in Western Anatolia and would pave the way for the prospective Greek administration.[29]

Greek Administration in Western Anatolia

Stergiades would try to reassure the provincial Ottoman authorities about the goodwill of the Greek government and normalise everyday life in the city, which had been devastated by the violence directed against the Muslims on 15–16 May. His most immediate task was the restoration of harmony disrupted by these violent events among the different communities in the city. Thus, the perpetrators of the landing-day incidents were severely punished by court martial.

Stergiades declared that the High Commission would pay compensation to those who suffered on the basis of damages estimated by a mixed commission of Greek, Ottoman and Allied representatives.[30] An affidavit published in the daily *Âhenk* on 21 May by the Greek Forces Command declared the following:

> It is imperative to respect the religious law and humanity (*hukuk-ı dîniyye ve insâniyyetine*) of all the people located in the city, and no person must be degraded (*izzet-i nefsine dokunulmamalıdır*). People who may dare this kind of an indecent attempt are going to be severely punished by a court martial.[31]

While governing the occupation zone around Smyrna, Stergiades had to cope with the challenges posed by a number of social groups. The first group, which was dissatisfied with the rule of the high commissioner, was the provincial notables of the Ottoman Greeks. The rise of Greek nationalism among the Greeks living in the *sanjak* of Smyrna after the landing was the first reason for conflict between the high commissioner and the Ottoman Greek communities. Claiming that they had a long tradition of autonomy in their communal life during the Ottoman period, the notables did not wish to accept any intervention from the High Commission and emphasised their local particularities. Therefore, this group, emboldened by the presence of the Greek armies in Western Anatolia, emerged as the major champion of the mobilisation of Greek nationalism in the region. Ironically, Greek nationalism had not become a dominant ideology among the members of this group until the Greek landing in May 1919. The rise of nationalistic feelings and the risk of intercommunal conflict can be best illustrated in the violent events directed at the Muslim habitants of Smyrna following the landing. The strict measures Stergiades had taken to establish the authority of the High Commission would result in accusations of his discrimination against the Ottoman Greek communities and alienating the notables of the Greek Orthodox communities. Thus, he would not find favour in the small – but effective – nationalist section of the Ottoman Greek communities on account of his unyielding attitude towards the reforms concerning the political and cultural rights of the Muslim communities.[32]

Ethnic Cleansing in Western Anatolia

Aware of the multi-religious and multi-ethnic character of the region, the Greek administration had to secure the rights of each community equally and maintain public safety. However, the notables of the Greek Orthodox communities did not want to accept the fact that the establishment of the Greek administration and its attempts at centralisation meant the end of their community's traditional privileges. Both the Greek government and the High Commission held the view that the uncompromising stance and even excessive nationalistic feelings of the Ottoman Greek notables would not obstruct the incorporation of Western Anatolia into Greece. Another problem was the limited participation of Ottoman Greek notables in the administration of the province. The impression of the Ottoman Greeks was that Stergiades's former staff from Epirus and civil servants from Athens were mainly employed by the High Commission. All the same, the arrogant attitude of some officers in the Greek administration disturbed members of the Ottoman Greek communities.[33]

The second group which disapproved of Stergiades was the hierarchy of the Orthodox Church. Since Stergiades was considered the sole responsible authority to both the Greek government and Allied representatives, his political power was envied by the metropolitan bishops, who did not approve of official interference in communal organisations, such as schools, hospitals, orphanages and charitable institutions.[34] As the most powerful metropolitan bishop in Aydın Province, Chrysostomos, metropolitan bishop of Smyrna, had the right to have a say on the management of the financial resources of the Orthodox communities, as well as that of the communal organisations in cooperation with the General Committee of the Greek Orthodox community in Smyrna.[35] Thus, a clash of authority arose between the high commissioner and the metropolitan bishop. Venizelos was also not pleased with the nationalist rhetoric of the clergy. He asked Stergiades to convince the metropolitan bishop and other clerics not to make nationalist remarks, which could be directed at other communities, especially the Muslims, in their sermons and to limit themselves to religious duties. It is almost obvious that Stergiades had never approved of the political acts of the metropolitan bishop, and he regarded priests who employed nationalist rhetoric to be a menace. Stergiades allowed Emîn Bey, the governor-general, to monitor Chrysostomos's activities in the countryside during his tour in the summer of 1920.[36] There was no delay in the reaction from the Ecumenical Patriarchate. In a letter written to Venizelos, Patriarch Meletios stated that 'no governor has exceeded Stergiades in his measures against the higher clergy ...'[37]

The third group was made up of the Allied representatives in the region who opposed any expansion of the Greek zone since the Greek military advance might be accompanied by intercommunal conflict.[38] They declared that they would supervise the activities of the High Commission, and compelled the High Commission to send the public prosecutor to investigate the violent incidents that took place in Menemen after the occupation in June 1919. Moreover, various Inter-Allied boards, which supervised the activities of the High Commission, were engaged in disputes with the Greek authorities on the administration of the occupation zone. The most problematic issues between the Inter-Allied boards and the Greek authorities were commercial quotas, passport control, censorship and medical service aggravated by overlapping scopes of authority.

The last source of conflict for Stergiades after changes in the Greek government in November 1920 was the newly appointed royalist generals in the Greek armies in Western Anatolia. The November 1920 elections gave a clear victory to the Royalists over the Venizelists, surprising the staff of the High Commission and the Christian populations in Western Anatolia. The new government enforced no major changes in the lower ranks; nonetheless, some 150 pro-Venizelist high-ranking officers in the Asia Minor Army left their posts or resigned. The result of these appointments was the creation of an experienced Venizelist army with anti-Venizelist leadership with no knowledge of the conditions prevailing in Western Anatolia.[39] However, Stergiades did not enter into open conflict with those generals, believing that favouritism played an important role in these appointments and that the merits of the generals were not regarded by the new government in Athens.[40] While he did not object to the changes in the military, he resisted any changes in civil personnel serving in Western Anatolia. Thus, the new government would not dare to make any crucial changes in the organisation of the High Commission.

Organisational Structure of the Greek High Commission and Administrative–Social Reforms

The careers of the officers that Stergiades brought with him to Smyrna reveal how meticulous he was in terms of his selection. Petros Gounarakis, who was Stergiades's general secretary during his governorship in Epirus, took on the same duty in the High Commission. Ali Nâîbzâde, the former prefect of Drama and a Muslim Cretan himself, was put in charge of Muslim affairs in the Commission.[41] Furthermore, starting from August 1919, Stergiades was to be assisted by Triantafyllos Krionas, prefect of Preveza, and Evangelos Koufidakis from the General Accounting Office. These people formed the nucleus of the Greek High Commission.

Ethnic Cleansing in Western Anatolia

The High Commission was organised into twelve departments including (1) the Office of the High Commissioner, (2) the General Secretariat, and the Departments of (3) Foreign Affairs, (4) Internal Affairs, (5) Repatriation and Rehabilitation of Refugees, (6) Post Offices, (7) Prisons, (8) Finance, (9) Public Works, (10) Muslim Affairs, (11) Public Health and (12) Translation.[42]

Some of the problems that this expansion needed to address were the repatriation of refugees, the founding of a university, the organisation of a well-developed health service and the care for Muslim institutions. It did not take the High Commission long to reason that it could not surmount these problems miles away from Smyrna with its existing organisation and staff. Therefore, Stergiades took the first step to firm up the provincial organisation of the High Commission by founding so-called diplomatic missions in places other than Smyrna in the summer of 1919.[43] Between then and the summer of 1920, diplomatic offices were opened in the cities of Manisa and Aydın, and as well as all of the *kaza*s of the Smyrna *sanjak*, excluding Kuşadası, which was under Italian occupation. To these offices were sent people who had previously served as regional governors (*nomarchoi*) or prefects (*eparchoi*) in Greece. By solving problems on the spot with the help of the Greek military forces and by opening these offices, it was intended to lighten the heavy workload of the central organisation in Smyrna. This would then lead to the High Commission adopting a centralist administration policy expanding from Smyrna to its environs with diplomatic missions rotating among branch offices.

In the first weeks of the Greek occupation, the international press had foreseen that it would not be an easy task for Greece to administer Smyrna and its environs. The Greek administration would need the goodwill of the various communities in the region and at least the consent of the Muslim population. Greek authorities, having taken over the control of the region right after the occupation, motivated the other communities to participate in the administration,[44] yet also allowed the continuation of some autonomy for different ethno-religious communities.

The High Commission initially tried to restore the political normalcy after the landing. First, Muslim civil servants who had left the region after the occupation were called back to duty by a directive from the Ministry of the Interior to all the other ministries in Constantinople on 9 November 1919. This directive warned that officers who had left their places of duty in Aydın Province would not get their salaries and lose their right to civil service work unless they did return.[45] Moreover, Stergiades, in an effort to encourage Muslim officers to return, made a short-term offer of a significant pay rise.

92

Greek Administration in Western Anatolia

As the new regime was institutionalised, more people from the Muslim community were encouraged to take part in the administration. Muslim civil servants would be able to keep their former positions until it became definite that they had new positions in accordance with their skills.[46] In that case, they could be integrated into the Greek administration and play an important role in the control of the Muslim population in the region. However, there would be no change in the mufti's office, the municipality,[47] the heads of Muslim schools or the personnel of the Ottoman Bank. The pious endowments (*vakfs*), orphanages and the Muslim foundations preceding the Greek administration would continue their function.[48] The pious endowments, which were administered by the Ministry of Pious Endowments (Evkaf Nâzırı) in the Ottoman period, went under the jurisdiction of the Department of Muslim Affairs. While Greek civil servants attended a swearing in ceremony at the beginning of their career, Muslim civil servants were required only to sign an affidavit.

In the Smyrna *sanjak*, it was determined that the official written correspondence would be carried out in both Greek and Ottoman Turkish, and a special translation department was created at the High Commission.[49] In addition, Stergiades directed that Turkish courses were to be given in the government office and that knowledge of Turkish would be a significant factor in promotions.

In order to fill the vacancies in the staff of the Greek administration in Western Anatolia, Venizelos wanted the Ottoman Greek, Armenian and Muslim youth prepared for significant posts as much as young people from Greece. Those people interested in civil service were sent to Athens for a short period of education and then returned to the province to serve in appropriate positions. Several local Muslims began to serve as drivers, clerks and translators in the High Commission.

With priority for reorganising the Ottoman gendarmerie, police and courts, the High Commission sought ways to reshape the administrative structure and the central and provincial organisations it had taken over rather than eliminate them.[50] Stergiades believed that the Unionist officers in the Ottoman gendarmerie posed a crucial threat to intercommunal peace, and so some limitations were imposed on it. This was because many local gendarmes kept their close ties with the CUP and objected to the reconciliation of Muslim and Greek elements. Furthermore, some of them cooperated with the National Forces (Kuvâ-yı Milliye) and put pressure on Muslims who appealed to the Greek gendarmerie. Indeed, the Ottoman gendarmes in the rural areas typically surrendered to the National Forces with their weapons or joined them with their military equipment.[51]

Stergiades preferred establishing full control over the Ottoman gendarmerie instead of dissolving it. Whereas the forces of the Ottoman gendarmerie were replaced by Greek troops in the towns close to Smyrna, they were permitted to serve under Greek supervision in rural settlements. Since the Ottoman gendarmerie's equipment was limited to only knives and revolvers, and no heavier weapons, and were required to report regularly to the nearest Greek military authority.[52]

During the Ottoman period, the chief of police (*emniyet müdürü*) was appointed by the sultan upon the recommendation of the Ministry of the Interior and was responsible directly to the government in Constantinople. During the Greek occupation, Ottoman police forces continued their duties for a while; however, this ended when they were disarmed by the High Commission in early November 1919[53] and their salaries were entirely cut off by the Ottoman government.[54] The remaining Ottoman police were encouraged to team up with the Greek gendarmerie by the High Commission and the Ottoman chief of police, Zeki Bey, in March 1920.[55]

Reforms conducted by the Greek Administration of Smyrna impressed observers. Prior to 1920, Ralph Harlow had described in his contribution to a report by the professors of the International College, after a visit to a prison, the inhuman conditions therein and gave, to some extent, an exaggerated depiction of the widespread use of torture as a means of punishment in his report.[56] Harrow appreciated the reforms made by the High Commission in the police stations and sharply highlighted the differences between the previous administration of the Directorate of Prisons (Hapishaneler Müdüriyeti), a branch of the Ottoman Directorate of Public Security (Emniyet-i Umûmiye Müdüriyeti), and the current conditions of the prisons.[57]

After Sèvres: Consolidation of the Greek Administration

On 10 August 1920, twenty-two months after the armistice, a peace treaty with the Ottoman Empire was signed in the Parisian suburb of Sèvres.[58] The Treaty of Sèvres was divided into thirteen parts with various clauses ranging from the prospective League of Nations mandates in the Ottoman lands to the protection of the other ethno-religious communities in the Empire. It also included the Ottoman Empire's military and political obligations from the prisoners of war to the detailed formation of the new borders. The sections concerning Smyrna were included in the third part under the heading 'Political Clauses', defining the boundaries and the legal status of the Greek occupation zone around Smyrna.[59]

Greek Administration in Western Anatolia

Contrary to the interpretations of mainstream Turkish and Greek historians, the Greek government was not granted the right to annex the Smyrna zone; however, it was allowed a mandate to maintain the zone in accordance with the Treaty of Sèvres. At the end of a five-year period the local parliament in Smyrna would be able to vote on an appeal to the League of Nations for the annexation of Smyrna to Greece. While Article 69 of the treaty stipulated that the city of Smyrna and its adjacent territory would remain under Ottoman sovereignty, the Greek government was allowed to exercise sovereignty in this territory. The next two articles (Articles 70 and 71) outlined the responsibility of the Greek government in the administration of the region. The government put into effect this administration by means of a specially appointed body of officials. It was also allowed to appoint any military forces required for the maintenance of public security. Article 72 stipulated the formation of a local parliament in which all nationalities in the region were to be proportionately represented. Article 79 stated that the inhabitants of the region would still hold Ottoman citizenship and that Greece had to follow an egalitarian policy for both Ottoman and Greek citizens.[60]

Following the signing of the treaty, the *sanjak* authorities were to submit formally to the Greek administration by way of a signed protocol in the government office in Konak. However, before signing this protocol, Stergiades asked Câvîd Bey, the vice-governor, to seek instructions from Constantinople. Since the Ottoman government did not send any written documents, a group of Muslim civil servants were then dispatched to Constantinople. The imperial government informed them that they had to recognise the Greek administration; however, they were allowed to keep their offices on the condition that the new regime could ask for their assistance.[61] Hence, the signing of the peace treaty did not mean that the Ottoman authorities were abrogated in the Greek administration zone. Stergiades declared that Muslim civil servants could continue to perform their duties and that their incorporation into the new Greek administration would be highly appreciated. Except for the gendarmerie and police, all Ottoman personnel kept their positions. Whereas the duties of the police were assigned to Greek troops, the gendarme forces were encouraged to take part in the Greek gendarmerie after resigning from the Ottoman gendarmerie. In the countryside, the Greek gendarmerie became the most important means of enforcing the new laws.[62]

After the signature of the Sèvres Treaty, the zone under the Greek occupation was *de jure* divided into two parts. The first of these was a zone of direct administration, which roughly covered the Smyrna *sanjak*, where the High Commission was influential. The high commissioner directly

Ethnic Cleansing in Western Anatolia

governed the *kaza* of Smyrna and Ayasuluk. The remaining area was divided into a province and fourteen counties: the province of Manisa, and the counties of Ödemiş, Tire, Bayındır, Nif (Nymfaion), Çeşme, Karaburun, Seferihisar, Urla, Foça, Menemen, Kasaba, Bergama and Ayvalık[63] (see Map 2.1). The Greek administration, which shut down all its diplomatic offices in the Smyrna zone, transferred the Greek personnel working in these places into the staff of the district governorships. Muslim district governors were discharged and replaced by Greek diplomatic representatives.

On 23 September 1920, the Greek government gazette published the official renaming of the High Commission of Smyrna to the Greek Administration of Smyrna.[64] The person at the head of this administration continued to be known as high commissioner and was put in charge of all authorities as the official representative of the Greek administration in Smyrna. This administrator was to be appointed by a royal decree upon nomination by the Council of Ministers. Until the local parliament anticipated in the treaty was founded, the high commissioner assumed

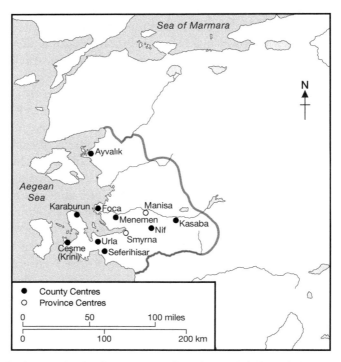

Map 2.1 Territory under the direct control of the Greek High Commission in the Treaty of Sèvres, August 1920.

Greek Administration in Western Anatolia

absolute control over all aspects of government: administrative, judicial and legislative.[65]

The Greek Administration of Smyrna was comprised of the following branches: Office of the High Commissioner and General Secretariat, Department of the Interior, Department of Finance, Department of Justice, Department of Education, Department of Public Health, Department of National Economy, Department of Public Works, Department of Muslim Affairs and the General Inspectorate. Subsequent to the Greek military advance in Anatolia and the expansion of the Greek occupation, the Greek Administration of Smyrna was reorganised in the summer of 1921.[66] One of the most important changes was the transformation of the General Inspectorate into the Department of the Military Occupation Zone. Additionally, the Department of Telecommunications was founded.

Faithful to its promise, the Greek administration did not change the staff of the sharia courts and government offices in the period following the Treaty of Sèvres but preferred to bring these together under one umbrella organisation named Department of Muslim Services, appointing Dimitrios Voudouris as its director and Ahmet Hulûsî Bey as counsellor.[67] The mufti offices[68] were also added to the jurisdiction of this department. The High Commission, which facilitated the administration by bringing all Muslim institutions under the same roof, explained through public declaration that this reorganisation intended the prevention of the estrangement of Muslims from the Greek Administration of Smyrna and ensuring the integration of the Muslim community into the new administrative system.

The question of who would pay the Muslim civil servants' salaries turned into a dispute between the Greek and Ottoman administrations for a while. The Ottoman government, which stopped paying salaries to civil servants in the *sanjak* of Smyrna on 13 August 1920, considered financial assistance with funds from the state treasury, and Rahmetullah Efendi, the mufti of Smyrna, announced that a committee organised for the distribution of money would start in that same month, but this attempt remained fruitless. At the end of March 1921, the Ottoman government declared that it would send a limited amount of money for the payments.[69] Finally, the High Commission guaranteed to meet all the expenses of personnel serving in these institutions, including their salaries. These payments continued without disruption for the next two years. Moreover, all the Muslim civil servants who continued to serve under the roof of the Greek administration, excluding those working in the offices of education, charity foundations, orphanages and sharia courts, would benefit from pay rises the same as their Greek colleagues.[70]

Ethnic Cleansing in Western Anatolia

The second zone, the interior of the province where the delegates represented the High Commission, benefited from the expansion of the occupation in the summer of 1920. This area, which was regarded as a buffer zone between the nationalist-controlled zone and the Smyrna *sanjak*, was referred to as the Military Occupation Zone. In the summer of 1920, the zone occupied by the Greek troops in Western Anatolia included approximately twenty representatives offices (*antiprosōpeies*). At least six of these (Soma, Salihli, Alaşehir, Kırkağaç, Kula and Aydın) were situated within the borders of Aydın Province.[71] The rest of these representatives were located in southern Marmara and the interior (see Map 2.2). The primary duty of these representatives was the systematic observation of the Ottoman administrative authorities who kept their positions in the Military Occupation Zone. In addition, the representatives had to apply the directives from the high commissioner and mediate between the Greek military authorities and the Ottoman administrators to secure provincial peace. Apart from the Ottoman administrative authorities, the Ottoman police, gendarmerie and courts also continued to function in this region.

The government change in Greece in November 1920 constituted the primary and most difficult problem in the post-Sèvres period of Stergiades's rule. Stergiades presented his resignation as soon as the Liberal Party lost the general elections on 14 November 1920. Nonetheless, Dimitrios Rallis, the new prime minister, refused to accept his resignation.[72] The new government declared that the Greek policy in Western Anatolia would not change and an amnesty would be announced for all political opponents.

A short time after the reorganisation of the High Commission in September 1920, political turmoil and government change became the main obstacles for the Greek administration. Although the change in government affected the administrative agenda of the High Commission, Christian townspeople continued to support Venizelism, fearing that Royalism might mean, from their point of view, the Allied Powers' intention to suppress Greece. The Ottoman Greeks in Smyrna continued to see Venizelos as their national saviour in the face of the lukewarm relationship between the local Christians and the High Commission led by Stergiades. Thus, the Liberal Party managed to gain the majority of votes in Crete, a few pockets in Epirus, some Aegean islands and Thrace in November 1920, though it was evident that they would lose overall. As expected, most of the Smyrniote population, which had a liberal affiliation, supported the Venizelist government, though the elections were not held in the Smyrna zone. The defeat of Venizelos was a real shock for Smyrniotes who held profound admiration for him.[73]

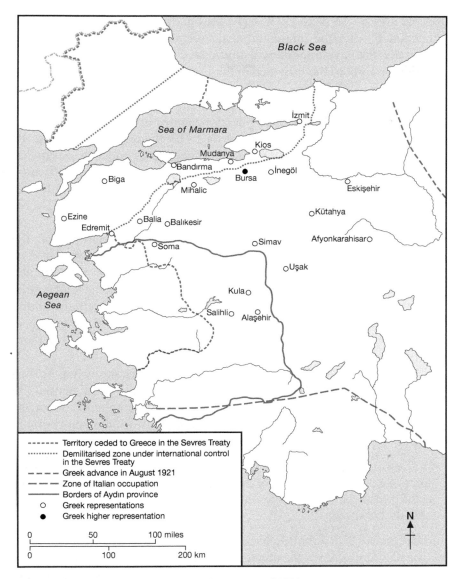

Map 2.2 Military Occupation Zone in the summer of 1921.

Establishment of the Court Martial and the Judicial System

The High Commission established the Extraordinary Court Martial (Ektakto Stratodikeio) though civil courts continued to be controlled by the Ottoman administration. This court martial commenced its proceedings on 16 May 1919 in the Fasoula neighbourhood of Smyrna immediately after the intercommunal violence during the landing, and constituted the most important institutional change that the Greek administration brought to the province in the judicial system. The court martial was made up of five or six judges, all officers being legally trained. The court's decisions were considered too strict. On 18 May, two Hellenes, a civilian and a soldier, received death penalties due to their roles in the mobs and were executed on the same day.[74] By the middle of August, the court martial had almost completed its proceedings about the events on the landing day: seventy-two individuals were convicted, three of whom received capital punishment, four life imprisonment and sixty-five lighter sentences. Forty-nine of them were Greeks, thirteen Muslims, twelve Armenians and one Jew.[75]

Because of positive remarks about the extraordinary court martial, the Muslim population started to prefer the court martial, believing that they would receive more lenient treatment than they would in the Ottoman sharia courts and modern (*nizâmiyye*) tribunals.[76] This leniency towards Muslim defendants might have been because the Greek administration was trying to win favour with the Muslim population of the province. Furthermore, there was no restriction on the use of Turkish in these courts.

Meanwhile, the Ottoman administration reacted harshly when its own courts were suspended because of the extraordinary court martial. In August 1919, Ahmet İzzet, the governor-general, complained about the encroachment of the court martial on the functions of Ottoman courts in Smyrna.[77] Stergiades sent a response on 5 September affirming that

> in accordance with the instructions received from the Allied Powers, the Greek forces are obliged to maintain order in the occupation zone in Asia Minor, and entitled to declare martial law and establish courts to investigate the crimes after the occupation.[78]

In December 1919, John Michael de Robeck, British high commissioner at Constantinople, drew the attention of the Foreign Office to the interference of the Greek authorities in the jurisdiction of the Ottoman courts, and alleged that

> If the Greeks eventually evacuate Asia Minor and make room for some other form of administration, or even, to a lesser degree, if they are maintained there by the decisions of the Peace Conference, there is danger of serious confusion arising, especially in civil cases, from the existence of judicial decisions of the Turkish courts, which are legally valid but have been set aside by the Greek military.[79]

Greek Administration in Western Anatolia

At the beginning of 1920, the High Commission appealed to the Aydın Governorship and suggested that a committee consisting of both parties' jurists be formed for the purpose of determining the duties of the Ottoman courts and the Greek court martial. The government attorney in the provincial court of appeal (*vilâyet istinâf müddeî-i umûmîsi*) wrote a petition to the Ministry of the Interior on what could be done. The Ministry declared in the memorandum, dated 26 February 1920, that the High Commission, having ordered the foundation of the court martial in Smyrna, had suspended the Ottoman courts, which signified an encroachment on the Ottoman rights of sovereignty. The Ministry of Justice, via a memorandum sent to the Ministry of Foreign Affairs on 21 February, highlighted the fact that the Greek Army Command forwarded every crime committed in the occupied territories to the court martial by relating them to security and public order. Thus, the Ministry of Justice objected to this application.

The court martial, however, would operate in the province throughout the three years of Greek administration. This court examined and ruled on various cases, such as disobeying the prohibitions imposed by the Greek military authorities, including theft, revenge, murder, pick-pocketing, banditry and supporting the National Forces. Those who committed the crime of aiding and abetting the National Forces were sentenced to life imprisonment or hard labour.[80] These people, who were thought to provoke the Muslims against the Greek administration, were generally put in the prisons of Urla and Stavros near Smyrna, or the central prison buildings in the Konak neighbourhood.[81]

The High Commission claimed that the court martial had the authority not only over the Ottoman population, but also over people of foreign origin. This, in some cases, incurred problems between the High Commission and the consuls of the Allied States and resulted in the mitigation of punishments by the Greek court martial.[82] For example, Raphael de Ciaves, a Dutch subject of Jewish origin residing in Smyrna, was sentenced to eight years imprisonment by the court martial on account of theft committed during the events on 15–16 May 1919. Arguing that the actions of the Greek authorities constituted a contravention of the existing capitulatory regime, the Dutch government made an appeal to the British and French representatives in Smyrna.[83] Although British documents do not tell much about Ciaves' fate, the Quai d'Orsay admonished the French representative in Smyrna that he should 'refrain from any intervention or protest'.[84] In another case, Emanuel Tazartes, a British subject of Jewish origin, was condemned to three months' imprisonment for refusing to swear on the Old Testament.[85] With the involvement of the British representative, he was released. After the Treaty of Sèvres was signed, the High Commission claimed that the court martial had the right to try subjects of the Allied Powers in Smyrna for crimes against the security of the army and even against the common law. Nonetheless, Harry Lamb, the British representative at Smyrna, insisted that the court martial should keep the consulates informed, and also invite the diplomatic representatives of the concerned person.[86]

In the post-Sèvres period, the Greek administration allowed the functioning of Ottoman secular courts, which had been established in 1840. Aside from these, the sharia courts, which were interested in family and inheritance law, as well as the law of pious endowments, maintained their function. The High Commission left all the sharia courts in the occupied region under the authority of the Muslim judge (*kadı*) of Smyrna and began to fill the vacant posts in accordance with his suggestions.[87] The salaries of the Muslim judges and the running costs of these courts were to be paid by the Department of Muslim Affairs. The Greek administration established its own civil courts in Smyrna, which came into operation after 1 August 1921.[88]

In the countryside, the involvement of Greek representatives in the juridical matters of the Muslim communities was not welcomed by the Ottoman judges. In the summer of 1921, the Ottoman courts in Salihli sent a complaint to Gounarakis, the general secretary, to point out that they were bothered by the interventions of Konstantinos Mitakos, the High Commission representative. Gounarakis openly stated that he would never approve of the Greek representative's interference with the functions of the Ottoman religious and civil courts, and that a representative only had the authority of supervision in the region. He underlined that the High Commission actually did not have the right to modify the members of the current Ottoman institutions. If there was evidence of any crime a Muslim judge was charged with, it was to be presented to the General Secretariat for the final verdict. Gounarakis also urged people to take necessary measures so as to prevent the waste of the Ottoman public income.[89]

Commercial Regulations in Regional Economy: Formation of Two Commercial Zones

From an economic aspect, the period of the High Commission was marked by continuities with the previous period rather than with changes. Since Stergiades's administration provided stability, numerous European citizens who had left the province during World War I were able to regain the courage to return to Smyrna. Among those who rushed back to the city were merchants, craftsmen and prominent local people.[90] Moreover, the High Commission reassured the prerogatives of the European citizens in the *sanjak* within the framework of the capitulations.[91] Apart from commercial privileges, European citizens continued to hold extraterritorial status in jurisdictional affairs and the local gendarmerie could not interfere with the properties of European citizens.[92]

The lucrative commercial activity between Aydın Province and Constantinople was revived, and the Ottoman lira remained valid currency in the region despite pressure from Athens. After February 1921, the salaries of civil servants were paid in Greek drachmae rather than the Turkish liras as part of the financial policy launched in the same year, necessitating the use of the Greek drachma along with the Turkish lira as the valid currencies in the Smyrna zone.

The Greek administration imposed some restrictions in spite of this commercial boom, since administration and military expenses were totally funded by the Kingdom.[93] After the Greek landing, Greek seamen and police under the leadership of the Greek harbour master started to control the customs houses, ports and piers, even though the Ottoman custom authorities also continued to function in the occupied zone.[94] The High Commission exercised the policing of the ports with the exception of passport and travel permits control in Smyrna, which were the responsibility of the Inter-Allied Port Police, consisting of British, French, Italian and Greek officers. However, a small Ottoman police contingent served in the port of Smyrna as an ostensible sign of Ottoman suzerainty.[95]

It did not take long for the Allied high commissioners in Constantinople to complain that the Greek authorities were interfering with the duties of Ottoman customs officers. The main problem was related to the exportation of certain products from the region. In July 1919, the Supreme Military Command of the Greek forces in Western Anatolia published a list of goods whose exportation from Smyrna to any other port, including Ottoman ports and even the capital, was prohibited.[96] The Allied high commissioners instantly objected to this decision and stressed that the Supreme Council had not decided about the status of the Smyrna zone yet. This prohibition was annulled due to the efforts of the British and French high commissioners in Constantinople.[97]

Due to the intensifying conflict over exports, the Allied representatives in Constantinople recommended to the High Commission in Smyrna in January 1920 the establishment of an Inter-Allied Authority for the port of Smyrna. Its main tasks would be the prevention of smuggling of arms and munitions in and out of the occupation zone; arranging exports and imports under the guidance of the Inter-Allied Commission of Exports based in Constantinople; inspecting ships arriving at the port, in cooperation with the Inter-Allied Commission on Health and Hygiene; and the policing of the port and ensuring security for the ships on the port.[98]

Complaints about the restrictions on exports from Aydın Province continued and even permeated the foreign chambers of commerce in Smyrna. Stating that members of their respective chambers were harmed financially, the presidents of the British, French, Italian, American and Dutch chambers of commerce in Smyrna protested these restrictions to the British High Commission.[99] The British and French high commissioners in Constantinople then protested the restrictions imposed on the export of olives, olive oil and livestock to the Greek Foreign Ministry, and claimed that the restrictions created shortages in the Constantinople market. Owing to the incessant condemnations, Rallis, the Greek foreign minister, asked Stergiades to inform his ministry about this issue and give the necessary orders for the appropriate regulation of the exportation of olives and olive oil.[100] In his response, Stergiades stated that the Greek High Commission never prohibited the exportation of olives and olive oil to Constantinople or any other Ottoman port, and as for the issue of cattle and sheep, the most appropriate solution would be reached only after the Greek troops returned from the front, which would take two to three months.[101]

The Asia Minor Army Command revised the regulation of the transportation of cattle by dividing the Greek occupation area into two zones. In the first zone, including all of the occupied area of Aydın Province and the Karesi *sanjak*, the transportation of cattle was sanctioned and no restrictions on exportation were applied. In the area east of Aydın Province, which formed the second zone, the cattle that were not required by the army were placed at the disposal of the Greek administration. The High Commission was allowed the transportation of cattle from the second zone to the first zone given the owners of the animals had proven in advance their inability to pasture them in the second zone during the winter. To be more specific, local herders whose traditional grazing lands were broken up because of war were limited to transport up to five oxen and twenty-five sheep per transit from the second zone to the first.[102] The British representative in Smyrna, however, suspected that these regulations would be abused by the Greek civil servants. In his written communication, he demonstrated, as an example, the needless requisition by Greek authorities of the entire stock of mohair for the army.[103]

Despite continuous objections by the Greek high commissioner, the Allied representatives in Smyrna maintained that the Allied high commissioners' jurisdiction extended over all Ottoman territories, including

Greek Administration in Western Anatolia

Aydın Province.[104] In order to solve this problem, Stergiades was compelled to convince the British representative in Smyrna of that. The Allied representatives in Constantinople abandoned the idea of establishing the Inter-Allied Authority for the port of Smyrna, but the Inter-Allied Port Police continued to function. Nonetheless, the presidents of the American, British, French, Italian, Belgian and Dutch chambers of commerce in Smyrna continued to complain about limitations on trade. In a dispatch dated 20 February 1922, they informed the Allied high commissioners in Constantinople that the restrictions on the movement of grain, the ban on exportation of olive oil, and the requisition of wool and sugar were still enforced by the Greek military authorities. They also stated that the establishment of two trade zones – 'the first one with full freedom of trade, but with almost no goods, and the second one with severe restrictions and the prohibition of transport for traders' – was an attempt to replace the traders in favour of the Greek military authorities.[105]

The High Commission was wary of possible conflict with the interests of the Allies in the region. On 15 November 1921, Gounarakis, the general secretary of the High Commission, requested that Greek representatives in the Military Occupation Zone notify him of available offices of the Imperial Ottoman Bank, the OPDA and the Tobacco Monopoly (Régie des Tabacs) in their region. The Department of Finance of the High Commission warned the Greek representatives not to interfere with the aforementioned institutions since they 'represented the economic interests of the Great Powers in Anatolia', and that no conflict with them would be beneficial. Therefore, the Greek representatives had to provide unlimited help in the activities of these offices.[106] Additionally, the High Commission supported the activities of the OPDA in the Smyrna zone. Stergiades demanded continued supervision of the Public Debt Administration in the zone, and that the revenues of olive oil in Bergama and Ayvalık be allocated to the administration in payment of outstanding debts.[107]

The imposition of a stamp tax added to problems between the Allied high commissioners in Constantinople and the High Commission in Smyrna. By a joint diplomatic note, Allied high commissioners complained to the Greek representative (*antiprosōpos*) in Alaşehir about the imposition of a stamp tax by the Greek Kingdom on the export of Bursa silk in November 1921. The Greek higher representative (*tōn anōterōn antiprosōpos*) in Bursa stated that enforcement of this tax in the occupied regions of Western Anatolia was due to misunderstanding. On 30 November 1921, the Department of Finance notified all military representatives that the Greek stamp would be used only in dispatches related to military affairs, for in an occupied country, taxation rules peculiar

Ethnic Cleansing in Western Anatolia

to that country – in this case, the Ottoman taxation rules – had to be in force.[108]

Refugees and Housing

The High Commission had jurisdiction over the various aspects of the return of refugees, such as the resettlement and restitution of confiscated properties. This was overseen by a branch of the High Commission known as the Department of the Repatriation and Rehabilitation of Refugees. These refugees can be classified as either Ottoman Greeks who were expelled from their homelands before and during the Great War; Balkan Muslims forced to migrate to the Ottoman Empire and who carried the risk of potential conflict with the provincial Christians; and Anatolian Muslims (Turks, Kurds and Circassians) and Christians (Greeks and Armenians) evading the National Forces and sheltering in the Greek occupation zone.

Demographic engineering by the Unionist government during the war years had altered the balance of population in the littoral of Aydın Province. Heathcote-Smith, a former British consul at Smyrna, reported that almost 250,000 Ottoman Greeks had been expelled from the province.[109] To assist in the return of these refugees, Venizelos, after meetings in the Supreme Council of the Paris Peace Conference, instructed Greek troops to invade the coastline stretching from Ayvalık to Ayasuluk. However, the return of 300,000 Orthodox refugees from Greece back to land that had been seized and distributed to new settlers would trigger a reaction amongst those new settlers.[110]

One aim of the Department of Repatriation and Rehabilitation was to intervene between returnees and the Muslims who had settled in the abandoned districts and who were asked to leave. The department determined that out of 45,000 residences belonging to the Ottoman Greeks along the coasts of Aydın Province, 23,000 had been demolished, 18,000 were damaged and only around 4,000 were available.[111] Another report prepared by Heathcote-Smith, who toured the coastal settlements in the Smyrna *sanjak* in February 1919, presented that most of the houses were uninhabitable or completely destroyed (see Table 2.1).[112] In the absence of housing facilities, many refugees were compelled to stay in makeshift tents in the towns of Çeşme, Karaburun and Urla during the summer months of 1919.

It had been a difficult task for the Department of Repatriation and Rehabilitation to transfer crowded refugee groups to the coast of Western Anatolia in such a short time. Although more than three months had elapsed since the occupation of Smyrna, the High Commission had failed to

Greek Administration in Western Anatolia

Table 2.1 Numbers of pre-war and habitable houses in the coastal settlements of the Smyrna and Karesi *sanjak*s in February 1919

Towns	Pre-War Houses	Habitable
Alatsata (Alaçatı)	2400	900
Tchesme (Çeşme)	2100	900
Nohout Alan (Nohutalan)	40	Nil
Narli Dere	100	10
St George Tchiftlik (Çiftlikköy)	350	4
Dikili	600	400
Ismailar	80	10
Aivali (Ayvalık)	5100	3500
Mosco Island (Cunda)	1500	400
Yenitsarihori (Sarıköy)	650	300

procure vessels that would carry the Ottoman Greek refugees from Athens and the Aegean islands to the harbours of Aydın Province. Accordingly, the Greek government took action and invited seafaring companies and ship owners to arrange transport to the ports of Urla, Dikili, Çeşme and Smyrna. A published notice said that Ottoman Greek refugees, whose number would be determined by the High Commission, were to come to Smyrna by ship; nonetheless, the Allied high commissioners announced that the resettlement of large refugee groups would not be permitted.[113] As it was not possible to find accommodation, the Ottoman Greeks would by no means be allowed to enter the city. In order to obtain their permit documents, the Greek refugees had to certify to the Inter-Allied Port Police units that they had adequate means of support to return to their homelands.[114] The refugees who received a permission slip from the Inter-Allied Port Police would then be transferred to their hometowns, such as Çeşme, Urla and Foça. The ships that received permission slips in Smyrna for Ottoman Greeks returning from the islands were welcomed at the port by Greek resettlement clerks who worked in the nearest central districts.[115] Since most of these districts lacked permanent High Commission representatives in the summer of 1919, these resettlement clerks tried to solve various refugee problems, such as transport, housing or catering, in cooperating with local resettlement committees consisting of priests, teachers and Ottoman Greek tradesmen in the towns of relocation. These clerks continued to function as affiliates of the High Commission even though representatives of the High Commission would later be established in the places they served.

Official documents of the High Commission claimed that public health was better in the occupation zone than it had been during the war years.

In addition, the Department of Public Health had made every effort to protect the health conditions of the refugees. Doctors were sent to refugee camps and free medicine was distributed at camp dispensaries.[116] In spite of the optimistic tone of these Greek documents, the situation faced by Ottoman Greek refugees in some regions was disappointing. A contemporary report described terrible sanitation problems in shelters where the refugees were resettled:

> In a khan near *Ayo Voukla*, nine families occupied a nine-room house. No room was large. There were twenty-seven persons in the nine families. All used a common privy, a common well, and a common laundry, in the central court, out of doors. Cooking was done usually out of doors in front of the rooms. It should be said to the credit of the people in this khan, that the rooms were in a cleanly condition, much pains evidently being taken to keep them so, under difficulties. They were on the whole, people of fair intelligence and refinement, some of them refugees. This khan has no sewer connection.
>
> Another khan is inhabited wholly by refugees. It is of two stories. The upper story contains 24 rooms, the lower 17. There is a family in each room. There is fair ventilation because the rooms are located about an open court. The maximum number of persons living in one room is 8.
>
> There is no central kitchen. Some of the cooking is done in the rooms, some of it on the door steps. Charcoal and wood are used. The burning wood fills the room with smoke. There is one well for forty families.[117]

In the countryside, the situation of the returnees was worse. A British captain named M. A. B. Johnston, having visited the towns and villages on the southern littoral of the province between 19 and 30 April 1919, related the destitution of the Greek refugees in Kuşadası:

> The condition of Greeks in Scala Nova is very bad. On May 20th 1916 nearly the whole of the Greek quarter comprising half the town was burnt down and completely ruined.
>
> There had been about 7000 Greeks there before the war. At the time of the Armistice there remained between 150 and 200. About 1300 of those deported have returned since then.
>
> They are living in a most direful state of poverty, families of ten or twelve being herded in small rooms without light or ventilation. The little money they have is not enough to enable them to buy food, let alone medicines and many of them are very ill.[118]

On the other hand, the Muslim refugees coming from the former Balkan territories of the Empire, whom the Ottoman administration had settled in abandoned properties, were to be evacuated from these properties and relocated in a more appropriate place. As reported by the Ottoman

Greek Administration in Western Anatolia

authorities, 22,000 out of 90,000 Muslim refugees who had been settled in the province since 1913 were resettled in the abandoned properties of Ottoman Greeks.[119] Some of those Balkan migrants did not give consent for the return of these properties to their former owners. Thus, the High Commission had also taken upon itself the duty of resettling the Muslim refugees. For instance, in October 1919, the High Commission requested the Inter-Allied Commission of the Railways to transport and resettle fifty Muslim families which had been expelled from eastern Macedonia by Bulgarian authorities.[120] Their travel expenses would be paid by the High Commission.[121]

In some localities, encounters between returning Greeks and Balkan migrants led to friction and special patrols were called in. For example, 8,000–12,000 Orthodox refugees who had crossed from Mytilene to Ayvalık and Edremit tried to reoccupy their properties by forcibly evicting the Balkan migrants. After conflicts escalated, the High Commission declared that no Balkan Muslims should be evicted without its permission. The Ottoman district governor would be responsible for the preparation of adequate housing for the Balkan Muslims, mostly Bosniaks and Pomaks.[122] In another case, upon the return of Ottoman Greeks to Çeşme in January 1920, the Bosniaks dispersed inland.

Moreover, large groups of Anatolian Greeks, Armenians and Muslims (Turks, Kurds and Circassians) who wanted to escape the menace of the nationalists, were resettled in the occupation zone, especially in Smyrna and its environs. Roughly 65,000 Greeks, Armenians and Circassians from the interior of Anatolia had applied to the High Commission for resettlement in areas under its control.[123] In the Bahri Baba refugee camp, Muslim refugees were housed with Anatolian Greek refugees, and the High Commission facilitated a dining hall that served both groups. The Department of the Repatriation and Rehabilitation of Refugees made efforts to cater to the needs of these groups irrespective of religion and ethnicity. The donation campaign launched for the refugees of Aydın was gathering speed, and donations were recorded in the Greek newspapers published in Smyrna.[124]

As Greek troops advanced and armed conflicts in the interior increased, tens of thousands of Muslims rushed to Smyrna. In response to demands for food, clothing and housing, the Ottoman government institutions in both Constantinople and Smyrna began cooperation with the municipality in July 1919 in their response to the refugee crisis. The Commission of the Refugees (Muhâcirîn Komisyonu), which consisted of the mayor Hacı Hasan Pasha, Mufti Rahmetullah Efendi, tradesmen Halil Zeki and Sâlepçizâde Refik, the Turkish Company manager Mustafa, Tokadîzâde Şekip and Ömer Lütfi Bey, held its first meeting in the mayor's office on

Ethnic Cleansing in Western Anatolia

4 July 1919. Mufti Rahmetullah Efendi, the head of the commission, urged local people to help the refugees.[125]

Forming an Official Regional Identity: Autonomous State Formation and Asya-yı Suğrâlılık *(Asia Minorism) Movement as a Response to Nationalisms*

Right after the elections in November 1920, a group of Venizelist officers, unable to reconcile themselves with the new government, abandoned their posts in Western Anatolia and settled in Constantinople where, in January 1921, they formed the military core of the National Defence League (Ethniki Amyna), with support from prominent liberal members of the Greek Orthodox community there.[126] Intending to guarantee the British support mediated by Venizelos, the League planned to declare Smyrna and its environs an autonomous region. Although Venizelos did not explicitly back the movement, he brokered a meeting between representatives of the movement and Lloyd George in London in January 1921. Nonetheless, a compromise between the High Commission and Amyna was impossible in Western Anatolia. Stergiades categorically rejected the idea of creating an autonomous government under the leadership of Amyna. Venizelos surmised that the movement had no chance of success unless Stergiades would lead it, but Amyna rejected Stergiades's leadership.[127]

Another attempt at creating an autonomous state which would include all the ethno-religious elements of Western Anatolia in its governance mechanisms had taken place during the Conference of London in February 1921. According to this proposal, Smyrna and its environs should be consigned to an autonomous administration for at least twenty-five years. By the same token, local ports would be open to free trade, and Muslims and Orthodox Christians would be allowed to settle wherever they chose. Stergiades would serve as the administrator of the autonomous region rather than on behalf of the Greek government. Moreover, this administration – from the security forces to the ministers – would be elected 'from the various local nationalities', and the regional revenue would be 'allotted proportionately'.[128]

As the power of the Ottoman Empire in the region diminished with the signing of the Sèvres Treaty, a controversy arose among the High Commission, the local Christian and Muslim communities, and the Allied Powers with regard to the new political structure for the occupation zone. The apprehensions behind all these discussions were to defuse Turkish nationalism, which was strengthening during the military conflicts in

Greek Administration in Western Anatolia

Western Anatolia, and the creation of a sentiment of regional belonging through the establishment of an autonomous administration in the province. These discussions spread to the provincial press in the spring of 1921. *Âhenk*, one of the most influential newspapers in Smyrna, asserted that nationalism would not have a future in the Anatolian land.[129]

The Greek government increasingly supported this project, provided that it maintained its power in the shaping of the foreign and security affairs of the new political formation. Besides, it expected to shift a certain amount of political and, above all, financial burden to the autonomous province.[130] When Stergiades returned to Smyrna, rumours about the declaration of autonomy were already widespread. The editor-in-chief of *Islahât* confirmed rumours about autonomy and stated that the basic features of this administration had not yet been determined:

> The definitive decision taken by the Greek government in Athens was not reported in yesterday's telegrams. Nonetheless, it can be absolutely inferred from the rumours spreading here and there that Athens wants to declare autonomy (*muhtâriyyet*) in Smyrna and in the occupation zone. Still, the shape and content of the autonomy is yet to be known. What kind of qualities and implementations will it have? How will this autonomy be encountered by the Great Powers? Even though it is said that the people (*ahâlî*) will be informed through an affidavit, it is not possible to be certain about that. That is because there is nothing in sight to appear officially true.[131]

Finally, the Greek government authorised the reorganisation of the occupation zone with greater autonomy for local ethno-religious communities. On 28 July 1922, Stergiades informed the public of the Greek government's decision to form an autonomous state, announcing that as the high commissioner he was the sole authority in the region and in charge of devising the constitution. The new state would run by itself, that is, as a mandate under Greece, and the support of the Greek army would be received if necessary, though this state would never be united with Greece.[132] Stergiades also emphasised that the replacement of any religious or nationalist fanaticism with the new concepts of working in peace and economic progress was the duty of the peoples of Western Anatolia. Through this declaration, the High Commission proclaimed that the autonomous state would not endorse homogenisation policies, which could transform the religious or ethnic structure of the region for the worse. Conversely, equal representation among diverse populations was going to be one of the most important founding principles of the autonomous state.

This declaration also implied that the local Muslim communities would not be excluded from the administration but be granted the right to play an

Ethnic Cleansing in Western Anatolia

equal role like the other communities. The religious leaders and notables of the Muslim community, as well as Ali Nâîbzâde, the superintendent and executive assistant of the general secretary, were invited to the municipal building of Smyrna to be informed of the related measures. Stergiades asked them to guarantee the support of the Muslim community for a rally to declare autonomy on 31 July.[133] Two days later, this announcement was verified by Petros Protopapadakis, the prime minister of Greece. This autonomous region would encompass the *sanjak*s of Smyrna, Saruhan and Aydın, comprising a wider zone than the plan contemplated in the Treaty of Sèvres. On the day of the rally, some prominent members of the Greek Orthodox, Muslim, Armenian and Jewish communities were present in front of the office of the governor-general. Hacı Hasan Pasha, the mayor of Smyrna, and Ahmet Şükrü, the mayor of Cordelio, also attended the ceremony, and the former expressed, on behalf of all peoples, his gratitude (*nutk-ı şükran îrâd eylemişdir*) to Stergiades.[134]

In an attempt to win the support of the Muslims, Stergiades stressed that the sultan continued to be caliph, and would retain intact all of his prestige throughout the Islamic world.[135] The idea of an official regional identity, that is, belonging to Asia Minor or *Asya-yı Suğralılık*, was possibly seen as an alternative to Greek or Turkish national identities. A considerable number of Muslim notables supported the idea of founding an autonomous state in Western Anatolia. These people were generally Muslims who had a rift with the nationalist organisation in Ankara or who were loyal to the sultan and apprehensive of the radicalism of the movement in Ankara. They preferred the establishment of an autonomous multi-ethnic state around Smyrna, which would be a *de jure* province of the Ottoman Empire under the protection of the Allied States and Greece, rather than the presence of Turkish nationalists in Smyrna. Indeed, the fact that crowds rushed to the squares for meetings held in the cities and towns of Western Anatolia after the possibility of autonomy was brought up could not have been a coincidence or a result of Greek pressure or the numerical superiority of the Christians. For example, it is evident in the letter dated 13 July and sent to the Greek representative in Kasaba by Arif Hikmet, the Muslim mayor of this important town in the Saruhan *sanjak*, that the municipal authorities supported the autonomy resolution:

> We have been notified about the decision of the Greek government in regard to the autonomy of Western Asia (Asya-yı Garbînin *muhtâriyyet idâresi*) and the affidavit by His Excellency Mr Stergiades, the high commissioner of Smyrna. We present our most profound thanks to him, who from the minute he honoured Smyrna through his appointment as an officer up until now did not deprive anybody or Muslims of his fatherly and compassionate grace and

Greek Administration in Western Anatolia

good deeds, but rather lavished upon them. We hope that the new regime will provide freedom (*hürriyyet bahş olmasını*) and we submit our respects to the High Commissioner in the name of the people.[136]

The Armenian communities, whose destiny in a way depended on the Allied and Greek presence, did not need to conceal their support for the new regime since the Treaty of Sèvres anticipated an independent Armenian state in the eastern part of the Ottoman Empire. They expected to take part in the new administration and obtain compensation for the survivors of the Armenian communities decimated during World War I. However, the response by the Jewish communities to the declaration of autonomy was quite different. Although the representatives of the Jewish community in Smyrna had gained the favour of the High Commission, they showed in various ways that they did not approve of the new regime. Blood libels and religious enmity contributed to the distrust the Jews sensed regarding possible Greek-sponsored rule in the future.[137]

Another rally was arranged by the Supreme Military Command of the Greek forces in Asia Minor on 13 August. Early that same morning, people started to mass along the Quay. Then, at around nine, notables of the Muslim community who had convened in the municipal office headed for the Hunters' Club in horse-drawn coaches. Carrying a large portrait of Lloyd George, they were sincerely welcomed by non-Muslims along the way. When the cortege came before the British Consulate, the crowd shouted 'Long live Britain!' and 'Long live Lloyd George!', and a decree was presented to the consulate. Among the people who signed the decree praising Britain's efforts for the establishment of peace in the region were Hacı Hasan Pasha, the mayor of Smyrna; Ahmet Şükrü, the mayor of Cordelio; Hoca Sabri, imam of the Hisar Mosque; İsmail Hakkı, the leader of the Circassian Society; Mehmet Sait, the legal consultant of the same society; Mehmet Samih, a member of that society; Alagözyan, a clergyman from the Armenian community; and various figures from the Greek Orthodox community.[138]

After two weeks of silence following these rallies, the Allied Powers announced in mid-August their refusal to accept the proclamation of an autonomous state, declaring that the status of Western Anatolia would be determined after the end of the military conflict in the region. On 24 August, two days before the attack of the nationalists in Ankara, the Greek Ministry of the Interior declared that the decisions made about the autonomy of Western Anatolia would begin to be enforced. However, towards the end of August, news about the defeat of the Greek army started to arrive in Smyrna. The attempt to establish an autonomous administration in Western Anatolia was treated with indifference by the Ottoman Christians and with distrust by the Allied Powers over the summer of 1922.

One of the general opinions in mainstream literature in regard to the formation of an autonomous state in the region is that Greece's quest for a new Hellenic presence in Western Anatolia actually 'threatened Turkey's existence as a nation'.[139] In contrast to mainstream literature, it is more plausible to think that rather than imposing a Hellenic presence in the province the Greek authorities sought the formation of a regional and supranational identity which could constitute a feasible alternative to competing Greek and Turkish nationalisms. Therefore, the Greek administration needed the support of the whole population of the province, including Muslims, and was careful to avoid equating Muslim communities with Turkish nationalists. As will be discussed in more detail in Chapter 4, the best method for guaranteeing this support would have been the co-optation to the Greek administration of all those high-ranking provincial officials whose legitimacy had been recognised by the Ottoman government.

The achievements of the High Commission displayed obvious limitations. The Greek administration in Smyrna tried to maintain public order and implement the administrative directives received from Athens at the same time. The delayed operationalisation of the High Commission due to staff shortages, combined with the inefficiency of many of its officials and the absence of coordination between the High Commission and various Allied boards, resulted in loose and inactive control over the occupied Ottoman territories. Since the day it was founded, the High Commission had very limited authority to consolidate its rule in the region. As a result of its fragile relations with the Allied boards and regional actors, the High Commission gradually began to consider establishing an autonomous administration in Western Anatolia to be more convenient than being under the direct rule of Greece.

Throughout the Greek administration in Aydın Province, Ottoman and Greek institutions coexisted, although the influence of the former relatively decreased after the Treaty of Sèvres in August 1920. The existence of this dual system was considered necessary by the authorities of the Greek state due to the multi-ethnic and multi-religious character of the region. Moreover, the Greek authorities never actually tried to establish strong control in the province in order not to agitate the non-Greek populations, even though the Greek political presence in Western Anatolia is nevertheless portrayed as an 'agent of British imperialism' by mainstream Turkish historiography. Contrary to this approach, it could be said that the Greek administration was poorly defined, caught between nationalist

Greek Administration in Western Anatolia

and colonialist policies and unable to define itself, and it had an ambiguous character in the region. The vacillation of Greece between nationalist and colonialist policies in Western Anatolia can be best observed in the memoirs of Konstantinos Zavitzianos, a former Venizelist who stood as an independent candidate in Corfu during the legislative elections of 1920:

> The majority of the new Chamber in the pre-election period had attacked the whole policy of Venizelos, both foreign and internal, with exceptional harshness. They stood for the programme of a 'small but honest Greece' as they put it. They would not want Asia Minor even if it were offered to them. They would never have made war in order to win it because, according to them, Asia Minor was a burden on Greece. They said it was a colony, and they were not disposed to pursue a colonialist policy. It was inhabited for the most part by foreign populations hostile to Greece. Greece, they said, did not have the strength to govern so extensive a tract of territory, however rich and productive, if it were inhabited by enemies.[140]

The reflection of this vacillation between nationalist and colonialist policies in the decision-making processes of the newly established High Commission became manifest in the ambiguous character of its administrative structure and in the clashes that sometimes occurred between the regional policies it was trying to conduct and Greek national policies.

Notes

1. Llewellyn Smith, *Ionian Vision*, 89–90.
2. TNA FO 608/104, 20 May 1919, James Morgan, Representative of the British High Commissioner in Smyrna, to Calthorpe, British High Commissioner in Constantinople. In some exceptional places, ethnic violence did not break out. The leading Greek Orthodox notables had forbidden plundering and only a few cases of pillaging were seen in Boudjah.
3. Clogg, 'The Byzantine Legacy', 253–4.
4. Richard Clogg, 'The Greek *Millet* in the Ottoman Empire', in *Christians and Jews in the Ottoman Empire: The Functioning of a Plural Society*, ed. Benjamin Braude and Bernard Lewis (London: Holmes & Meier, 1982), vol. I, 193.
5. Stouraiti and Kazamias claim that the *Megali Idea* forming a polyvalent notion accomplished accommodating four indispensable components: an irredentist ideology, a Western civilising mission, an ethno-religious concept of nationhood and an imperialist project of reviving the Byzantine Empire, Anastasia Stouraiti and Alexander Kazamias, 'The Imaginary Topographies of the *Megali Idea*: National Territory as Utopia', in *Spatial Conceptions of the Nation: Modernizing Geographies in Greece and Turkey*, ed. Nikiforos Diamandouros et al. (London: I. B. Tauris, 2010), 11–34. As a follow-up

Ethnic Cleansing in Western Anatolia

to these four different components of a stable interpretation of the *Megali Idea*, the idea that the conception of the *Megali Idea*, whose alternative facets were consciously or unconsciously put forward at different moments by Greek politics, is much more explanatory.

6. On the life and works of Rigas, see Leandros Vranousēs, 'Ē sēmaia, to ethnosēmo kai ē sfragida tēs "Ellēnikēs Dēmokratias" tou Rēga', *Deltion Eraldikēs kai Genealogikēs Etaireias Ellados* 8 (1992): 347–88; and Apostolos V. Daskalakēs, *To politeuma tou Rēga Velestinlē* (Athens: Vagionakēs, 1976). For an English biography of Velestinlis, see C. M. Woodhouse, *Rhigas Velestinlis: The Proto-martyr of the Greek Revolution* (Limni: Denise Harvey, 1995).

7. In the second half of the eighteenth century, members of the Phanariot elite were appointed as *hospodars* (tributary rulers) of Wallachia and Moldavia by the Ottoman sultan.

8. Clogg, 'The Greek *Millet*', 188. This political structure shared a group of common principles with the ideology of the modern state in terms of equality of citizens before the law, freedom of the press, security of citizens, the right of ownership and abrogation of slavery.

9. Rigas Velestinlis, *Revolutionary Scripts*, trans. Vassilis K. Zervoulakos (Athens: Scientific Society of Studies Pheres-Velestino-Rhigas, 2008), 99.

10. Ibid. 79.

11. Stephen G. Xydis, 'Modern Greek Nationalism', in *Nationalism in Eastern Europe*, ed. Peter F. Sugar and Ivo J. Lederer (Seattle: University of Washington Press, 1969), 238–40.

12. Costa Carras, 'Greek Identity: A Long View', in *Balkan Identities: Nation and Memory*, ed. Maria Todorova (New York: New York University Press, 2004), 318.

13. Andreas Nanakis, 'Venizelos and Church–State Relations', in *Eleftherios Venizelos: The Trials of Statesmanship*, ed. Paschalis M. Kitromilides (Edinburgh: Edinburgh University Press, 2006), 349.

14. *The Cretan Drama: The Life and Memoirs of Prince George, High Commissioner in Crete*, ed. A. A. Pallis (New York: Robert Speller & Sons, 1959), 46.

15. Ion Dragoumis was born in Athens in 1878. His father Stefanos Dragoumis had served as the prime minister of Greece from January to October 1910 before Venizelos took over.

16. Vangelis Kechriotis, 'Greek Orthodox, Ottoman Greeks or just Greeks? Theories of Coexistence in the Aftermath of the Young Turk Revolution', *Etudes Balkaniques* 1 (2005), 60–4.

17. Diogenis Xanalatos, 'The Greeks and the Turks on the Eve of the Balkan Wars: A Frustrated Plan', *Balkan Studies* 3 (1962), 282.

18. Michalis Katsikas, 'Dragoumis, Macedonia, and the Ottoman Empire (1903–1913): The Great Idea, Nationalism, and Greek Ottomanism',

Greek Administration in Western Anatolia

unpublished PhD thesis, Centre for Byzantine, Ottoman and Modern Greek Studies, University of Birmingham, 2008, 162–3.

19. Nonetheless, the organisation lost its influence on the Ottoman Greek communities in the 1912 elections. Most of the Greek delegates were elected through cooperation with the CUP, see Catherine Boura, 'The Greek Millet in Turkish Politics: Greeks in the Ottoman Parliament (1908–1918)', in *Ottoman Greeks in the Age of Nationalism*, ed. Dimitri Gondicas and Charles Issawi (Princeton: The Darwin Press, 1999), 198–9.

20. Gerasimos Augustinos, *Consciousness and History: Nationalist Critics of Greek Society, 1897–1914* (New York: Columbia University Press/ East European Quarterly, 1977), 115.

21. Ion Dragoumis, *Osoi Zōntanoi* (Athens: Nea Zoi, 1926), 128.

22. Stefanos Katsikas, '*Millet* Legacies in a National Environment: Political Elites and Muslim Communities in Greece (1830s–1923)', in *State-nationalisms in the Ottoman Empire, Greece, and Turkey: Orthodox and Muslims, 1830–1945*, ed. Benjamin C. Fortna et al. (London: Routledge, 2013), 50.

23. Ioannis Glavinas, 'In Search of a New Balance: The Symbiosis between Christian and Muslim Inhabitants of the Greek State, 1912–1923', in *Balkan Nationalism(s) and the Ottoman Empire, vol. I: National Movements and Representations*, ed. Dimitris Stamatopoulos (Istanbul: Isis Press, 2015), 159–64. The so-called New Lands are the territories incorporated into Greece after the Balkan Wars in 1912–1913, namely Macedonia, Epirus, Crete and other Aegean islands.

24. An important factor about these efforts of normalisation was the fact that during the Balkan Wars the Greek army was far less violent towards Muslim civilians than its Serbian and Bulgarian allies, see Mazower, *Salonica, City of Ghosts*, 313.

25. On 30 December 1918, Venizelos submitted a memorandum to the Committee on Greek Affairs. According to this memorandum, Greek claims included the Karesi *sanjak* and Aydın Province, with the exception of the Denizli *sanjak* where the population was exclusively Muslim, see Paul C. Helmreich, *From Paris to Sévres: The Partition of the Ottoman Empire at the Peace Conference of 1919–1920* (Columbus, OH: Ohio State University Press, 1974), 39–40.

26. Victoria Solomonidis, 'Greece in Asia Minor', 133–4.

27. Roughly one and a half months after the treaty, on 4 October 1920, the Ottoman Ministry of the Interior redetermined the borders of Aydın Province. According to this new reorganisation, the province of Aydın, whose centre had been transferred to Alaşehir, consisted of only the Alaşehir, Aydın and Denizli *sanjak*s, while the Greek administration of Smyrna was recognised by the Ottoman authorities, see BOA DH. İ-UM. EK 122/16.

28. Harris Mylonas, *The Politics of Nation-building: Making Co-nationals, Refugees, and Minorities* (Cambridge: Cambridge University Press, 2012), 126.

Ethnic Cleansing in Western Anatolia

29. MOFA A/ 5VI tel. no. 3890, 24 April 1919, from Venizelos to MOFA.
30. BOA DH. İ-UM. EK 51/114. Adil Bey, a Finance Inspector (*Mâliye Müfettişi*), and Kemal Bey, a Lieutenant of the General Staff (*Erkân-ı Harbiye Kaymakamı*), were appointed to this commission as Ottoman representatives.
31. 'Havâdis-i Vilâyet', *Âhenk*, 21 May 1919 (R. 21 Mayıs 1335).
32. See Evangelia Achladi, 'De la guerre à l'administration grecque: la fin de Smyrne cosmopolite', in *Smyrne, la ville oubliée?*, ed. Marie-Carmen Smyrnelis (Paris: Editions Autrement, 2006), 187–9.
33. Ibid. 190–3.
34. TNA FO 608/271, 16 December 1919, James Morgan to the British High Commissioner in Constantinople. Morgan noted, in the earlier days of the occupation, that the ecclesiastical leaders were annoyed with Stergiades for his curbing 'the power of the church, and treating metropolitans roughly'.
35. Despite the fact that following the re-proclamation of the constitution in 1908, the abolition of the *millet* system targeted the undermining of the roles and privileges of the religious leaders in communal affairs; Chrysostomos had a great support within the Greek Orthodox community in Smyrna, see Chrēstos Solomōnidēs, *O Smyrnēs Chrysostomos*, 2 vols (Athens: Ethnikis Mnimosynis, 1971).
36. BOA DH. EUM. AYŞ 75/118. According to this report, he stayed in Nif (Nymfaion) two nights and arranged meetings with the prominent people from the Orthodox community as well as his brother. The Ottoman authorities were aware of the conflict between the high commissioner and Chrysostomos, cf. BOA DH. İ-UM 20-30/14-07. The Ottoman authorities, particularly vice-governor Subhî Efendi, favoured Stergiades in this conflict. In a letter delivered to the Ottoman Ministry of the Interior, he clearly sided with Stergiades and described the High Commission as an institution that 'weakened Chrysostomos, who was renowned for his incitements and maltreatments (*tahrikât ve iğvaât*) in the name of religion (*din namına*), and hence attempted to win the hearts of Muslims through fondling their wounded lives'.
37. Llewellyn Smith, *Ionian Vision*, 269–70. Stergiades's distant approach towards the Patriarchate and Orthodox clergy was supported by the monarchist Gounaris government in Athens. From the time of the election of Meletios IV as the Patriarch of Constantinople in December 1921, the tension between the Patriarchate and the government had escalated. Meletios was born in Crete and served as metropolitan bishop of Athens from 1918 to 1920 before the second reign of King Constantine. This election was considered as a Venizelist conspiracy by the newly elected Royalist government in Athens. Since the Royalist government interrupted all telegraphic communication with Constantinople during the elections, the Orthodox clergy in the Smyrna zone were able to learn limited details about the patriarchal elections by the end of the month. See J. Lacombe,

'Chronique des Eglises Orientales', in *Echos d'Orient* 21, no. 125 (January–March 1922), 105.

38. After the expansion of the Greek zone of occupation, British naval representatives were appointed in order to keep the commodore of the British Aegean Squadron informed of the situation in the inner settlements such as Manisa, Ödemiş and Aydın, see TNA ADM 137/1762, 22 June 1919, Commodore M. Fitzmaurice to Stergiades.

39. Victoria Solomonidis, 'Greece in Asia Minor', 124; and Llewellyn Smith, *Ionian Vision*, 173.

40. GAK. EDS., 8d tel. no. 2243, 11 November 1921 (J. C. 29 October 1921), from Stergiades to High Command.

41. Mihail L. Rodas, *Ē Ellada stēn Mikra Asia (1918–1922): Ē Mikrasiatikē Katastrofē* (Athens: Kleisiouni, 1950 [Reprinted Lavyrinthos, 2019]), 80.

42. Victoria Solomonidis, 'Greece in Asia Minor', 136.

43. Initially, in the summer months six diplomatic offices affiliated with the High Commission were opened in Ayvalık, Kasaba, Ödemiş, Bergama, Menemen and Tire. The last four of these were sub-units dependent on the Smyrna *sanjak* in the Ottoman provincial organisation.

44. Victoria Solomonidis, 'Greece in Asia Minor', 135. The leaders of the Armenian and Jewish communities in Smyrna were informed that the Greek administration intended to employ an important number of qualified Armenians and Jews. Thus, similar to the Ottoman administration, the new regime continued to have a multi-ethnic and multi-religious character, reflecting the nature of the society to be governed.

45. BOA BEO 4600/344941. The Ottoman Ministry of the Interior worried that the administrative offices would be occupied by the Greeks and therefore the Ottoman rule in the region would lose its credibility.

46. Victoria Solomonidis, 'Greece in Asia Minor', 133–4.

47. Hacı Hasan Pasha remained in office as the mayor of Smyrna during the rule of the High Commission.

48. TNA FO 371/ 7921, 20 March 1922, 'A Year of Greek Administration in Smyrna', Greek Chargé d'Affaires in London to Curzon, Secretary of State for Foreign Affairs.

49. Victoria Solomonidis, 'Greece in Asia Minor', 133.

50. Ibid. 144–6.

51. Rodas, *Ē Ellada stēn Mikran Asia*, 127–30. In an early example, the Ottoman gendarmes threatened the district governor of Aydın with leaving their duties and joining the National Forces in December 1919 unless their salaries were paid in time, see BOA DH. ŞFR 642/69.

52. Victoria Solomonidis, 'Greece in Asia Minor', 145–6.

53. BOA DH. ŞFR 104/144.

54. TNA FO 608/104, 6 June 1919, James Morgan, Smyrna representative of the British High Commission, to British High Commissioner in Constantinople. The Ottoman police were placed at various police

Ethnic Cleansing in Western Anatolia

stations in downtown Smyrna along with Greek soldiers. Furthermore, the High Commission allowed the use of Ottoman flags in official buildings, cf. TNA FO 608/86, 26 August 1919, British High Commission in Constantinople to Astoria. All Ottoman flags would be replaced by Greek ones after the signing of the Sèvres Treaty, see the memoirs of Süleyman Vasfi (Adıyaman), who was chief clerk (*başkâtib*) at the Smyrna customs and taken captive during the day of landing, 'Bir Gümrükçünün İşgal Yılları Anıları: İzmir Gümrükleri Başmüdürlük Tahrirat Başkatibi Süleyman Vasfi Bey'in Anılarından', in *Üç İzmir*, ed. Enis Batur (Istanbul: Yapı Kredi Yayınları, 1992), 243.

55. BOA DH. EUM. AYŞ 35/49. Zeki was appointed as the chief of police of Aydın Province in mid-August 1919 shortly after the Greek occupation, see BOA BEO 4586/343944.

56. *A Survey of Some Social Conditions in Smyrna, Asia Minor – May 1921*, ed. Rıfat N. Bali (Istanbul: Libra Kitap, 2009), 143–5. The International College is the outgrowth of a school founded in Smyrna by the American Board of Commissioners for Foreign Missions (ABCFM) in 1879. Throughout the whole period of the war, the college continued its work without interruption and, in addition, it carried out considerable relief activities.

57. Ibid. 149.

58. The nationalist government in Ankara immediately announced that the Turkish signatories of the treaty were traitors and the National Assembly, again, called the Muslims to take up arms against the occupation forces and their supporters.

59. For the full text of the treaty, see *Treaty of Peace with Turkey* (London: His Majesty's Stationery Office, 1920).

60. Ibid. 21–4.

61. BOA DH. ŞFR 108/84 and BOA DH. ŞFR 660/158.

62. Victoria Solomonidis, 'Greece in Asia Minor', 152–4.

63. Ibid. 154.

64. *Efēmeris tēs Kyvernēseōs*, Teuchos A, Nomos 2495, 10 September 1920 (J. C.).

65. Victoria Solomonidis, 'Greece in Asia Minor', 156.

66. Ibid. 157.

67. The integration of the Ottoman sharia courts into the Greek judicial system depended on some legal regulations. Following these regulations, the officers of the Ottoman sharia courts would be asked whether or not they would serve in the Greek administration. *A Survey of Some Social Conditions*, 133–5.

68. The muftis, who were responsible for the operation of the mosques and had the right to interpret sharia on the basis of his own examination of the Islamic sources (*fatwa*), would continue to serve under the Greek administration.

69. BOA BEO 4678/350814.

70. In the specific case of Salihli, it was stressed that the High Commission made the monthly payments on time, but the district governor and the Greek

Greek Administration in Western Anatolia

representative were responsible for the Ottoman civil servants' delayed salaries. See GAK. EDS., no. 126, 11 February 1922 (J. C. 29 January 1922), Samarakis, Head of the Department of Finance, to the representative of the High Commission in Salihli.

71. Victoria Solomonidis, 'Greece in Asia Minor', 154.

72. Rodas, *Ē Ellada stēn Mikran Asia*, 189.

73. Even after the fall of his government, many Orthodox Greeks in Western Anatolia continued to close their shops on the occasion of Venizelos's name day as a sign of respect. Against long odds, there were few incidents between them and the higher ranks of the Greek army, who clearly had Royalist allegiance, see TNA FO 286/758, 10 January 1921, James Morgan to British High Commission. Moreover, the Allied Powers, which had supported Venizelos almost unconditionally, did not maintain the same support for the Royalist government under the new circumstances.

74. TNA FO 141/444/8, 15 October 1921, Horace Rumbold to Curzon.

75. Victoria Solomonidis, 'Greece in Asia Minor', 63.

76. *A Survey of Some Social Conditions*, 141–2. First modern tribunals of the Empire were used to deal with cases in accordance with the 1858 Ottoman Criminal Code, and both Muslim and non-Muslim citizens could enrol them, see Carter Vaughn Findley, 'The Tanzimat', in *The Cambridge History of Turkey, vol. 4: Turkey in the Modern World*, ed. Reşat Kasaba (Cambridge: Cambridge University Press, 2008), 17–21.

77. TNA FO 608/103, 17 September 1919, İsmail Cenani to the British High Commissioner in Constantinople.

78. BOA DH. EUM. AYŞ 22/77.

79. TNA FO 608/273, 14 December 1919, J. M. de Robeck, British High Commissioner in Constantinople, to Earl Curzon.

80. *Âhenk*, 12 April 1922 (R. 12 Nisan 1338).

81. TNA FO 608/ 103, 13 November 1919, Vali Ahmed İzzet to the Smyrna Representative of the British High Commissioner.

82. MOFA 12e tel. no. 6484, 12 October 1919, from Diomidis to Venizelos.

83. TNA FO 608/103, 8 August 1919, Balfour to Lord Curzon.

84. CADN, Izmir 643 PO/1, 26, 23 October 1919, 'C. M. 14 Compétence militaire-Grèce de Ciaves/ Raphaël'.

85. TNA FO 608/103, 16 July 1919, James Morgan, Smyrna representative of the British High Commissioner, to the British High Commission in Constantinople.

86. TNA FO 141/444/8, 9 September 1921, H. Rumbold to Curzon.

87. Victoria Solomonidis, 'Greece in Asia Minor', 179.

88. TNA FO 286/758, 11 August 1921, Harry H. Lamb, Smyrna Representative of the British High Commission, to Sir Horace Rumbold.

89. GAK. YAS., no. 2150, 29 October 1921 (J. C. 16 October 1921), from Gounarakis, General Secretary, to the representative of the High Commission in Salihli and BOA DH. İ-UM 20/29-14/47.

Ethnic Cleansing in Western Anatolia

90. Achladi, 'De la guerre à l'administration grecque', 186–8.
91. Following his appointment, Stergiades announced that when Greece annexed the Smyrna zone, capitulations and consular courts would be abolished, see TNA FO 141/444/8, 26 May 1919, James Morgan to Earl Curzon. It was only after some weeks of correspondence that Stergiades was forced to admit in writing that the capitulatory regime would continue, see TNA FO 141/444/8, 12 September 1919, James Morgan to British High Commissioner.
92. For instance, Georgios Kyriakidis, an Ottoman Greek, had rented out his house located in Mehpare Street of the Basmane district to Miran Gkianigkian, a clerk in the Smyrne–Cassaba et Prolongements Railway Company. Nonetheless, the former tenant, Maria Kassar, a British subject, did not accept the order to evacuate the house and displayed a British flag in the garden of that house. Even though Gkianigkian made a complaint about both Kyriakidis and Kassar, the colonel (*antisyntagmatarchēs*) had to admit that he could do nothing as Kassar was a British citizen. See GAK. YAS., no. 11527/210, 12 October 1919 (J. C. 29 September 1919), from the Chief of Gendarmerie in Basmane to the High Commission.
93. Mark Mazower, *Greece and the Inter-war Economic Crisis* (Oxford: Oxford University Press, 1991), 63–5.
94. TNA FO 608/ 103, 19 November 1919, J. M. de Robeck, British High Commissioner in Constantinople, to Earl Curzon.
95. TNA FO 608/103, 7 November 1919, C. M. Staveley, British Naval Attaché in Constantinople, to British High Commissioner in Constantinople.
96. TNA FO 608/92, 20 June 1919, English copy of the communiqué of the [Greek] Army Headquarters. According to this communiqué, exportations of foodstuffs (wheat, maize, lentils, all kinds of animal food, olive oil), fuels (petroleum, benzene, coal), timber, cotton, gold and money were prohibited from the occupation zone. The people who did not obey this order would be judged by the court martial and punished in accordance with the provisions of the martial law.
97. TNA FO 608/108, 17 July 1919, Conférence des Hauts Commissaires.
98. Victoria Solomonidis, 'Greece in Asia Minor', 149–51.
99. TNA FO 286/756, 10 January 1921, the Presidents of the Chambers of Commerce to the British High Commission. Most of the members of these chambers were the European subjects who benefited from the capitulations. In spite of the reassurance of the capitulations by the High Commission, the European merchants and Levantines held the opinion that the High Commission would promote the Greek capital in the region.
100. TNA FO 286/756, 13 January 1921, Rhallys to Stergiades.
101. TNA FO 286/756, 19 January 1921, Stergiades to Council of Ministers.
102. TNA FO 286/758, 22 November 1921, Asia Minor Army Command to the Greek High Commission.
103. TNA FO 286/758, 9 December 1921, Harry Lamb, Smyrna Representative of the British High Commission, to the British High Commission.

Greek Administration in Western Anatolia

104. Victoria Solomonidis, 'Greece in Asia Minor', 151.
105. TNA FO 280/790, 20 February 1922, American, British, French, Italian, Belgian and Dutch Chambers of Commerce to British High Commission.
106. GAK. YAS., no. 3840/52, 15 November 1921 (J. C. 2 November 1921), from the General Secretariat to the representatives of the High Commission in the Military Occupation Zone.
107. TNA T 160/50, 24 January 1921, Sallandrouse de Lamornaix, President of the Administrative Council of the OPDA, to Horace Rumbold, British High Commissioner.
108. GAK. EDS., n. n., 30 November 1921 (J. C. 17 November 1921), from Samarakis, head of the Department of Finance to the General Secretariat.
109. TNA FO 608/92, 23 February 1919, Commander Heathcote-Smith to the British High Commission in Constantinople.
110. 'Eortē yper tōn Prosfygōn-Eis to stadion tou Paniōniou', *Kosmos*, 22 July 1919 and 'Prosfygikai Engatastaseis', *Kosmos*, 24 July 1919. The Department of Repatriation and Rehabilitation of Refugees, which was headquartered next to the Agios Haralambos Ottoman Greek hospital and under the presidency of Haralambos Roïlos, was to conduct research and make preparations that would facilitate the refugees' resettlement.
111. Victoria Solomonidis, 'Greece in Asia Minor', 165.
112. TNA FO 608/92, 23 February 1919, Heathcote-Smith to the British High Commission.
113. Victoria Solomonidis, 'Greece in Asia Minor', 164–5.
114. TNA FO 608/ 103, 13 February 1919, W. Lewis Bailey, British vice-consul in Mytiline, to Lord Granville.
115. Kâmil Su, *Sevr Antlaşması ve Aydın (İzmir) Vilayeti* (Ankara: Kültür Bakanlığı Yayınları, 1981), 8.
116. Victoria Solomonidis, 'Greece in Asia Minor', 164, citing MOFA 116 a5.
117. *A Survey of Some Social Conditions*, 89–90.
118. TNA FO 608/102, 24 May 1919, Calthorpe to Curzon.
119. TNA FO 608/92, 23 February 1919, Commander Heathcote-Smith to the British High Commission in Constantinople.
120. GAK. YAS., No. 11164, 27 October 1919 (J. C. 14 October 1919), from Stergiades to the Director General of the Ottoman Railway.
121. GAK. YAS., No. 13406, 13 November 1919 (J. C. 31 October 1919), from the Director General of the Ottoman (Aidin) Railway Stergiades.
122. GAK. YAS., No. 20545, 13 July 1920 (J. C. 31 June 1920), from Gounarakis to Greek representative at Adramyt (Edremit).
123. See Victoria Solomonidis, 'Greece in Asia Minor', 169.
124. 'Apo ton Prochthesinon Eranon', *Kosmos*, 20 September 1919.
125. 'Te'âvün', *Âhenk*, 5 August 1919 (R. 5 Ağustos 1335).
126. See Alexis Alexandris, 'The Constantinopolitan Greek Factor during the Greco-Turkish Confrontation of 1919–1922', *Byzantine and Modern Greek Studies* 8 (1982), 159.

Ethnic Cleansing in Western Anatolia

127. In the spring of 1922, Stergiades managed to expel Amyna's leaders from Smyrna. General Anastasios Papoulas had tendered his resignation, and Mr Lambros, a Venizelist lawyer from Thessaloniki who had been collecting donations for Amyna in European capitals, was barred from the Smyrna zone, CADC, 51CPCOM, P1533, 10 June 1922, La situation.

128. *The Manchester Guardian*, 'Future of Smyrna', 23 February 1921, 7.

129. *Âhenk*, 25 May 1921 (R. 25 Mayıs 1335).

130. TNA FO 286/790, 1 August 1922, Harry Lamb to the British High Commission in Constantinople.

131. Sâmi Lûtfi, 'Olanlar Bitenler', *Islahât*, 21 July 1922 (R. 21 Temmuz 1338).

132. TNA FO 371/ 7868, 31 July 1922, Harry Lamb to Rumbold. A French copy of this declaration can be found in *La Réforme*, the French newspaper of Smyrna. See *La Réforme*, 30 July 1922 (J. C. 17 July 1922).

133. GAK. EDS., 17h2, No. 2645, 9 August 1922 (J. C. 27 July 1922), Intelligence Report, No. 2645.

134. 'Sabah ve Akşam Yerli Rumca Gazetelerin Dediği', *Şark*, 1 August 1922 (R. 1 Ağustos 1338).

135. The British documents mention that Stergiades addressed the notables of the Muslim community. See TNA FO 286/790, 1 August 1922, Harry Lamb to the British High Commission in Constantinople. According to this document, he made the following statement: 'In view of the malicious rumours that have been put in circulation, I take this earliest opportunity of assuring the Mussulmans that the Sultan of Constantinople is above all the Caliph of all Mussulmans; the prestige which he rightly enjoys throughout the world of Islam will remain intact and he will similarly preserve the religious bond which unites him to all believers. Let me add that the prestige of the Caliph will be far higher here than it is in Angora, where all are behaving as rebels against the Sultan and as apostates from the Caliph.'

136. 'Kasaba Kaymakamlığı Cenâb-ı Âliyyesine', *Islahât*, 13 August 1922 (R. 13 Ağustos 1338).

137. Henri Nahum, *Juifs de Smyrne, XIXe–XXe siècle* (Paris: Aubier, 1997), 167–8. The Greek High Commission's earlier attempts to found the Ionian University on a land that belonged to the Jewish community of Smyrna proved the predictions of the Jewish community true. This land was a large Jewish cemetery before Rahmî Bey had sequestrated it in 1914. When the Greek administration started to construct the Ionian University on this land instead of handing the cemetery back, the notables of the Jewish community in Smyrna wanted to discuss this with Stergiades. Upon his refusal, the Jewish notables appealed to the representatives of the Allied High Commission, see TNA FO 286/761, 3 January 1921, Note of the Jewish Community to James Morgan (in French).

138. 'Vilâyât Haberleri: Dünki Miting Tafsîlâtı', *Islahât*, 14 August 1922 (R. 14 Ağustos 1338).

Greek Administration in Western Anatolia

139. See Peter Kincaid Jensen, 'The Greco-Turkish War, 1920–1922', *International Journal of Middle East Studies* 10, no. 4 (November 1979), 553. See also Michael M. Finefrock, 'Atatürk, Lloyd George and the *Megali Idea:* Cause and Consequence of the Greek Plan to Seize Constantinople from the Allies, June–August 1922', *The Journal of Modern History* 52, no. 1 (March 1980), 1047. Finefrock depicts the Turkish War of Independence as 'a war against Hellenist imperialism in Asia Minor'.
140. Llewellyn Smith, *Ionian Vision*, 153, citing Kōnstantinos G. Zavitzianos, *Ai anamnēseis tou ek tis Istorikis Diafōnias Vasieleōs Kōnstantinou kai Eleutheriou Venizelou opōs tēn ezēse (1914–1922)*, vol. II (Athens: Rodis, 1947), 100.

Chapter 3

Zoi: A Survey of Social Life under the Greek Administration

Throughout most of the Ottoman Empire, in contrast to what is contended, city quarters were not divided in accordance with communities, nor in a discriminating manner. Urban maps of Smyrna at the end of the nineteenth century depict distinct neighbourhoods of Greeks, Muslims, Armenians, Jews and Europeans (Frenks).[1] In fact, settlement patterns were much more heterogenous with, for example, Greek Orthodox churches in the Armenian quarter and Armenian churches and schools in the Jewish quarter. While European neighbourhoods accumulated along the coastline of the city, Greek districts encompassed a vast area to the north and northeast of the city right behind them. Muslim neighbourhoods are shown as clustered around the traditional bazaar and Konak, where the administrative offices of the city were situated (see Figure 3.1).

The settlements of these five distinct religious communities were in fact scattered in such a way as to challenge the validity of this pattern of the city, however. It so happened that while an Orthodox church and its parish appeared in the middle of Basmane, which was known as the Armenian neighbourhood, at least one Armenian church, school and its parish were located in the coastal suburb of Karatas, which was known as the Jewish district. It is also obvious that the places marked as Greek, Muslim or Jewish districts on the map had inhabitants from other religions. In addition, new prosperous suburbs, such as Cordelio and Goztepe, connected to the centre by proper roads and steam ferries, were even less distinct in ethnic and religious make-up. For instance, Cordelio was a settlement where Catholic and Orthodox Greeks lived very close to the affluent Armenians and Muslims. Similarly, in Aydın, a smaller urban centre in the interior, many Jews owned houses in the Muslim district. In general, neighbourhoods displayed homogeneity with regard to social and economic status instead of having boundaries on the basis of the dwellers'

Social Life under the Greek Administration

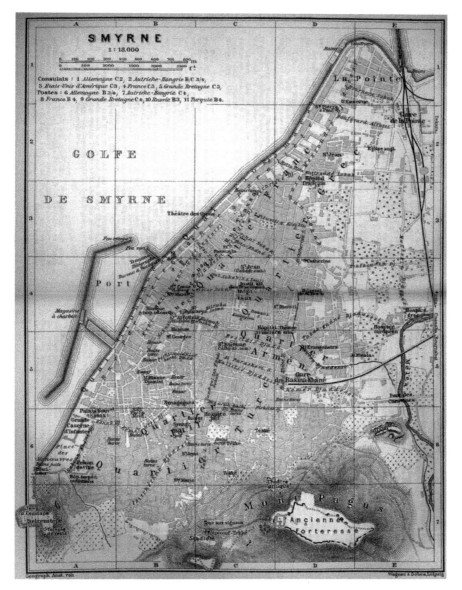

Figure 3.1 Karl Baedeker's map of urban Smyrna, 1905. Karl Baedeker, *Konstantinopel und das westliche Kleinasien: Handbuch für Reisende* (Leipzig: Baedeker, 1905), 194–5.

religious affiliation. There were no walls separating districts in Ottoman Smyrna, nor was there anything in the everyday lives of the people or in the administrative functioning of the Empire that made it necessary to divide into districts.[2]

Ethnic Cleansing in Western Anatolia

Despite the blurred social boundaries in these neighbourhoods, they did not share the same communal institutions such as hospitals, schools and associations. For this purpose, the High Commission, which emphasised the special status of the Smyrna *sanjak*, tried to modernise social life and cultivate a new kind of regional belonging. Therefore, the differences between Greece and the *sanjak* were underlined by the high commissioner. Nonetheless, the Greek civil servants appointed by the Kingdom interpreted the diversity as the sign of the inferior position of the peoples in Western Anatolia. In certain cases, Greek authorities claimed that Greece had a duty, a *mission civilisatrice*, in the region.[3] According to this idea, the cultural superiority and the European character of the Greek administration in Western Anatolia would consolidate the prospective dominant position of the Greek Kingdom in the Levant. In a discourse underlining the differences between 'self' and 'other', Asia Minor/Western Anatolia was being reconstructed as a geographical region that required the guidance of the Kingdom. The introduction of European-style novelties to the region in education, agriculture and health issues were considered as a moral obligation of the Kingdom.

In his seminal essay, Edward Said pointed out that 'to be colonized is potentially to be a great many different, but inferior things, in many different places, at many different times.'[4] In essence, the term colonisation pertains to the actual process of occupying, controlling and exploiting a foreign country. This concept coined in nineteenth-century Europe gained a central position in the designation of governments in much of the twentieth century. Similar to colonised people, colonised societies were also seen as objects that could be opened to survey, regulation and sanitisation.[5]

The colonialist vision of Greece could be understood best in the High Commission's administration of public health and education. To illustrate, some postcards show the zeal of Greek officials in vaccine campaigns and other services organised by the Department of Health, a branch of the High Commission (see Figure 3.2). The Greek Red Cross used to carry the banner in these campaigns, which did not exclude the Muslim inhabitants of the province. Moreover, on some postcards, members of this institution can be seen offering food and shelter to poor refugees (see Figure 3.3). These representations attempt to legitimise the authority of the occupying forces over the indigenous groups. Likewise, in the realm of education, the formation of the Ionian University, which would welcome 'all students from every race and nation', could be considered as a sign of this policy since that institution undertook the duty of production of knowledge in the region. Moreover, this university was

Social Life under the Greek Administration

Figure 3.2 Greek Red Cross vaccine campaign. ELIA/MIET Photographic Archive – Photos Zographos, 84.

Figure 3.3 Greek Red Cross and the refugees. ELIA/MIET Photographic Archive – Photos Zographos, 67.

to have a School of Oriental Ethnology and Languages, where research could be conducted on the so-called different and exotic cultures of the Orient.

The internal colonialist vision of the Greek administration, which sought to introduce new methods and representations in Western Anatolia, was especially evident in daily life. This chapter, which addresses different aspects of daily life, primarily aims to present a panorama of the associations and clubs in the region. Later, public health and education in this period will be covered, and finally censorship conducted by both the Greek administration and the Allied representatives will be demonstrated.

Urban Life: Social Organisations, Labour Unions and Missions

The number of Ottoman Greek organisations multiplied under Greek rule and can be classified into three main groups: charity foundations, sports clubs and cultural associations.[6] The degree of inclusivity of these social networks bear vital significance for the comprehension of the social structure in the cities and towns, particularly in Smyrna. Whereas charity foundations operated within the local Greek Orthodox communities and had an exclusivist structure, occupational organisations and cultural associations were more open to outsiders and could even have multi-religious and multi-ethnic structures. It was overtly stated in the regulations of such associations who would or would not be accepted as a member.[7]

In the period following the armistice, the number of women's organisations also increased; however, most of these had a stark nationalist character. Greek nationalist discourse had asserted that Greek women would play an important role in the modernisation of the nation and in the *mission civilisatrice* of the Kingdom. In this context, women's presumed civilising and charitable qualities would rehabilitate society,[8] which was believed to have lost its moral values during the long war. By the same token, a correlation between womanhood, particularly motherhood, and charity was established. Charity campaigns within the Orthodox communities were usually carried out voluntarily by women from urban and upper-class backgrounds.[9] It is not a coincidence that the main target of women's associations founded in this period was charitable work, especially in educational and ecclesiastical matters. The most important of these associations were the Greek Female High School Students' Association of Smyrna and the Smyrna Women's Association League, both of which made financial contributions to the girls' high schools and their students in the city. The Smyrna Women's Association League would later expand to open offices in Menemen and Kasaba. Aside from these two groups, the Women's Religious Sisterhood Organisation and Alaçatı Women Friends of the Poor Association, established in 1921 by Pinelopi Iliadis with the aim of restoring the Agios Georgios Church, could also be added to this list. Moreover, the Benevolent Sisterhood of Ladies (Agathoergos Adelfotēta Kyriōn), founded in 1899 by a former Greek consul's wife, Ekaterini Laskaris, continued its activities for educating orphaned girls in the region.[10]

Social Life under the Greek Administration

Aydın Province, particularly Smyrna, became one of the urban centres in the Ottoman Empire where modern sports clubs started to be founded since it hosted merchant groups having ties with European capitals. By the end of the nineteenth century, several types of sports had already arrived in Smyrna. There were two prominent sports clubs: Panionios and Apollon.[11] The Panionios Gymnastic Club, established through the unification of the Orpheus and Gymnasion Clubs in 1898, had the largest membership in the province. The more bourgeois Apollon Club was founded in 1891 and rivalled Panionios. Although these two clubs were famous for their football teams, they were also active in gymnastics, swimming, fencing, hiking and cycling.

Apart from these two prominent sports clubs, there were other clubs serving wealthier city-dwellers. The Sporting Club, founded in 1894 by Polycarpos Vitalis, had Ottoman Greeks, Levantines and Armenians on its administrative board, and appealed to the crème de la crème of Smyrniote society.[12] This club, which lost some of its members because of the war conditions and financial crisis, regained its members and altered its name to Asia Minor Club in 1920. Even though Muslims did not take part in its administrative body, the Asia Minor Club went beyond the borders of ethno-religious communities and provided an environment for all members who had a certain level of welfare.[13]

From its establishment, the High Commission supported Muslim social organisations. The Red Crescent (Hilâl-i Ahmer) Society, the Teachers Association (Muallimîn Cemiyeti), and the Farmers Association (Çiftçiler Cemiyeti) all continued in Aydın Province under Greek rule.[14] Additionally, Smyrna's Muslim community was permitted to found new educational organisations after May 1919, which made efforts to systematically guide schools and teachers in self-improvement. For example, the Association for Support of Education (Teşvîk-i Maârif Cemiyeti) was founded as a Smyrna-based organisation in May 1920 with the aim of bringing modernised educational institutions to the Muslim population of the city.[15] Muallim Celâl, the chairman of the association, and Mehmet Tahirü'l Mevlevi, the general secretary of this society and a columnist in *Islahât*, had embarked on the venture in full cooperation with the Islamic Library, formerly the Milli Kütüphane.[16]

The labour unions, which were powerful, particularly in the Greek Orthodox[17] and Armenian communities of the Smyrna *sanjak*, continued to thrive under the Greek administration after the constraints of the war years. Indeed, the Pharmacists Association, the Bakers Association, the Coffee and Beer Salesmen Association, the Barbers Association and the Trade Officers Association had been active in the city since the second half of the nineteenth century. To these were added, under the Greek administration, the Painters Association; the Grocery Association of Greater Smyrna, which was organised in every neighbourhood of Smyrna; the Military Club, which was opened in the former building of the Austro-Hungarian Consulate and served Greek military officers; the Port Workers Association, among the founders of which were Ottoman Greeks, Levantines and people from the Muslim community; the Port Boatmen Association; and the Smyrna Railway Workers Association. A survey prepared by the professors from the International College of Smyrna revealed the situation of the Greek-dominated occupational organisations:

> There are many unions of various kinds in the city, though most of these were inactive during the war, due to the suspicion that they would naturally attract in holding meetings. Since the armistice these unions have been gradually recognized until there are now 20 Greek unions with 3120 members. The Greek unions are of tobacco workers, bakers, druggists, employers, philologists, barbers, editors, millers, railway clerks, grocers, painters, lawyers, cooks and waiters, boatmen, coffee house proprietors, macaroni workers, confectioners, clerks, distillers and merchant tailors.[18]

During World War I, Armenian unions of every kind were considered a threat to the state and so their activities were severely curtailed. After the war, these Armenian unions were slowly able to form a general union of Armenian artisans with only 193 members. This organisation had a nationalistic overtone in its regulations, with the primary purpose 'to unite to rebuild and upbuild our own native country of Armenia'. Moreover, it aimed 'to establish fraternal relations among the different tradesmen, for mutual protection and help, and to keep in touch with similar unions in Armenia, so as to distribute artisan labour in the most equitable manner where needed'.[19]

Remarkably, the labour unions and occupational organisations in the province of Aydın all failed to find a remedy for the division of Ottoman society on an ethno-religious basis.[20] Muslims, Jews and Christians from different denominations had been separately organised in different labour unions. Consequently, it is quite possible to observe strong ethno-religious polarisation in the unions.

A Clock in a Thunderstorm: Health Facilities

Smyrna, as the administrative centre of Aydın Province and the major port city in the region, offered a well-developed health and medical system thanks to the reform programme of the Empire, as well as the

Social Life under the Greek Administration

efforts of non-Muslim communities. Although Aydın Province did not suffer from a lack of health facilities after the war, high prices and poor transportation conditions in the interior affected the health services offered there.

Following the Greek landing, the Department of Public Health was founded under the jurisdiction of the High Commission for the establishments of new hospitals, dispensaries, surgeries and clinics throughout the province, and to control infectious diseases, such as malaria and smallpox.[21] Needless to say, the Department of Public Health rendered service with no ethnic or religious discrimination in urban Smyrna.

Smaller urban centres, such as Aydın, Akhisar, Bayındır, Ayasuluk, Manisa, Kuşadası and Söke, also had their own hospitals. In each of these towns, there were two hospitals, one established by the Empire and the other established by the local Greek Orthodox community in the war years. In the late Ottoman period, there were more than ten hospitals and clinics located in various parts of the city of Smyrna.

According to *Annuaire Oriental*, edited in 1921, there were ten hospitals and five hospices in downtown Smyrna. The biggest hospitals were the St Antonio Catholic Hospital, the Agios Haralambos Greek Orthodox Hospital and the Dutch Hospital in the Spitalia neighbourhood; the French Military Hospital, the St Roch Catholic Hospital and the British Seaman's Hospital in the Punta neighbourhood; the Surp Krikor Armenian Hospital in the Basmane neighbourhood; the Jewish Hospital in the İkiçeşmelik neighbourhood; and the Hopitaux Impérials Ottomans in the Konak neighbourhood.[22] They were followed by the establishment of a rabies hospital and an infants' hospital in Smyrna in August 1919. In the same period, the first ever Dermatology and Venereal Diseases Hospital in Western Anatolia, which would be the champion of personal hygiene in the camps, was founded in Manisa.[23]

Throughout the years of Greek administration, the Department of Public Health deployed remote mobile teams, composed of a doctor, vaccination and disinfection specialists, nurses and technicians, through the Greek occupation zone. Disease control crews carried out disinfection projects in the refugee camps.[24]

The Greek Red Cross, which continued its activities in the region in cooperation with the Department of Public Health, also opened a hospital connected to the Agios Haralambos Hospital in Smyrna. The branch of the Greek Red Cross in Aydın Province had treated nearly 25,000 patients within the first eighteen months of the occupation and served people of all nationalities and religions at no expense.[25] Furthermore, the Greek Red Cross instituted another hospital to provide health care to Anatolian refugees, as well as to those who suffered from the armed conflict, including Muslims.

As Michel Foucault asserts, a regulatory discourse on sex as a form of science in the modern period embraced 'old fears of venereal affliction', 'combining them with the new themes of asepsis, and the great evolutionist myths with the recent institutions of the public health' and claimed 'to ensure physical vigour and moral cleanliness' of the body.[26] Late nineteenth-century hygienic rationale contended that prostitutes, who were believed to be vectors of venereal diseases, had to be examined on a regular basis to ensure public health. Thus, a regulatory approach was justified by science and supported by health authorities and the judiciary. As well as being a means of maintaining hygienic control over the population, regulated prostitution emerged as a platform for the enforcement of normative practices regarding gender, race and sexuality.[27]

According to a report by the municipality of Smyrna in 1919, venereal diseases, intestinal diseases, heart disease and pneumonia were, in order of prevalence, the most frequent causes of death by disease in Smyrna.[28] Venereal diseases ranked highly because they were often concealed by patients, their family members and even physicians.[29] Considering the spread of venereal diseases to be a serious risk that would affect the local population as well as the Greek soldiers, the High Commission undertook forming a segregated zone for prostitution, and brothels that were scattered all around the city were moved to the Chiotika neighbourhood by November 1919.[30] Thus, their control was intended. The Americans and Europeans in the city were eager to establish a connection between immorality and venereal diseases in an explicit manner. Therefore, they spoke highly of the Greek administration's efforts:

> Immorality is also very wide-spread in the city. Before the Greeks came into power, one red light district was established in the very center of the shopping and business quarter of the city where it was not only so accessible as to be a constant temptation to the young men, but also to be conspicuously before children and those adults who were desirous of avoiding it. The new Greek government moved this district to a region on the outskirts of the city where it is less easily reached and much less in evidence. At present, the houses of prostitution are quite well segregated.[31]

Undoubtedly, this imagined connection between immorality and venereal diseases constituted an indispensable element of the way the Orient was perceived by Western mindset.

Sanitation services were also affected by the conflict between the Greek administration and the Allied authorities. Overcrowding in urban

Social Life under the Greek Administration

settlements of the province, particularly Smyrna, was a major threat to sanitation. After the Spanish flu epidemic in September 1919 and the inability of the Ottoman government to respond adequately, an Inter-Allied Commission on Health and Hygiene was founded by the decision of the Allied representatives.[32] This body, whose duty was to control the health conditions in Smyrna zone, consisted of American, British, French, Italian, Greek and Ottoman doctors. The Ottoman governorship was still regarded as legally responsible to meet the measures suggested by this commission; however, the insufficient funding prevented the Ottoman governor-general from performing these duties. Therefore, the High Commission had to establish its own public health department. The Public Health Department and the Inter-Allied Commission on Health and Hygiene continued their services in the province as long as the Greek administration remained in power.[33]

Health facilities supported by the ethno-religious communities, as well as the American and Greek Red Cross, assisted the Public Health Department in this tremendous responsibility. As in the Ottoman period, patients continued to have access to medical care regardless of religion, ethnicity and wealth in the hospitals run by different communities, Red Cross institutions or the Empire itself. The Public Health Department also followed an open policy for the activities of Red Cross institutions due to the scarcity of financial and personnel resources.[34]

The main target of the Public Health Department and Inter-Allied Commission on Health and Hygiene was to control the inhabitants' hygiene and health conditions. These multiple bodies replaced the Ottoman health institutions because of the lack of financial resources of the latter.[35] The activities of the Public Health Department, such as preparing detailed statistics about the population and providing health services escorted by the police, can be regarded as yet another sign of the colonialist vision of Greece in Western Anatolia. Although the Inter-Allied Commission on Health and Hygiene, along with the American and Italian Red Cross, supported decentralisation efforts for the health services, their participation in the services remained limited.

A Realm under the Control of the High Commission: Educational Institutions

Aydın Province was one of the administrative units of the Ottoman Empire that had the greatest number of educational institutions, and was second to none other than the capital in terms of the number of institutions and students.[36] Smyrna, as the most important urban centre in Anatolia, was naturally many steps ahead of the other settlements in the province on the basis of the multiplicity and level of educational facilities. Several schools that were founded either by private enterprise,[37] or imperial efforts for modernisation,[38] or officially supported by non-Muslim communities and missions[39] served both wealthy and poor students in various neighbourhoods.

Although Aydın Province had a high number of schools when compared to the other provinces of the Empire, the school enrolment rate was very low in Muslim communities. Even in the capital *sanjak* of Smyrna, only 5,630 children attended school.[40] There were two main reasons for this low rate of schooling. Firstly, financially strapped parents with difficulties had to take their children out of school during the chaotic atmosphere of the Great War. Secondly, many young men who had joined the army did not return to their schools.

Even without adequate data on the ethno-religious composition of students attending the imperial schools at the time of the Greek administration, it is obvious that most of the students were Muslim. Although there was actually no legal restriction in imperial schools regarding the religious affiliation of students, these schools were not preferred by non-Muslim families in Smyrna in the early twentieth century. It must also be remembered that the Ottoman Christian families preferred imperial schools in towns, such as Aydın and Manisa, where education institutions of the Ottoman Christian communities could not compete with the imperial schools, and in the interior of the province that lacked Christian schools.

In order to recover from the decline in quality of education due to post-war scarcity of resources and bureaucratic insufficiency, the High Commission started a reform of Ottoman imperial educational institutions. Early in its tenure, the High Commission had promised that the staff serving in the imperial schools would not be changed, and it can be inferred from the newspapers of the period that the High Commission actually tried to fill teaching vacancies in the schools.[41] Because of low enrolment, the Commission extended the admission period. For example, the daily *Âhenk* announced on 18 August 1919 that student registration for the Teacher Training College for Boys (Dârü'l Muallimîn) and the Teacher Training College for Girls (Dârü'l Muallimât) had not yet begun.[42] On 28 September 1919, *Âhenk* announced that the registration for the Muslim Teacher Training College for Girls was extended until 1 October since no students had applied.[43]

In August 1920, when the Greek administration *de jure* took over the *sanjak* of Smyrna, the High Commission turned the Inspectorate

Social Life under the Greek Administration

General of Education (Maârif Müdürlüğü), which would be later renamed Administration of Muslim Schools (Mekâtib-i İslâmiye Maârif İdâresi), into a sub-unit under the Department of Muslim Affairs. The fact that this sub-unit was not under the Department of Education demonstrates that the Greek Administration of Smyrna, which followed a centralising policy in educational matters, carefully approached the Muslim population's needs. Pursuant to this centralising policy, Greek language courses were introduced in the imperial schools, where previously only French was taught as a foreign language.[44]

The High Commission's policies targeting the education of Muslim students also aimed to increase of the number of students attending school.[45] The augmentation of the number of Muslim students at educational institutions and the institution of new Muslim schools would inevitably have a modernising influence on the Muslim population. In spite of these modernisation efforts, the High Commission kept an eye on these institutions in case Turkish nationalism took root and gained adherents there.

In some cases, problems did occur between the Greek administration and principals of the imperial schools due to the activities of Turkish nationalist students. The Smyrna Sultânî Lycée, known to be a place of anti-Greek propaganda before the landing of the Greek army, and a majority of whose students participated in the demonstrations organised on the evening of 14 May, came to be a blacklisted school in the sight of the High Commission. This was the only imperial school to be evacuated during the Greek landing, with its students and teachers being arrested. The High Commission thought of using the building of Smyrna Sultânî Lycée, which had started receiving students in mid-September, like the other Muslim-dominated schools in Smyrna.[46] The court ordered the principal to turn the school building over to the Department of Education on 19 October 1920, which deeply worried its teachers and students. Alongside this demand, Ferit Efendi, a teacher of Arabic, and Kenân Efendi, a teacher of French, were discharged from their offices.

A committee consisting of the schoolteachers Ahmet Nâilî, Ahmet Nazmî and Hasan Vasfî, and led by Mufti Rahmetullah Efendi, paid a visit on 17 November to the High Commission asking Gounarakis, the general secretary, to withdraw this decision. To their dismay, they returned empty-handed. As a final resort, Hasan Vasfî and Hüsamettin Bey, the former head clerk of judicial matters in the province, wrote a petition of complaint that would be submitted to the American and British representatives on 22 November. Even though the petition reached the representatives, there was no change in the outcome. It was then announced by the Administration of Muslim Schools that it would be most convenient for

Ethnic Cleansing in Western Anatolia

the students of this school, which was closed in December, to continue their education in Hilâl İdâdî Lycée and that the students were supposed to register themselves at that school without delay.[47] Smyrna Sultânî Lycée was never to be opened again under Greek rule.

The Department of Muslim Affairs worked in tandem with the remaining Ottoman civil servants. The Greek Administration of Smyrna announced that it would not pay the salaries of the teachers serving in the imperial schools from October 1920 onwards and instructed the teachers to demand wages from the Ottoman government by the following month. The Greek authorities stated that the salaries which were paid up to this date were a donation of the Kingdom. Thereupon, Mufti Rahmetullah Efendi arranged four different meetings with the teachers and notables of Smyrna, but failed to find a concrete solution to this problem.[48] After it became clear that these efforts were futile, the High Commission decided to pay salaries to the teachers from the imperial schools in Smyrna zone.[49] In fact, the imperial government in Constantinople had added a special tax to the tithe collected by the Ottoman Public Debt Administration (OPDA) that was supposed to be spent on the needs of secondary schools. As required by the agreement, the income obtained from this tax, which was collected by the OPDA for the government, was used to eliminate deficits in the accounts of the provinces for the aforementioned schools. As the High Commission had not collected this tax, it started meeting the expenses of the Muslim secondary schools from its own budget.

The modernising attempts of the High Commission indeed influenced the imperial schools in the *sanjak*. At the beginning of the school year of 1921–22, the Administration of Muslim Schools tried to reorganise the structure of the senior high schools (*idâdî*) in Smyrna. This reorganisation was probably linked to the need for financial aid from the High Commission for the general expenses of these schools. The High Commission, which paid the salaries of the principals and teachers, started to consider itself the authority on the reform activities that would be carried out. In accordance with this reorganisation, the High Commission gathered the senior high schools, one of which served girls and two of which served boys, under the roof of two schools, one for girls and one for boys. The reforms made in the boys' senior high school were particularly praised in Turkish newspapers:

> The progress that can be seen in İzmir High School this year is seriously dazzling (*gözleri kamaştıracak derecede*). Zeal and perseverance do accomplish so many things! The existence of this institution of culture (*bu irfân müessesemizin mevcûdiyyeti*), which brings education and every sort of similar virtues (*her*

Social Life under the Greek Administration

türlü meziyyet) in itself as senior high school makes us proud. It creates in our souls waves of growth and greatness (*neşet ve server*). The senior high school is by no means similar to the schools of yesterday! Not only are weaknesses that have nothing to do with school, such as charlatanism and wantonness (*şarlatanlık ve hafifmeşreblik*), absent from there, but also not accepted as fundamental in formal education.[50]

The Greek Orthodox communities in Aydın Province, particularly Smyrna, had a well-developed network of community and private schools. Although not of uniform quality and capacity, the schools of the Greek Orthodox communities, at least in Smyrna, tried to meet the educational needs of Ottoman Greeks from every economic level. To illustrate, in the school year of 1921–22 there existed in the region under the rule of the High Commission approximately 190 elementary and secondary schools that belonged to the Ottoman Greek communities. The places with the highest rate of enrolment were Smyrna and the *kazas* of Urla, Çeşme and Bergama. All of the seven ordinary high schools and two teacher training schools were located in downtown Smyrna. These were Evangeliki Scholi (the Evangelical School), Omerion School for Girls, Kentrikon Parthenagogeion (Central School for Girls), High Commission's School, Aroni Commercial School and Ionian School. Whilst a new building was assigned for the Male Teacher Training School, the Female Training School and the Nursery Training School availed themselves of the large campus of the Kentrikon Parthenagogeion.[51] In addition to these schools, most of which had been established in the nineteenth century, the High Commission also supported the other educational institutions in the province. Five months after the occupation of Smyrna, Stergiades invited to the city Dimitris Georgokakis, a consultant of the Greek Ministry of Education, to investigate opening a Greek Teacher Training School for Boys with three grade levels. This was the first step taken by the High Commission for the improvement of education in the Ottoman Greek communities. The Greek Teacher Training School for Boys, which had been previously operated within the Evangeliki Scholi and then shut down during wartime after a short-term period of activity with its students being scattered, was officially reopened in October 1919.

Apart from its modernisation attempts, the High Commission emerged as the main institution that regulated and supervised the education of the Greek Orthodox communities in the province. In some respects, the High Commission intended to play the supervising role of the state in the late Ottoman period.[52] Nonetheless, the importance of the Orthodox prelates did not cease in the decision-making mechanisms of these schools.

All appointments of professional teachers to the Greek Orthodox community schools had been made by the High Commission with the consent of the metropolitan bishop of Smyrna. These schools had a wide spectrum of courses, though religion and language courses, which played a crucial role in the formation of a concept of nation in the minds of students, dominated their syllabi instead of courses related with commercial skills. As before, the community schools continued to enrol exclusively Greek Orthodox students. Essentially, the Greek Orthodox community schools continued to remain the institutions where the self of the Greek nationalism was cultivated.[53]

The Christian community schools in rural areas, which provided primary education and often operated directly or indirectly under religious guidance and were less influenced by the educational reforms of the High Commission, had disadvantages when compared to the schools in the urban centres. Firstly, they suffered from the scarcity of financial resources, and had to rely on the local church or donations from benefactors. Secondly, they did not have sufficient equipment, teachers or space. The school building was usually operated by the local church and located in the courtyard of the church.[54] The courses were taught by local priests or teachers who had graduated from higher educational institutions of the community located in Constantinople and Smyrna, or by those who had earned their degrees from Athens. Thirdly, students in the rural settlements had more important responsibilities than attending school. Many of them had to participate in family labour – whether agriculture or husbandry – therefore, they could not attend school regularly.

Under the High Commission, the policies that had restricted the scope of non-Muslim community schools in the period of Unionist dictatorship were abandoned, but the High Commission had its own disciplining approach for the Orthodox Christian community schools. In this period, the High Commission did not allow Greek Orthodox schools to use the term Hellene in their name. That a school in Bournabat took down the sign that read 'Boys' School of Bournabat Orthodox Community' and hung in its place a sign that read 'Hellenic Boys' School of Bournabat' would cause problems between the High Commission and the school in 1919.[55] A number of similar incidents with regard to the renaming of the schools after the occupation indicated changes in the way local Greek Orthodox communities viewed their official status in the Ottoman structure. Despite the High Commission's protests, these communities would gradually tend to refer to their educational institutions with Hellene rather than Greek Orthodox (Rum).

In addition to the pivotal role of the High Commission in the establishment of new schools in the province, its Education Department exercised

Social Life under the Greek Administration

control over both Muslim community schools and Greek Orthodox community schools. For example, in accordance with a document written by the director of the Department of Education in February 1922, the following information about the teachers and the students was demanded from the principals of primary and secondary schools:

1. The name of the school principal
2. The type of the school (boys, girls or mixed)
3. The degree of the school (kindergarten, primary, semi-secondary, secondary or college)
4. The number of classes
5. Enrolment in those classes
6. Teachers' names
7. Teachers' qualifications
8. Teachers' birth year
9. Teachers' marital status
10. Teachers' terms of service
11. Teachers' salaries

As well as this information, the income and expenses of the schools were also demanded in the document.[56]

In the same period, the Department of Education increased its disciplinary standards on the Ottoman Greek communities outside of the Smyrna *sanjak*. This body was the highest office that would be appealed to for the settlements of controversies that were likely to arise between the community and individuals. One such case occurred in February 1921 when the district attorney of the court in Edremit sent in a case file regarding a controversy between the local Orthodox community and a teacher by the name of Klemenoglou. The subject of controversy was that the community refused to pay the teacher his salary. On 4 February 1921, the head of the Department of Education cabled instructions to the Greek representative (*antiprosōpos*) in Edremit, asking for the documents of this assignment along with a copy of the decision of the assignment in community registers in the period between July and November 1920. The Greek representative was asked to find out when the community and Klemenoglou had made an agreement, and in particular, if they had come to an agreement before or after September, and if the payment was agreed to be made on a monthly or annual basis.[57]

Besides the controlling zeal of the High Commission, foreign schools also posed a serious challenge to the Christian community schools. This challenge continued to be a reason of anxiety for the notables of the local

Ethnic Cleansing in Western Anatolia

Christian communities who did not want to lose their vital control on educational matters. The majority of foreign schools in the province were French, numbering more than all other foreign schools combined. Despite the fact that most of the French schools were located in Smyrna, as were all other European educational institutions, their networks had expanded through urbanisation, reaching even the suburbs of the city.[58] The expansion of the French school network in the province continued under the Greek administration, with a St Vincent School for Girls as far away as Aydın opening in 1921.[59]

The American Board of Commissioners for Foreign Missions, a Boston-based missionary organisation that had decided at the beginning of the twentieth century to support higher education in the Ottoman territories, started to follow a strategy that required leaving primary education to Christian community schools and concentrating all its facilities on higher education. The American Collegiate Institute in Basmane, a neighbourhood densely inhabited by Armenians, had a secondary school and a teacher training school that served girls. The International College, its sister institution, had three large college buildings and residences in the attractive suburb of Paradiso.[60] In this school, English was the language of instruction, whereas French, Greek and Armenian were offered as optional courses.[61]

The foreign schools drew most of their students from among local Christian communities.[62] Although Muslim students were few in numbers, foreign schools were rare places that provided a mixed environment for education. There were fifty Muslim male students attending the International College in 1913. The Muslim male pupils constituted a noticeable group in the French schools as well.[63] The number of Muslim female students was also significant in these institutions during wartime,[64] and the American Board made efforts for their schooling with the foundation of the Turkish Girls School in 1921.[65]

In spite of their strong presence in Smyrna, the Protestant missionary groups were not successful in converting large numbers of Greek Orthodox to Protestantism. Therefore, they were left with no choice other than concentrating their activities on Armenian and Jewish communities.[66] Still, the schools founded by the missions, particularly American missions, functioned as a magnet, drawing even the Orthodox who did not intend to change their religious affiliation. By all means, the American Board schools kept an important place in the education of Christian communities.

In short, every ethno-religious community in the province appeared to have improved its respective institutions of education under the control

Social Life under the Greek Administration

of the High Commission. Despite the fact that the educational institutions remained under the nominal supervision of the communities, the controlling and reorganising tendencies of the High Commission created a palpable tension between the communities and the Department of Education in some cases.

Ex Oriente Lux: *Foundation of the Ionian University*

One of the most striking developments to happen in the province under the Greek administration was the establishment of a university in Smyrna. The Venizelos government had envisioned a university since the Paris Peace Conference, and on 1 August 1919 delegated Constantin Carathéodory,[67] professor of mathematics from Göttingen University, to realise this project. This university was seen as an attempt to meet the higher education needs that had increased in the region. Carathéodory was invited to Paris in October 1919 to exchange views with Venizelos on this issue and presented to the prime minister a report on the required university departments.

The memoirs of Ioakeimoglou, who was to serve as professor of chemistry at the Ionian University of Smyrna, revealed that the foundation of this university was related to the role of *mission civilisatrice* that Greece wanted to undertake in this region: 'For the purpose of encompassing cultural differences among diverse populations and similarly for Greece to convey her high civilisation to the foreign communities in Asia Minor rather than take them under hegemony ...' This university would be a landmark of Greece's increasing interest 'in the Orient and its various peoples and cultures' and, as mentioned earlier, her self-designated mission to bring 'the light of Western civilisation to the Orient'. As such, the university's staff and students would make efforts to reconcile the differences of the various groups in the region through the creation of a genuine *Universitas Litterarum* in Smyrna.[68]

Carathéodory also envisaged a Greek Empire dominating the Slav, Turkish, Jewish and Armenian elements as an outpost of the European civilisation in the Levant. As Maria Georgiadou points out, 'the leitmotif in Carathéodory's conception of the university was Greeks' civilizing mission in the Orient, an aspect of the Great Idea encompassing the ideas of enlightenment while at the same time absorbing modified national elements.'[69] Carathéodory was invited to Smyrna in April 1920 by Stergiades upon Venizelos's suggestion. He travelled to Athens from the University of Berlin, his former workplace, as soon as the academic year of 1920–1 was over. While he was in Athens, the Greek government issued a set of laws and regulations for the foundation of the university in Smyrna.

According to Carathéodory, who settled in Smyrna in the autumn of 1920, the university would adopt a modern mentality of education that would take regional needs into account rather than apply the British or German educational system. The language of instruction would be Greek, but Turkish and other languages could also be used in some courses. 'Students from every race and nation' would be able to apply, and auditors as well as guests would be welcomed. The university would be run by a president on the condition that they would be liable to other administrators, who would be deans and heads of departments as well as members of the university senate. The High Commission deemed it suitable for the Ionian University to be located in the incomplete buildings that Rahmî Bey, the former governor-general, had started to get constructed for the School of Union and Progress (İzmir İttihâd ve Terakkî Mektebi) in 1911.

Carathéodory began to purchase the educational equipment required for the university, the first of which were books for the library. With the help of Dr Richard Ochler, who had been serving in the Berlin State Library, thirty-six trunks of books were dispatched to Smyrna. A group of books compiled about Western Anatolia by Austrian archaeologists who had carried out excavations in Ephesus during World War I were also bought for the library. Furthermore, the library was to receive copies of all the newspapers published in Western Anatolia, including those published at the front.[70]

Carathéodory, who thought that the Ionian University of Smyrna would rival the University of Athens and enlighten the East with the spirit of science and technology, chose the phrase *Ex Oriente Lux* as its motto. Appointed as founding president of the university for five years through a decree published by Stergiades on 28 October 1920, Carathéodory embarked on activities to fill academic vacancies and procure equipment.[71]

In general, Carathéodory suggested to Stergiades those whom he wanted to employ at the university. For example, Georgios Ioakeimoglou,[72] professor of microbiology from the University of Berlin, was invited in September 1920 to serve in the Ionian University for five years from 1 January 1921 onwards. Likewise, along with Ioakeimoglou, who would be the head of the Institute of Hygiene, several instructors were employed upon Carathéodory's recommendation.[73]

Academically, four principal schools would constitute the basis of the university.

1. The School of Natural and Technical Sciences: this school consisted of the departments of civil engineering, chemical engineering, geology, botany, zoology and physics. It was intended that the school

Social Life under the Greek Administration

would educate scientists who would be entrusted with the planning and implementation of public affairs. Frixos Theodoridis, who had graduated from the Zurich Institute of Technology, was appointed professor in the department of physics. Nikolaos Kritikos, professor of mathematics from Athens Polytechnic and who was doing his military service in Western Anatolia, also took part in the studies concerning the establishment of this school through a special permission granted by the Greek army.[74]

2. The School of Agriculture: this school would give lectures for two or four years to students who were interested in practical agriculture and to those who aimed for a scientific career. The school would organise seminars for farmers and landowners, and scientific research would be conducted in well-equipped laboratories in association with a model farm in Tepeköy. Theologos Kesisoglou, who was originally from Kayseri, Cappadocia, and had graduated from the Agronomic Institute of Gembloux in Belgium, was employed to establish the School of Agriculture.[75] The Experimental Farm in Tepeköy, which had been in existence since 1920, would be the place where practical lessons were given to students from all levels from the School of Agriculture. Simultaneously, at this school, applied and mechanical farming methods would be tested, and the farmers would be taught how to use and maintain tractors, ploughs and other farming machines imported from the United States.[76]

3. The School of Oriental Ethnology and Languages: this school would offer courses on the history, literature, culture and languages of the various ethno-religious communities in the Orient. The vision of the school was that various cultures would live together in peace through understanding and getting to know one another. In this respect, Turkish, Arabic, Persian, Armenian, Hebrew and Greek would be taught, and special seminars would be organised for the students affiliated with the other schools of the university. As Agelopoulos indicated, this school was established in order to conduct scientific studies on the so-called 'others' in Western Anatolia. To illustrate, Dr Dinos Malouchos, a civil servant in the High Commission and founder of this school, undertook an ethnographic mission to the interior of Anatolia in the winter of 1922 and categorised the Muslim societies in his investigation area – as Circassians, Kurds, Tatars and Africans – in his memorandum to the Ministry of Foreign Affairs.[77]

4. The School of Civil Service: Greece faced the problem of inadequate administrative personnel because of the vast territories included in her borders after World War I. This school was designed to be later

Ethnic Cleansing in Western Anatolia

transformed into a faculty of administrative and financial sciences for the purpose of educating high-quality civil servants.[78]

Aside from these four schools, the university would have a number of supplementary departments, institutes and facilities.[79]

In the spring of 1922, the construction of the university was almost finished with its roughly seventy lecture rooms, an amphitheatre and a group of laboratories. The Ionian University, which was preparing to open for the academic year of 1922–3, would never be able to start education due to the arrival of the Kemalist forces in Smyrna. While leaving Smyrna on 8 September 1922, Carathéodory, the president of the university, was only able to take with him the university's archive, a small section of its library and the laboratory equipment.

Provincial Press

Under the Greek administration, the provincial press witnessed a revival as the number and variety of the newspapers and magazines increased, especially those published in Greek, Ottoman Turkish and Ladino.[80] By 1922, there were seven Greek (*Amaltheia, Kosmos, Estia, Patris, Synadelfos, Tēlegrafos* and *Tharros*), six Turkish (*Âhenk, Islahât, Hikmet, Köylü, Sadâ-yı Hakk* and *Şark*), four Ladino (*La Boz de Izmir, El Novelista, El Pregonero* and *Shalom*), three French (*La Réforme, Le Levant*[81] and *L'Impartial*) and three Armenian (*Arevelian Mamoul, Tashink* and *Horizon*) daily newspapers in Smyrna.

Apart from the daily newspapers, weekly newspapers and journals were also published in Smyrna. *Ieros Polykarpos*, the weekly paper of the religious brotherhood Euseveia, resumed publication in 1919 under Metropolitan Chrysostomos's patronage. Publication of this paper had halted in 1914 upon the exile of Chrysostomos to Constantinople. In addition, the magazine *Efesos* was published in Cordelio as an organ of the Metropolis of Ephesus.

The Greek administration indulged the Allied representatives in Smyrna with the formation of an Inter-Allied Board of Censors (IBC). In order to prevent the domination of the provincial press by this Allied board, a Greek Board of Censure, which was a parallel board and independent of the Greek military authorities, was also established. The High Commission stated that this double-headed system of censorship in Smyrna had similarities with the model in wartime Salonica where the leader of the Allied military forces reserved the right to censor.[82] Of the Greek members of the IBC, Periklis Skeferis and Mihail Rodas obtained from Colonel Nikolaos

Social Life under the Greek Administration

Zafeiriou the release of Muslim journalists who had been arrested during the occupation. Skeferis and Rodas thought that if the newspapers *Köylü*, *Âhenk* and *Müsavat*, the publication of which had been suspended right after the occupation, began to be published again, this would indicate to the Muslim community that nothing was actually different from what used to happen in the past except for giving space in their pages to the notices of the Army of Asia Minor.

The Ottoman censorship was maintained during World War I and the post-armistice period,[83] and censorship continued under the Greek administration after May 1919.[84] The type of news that could be published had depended on the censure either from the High Commission or the Inter-Allied Board. In September 1919, General Konstantinos Nider, the commander of the occupation forces, issued an order forbidding the publication of any new newspapers except by the permission of the high commissioner. Nonetheless, the British representative claimed that this measure constituted an encroachment on the authority of the IBC.[85]

The Turkish press in Smyrna, however, was divided into two hostile camps: supporters of the Unionists and the supporters of the Freedom and Accord Party. The outstanding figure of the pro-Unionist press was Haydar Rüştü, owner of the papers *Anadolu* and *Duygu* and a member of the Turkish Hearth. According to his memoirs, the High Commission had promised a 100,000 drachmae reward to the person who would deliver Haydar Rüştü to the authorities. After hiding in various places in Smyrna for three months following the occupation, Haydar Rüştü left the Greek occupation zone and continued to publish *Anadolu* in Antalya in the Italian occupation zone.[86]

After the armistice was signed in October 1918, newspapers like *Islahât* and *Müsavat*, which supported the Freedom and Accord Party, began being published or managed to be revived following the weakening of Unionist pressure. The prominent theme in the Turkish provincial press was the examination of wartime politics, such as the destructive policies propagated by the CUP against different ethnic elements, the necessity for the judgement and punishment of Unionist leaders, the suffering of several Muslim groups due to the same destructive policies that the Ottoman Greeks and Armenians had been exposed to, and the dissociation of the majority of Muslims from what had actually happened.[87]

After the Greek landing, the themes started to change gradually, and the presence of the Greek troops in the city became the new focus of the Turkish newspapers. *Köylü*, Mehmet Refet's newspaper, managed, though, to continue its advocacy for the Freedom and Accord Party. Again, the paper *Islahât*, another supporter of the same party, in the issue published on the evening of the Greek landing, used the headline 'a rather unimportant occupation' and encouraged the Muslim community to remain calm. The following day the owner of the newspaper, Sabitzâde Emin Süreyyâ, used as its headline the Arabic proverb 'el cezâ-yi min cinsü'l-amel', which means 'you reap what you sow', stating that the occupation was repayment for the evil done by the Committee of Union and Progress in the past. Nonetheless, it is not easy to claim that Emin Süreyyâ supported the Greek landing. On the contrary, he attached credence to the idea that this landing would trigger animosities between the Orthodox Greeks and Muslims.[88] The daily *Âhenk*[89] managed to keep up its moderate publishing policy, though it too was censored many times.

Upon his arrival in Smyrna, Stergiades stated that the press would not be allowed any activities that would harm the Greek administration and asked the officers of the Greek Board of Censors to hinder the publication of articles that would provoke Muslims.[90] A satirical poem published in the weekly humour magazine *Kopanos*, which mocked Muslims, did not escape the attention of the High Commission. Feeling exasperated, Stergiades dismissed from office not only the censorship officer, but also Skeferis, whom he considered responsible as the head of the censorship committee, replacing him with Skeferis's assistant, Mihail Rodas.[91]

Nevertheless, sharing authorised newspaper inspections with the IBC concerned the Greek authorities, reaching its peak with articles published in the Greek newspapers on an armed conflict between the Greek troops and Muslim irregulars in Aydın in July 1919. The articles were translated into English upon the suggestion of Second Lieutenant Enia Brunetti, an Italian member of the IBC and a Levantine originally from Smyrna, and were sent along with a report to the Allied high commissioners in Constantinople. Rodas, the Greek representative on the IBC, suggested that the Levantine members representing the Allied States on the board supported the Turkish newspapers and made extraordinary efforts to permit the publication of articles that would encourage anti-Greek activities.[92]

Tension between the IBC and the Greek High Commission then flared because of an article that the recently established newspaper *Şark* attempted to publish. In the report he sent to the IBC on 15 October 1919, Rodas objected to the publication of this article, which described Greeks as 'vermin that had been sucking Turkish blood for one and a half centuries' ('bir buçuk asırdan beri Türklerin kanını emen zehirli haşerât'). Brunetti, the Italian representative of the committee, tended to favour the publication of the article, and through the other members' support the article was permitted unanimously, despite Rodas's objections. Having been notified by Rodas, Stergiades ordered that Halil Zeki, a prominent

Social Life under the Greek Administration

Muslim merchant and publisher of the newspaper, and Kenan Tevfik, its acting director, be arrested and appear at the extraordinary court martial.[93] The publication of this article gave an impression among Turkish nationalist circles that the IBC had a pro-Turkish stance. The Greek officers came to the editorial room of *Şark* on 18 October, arrested and took away the people in view after a search.[94]

Major Haralambos Tamiolakis, a military prosecutor, accused the defendants of 'publishing provocative news and arousing enmity against the Greek administration' at the trial on 23 October. After testimonies from Mihail Rodas, the director of the Greek Press Office and the gendarme officer who searched the newspaper editorial room on the day of the arrests, the defendants spoke and denied the accusations. The court martial found the defendants guilty; Halil Zeki was sentenced to imprisonment for one year and Kenan Tevfik for six months.[95] The court also declared that these sentences were justified against any possible uprising in the occupation zone. Thereupon, the representatives of the Allied States in Smyrna went to Stergiades's office to protest this decision by the Greek authorities.[96] In order to please the Allied high commissioners in Constantinople, Stergiades dismissed Halil Zeki's sentence on 23 December.

This clash of authority indicated that a consensus for power-sharing was required between the IBC and the High Commission. As a result of talks between Stergiades and the Allied representatives, an agreement took shape on 22 December 1919, wherein no new newspapers in Greek and Turkish were to be published until the final peace treaty was signed. The publication of newspapers in other languages (English, French, Italian, Armenian and Ladino) would depend on permission of the IBC. Moreover, the IBC had the absolute right to suppress any publication that could 'harm the interest of the Allied representatives and the public order'. A majority of votes on the IBC would be decisive in the censoring of articles. Nevertheless, in case of the objection of the Greek delegates on this board, the opinion of the high commissioner would be requested.[97]

This agreement sought a modus vivendi for each party 'regarding the functioning of censorship that was paralysed by the control of the Greek organ'. Stergiades insisted that the number of Turkish newspapers should be limited 'until the conclusion of peace with the Ottoman Empire'. Although the British and French representatives raised no objection, the Italian representative stated that he had strong reservations about the proposal.[98]

Contrary to Stergiades's expectations, the agreement failed to resolve the conflict among the members of the IBC, in particular between Rodas and Brunetti. According to Rodas, the only person responsible for the tensions in relations during the following days was Brunetti, who was trying to provoke the Muslim people to sedition. In fact, Brunetti, who had knowledge of Greek and Turkish as he had studied at the Evangeliki Scholi in Smyrna, strove to get the support of the most provocative Turkish newspapers sanctioned by the board.[99]

Nonetheless, it is rather difficult to say that the censoring of the IBC targeted only Turkish newspapers. Large gaps in the Greek newspapers caused by censorship are also noticeable. The Greek papers, including *Amaltheia*, which had the largest circulation in the city, were censored several times for criticising the administration or provoking Muslims.[100] Stergiades deemed Rodas a failure and discharged him from office early in February 1920, replacing him with Stylpon Pittakis, curator of the Evangeliki Scholi museum. After the Treaty of Sèvres was signed, the IBC was liquidated, and from that time on the press would be inspected by the Press Office of the Greek Administration of Smyrna.[101]

From the very beginning, Greek statesmen realised that they would face different problems in Western Anatolia because of its heterogeneous population. Furthermore, the Greek Administration of Smyrna, established after the Sèvres Treaty, had a different status compared to other governorates (*nomarchies*). As such, Asia Minor/Western Anatolia was constructed as the so-called Orient in the mentalities of Greek policymakers, to which the policies of the Greek Kingdom had both colonialist and nationalist tendencies. The colonialist vision of the Kingdom was reflected in reforms of health care and education, as well as the censoring attempts to the provincial press.

Even though Greek authorities claimed that Greece had a *mission civilisatrice* to bring Western civilisation to the Orient, this effort could not develop into a comprehensive programme. Indeed, the High Commission modernised everyday life by reorganising health services, educational institutions (including a university), associations and labour unions. It also resettled refugees, censored the press and reshaped the cities and towns of the Smyrna *sanjak*, as in the cases of the segregation of brothels and the foundation of new public offices. Nonetheless, these reforms were radically different from those conducted in Greece in terms of the ideology behind them as they were implemented in an ethnically heterogenous region and the Greek Administration of Smyrna had a *sui generis* administrative and legal structure compared to the governorates in the Greek mainland.

Social Life under the Greek Administration

Notes

1. Karl Baedeker's map of Smyrna (1905) is one well-known example of these maps. It names the neighbourhoods after ethno-religious groups. Edward Weller (1882) and Charles E. Goad (1905) also prepared urban maps of Smyrna.
2. Reşat Kasaba, 'Izmir 1922: A Port City Unravels', in *Modernity and Culture: From the Mediterranean to the Indian Ocean*, ed. Laila Tarazi Fawaz and C. A. Bayly (New York: Columbia University Press, 2002), 210.
3. Georgios Agelopoulos, 'Contested Territories and the Quest for Ethnology: People and Places in İzmir 1919–22', in *Spatial Conceptions of the Nation: Modernizing Geographies in Greece and Turkey*, ed. Nikiforos Diamandouros et al. (London: I. B. Tauris, 2010), 187; and Ioannis N. Grigoriadis, *Instilling Religion in Greek and Turkish Nationalism: A 'Sacred Synthesis'* (New York: Palgrave Macmillan, 2013), 21–3.
4. Edward W. Said, 'Representing the Colonized: Anthropology's Interlocutors', *Critical Inquiry* 15, no. 2 (Winter 1989), 207.
5. Robert Shannan Peckham, 'Internal Colonialism: Nation and Region in Nineteenth Century Greece', in *Balkan Identities: Nation and Memory*, ed. Maria Todorova (New York: New York University Press, 2004), 42–3.
6. For more information about the Ottoman Greek societies and associations in Constantinople and Western Anatolia, see Ayşe Ozil, *Orthodox Christians in the Late Ottoman Empire: A Study of Relations in Anatolia* (London: SOAS/Routledge Studies on the Middle East, 2012); Yusuf Ziya Karabıçak, *The Development of Ottoman Policies towards Greek Associations (1861–1912)* (Istanbul: Libra Kitap, 2014); and George A. Vassiadis, *The Syllogos Movement of Constantinople and Ottoman Greek Education, 1861–1923* (Athens: Centre for Asia Minor Studies, 2007).
7. Vangelis Kechriotis, 'La Smyrne grecque: des communautés au panthéon de l'histoire', in *Smyrne, la ville oubliée?*, ed. Marie-Carmen Smyrnelis (Paris: Editions Autrement, 2006), 63–79.
8. Efi Avdela, 'Between Duties and Rights: Gender and Citizenship in Greece, 1864–1952', in *Citizenship and Nation-state in Greece and Turkey*, ed. Faruk Birtek and Thalia Dragonas (London: Routledge, 2005), 121.
9. Haris Eksertzoglou, *Nostaljinin Ötesinde Kaybedilmiş Memleketler: Osmanlı İmparatorluğu'ndaki Rumların Toplumsal ve Kültürel Bir Tarihi* (Istanbul: Tarih Vakfı Yurt Yayınları, 2015), 185.
10. Stavros Th. Anestides, 'The Church of Smyrna', in *Smyrna: Metropolis of the Asia Minor Greeks*, ed. Nikos Hatzigeorgiou (Athens: Ephesus Publishing, 2004), 130–1. See also *Appels des femmes de Thrace et d'Asie Mineure* (Athens: Conseil National de Femmes Hellènes, 1922).
11. Stavros Th. Anestides, 'Education and Culture', in *Smyrna: Metropolis of the Asia Minor Greeks*, ed. Nikos Hatzigeorgiou (Athens: Ephesus Publishing, 2004), 156–8.

Ethnic Cleansing in Western Anatolia

12. Oliver Jens Schmitt, *Les Levantines: Cadres de vie et identités d'un groupe ethno-confessionnel de l'Empire Ottoman au 'Long' 19e siècle* (Istanbul: Isis Press, 2007), 454–5.
13. Emilia Themopoulou, 'The Urbanisation of an Asia Minor City: The Example of Smyrna', in *Smyrna: Metropolis of the Asia Minor Greeks*, ed. Nikos Hatzigeorgiou (Athens: Ephesus Publishing, 2004), 103–5.
14. The Red Crescent also managed to continue its work and the Teachers Association elected a new administrative council in July 1921, see Yaşar Aksoy, *Bir Kent, Bir İnsan: İzmir'in Son Yüzyılı, S. Ferit Eczacıbaşı'nın Yaşamı ve Anıları* (Istanbul: Eczacıbaşı Vakfı Yayınları, 1986), 166.
15. 'Teşvîk-i Ma'ârif Cem'iyetinin Nizamnâme-i Esâsîsi', *Âhenk*, 12 May 1920 (R. 12 Mayıs 1336).
16. Zeki Arıkan, 'İşgal Sırasında İzmir'de Kurulan Bir Dernek', *Atatürk Yolu* 3 (1989), 359–62. In contrast to the daily *Âhenk*, biographies on Mehmet Tahirü'l Mevlevi do not mention his membership in this association and covers only his pursuits in the imperial capital.
17. For the role of the Greek community in the socialist movements in the Empire, see Panagiotis Noutsos, 'The Role of the Greek Community in the Genesis and Development of the Socialist Movement in the Ottoman Empire, 1876–1923', in *Socialism and Nationalism in the Ottoman Empire*, ed. Mete Tunçay and Erik Jan Zürcher (London: I. B. Tauris, 1994), 77–88.
18. *A Survey of Some Social Conditions*, 47.
19. Ibid. 47–8.
20. Noutsos, 'The Role of the Greek Communityu', 85–8.
21. Victoria Solomonidis, 'Greece in Asia Minor', 173–4.
22. While some of these institutions were general hospitals, others were small hospitals that specialised in certain branches of medicine. The largest hospital in the city was the Agios Haralambos Greek Orthodox Hospital founded in 1748. It had facilities for the care of approximately 400 patients and its staff consisted of sixty-two people. The Hopitaux Impérials Ottomans or Muslim hospitals, which were operated by the municipality and located very close to Konak Square, had comparatively new buildings and equipment. The hospital complex had forty-eight beds for the treatment of contagious diseases. Apart from this hospital, there was a military hospital for Ottoman soldiers. See *1921 Annuaire Oriental: Oriental Directory*, ed. Alfred Rizzo (Constantinople: Imprimerie de l'Annuaire Oriental, 1921), 1463.
23. Victoria Solomonidis, 'Greece in Asia Minor', 174.
24. Ibid. 173.
25. *A Survey of Some Social Conditions*, 64–5.
26. Michel Foucault, *The History of Sexuality, vol. I: An Introduction* (New York: Pantheon Books, 1978), 54.
27. Mark David Wyers, *'Wicked' Istanbul: The Regulation of Prostitution in the Early Turkish Republic* (Istanbul: Libra Kitap, 2012), 21–2.

Social Life under the Greek Administration

28. According to Akder, the most widespread disease of the war years was malaria, while dysentery and typhus were the deadliest in the Ottoman Empire. The major causes of typhus epidemics were poverty, overcrowding and lack of adequate housing facilities, see Halis Akder, 'Forgotten Campaigns: A History of Disease in Turkey', in *Turkey's Engagement with Modernity: Conflict and Change in the Twentieth Century*, ed. Celia J. Kerslake et al. (Basingstoke: Palgrave Macmillan, 2010), 219.

29. *A Survey of Some Social Conditions*, 55–7. Moreover, there was a widespread phobia of hospitals, which were designated as *mortakia*, meaning houses of death, in the early 1920s throughout the province.

30. This neighbourhood was also previously famous for the presence of brothels, see Kosmas Politis, *Stou Chatzēfrangou* (Athens: Estias, 2001), 54–5. In a particular scene in this novel, which consistently depicts the social life in Smyrna prior to the Great Fire in 1922, young men talk among themselves in the house and say that they are not allowed to walk around Caravan Bridge or go to Agios Konstantinos Church in the Chiotika neighbourhood.

31. *A Survey of Some Social Conditions*, 123. On the other hand, when the High Commission resolved to shut down the brothels in the central neighbourhoods on 28 October 1919, several brothel owners had to evacuate their properties at the heart of the city. Brothel owners who were planning to move to Chiotika could not maintain their businesses when they failed to meet the demands put forward by the High Commission. In this period, the High Commission had to deal with tens of complaints of the people managing brothels. For instance, Loukia Nikolaou, the patroness of the brothel in rue Parallèle, had to shut down her workplace where she also stayed at nights, and she asked her tenant Georgios Petroheilos in the Fasoula neighbourhood to leave the house for her under the pretext that their contract was over. She also asked the High Commission to provide a place where she could leave her furniture that she had removed from the brothel, cf. GAK. YAS., no. 11909, 31 October 1919 (J. C. 18 October 1919), Loukia Nikolaou to the Chief of Police.

32. Victoria Solomonidis, 'Greece in Asia Minor', 147–8.

33. Ibid. 147–8 and 164–5.

34. Actually, the Ottoman paramedics seemed to have worked in these kinds of vaccination campaigns together with foreigners. For example, the Germans conducted a vaccination campaign in Smyrna during the war years, see Akder, 'Forgotten Campaigns', 220. The foreign institutions constituted the Empire's connection to developments in microbiology.

35. Victoria Solomonidis, 'Greece in Asia Minor', 174–7.

36. Georgelin, *La fin de Smyrne*, 55.

37. Ibid. 62–72.

38. The network of the imperial high schools had expanded to the province in the reign of Abdülhamit II. For the modernisation of Ottoman educational

Ethnic Cleansing in Western Anatolia

system and the place of Islamic symbols and values in this process, see Fortna, *Imperial Classroom*.

39. Since the second half of the nineteenth century, foreign schools established by Protestants or Catholic missions and community schools belonging to native Christians had provided Ottoman Christians with new ideas, models and career opportunities. These schools played a significant role in the emergence of a Christian bourgeoisie in the Ottoman social structure. For the roles of these schools in the transformation of the Ottoman society, see Göçek, *Rise of the Bourgeoisie*, especially Chapter 3.

40. *A Survey of Some Social Conditions*, 188.

41. See 'Havâdis-i Vilâyet', *Âhenk*, 21 October 1920 (R. 21 Teşrîn-i Evvel 1336). Since Hilâl Sultânî Lycée did not have any teachers of Arabic and Persian, two teachers were assigned there to open these classes. A music teacher was also appointed to Karantina Primary School.

42. 'Havâdis-i Vilâyet', *Âhenk*, 18 August 1919 (R. 18 Ağustos 1335).

43. 'İzmir Ma'ârif Müdüriyetinden', *Âhenk*, 28 September 1919 (R. 28 Eylül 1335).

44. Melih Tınal, 'Yunan İşgali Döneminde İzmir Mekteb-i Sultanisi', *Tarih ve Toplum* 188 (August 1999), 8.

45. Victoria Solomonidis, 'Greece in Asia Minor', 180.

46. 'Havâdis-i Vilâyet', *Âhenk*, 6 September 1920 (R. 6 Eylül 1336).

47. *Âhenk*, 26 December 1920 (R. 26 Kânûn-i Evvel 1336).

48. Su, *Sevr Antlaşması*, 26–9.

49. 'Oi Misthoi tōn Tourkōn Didaskalōn', *Kosmos*, 7 December 1920.

50. *Islahât*, 26 June 1922 (R. 26 Haziran 1338).

51. Similar to all of the other schools belonging to the Greek Orthodox community, these schools continued to enrol only Orthodox Christian children. High schools of the Greek Orthodox community in Smyrna did not only serve the needs of Smyrniote Orthodox Christians, but also kept their doors open for the Orthodox Greeks who came to the city for education from the inner and more disadvantaged parts of the province, see Anestides, 'Education and Culture', 139–45.

52. After the coup in 1913, the educational committees of the non-Muslim schools were made receptive and answerable to the state, though the authorities of the patriarchs and the chief rabbi over these schools were preserved.

53. Georgelin, *La fin de Smyrne*, 73–5.

54. Ibid. 74–6.

55. Nikos Kararas, *O Bournovas* (Athens: n.p., 1955), 151–4.

56. GAK. YAS., No. 112/3, 11 February 1922 (J. C. 29 January 1922), from the Department of Education to the school principals.

57. GAK. YAS., No. 113, 4 February 1921 (J. C. 22 January 1921), from the Department of Education to the representative in Edremit.

58. There were nine French schools for boys and two for girls in Smyrna. See *1921 Annuaire Oriental*, 1461.

Social Life under the Greek Administration

59. Ibid. 1258–9.
60. *A Survey of Some Social Conditions*, 208–9.
61. Chrēstos Solomōnidēs, *Ē Paideia stē Smyrnē* (Athens: n.p., 1961), 372.
62. In 1913, there were 240 Orthodox and thirty-two Armenian Apostolic students in the International College and 103 Armenian Apostolic and eighty-three Orthodox students in the American Collegiate Institute. See Hans-Lukas Kieser, *Iskalanmış Barış: Doğu Vilayetleri'nde Misyonerlik, Etnik Kimlik ve Devlet, 1839–1938*, trans. Atilla Dirim (Istanbul: İletişim Yayınları, 2005), 429. These communities continued to be the largest groups in the French schools as well. In 1920, of the 197 students of Notre Dame de Sion School for Girls in Cordelio, sixty were Greeks and fifty-six were Armenians. The third largest group that came after them were the Italians, with thirty-five students, CADN, Izmir, 643 PO/1, 75, 22 October 1934, 'Kız Fransız Mektebi-Nombre des élèves classés par nationalités'.
63. There were twenty Muslim students in Saint Germanicus School in the bourgeois suburb of Goztepe and sixteen in the Saint Joseph School in downtown Smyrna in 1912, see Maurice Pernot, *Rapport sur un voyage d'étude* (Paris: Firmin-Didot, 1913), 330–3.
64. Generally, 10–15 per cent of the students at the foreign schools were Muslim girls. In 1920, twenty-two out of 197 students of Notre Dame de Sion were Muslims, CADN, Izmir, 643 PO/1, 75, 22 October 1934, 'Kız Fransız Mektebi-Nombre des élèves classés par nationalités'.
65. Edward Hale Bierstadt, *The Great Betrayal: A Survey of the Near East Problem* (London: Hutchinson, 1924), 263.
66. In memoirs written at the end of the nineteenth century, it was recurrently stated with emphasis that of all the Christian communities, Armenians were the most willing to convert to Protestantism. In spite of the fact that Armenian communities objected to the activities of the American missionaries at the beginning, clergy and the lay members of these communities gradually changed their attitudes to them. In contrast, the Greek Orthodox communities were either indifferent to the missionary activities or protested against them. See Alexander Neil Somerville, *The Churches in Asia: Extracts from the Home Letters of A. N. Somerville (1885)* (Whitefish, MT: Kessinger Publishing, 2010). In 1905, a bilingual All Testament (Hebrew and Ladino) was published by the American Bible Company in Constantinople: *Sefer Torah Neviim v' Chetuvim/El Livro de La Ley Los Profetas: Los Eskrituras* [All Testament] (Constantinople: A. H. Boyadjian, 1905).
67. Constantin Carathéodory was born in Berlin in 1873. His father was Stephanos Karatheodori Pasha, a Phanariot and an Ottoman diplomat. Alexandros Karatheodori Pasha, who would be foreign minister of the Ottoman Empire, was a cousin of Constantin Carathéodory. Carathéodory served between 1913 and 1918 in the University of Göttingen after he had studied engineering at the Military School of Belgium. In 1919 he passed

155

Ethnic Cleansing in Western Anatolia

to the University of Berlin. He stayed in Smyrna between 1920 and 1922 in order to found the Ionian University of Smyrna. Between 1922 and 1924 he gave lectures at the University of Athens and Athens Polytechnic. In 1924 he returned to Germany and served at the University of Munich until his retirement. Two biographies on Carathéodory have been published: Maria Georgiadou, *Constantin Carathéodory: Mathematics and Politics in Turbulent Times* (Berlin: Springer, 2004) and Despoina Karatheodōrē-Rodopoulou and Despoina Vlachostergiou-Vasvatekē, *Kōnstantinos Karatheodōrē: O Sofos Ellēn tou Monachou* (Athens: Kaktos, 2001).

68. Geōrgios Iōakeimoglou, *Praktika tēs Akadimias Athēnōn*, vol. 25 (Athens: University of Athens, 1952), 80.
69. Georgiadou, *Constantin Carathéodory*, 147.
70. Victoria Solomonidis, 'Greece in Asia Minor', 188.
71. Ibid. 185.
72. Ioakeimoglou, who was born in the town of Kula in the Saruhan *sanjak* in 1887, graduated from the Evangeliki Scholi in Smyrna with a rather good degree. Upon his graduation from the Department of Chemistry in the University of Berlin in 1918, he started to serve in the Faculty of Medicine of the same university. He moved to Athens after the compulsory population exchange in 1923 and gave lectures in the University of Athens until his retirement. In 1951, he was elected vice-president of the Narcotics Control Board at the World Health Organisation.
73. Solomōnidēs, *Ē Paideia stē Smyrnē*, 399–400.
74. Victoria Solomonidis, 'Greece in Asia Minor', 185–6.
75. Georgiadou, *Constantin Carathéodory*, 159.
76. Victoria Solomonidis, 'Greece in Asia Minor', 188.
77. Agelopoulos, 'Contested Territories', 182–7.
78. Victoria Solomonidis, 'Greece in Asia Minor', 187.
79. Ibid. 186–7.
80. See *1921 Annuaire Oriental*, 1464–5. It seems that the post-armistice period enabled the publication of new Turkish newspapers: Haydar Rüştü's evening paper *Duygu*, the short-lived *Hukuk-ı Beşer* and the revived *Islahât*. Even after the Greek occupation in May 1919, new Turkish newspapers, such as *Sadâ-yı Hakk* and *Şark*, were allowed to be published.
81. First published in November 1918 by Raphael Amato, *Le Levant* was financially supported by the Italian Consulate in return for representing Italian interests in the region, see Fabio L. Grassi, *İtalya ve Türk Sorunu, 1919–1923* (Istanbul: Yapı Kredi Yayınları, 2003), 41.
82. Victoria Solomonidis, 'Greece in Asia Minor', 142–3.
83. The Censorship Ordinance (Sansür Talimatnamesi), which provided a legal base for the Unionist government to control the press, was promulgated in the autumn of 1914. Despite the fact that press censorship was abolished in all of the Ottoman provinces in January 1919, the Ottoman government did not abrogate military censorship in Aydın Province 'on the grounds of the Greek

Social Life under the Greek Administration

provocations and the bandit incidents' ('Rum tahrikâtı ve eşkıyâ vekâyi'i sebebiyle'), cf. BOA BEO 4551/341306 and BOA BEO 4552/341377.

84. TNA FO 371/ 4157, 7 April 1919, Ian M. Smith, Area Control Officer at Smyrna to General Staff Intelligence at Constantinople. Even though the censorship was abolished in all the Ottoman provinces, it was still in effect in Aydın Province even in the spring of 1919. The 17th Corps was responsible for implementing the censorship, cf. BOA BEO 4551/341306.

85. TNA FO 608/103, 19 November 1919, J. M. de Robeck, British High Commissioner at Constantinople, to Earl Curzon.

86. Haydar Rüştü Öktem, *Mütareke ve İşgal Anıları*, ed. Zeki Arıkan (Ankara: Türk Tarih Kurumu, 1991), 15. Haydar Rüştü's memoirs contradict what was written in many newspapers of the period. According to *Le Messager d'Athènes*, a newspaper published in Athens, Haydar Rüştü formed a party of 1,200 bandits, blew up the Ödemiş Bridge and was arrested while trying to set the Greek neighbourhood of Ödemiş on fire. As it would not have been possible for him to leave the occupation zone so easily while he was wanted by the High Commission (as he claimed in his memoirs), he most likely managed to get out of the region only through an agreement he had concluded with the Greek administration; see 'A Smyrne et aux Alentours', *Le Messager d'Athènes*, J.C. 23 May 1919, 2.

87. *Köylü*, *Islahât*, and particularly *Hukuk-ı Beşer*, published these kinds of articles. For example, on 14 February 1919, Hasan Tahsin, a columnist in *Hukuk-ı Beşer*, harshly criticised the wartime policies of the CUP in his article titled 'Poor us at the Beginning of the Catastrophe' ('Felâket Başında Herşeyden Evvel Zavallı Bizler').

88. *Islahât*, 23 May 1919 (R. 23 Mayıs 1335).

89. For the moderate publishing policy and politically noncommittal stance of *Âhenk*, see Ö. Faruk Huyugüzel, 'İzmir'in Uzun Süre Yayımlanmış İstikrarlı Bir Gazetesi: Ahenk', *Yeni Türk Edebiyatı*, 3, March 2011, 23–35.

90. Rodas, *Ē Ellada stēn Mikran Asia*, 87.

91. Chrēstos Solomōnidēs, *Ē Dēmosiografia stē Smyrnē (1821–1922)* (Athens: Ar. Mauridē, 1959), 353.

92. Rodas, *Ē Ellada stēn Mikran Asia*, 116.

93. Ibid. 117–18.

94. 'Syllēpsis Dēmosiografou', *Kosmos*, 19 October 1919.

95. 'Ē Chthesinē Dikē', *Kosmos*, 24 October 1919.

96. Rodas, *Ē Ellada stēn Mikran Asia*, 141–3.

97. CADN, Izmir 643 PO/1, 26, 23 December 1919, from Stergiades to Osmin Laporte, Representative of the French High Commissioner at Smyrna.

98. CADN, Izmir 643 PO/1, 26, 26 December 1919, A. s. de Censure interalliée de Smyrne et du Ht. Commissariat héllènique.

99. Rodas, *Ē Ellada stēn Mikran Asia*, 141–2.

100. Ibid. 266–7.

101. 'Havâdis-i Vilâyet', *Âhenk*, 22 October 1920 (R. 22 Teşrîn-i Evvel 1336).

Chapter 4

Roses and Hyacinths: Ottoman Provincial Officials under the Greek Administration

When the Greek soldiers set foot on the Quay of Smyrna in May 1919, they easily established control over the city and occupied the government offices. Except for an armed conflict in the afternoon of the landing day, they did not meet any serious resistance movement. A dozen towns in the province were occupied in less than a fortnight by the Greek army. Considerable parts of the local population surrendered to the occupying troops 'even without firing a single gun'.[1] News of the lack of nationalist resistance to the advancing Greek troops shocked the Unionist intellectuals and officers. The Ottoman Christians, particularly Greeks and Armenians, were portrayed by Unionist circles as agents and supporters of the occupying forces. While local Greeks and Armenians were regarded as the primary actor allying with the occupying powers, some Muslims, even high-ranking Ottoman provincial officials and notables (*eşrâf*), were also accused of allying with the Greek administration and obtaining critical positions.

As Gingeras clearly states, Mustafa Kemal's nationalist movement claimed to represent 'all Muslims and Turks' in the Ottoman Empire, even though some 'Muslims' and 'Turks' sought to defy his movement.[2] Unlike Gingeras, the mainstream works concerning this period tend to disregard Muslim opponents of the nationalist movement as insignificant anomalies. Accordingly, in nationalist historiography, these people were simply portrayed as so-called collaborators who were driven by their temporary personal interests and sacrificed the long-term welfare of their nation. More to the point, these works held a view that these people were Muslims who were unwilling to support the nationalist ideal, and instead sided with allegedly treasonous Ottoman Greeks and Armenians.[3]

The National Struggle (*Millî Mücadele*) did not only change the power structure in the province and lead to the purge of high-ranking provincial

Officials under the Greek Administration

officials remaining loyal to the sultan, it also revolutionised the ways in which the nationalist elites perceived other elites who did not support the nationalist cause. The scapegoating of 'enemies of the Kemalist regime', who were called traitors (*hâinler*), became an intrinsic part of Kemalist popular culture in the early republican period. Contemporary memoirs of prominent Unionist statesmen, civil servants and officers who managed to find important positions in the post-war Turkey of the 1930s contradict the official documents of this period and do not give a coherent account of the attitudes of these provincial officials, who kept their loyalties to the Ottoman sultan under the Greek administration. This conventional Turks versus Greeks frame has obscured the incongruency between civilian interests on the one hand, and interests of state and nationalist groups on the other.[4]

Loyalist or anti-nationalist high-ranking officials were reduced to nothing more than quislings in the memoirs of Unionist statesmen. In his memoir, Kel Ali Bey (Çetinkaya), commander of the 172nd Infantry Regiment stationed in the coastal town of Ayvalık at the time, included a caricatured dialogue that occurred between Governor-General İzzet Bey, who was taken captive during the occupation of Smyrna on 15 May 1919, and Colonel Nikolaos Zafeiriou – İzzet Bey's son being the interpreter of the conversation:

> Colonel: You are responsible as you did not carry out your duty and thus caused turmoil.
> İzzet Bey: You could ask His Eminence Metropolitan Chrysostomos how much I strove to promote the occupation of Smyrna by the Greeks. You could also view my written communication with the Sublime Porte.
> Colonel: Then they have mistakenly arrested you. You will be released and sent back to your office in an hour. Do not worry.
> İzzet Bey: Thank you.[5]

These recollections contradict documents in the Ottoman archives. Ahmet İzzet Bey would be able to get back to his job not one hour later, but on 17 May, the day the turmoil was allayed. Furthermore, Çetinkaya contends in his memoir that this conversation took place because İzzet Bey's son was an interpreter of French; yet as someone who had previously served in the Translation Office, İzzet Bey's knowledge of French did not require an interpreter. This particular section in Çetinkaya's memoirs is apparently a total fabrication because he was based in Ayvalık when this supposed event took place, miles away from Greek-occupied Smyrna.

Celâl (Bayar), the former secretary-general of the CUP in Smyrna, mentioned in his memoirs some groups of provincial notables who were

159

Ethnic Cleansing in Western Anatolia

getting ready to 'welcome the enemy with the bouquets of roses and hyacinths' in Aydın Province.[6] As another example, Rahmî (Apak) in his memoirs written in 1937–8, in the early republican period, criticised the inhabitants of towns in the Saruhan *sanjak* for considering their personal interests to be more important than the national interest when they admitted the Greek administration and did not organise any armed resistance against the Greek troops:

> People from every town and city came out with white flags in their hands to see these cruel battalions and regiments of occupation. Self-preservationists (*cankurtarma kafileleri*) consisting of Muslim pilgrims and hodjas (*hâcı ve hoca*), turbaned and bearded people (*sarıklı sakallılar*), mayors in loose pants (*bol pantolonlu belediye reîsleri*), loutish fake notables (*hantal eşrâf bozmaları*), et cetera, offered bread and salt to the commanders of the occupying forces after taking with them a Christian priest or a few Ottoman Greeks and walking for hours around the town. When they came back, they rejoiced, thinking that they had saved the lives, properties, dignity and honour of the Turks. Then the streets were adorned with Greek flags; when the Greek troops entered the town, Ottoman Greek girls threw flowers at them.[7]

This chapter centres on a group of high-ranking provincial officials who remained loyal to the sultan in Constantinople and continued to function in the government mechanisms of Aydın Province in the days following the Greek occupation, in relationship with the Greek administration in Western Anatolia. What brought these officials together to prevent the activities of the National Forces (Kuvâ-yı Milliye) and thus subvert the barriers obstructing the way to a peaceful environment where various ethnic and religious elements of the Empire could live together was their loyalty to the sultan and the intricate networks to which they had access through their affiliations within the public administration.

This section refutes the allegation that these provincial officials were so-called tools of the Greek state or collaborators blindly devoted to the sultan. It will be argued that they had to make difficult choices in a very chaotic political atmosphere in order to attain social order and guarantee the lives and properties of the people in their scope of authority. The cases of three high-ranking Ottoman provincial officials, one governor-general (*vâlî*) and two district governors (*mutasarrıf*), whose stories are essential to counterbalance official accounts of national history, will be investigated. Following these three cases, the Circassian Congress in Smyrna, which was mainly attended by Ottoman civil servants of Circassian origin, will be explored briefly as a case of collective action vis-à-vis the nationalist movement in Ankara.

160

Officials under the Greek Administration

How and why were these cases selected? Although they were members of a bureaucratic elite with close ties to the palace, they were of different ethnicities. The governor-general had Kurdish origins, whereas the district governor of the Saruhan *sanjak* was a Muslim Cretan, whose native tongue was probably Kritika, a variety of demotic Greek. An ethnic Turk and a Kurdish district governor administered the Aydın *sanjak* successively, while the participants of the Circassian Congress descended from various Caucasian ethnicities. The most significant characteristic shared by all these people was that they had served as high-ranking provincial officials in Western Anatolia during the Greek administration.

Case 1: Ahmet İzzet Bey, Governor-general of Aydın Province, 1919–20

Ahmet İzzet Bey, also known as Kambur İzzet Bey,[8] the governor-general of Aydın Province, penned, between 14 and 18 May 1919, a fourteen-page report that depicts the incidents beginning one day prior to the Greek landing and continuing in the following days. This report relates events before and during the occupation of Smyrna, the unpreventable extremism of the Greek army, and the written communication İzzet Bey had with the representatives of the Allied States and his government.[9] In addition to this report in Ottoman Turkish, there is similar report of twenty-six pages in the Ottoman archives that was probably written by İzzet Bey in French, which documents the violence of the first days of the occupation.[10]

İzzet Bey was not an ordinary bureaucrat.[11] He served as minister of imperial foundations (*evkaf-ı hümâyun nâzırı*) in the first Ahmet Tevfik Pasha government, which was formed on 11 November 1918 after the Armistice of Mudros was signed. He also served as minister of imperial foundations in the second Ahmet Tevfik Pasha government, formed on 12 January 1919, in addition to being the deputy minister of the interior. He most likely developed a close relationship with the sultan during his regular visits to the palace, particularly during this term of his ministry.[12]

After the armistice, Mehmed VI Vahdeddin, the last Ottoman sultan, increased his efforts to restore the authority of the sultanate, and sought to fill the cabinet with loyal political figures, especially in key ministries, such as the Interior, Foreign Affairs and War. He also sought allies against the remaining cadres of the CUP.[13] He appointed Ahmet Tevfik Pasha, an elderly bureaucrat, to form a new government on 11 November 1918. The Unionist ministers were to take no more part in the newly established cabinet, and İzzet Bey would be one of the indispensable members in the two consecutive cabinets established by Ahmet Tevfik Pasha.

Ethnic Cleansing in Western Anatolia

Vahdeddin managed to find this ally in the Freedom and Accord Party. The Freedom and Accord Party, which was never outlawed yet whose leaders were exiled or assassinated during World War I upon the orders of the CUP triumvirate, emerged as one of the most important political organisations in the post-war period. Nevertheless, it still lacked a base among the medium and lower ranks of the Ottoman bureaucracy and urban notables which could compete with the Unionists' own political machine. When the party was revived in 1918, it resembled an umbrella political institution, including devout conservatives, frustrated constitutionalists and members of non-Muslim communities. It was the second most effective political party after the CUP and, unlike the CUP, it offered seats to Ottoman Christians in provincial administrative councils. However, this political party had structural disadvantages, especially in the provinces. While inclusive, it would lack well-established ties with provincial officials, and Muslim artisans and craftsmen. In other words, after its revival in the post-war period, its organisation was weak in the provinces. In any case, Damat Ferit Pasha, the party leader, was looked down upon by the Unionist groups as a close ally of the Ottoman palace.

Damat Ferit Pasha was an outstanding figure among Ottoman statesmen of his period since he had not only a striking talent, a great educational background and adequate knowledge of French, but also established affinity with the palace through his marriage. He previously worked in the Ministry of Foreign Affairs and in several embassies in Europe, including London. He served as a member of the Council of State (Şura-yı Devlet) in the reign of Abdülhamit II. After the restoration of the constitution, he became one of the leaders of the Freedom and Accord Party and was elected as a deputy in the Senate (Meclis-i Âyân). He had close ties to the palace as he was married to Mediha Sultan, Abdülmecid's daughter and Vahdeddin's sister.

Upon Ahmet Tevfik Pasha's resignation on 3 March 1919, Damat Ferit Pasha was appointed grand vizier the next day. Ferit Pasha would hold this office during two periods (March–October 1919 and April–October 1920) under the reign of Mehmed VI Vahdeddin. When forming the cabinet, he preferred appointing ministers from the deputies of the Freedom and Accord Party.

İzzet Bey would be appointed governor of Aydın Province, a critical position during the meetings of the Paris Peace Conference. On 9 March 1919, he was made governor-general (*vâlî*) of Aydın Province[14] and took office approximately a week later. By appointing İzzet Bey governor of Aydın, Ferit Pasha aimed to break the power of the Unionist officers, who were supported by Nureddin Pasha, the previous governor-general in this

162

Officials under the Greek Administration

province. Moreover, by this appointment, he would assert loyalist authority at the highest administrative levels of Aydın Province. This assignment was also considered appropriate by the representatives of the Allies as İzzet Bey was not a Unionist.[15]

Particularly in Unionist circles there were negative views concerning İzzet Bey due to his closeness to the British representative in Smyrna and his tolerant attitude towards the Ottoman Greek communities. İzzet Bey would be accused by the nationalist and Unionist groups of impeding nationalist resistance and allowing the return of previously expelled Ottoman Greeks and Armenians. Nationalist circles would criticise him severely until his death in January 1920 because he favoured the Freedom and Accord Party during his term in the governorship, had frosty relations with the İzmir Association of Defence of Ottoman Rights, entertained a positive attitude towards the High Commission after the occupation of Smyrna, and was co-opted into the Greek administration. One of the strongest examples of such nationalist views could be found in the memoirs of Celâl, former secretary-general of the CUP in Smyrna:

> İzzet Bey was the paternal uncle of the notorious Şerif Pasha, who surrendered to the peace conference in Paris for the disintegration of the Turkish land (*Türk vatanının*). The reason for his pretended association with the Turkish land was that he was ascribed much benevolence and significance. If another country had given him or shown him the same dignity, he would have become a servant or slave to it. This was because he had no common patriotic feelings or love for his country (*vatan sevgisi*) in his soul. He was an inept tool of Vahdettin's grudge and vengeance, a volunteered enemy of nationalism (*milliyetçilik*), which kept the state (*devlet*) together.[16]

In his memoirs, Ali Çetinkaya also made exaggerated statements about İzzet Bey. It is argued in these memoirs that after İzzet Bey's arrival in Smyrna, a feeling of exuberance existed among the Ottoman Greek communities. There was an increase in the organisational activities of Freedom and Accord Party in the region, and there were efforts to tyrannise nationalist military officers. Governor İzzet Bey and 'his confederates (*hempâları*)' broke the power and influence of Ali Nâdir Pasha,[17] commander of the 17th Corps, 'through cursed tricks (*melûnâne hîleler*)', and caused the surrender of Smyrna to the Greeks without any resistance:

> After İzzet Bey had arrived in Smyrna, there was no limit to the Ottoman Greeks' joy. At the Divine Liturgy celebrated in the presence of Greek officers, Metropolitan Chrysostomos said that their national wishes (*millî emellerinin*) would come true in fifteen days.

Ethnic Cleansing in Western Anatolia

A cursed man (*melûn*) named Kalkandelenli Tahsin, who was discharged from the army and later elevated to the rank of chief of police (*polis müdürü*) in Constantinople, came to Smyrna after Governor İzzet Bey's arrival and organised Freedom and Accord clubs. He was also engaged in inspecting the officers of the Army Corps in order to settle the accounts of those who were likely to participate in opposing activities and incidents and dissociate them from the army.[18]

Nonetheless, İzzet Bey's written correspondence between 1919 and 1920 presents a very different account of his governorship. Not knowing any details prior to the occupation of Smyrna, İzzet relates in the following words how he was notified by James Morgan, the British High Commissioner's representative in the city, about the occupation of Smyrna, one day before the landing:

One day before the occupation of Smyrna, that is, on the morning of 14 May, the British military representative Colonel Smith came to the government office and gave me a diplomatic note written by Admiral Calthorpe that I was supposed to announce to the military representatives, as the bastions and fortresses in and around Smyrna would be occupied by the forces of several states. When I received this note, I felt extremely desperate and sorrowful since I had not been informed about the possibility of such an incident. At my meeting with both Smith and Morgan, as well as his friends four or five days earlier, none of them had given even the smallest hint of anything like this. As the note had been written by Admiral Calthorpe on behalf of the Allied States, I felt obliged to obey it. After I protested, I instantly summoned Ali Nadir Pasha, Commander of 17th Army Corps, and Abdülhamit Bey, representative of general staff, to my house; and I informed them of the content of the diplomatic note before Monsieur Smith and James Morgan and told them through my official memorandum what must be done under these circumstances.[19]

In the French version of the same report, İzzet Bey repeated the events in almost the same way but this time, the occupation of Smyrna and its environs by the Allied Powers was overtly stated:

One day before the occupation of Smyrna, that is, on the morning of 14 May, Lieutenant-Colonel Ian M. Smith, representing the British army, came to the government office and submitted to me Admiral Calthorpe's memorandum, which instructed me to tell the military authorities that the fortresses of Smyrna and its surrounding area would be occupied by the Allied Powers. As soon as I got this note, I was gripped by a deep sorrow and felt puzzled because I could never have foreseen anything like this. This memorandum had been written by Admiral Calthorpe on behalf of the Allied States. While expressing my absolute objection to it, I instantly summoned commander Ali Nadir Pasha and Abdülhamit Bey to my house. I revealed to them the content of the note in

Officials under the Greek Administration

the presence of J. Morgan and Colonel Smith. I told them to give their official response and indicated what must be done.[20]

After meeting Admiral Calthorpe in the afternoon of the same day on the battleship *Iron Duke*, İzzet Bey reported their conversation about the note:

> Admiral Calthorpe received me with great courtesy and reverence. During our conversation, James Morgan was present too. He explained to me the character and scope of the diplomatic note given in the morning. He told me he was expecting a telegram from Paris that evening and this meant the military occupation of Smyrna. In response to my question of by whom this occupation would be performed, he said it would be most likely by the Greek troops. When I heard this, I was shocked and devastated and I think I also started to cry. I said, 'Oh admiral, how is this possible?' He responded, 'What can I do? This is Paris' decision' (*'Ben ne yapayım, Paris kararı dedi'*). I said, 'Well, Admiral, Paris has given so unjust (*adâlete münâfî*) a decision that it is difficult to explain.' He said, 'I am a soldier; I cannot dispute in this manner.' I told him that it was also not my duty to dispute, but it would not be right not to state the havoc and disasters this would bring upon this country. I said, 'Although we committed murder by declaring war on you and are today in a position of getting its punishment, this punishment must be in a reasonable way. This measure is going to cause a disaster for this country; if it is possible, I request that this occupation not be allotted to Greeks.' He said, 'This is not among my duties. I can by no means intervene. This is not an annexation, but only a military occupation. Therefore, it is not necessary to be so sad about it.'[21]

Before noon, the Allied troops occupied the forts and sent guards to protect the consulates, banks and foreign post offices. An intelligence bureau, responsible to the Foreign Ministry in Athens, was established at the Greek Consulate to subdue disturbances. Although this bureau established successful contacts with Armenian and Jewish community leaders, the Catholic and Muslim communities were cool towards the bureau. The Greek propaganda may have won limited support of the Greek-speaking Muslim Cretan colony in Smyrna.[22]

When İzzet Bey came back to the government office, a crowd of Muslims was gathering, expecting an explanation. İzzet Bey addressed this crowd and ordered them to return to their homes, stating that the occupation of Smyrna would only be a temporary military measure and he was sure that the government would take precautions to defend the rights of Muslim population. Later, he wrote and sent a memorandum to the muftis and the mayors to say that, contrary to rumours, the annexation of the *sanjak* to Greece was out of question. He emphasised that it was only a matter of temporary military occupation and urged them not to be

Ethnic Cleansing in Western Anatolia

anxious about this and to calm the people in their jurisdictions. İzzet, who explained his views to the members of the provincial press, had aimed to avoid a possible clash between the Greek soldiers and local people, especially Muslims. For the same purpose, he summoned the chiefs of police and gendarmerie and strictly asked them to avoid provocations and not to allow the disturbance of law and order in the city.[23] Besides this, he wrote an article for publication in the provincial newspapers on the morning of the Greek landing to reassure the public.

A second diplomatic note from Admiral Calthorpe was delivered to İzzet Bey by James Morgan and Colonel Ian Smith at ten o'clock in the evening. The note announced that Smyrna was going to be occupied by the Greek army the next day at around eight o'clock in the morning and that Ottoman soldiers were urged to remain in their barracks during the landing on order of the commander of the Greek troops. Upon receiving this note, İzzet Bey requested that the Allied troops assign to him of a party of 200–300 soldiers in order to hinder any provocation and restore the Muslim inhabitants' morale. Morgan relayed this to Calthorpe and, although it was not accepted, Calthorpe allowed the patrolling of some Ottoman soldiers in various neighbourhoods.[24]

Despite the efforts of the British admiral and Ottoman governor-general to keep the peace, violence began to break out in the city. Apart from Calthorpe and İzzet Bey, Venizelos also wished to prevent any conflict between the Greek forces and local Muslims. Venizelos, therefore, sent a telegram to the Ministry of War on 10 May 1919 and asked Mavroudis, who was expected to be the commander of the landing in Smyrna, to 'absolutely avoid confiscation of the houses belonging to Turks for the settlement of officers and servants'.[25] In accordance with the orders of Venizelos, buildings belonging to Ottoman Greek individuals and communities had priority for expropriation.

A group of Unionist agitators made use of Muslim-owned printing presses to urge people to take arms against the Greek troops. Notices published by the printing house of the newspaper *Anadolu* calling Muslims to resistance were hastily distributed by the students of the Sultânî Lycée and members of the Fraternal Society for Reserve Officers (İhtiyât Zâbitleri Teâvün Cemiyeti).[26] As a consequence of the talks at the Turkish Hearth, a public declaration was penned just before the Greek landing by Moralızâde Halit, Ragıp Nurettin (Eğe) and Mustafa Necâtî (Uğurel), figures known from the so-called Association for the Rejection of Annexation (Redd-i İlhâk Cemiyeti).[27] This series of events and provocative rhetoric of the declaration revealed feelings of panic and vigilance among Unionist notables.

Officials under the Greek Administration

On the eve of the occupation, the so-called Association for the Rejection of Annexation, the Fraternal Society for Reserve Officers and the Turkish Hearth branch organised a rally on the hills of Bahri Baba, near the Jewish cemetery, to protest against the Greek occupation. The crowd of a few hundred people lit fires in the square with the wood taken from the construction site of the National Library (Millî Kütüphane).[28] After hearing several speakers, the participants proceeded to the central prison, broke in and released Muslim detainees with the complicity of Unionist officers and Major Carossini, Allied inspector of the Ottoman gendarmerie. The mob then broke the gates of the main armoury and seized arms and munitions, led by members of the Fraternal Society for Reserve Officers. As can be inferred, the formation of local armed resistance groups occurred only a day before the Greek landing in Smyrna.

Having asked for orders from the Ottoman government and spent the whole night of 14 May in the telegram room waiting for an answer, İzzet Bey could not get any response from Constantinople. He had to take the initiative, as he described:

> It was midnight, and I asked for orders by informing the government on duty of the situation via the telegram. I was busy until five in the morning either sending telegrams or answering the questions of local Muslims who appealed to me from time to time. I was engaged in taking precautions to calm the people and provide peace and order. I had not been able to get correspondence from the ruling government (*hükûmet mütevelliyesi*) so, when morning approached, I immediately wrote a memorandum to Admiral Calthorpe to say that until that very moment, that is, until five in the morning, I had not received instructions from the government and thus had to protest the occupation of Smyrna by the Greek troops. At six o'clock I sent the memorandum to the Admiral by James Morgan.[29]

İzzet Bey believed that the occupation would be carried out within sight of the Allied navies without any problems. In order to prevent armed conflict, he had collected all the guns of the gendarmes who happened to be in the government office on the day of the landing. However, he must have understood that this was futile when the Greek soldiers besieged his office. İzzet describes the occupation of the government office and military barracks in the following way:

> Upon the requests and wishes of the civil servants, we hung a white cloth from the window; they immediately opened fire. Then upon it we hung another cloth and opened the doors; they instantly raced into the room with bayonets. I went to my official seat (*mevki-i resmiye*), and my officers gathered around me. At that moment soldiers with bayonets came into the room; they made us walk in

Ethnic Cleansing in Western Anatolia

front of them by threatening us with their bayonets and took us all downstairs. They made us raise our hands and shout 'Zito Venizelos!', forcing us, with various insults, to walk away. The people had nothing left on them; they were stripped naked, and not a fez was left; they tore everything up.

I said I was the governor-general, but it was not possible to express myself to anyone. On the way I appealed to a few Greek officers, but they would not listen. Thus, I was exposed to various insults with all my officers on the pier. Someone recognised me, and Liadimis [Liatis in the French report], one of the civil servants at the Greek consulate who happened to be passing by there,[30] saw me. Through his intervention they took my son and me out of that group. We remained in the middle; they took the others away amid insults and violence.[31]

İzzet depicted the turmoil of the occupation:

I did not have a chance to find out who was the first person to fire his gun [at the Greek soldiers] in the street. According to what I heard later, some argued that this was done by an Ottoman Greek (Rum) whereas some others said that the first shot came from an Ottoman cavalryman. In short, who first fired the shot is unknown to me. I do not even suppose that Muslim people or soldiers opened fire. There are some who assert that shots were fired from the barracks; maybe this happened later. Yet I state and claim with certainty that not a single gun was fired from the government office. There exist in the government office 8 to 10 armed gendarmes ready to serve; I myself took their guns from their hands when they opened fire on the government office. I saw that day 7 or 8 officers, 3 or 4 of whom had ammunition in the hall. I am fully convinced with the help of appeals and complaints that on the first, second, and third day and at night Muslim houses were robbed or Muslims' dignity and chastity were molested with the claim that they opened fire.[32]

Returning to the government office to resume his duties the next day, that is, on 16 May, İzzet Bey was not allowed in by the Greek soldiers. He appealed to the Greek commander to say that his work was hindered and that he would report this to the British representative. Morgan sent a note to İzzet Bey to say that he was sorry about what had happened the previous day and the hindrance that had occurred on that day.[33] The governor waited outside his office all day and returned to his home at four in the afternoon, reporting how the turmoil in the city spread to his neighbourhood, and even to his own home:

I guessed that war had broken out in the streets. Bullets started to fly and enter the building through windows and the walls of the entrance floor, so we had to take refuge in the vaults. The glass of the upper windows was utterly shattered, and the walls fell apart. This was undoubtedly the worst we had seen so far. Exclamations were heard from outside: 'Turks, come out or else we shall burn

Officials under the Greek Administration

you.' Upon this threat, and also taking into account that the assault had been going on for almost an hour, we, first I and then my wife and my little children, rushed out. Nine Greek soldiers (*piyâde eri*) and someone who was wearing a blue jacket and holding a big knife in his hand came at us ... Some time towards midnight two Greek officers came by to investigate and express their sadness. I talked to them about the whole felonious outrage and showed them the damage done by the soldiers to my house.[34]

On Admiral Calthorpe's insistence, all Ottoman civil servants who had been arrested were set free the following day. A Greek battalion welcomed and saluted İzzet, who came to the government office. Zafeiriou went to his office to officially apologise for the harsh treatment that the governor-general received on 15 May.[35] That same day, İzzet announced that Zafeiriou assured him that 'no incidents will take place anywhere touching the feelings of the Muslim community.'[36] What could be the reason for this change of attitude in the Greek military hierarchy?

In order to allay the reactions to the brutality of the day of the landing and avoid repercussions from the Supreme Council of the Paris Peace Conference, the Greek administration called Ottoman administrators back to office under the presidency of İzzet Bey. Moreover, immediately upon the occupation, Damat Ferit Pasha presented a letter of protest to the British high commissioner in Constantinople, pointing out that there was no condition to validate and no evidence to justify this occupation; he then resigned from his post in the government.[37] His resignation may have played an important role in changing the attitude of the Allied representatives, who feared a possible shift in the political balance in Constantinople. Ottoman public opinion also started to show its reactions in the face of the events that had taken place during the occupation. Furthermore, in an interview published by one of the French newspapers in Constantinople on 17 May, Mehmet Ali (Gerede) Bey, the minister of the interior, said: 'It is not possible to snatch Smyrna from the Anatolian mainland. Hence, I hope that the Allied States would not assume the Ottoman Empire would stoop to that.'[38] On the same day, the Freedom and Accord Party protested against the occupation, and the next day, joined by the Ottoman Peace and Welfare Party (Sulh ve Selâmet-i Osmâniyye Fırkası), the Free Nationalist Party (Millî Ahrâr Fırkası) and the Ottoman Socialist Party (Osmanlı Sosyalist Fırkası), via memorandum, denounced the occupation to the representatives of the Allied States.[39]

Accompanied by a Greek officer–interpreter for communication with the Greek military and civilian authorities, İzzet Bey went to the government office on 17 May and convened the Administrative Council of

169

Ethnic Cleansing in Western Anatolia

Province.[40] At this meeting, attended by its Ottoman Greek, Armenian and Muslim members, some decisions were made concerning the re-establishment of public order and safety, and the Greek command was given instructions for the implementation of those resolutions. It seems that neither the Ottoman government nor İzzet accepted Greek control over Smyrna. On the day he resumed his position, İzzet received a telegram from Constantinople in which Mehmet Ali clearly did not recognise the Greek occupation:

> In your meeting with Sir Calthorpe, you should state that the Ottoman sovereign rights over the city of Smyrna and its province are invariable rules, though we do not object to an international occupation (*enternasyonel işgâline*) of this region. However, if the issue of Greek occupation is discussed, you must additionally declare that neither our beloved sultan, nor the nation, nor the government (*ne sevgili pâdişâhımızın, ne milletin ve ne de hükûmetin*) will ever welcome (this).[41]

Contrary to the stereotypical view about him in nationalist historiography, İzzet did not function as a puppet of the Greek administration. On 19 May, he sent messages to the Allied representatives in Smyrna protesting about the atrocities committed against Ottoman administrative and military officers during the occupation, and demanded that Allied troops join the Ottoman troops in order to guarantee public security.[42] In two different telegrams he dispatched to Constantinople on 20 and 21 May, İzzet reported that, after meeting with French consul-general, he made efforts to alleviate the local elites in Smyrna, and the Ottoman civil servants had resumed working.[43]

İzzet gave voice to the Ottoman claim that the Greek armies seized the Ottoman guns and ammunition in the armouries by force. On 9 July 1919, he presented to James Morgan a list of guns and material owned by the 17th Army Corps and asked what happened to them after the landing.[44] In another letter, he emphasised that this seizure by the Greek military would constitute a clear contravention of the provisions of the armistice.[45] On 29 July, in a third letter, he asserted that the Greek army retained some of these guns, which were warehoused close to the monastery of Prophet Elias, and took others to an unknown location, stressing that this act violated the provisions of the armistice.[46]

By mid-August 1919, it became clear that İzzet Bey had established friendly relations with the High Commission and appreciated Stergiades's conciliatory stance. While returning from a short investigative tour to Aydın in his own car, Stergiades barely escaped an assassination attempt. After meeting with him, İzzet informed the Ministry of the Interior

Officials under the Greek Administration

about this plot and the possible perpetrators behind it through conveying Stergiades's own words:

> He stated to me that 'I had stopped for four minutes to listen to a group of innocent Muslims' complaints. Now, I would be blown up (*ber-hevâ*). I donated a hundred lira for restoring a mosque there, and treated the desperate Muslims well. Who knows perhaps their prayer saved me. This is not a Muslim organisation (*Müslümân işi*).' As the aforementioned person was really and truly disliked by many Ottoman Greeks in Smyrna due to his pro-Muslim stance, he implied that this assassination was organised by either them or the Italians who more or less had influence in that area. He made people understand that it was most likely arranged by the Italians.[47]

Nonetheless, İzzet was cautious about the propaganda by the Greek Kingdom arguing that the local population had invited the Greek troops. He complained to James Morgan that after the bloody events in Birgi, the Muslims in Ödemiş were forced by Greek secret agents to sign memorials expressing their pleasure at the Greek occupation. He added that these statements were presented to Ali Nâîbzâde, the president of the Department of Muslim Affairs in the High Commission, during his trip to that region.[48]

While İzzet Bey did not object to the return of Ottoman Greek refugees, he struggled to protect the property rights of Muslims in the face of waves of returning refugees. He harshly criticised the role of the Greek army in the eviction of Muslims to make way for Greek returnees from the Aegean islands. He urged the Ottoman government 'to exercise its right of sovereignty and forbid the resettlement of the Hellenes'[49] and encouraged the Bank of Agriculture (Zirâat Bankası) to make loans to Muslim peasants around Urla whose properties had been abandoned or burned by the Greek troops.[50] In a letter dated 14 December 1919 to Milne, commander-in-chief of the British Army of the Black Sea, İzzet complained that the Muslim evictions were encouraged by the Greek army and stressed that this violated the rights of the Ottoman government protected by a special treaty.[51]

İzzet Bey carefully monitored the activities of the Greek troops in Western Anatolia. In a telegram to Constantinople on 21 May, he told the Ministry of the Interior that the Greek occupation forces had expanded their zone of invasion in disregard to Admiral Calthorpe's instructions and that he had attempted to intervene on behalf of the representatives of the Allied States to impede this expansion.[52] Being the chief Ottoman administrator in the province, he did not refrain from protesting about the fires set by Greek troops in the villages of Demirköprü and Kolhisar after

171

Ethnic Cleansing in Western Anatolia

their recapture of Aydın and while crossing the River Menderes.[53] He had also taken action by resorting to the commander of the Greek troops concerning Greek soldiers who had seized precious goods and money in the houses they had entered for various excuses, and requested ending such acts.[54] When the Greek troops started marching towards Akhisar in August 1919, İzzet met with Stergiades and General Nider at Stergiades's office and reminded them that their soldiers had been compelled to retreat in the previous June due to British pressure and stated that the Greek administration 'would be unable to limit the National Forces (Kuvâ-yı Milliye'yi *tutamaz bir hâle gelecekler*) even with a thousand obstacles (*bin müşkilâtla*)'.[55]

On 18 July 1919, the Supreme Council of the Paris Peace Conference, which had entertained rumours about Greek atrocities in Aydın Province, established an Inter-Allied Commission of Inquiry to investigate the incidents that had occurred during and after the Greek occupation of Smyrna. The commission was comprised of General Robert Hugh Hare for Britain, General Georges Hippolyte Bunoust for France, General Alfredo Dall'olio for Italy and Admiral Mark Lambert Bristol for the United States.[56] İzzet Bey played a critical role and emerged as the key Ottoman administrator to facilitate the work of the Inter-Allied Commission of Inquiry. He contacted the political representatives of the Allied States in Smyrna in order to gain information on the mission and the authority of the Inter-Allied Commission of Inquiry.[57] Once the visit of the commission was certain, the Ministry of the Interior entered into extensive correspondence with high-ranking Ottoman provincial officials in Aydın Province. A telegram from the Ministry of the Interior on 6 August provided İzzet with details about the Commission of Inquiry, its composition and it mission. In the telegram, the Ministry of the Interior urged him to build good relations with the commission members, taking into consideration that the Commission of Inquiry's final report would influence the verdict about the Ottoman Empire at the Paris Conference. Two days later, on 8 August, the Ministry of the Interior sent another telegram to İzzet demanding 'the strict prohibition of illegal organisations, such as nationalist circles and congresses (*teşkîlât-ı milliye ve kongre gibi mugayir-i kanûn harekâtın*), and the arrest of those venturing to do so'.[58]

When the Commission of Inquiry started its meetings on 23 August in Smyrna, İzzet Bey clarified his political stance siding with the government in Constantinople and put a reserve to the activities of the Greek troops in the city. In the telegram he dispatched to the Ministry of the Interior on that day, İzzet Bey stated that the Commission of Inquiry had held its first meeting and that he had presented a list of proposed witnesses.

Officials under the Greek Administration

He additionally remarked that, as the head of the provincial administration, he had completed the 'preparations for examination and had no doubt that the facts which could no longer be concealed would be accepted by European public opinion'.[59]

The Ministry of Interior requested via telegram on 26 August that İzzet Bey form another commission under his administration that would investigate money seized and damage caused by Greek troops in the Ottoman government offices in Smyrna. İzzet had already assembled such a commission and prepared a report of the damage before this order reached him, and he sent the report to Constantinople as soon as he had received the 26 August order.[60]

While the commission visited conflict points in the province, İzzet Bey cautioned commission members that the Greek authorities, especially the military, targeted Muslim witnesses testifying to the commission. Upon learning that Greek troops were arresting Ottoman officials who had witnessed the violence of the early days of the occupation, İzzet directed Kadrî Bey, the Ottoman observer in the Commission of Inquiry, to immediately call the Ottoman police chief in Smyrna and the other witnesses before the commission. Again, on 11 September, İzzet protested to General Milne his objection to the fact that the Greek authorities did not allow some Muslims to travel to Nazilli while the commission was in town.[61]

On 22 August, İzzet Bey met with General Georges Hippolyte Bunoust, the French member of the Inter-Allied Commission of Inquiry. During this conversation, İzzet stressed to him that Greek troops had taken part in acts of violence in the province and that their atrocities against Muslims were overt and even performed in sight of foreigners.[62] On the following day, İzzet cabled Constantinople that he did not have any doubts that 'the facts that are unable to be concealed will be accepted by the European public.'[63]

The Inter-Allied Commission of Inquiry began hearings at the Imperial School in Smyrna (İzmir Sultânî Mektebi) on 25 August. İzzet was invited to observe the talks presided over by Admiral Bristol. İzzet himself recounted how the occupation started, and how the Greek troops treated the military and civilian captives during the talks, which lasted more than two hours. He stated that he also was exposed to assaults twice, yet still endeavoured to fulfil his duties as governor-general. He also submitted a statement written by himself in French, in addition to a report containing the official documents and photographs of the atrocities the Greek troops had committed.[64] On the same day, İzzet sent a dispatch to the Ministry of the Interior about the content of the testimony he had delivered before the commission.

Ethnic Cleansing in Western Anatolia

In a report to the Ministry of the Interior on 6 September, İzzet described the hearings as congenial, and speculated that the commission would decide in favour of the Ottoman Empire, although the commission's decision was still secret at that point.[65] He underscored in his dispatches to Constantinople the possibility that a report reflecting negatively on the Empire because of actions by the adherents of the National Forces (*Kuvâ-yı Milliyeciler*) would endanger the relatively peaceful intercommunal relations in Smyrna and have adverse effects on domestic policies.[66] Through public notices, he asked the people not to help the National Forces and to support the anti-Nationalist policies of the Ottoman central government.

Having completed the process of hearing from witnesses of different ethnic groups, nationalities and professions, the Commission of Inquiry concluded the hearings on 26 September 1919. It heard from Ottoman public officials and military officers, the high commissioner, clerics from different religious communities, merchants and shopkeepers, prominent members of the Izmir Association of Defence of Ottoman Rights, and leaders of local militias who had affinity with the National Forces. İzzet sent a general report to the Ministry of the Interior on 27 September, suggesting that the annexation of the Smyrna zone to Greece would be disallowed, but conceding that public opinion in the Allied States could influence the final decision:

> Although it was not known by the governorship how the report that was going to be devised by the Commission would be evaluated in Paris, it was expected that the administration of Smyrna and its surrounding region would not be given to the Greeks and an appropriate decision appealing to the Ottoman State would also be taken. The contribution of the Allied States' public opinion to the formation of the decision should not be ignored. It is also apparent that the government is supposed to undertake remarkable duties in regard to this matter.[67]

The Commission's extensive report claimed that the Greek occupation was not required since no major violence against the local Christians had occurred after the Armistice of Mudros. It emphasised that despite persecution of Christian populations in the summer of 1914 and during the war years, peace had been restored under the governorship of İzzet Bey.[68] Nonetheless, it did not exculpate Ottoman responsibility for violence, and accused Ottoman officers of conspiring to smuggle weapons and release prisoners on the eve of the occupation. Some of these prisoners obtained weapons from the military depot through the help of Ottoman officers. Concerning incidents in Aydın, the report asserted that Muslim militias, especially that of Yörük Ali, were the main actors in the looting of Christian houses and the burning of the town on 30 June 1919.

Officials under the Greek Administration

Having suffered from ill health later that autumn, İzzet Bey succumbed to a heart attack on 5 January 1920. His funeral took place on the following day and was attended by the high commissioner, the representatives of the Allied high commissioners, Muslim civil servants and Greek troops. The appointment of his successor was delayed for a long while because of disagreements between the High Commission and the Ottoman government about the status of the Ottoman governor. Emîn Bey, former undersecretary of the Sublime Porte (*sadâret müsteşarı*), was appointed governor of the province on 7 January;[69] however, he could not take up office due to reasons that are unclear. After the Treaty of Sèvres in August 1920, the High Commission ceased to recognise the governors-general appointed by the Ottoman government in Constantinople, and Ahmed Besim Bey, the vice-governor, signed a protocol with the High Commission confirming his secondary position. Therefore, as in the case of Subhî Efendi, the Ottoman government changed the title to vice-governor.

Case 2: Hüsnü Bey, District Governor of Manisa, 1919–22

Colonel Kâzım Fikrî (Özalp), Unionist commander of the northern districts, immediately left Smyrna on 15 May 1919, the day of the occupation, and went by train en route to Menemen/Manisa. Colonel Kâzım Fikrî was planning to have a meeting with Unionist mayors in the region about 'the preparation of National Forces (Millî Kuvvetler)' and the establishment of a military base in Bandırma.[70] For this purpose, the following day they talked over the methods of resistance in the region at the meeting held in the house of Bahri Bey, the mayor of Manisa, the administrative centre of the Saruhan *sanjak*. Having considered the risk that Manisa would be occupied after the Greek landing at Smyrna, Bahri Bey invited the prominent Unionist officers who had fled from Smyrna, including Colonel Kâzım, Ömer Faruk, Dr Şükrü and Hüseyin Vâsıf (Çınar). At this meeting, the secret transfer of the guns and ammunition from Manisa to the interior of Anatolia and the foundation of a resistance organisation were discussed. Alim Efendi, the mufti of Manisa, who was also the president of Cemiyet-i İslâmiye, a nationalist organisation supported by Nureddin Pasha, was in favour of such a resistance organisation.[71]

According to the impression of the British control officer in Manisa, many wealthy Muslim landowners would leave the town in the event of the Greek occupation. Muslim public opinion in Manisa, excluding the CUP sympathisers, was in favour of the continuation of the Ottoman administration under European control, preferably British, whereas a considerable part of the Greek Orthodox community preferred a Greek

175

administration. The notables and elders of the Greek Orthodox communities in Manisa, Muradiye and Kasaba, inspired by the Wilsonian self-determination principle, had sent petitions to President Wilson expressing their desire to unite 'with the mother-country Greece'. All of these petitions were confirmed by Ioachim (Yovakim) Vafiedis, the metropolitan of Ephesus.[72]

The Ottoman government stated that it was doing what was necessary in reaction to the occupation to protect the rights of the state. It asserted that the occupation was illegal and inappropriate, but that it was imperative for the people to remain calm. The government particularly stressed that no activities in response to the occupation would be tolerated except for protests.[73] Therefore, Hüsnü Bey, district governor (*mutasarrıf*) of Saruhan, tried to gain the confidence of the non-Muslim population by taking measures in order to prevent ethnic conflict.[74]

Hüsnü Bey, whose family had migrated from the Cretan town of Chania at the end of the nineteenth century, had a good command of the Greek language and had earned a degree in law. Before he was assigned to this office on 7 April 1917, he served as attorney general (*müddeî-i umûmî*) and district governor of Aydın.[75] He was a senior officer from Damat Ferit Pasha's faction and had strong ties with İzzet Bey, the governor-general of the province and senior administrator.

Aside from the Denizli *sanjak*, Aydın Province hosted a considerable number of Cretan Muslims who migrated after the unilateral annexation of the island by Greece in 1908. According to statistics dating to 1881, 73,234 Muslims had composed 27 per cent of the total population of Crete. In 1911, the island had only 27,852 Cretan Muslims. It can be estimated that at least 45,000 Cretan Muslims migrated in a period of thirty years.[76] All the Cretan Muslims, who arrived in the Dodecanese islands, and then Aydın Province, spoke Kritika, a dialect of Greek. Some Cretan Muslims, such as Hüsnü Bey, attained senior positions in the provincial government.

Warned by İzzet Bey against the risk of nationalist provocation, Hüsnü Bey tried to restrict the Unionists' activities in the Saruhan *sanjak* and prevent an ethnic clash that could occur in the area around the time of the Greek occupation. In particular, he openly stated that he did not want to see Colonel Kâzım Fikrî in Manisa as he was bothered by his efforts to provoke people prior to the occupation.[77] In a memorandum he issued before the occupation, he made efforts to reduce the tension in the area under his jurisdiction. Hüsnü Bey's resolution to prevent armed resistance against the Greek occupation was supported by the municipal council and the local notables, who feared the risk of an armed conflict among different ethnic groups.

Officials under the Greek Administration

When the Greek troops entered Manisa on 26 May 1919 they were received without armed resistance. The Greek troops went to the government office through a ceremony attended by the notables from the Muslim, Armenian and Greek Orthodox communities, the last of which was led by Ioachim, the metropolitan of Ephesus, who resided in Manisa. Although Maurice Fitzmaurice, commodore of the British Aegean Squadron, claimed that the occupation of Manisa was carried out without permission, Stergiades emphasised that the occupation took place without any fighting against the Ottoman regular army or irregular forces.[78] As a response to British objections to the Greek advance, Stergiades stated that the peace in the north-eastern parts of the Smyrna zone could be maintained only through the occupation of Manisa. Indeed, the Greek administration imposed several measures in order to police the suburban parts of Manisa, with the gendarmes patrolling the town at night due to the lack of street lamps.[79]

Hüsnü also directed the district governors under his authority not to support armed resistance. His instructions have been interpreted as efforts to block resistance in his jurisdiction. On this issue Bezmi Nusret, district governor of Alaşehir, and İbrahim Ethem, district governor of Demirci, opposed his order.[80] On the other hand, the governors in the districts of Kasaba, Salihli and Akhisar did not deviate from his order. The commander of the 56th Division, Bekir Sâmî (Günsav), who failed to find the support he had expected in Akhisar, accused the Muslims of Akhisar of welcoming the Greek occupation. In his memoirs, he describes with some hyperbole the situation in Akhisar on the morning of 24 May 1919:

> Greek flags are hung in every street, and everybody is expecting the Greeks. Several local Turkish people have got close to native Greeks and are flattering them. They think that in so doing they will assure the safety of their lives, goods and properties when the Greek army enters the city. All tailors are busy with sewing big Greek flags.[81]

Hasan Fikret, the district governor of Salihli, was present at the ceremony of the Greek army's entrance into the town. On 29 May, there was no resistance in Kasaba while the occupying forces were entering the city, and Hamdi Bey, the district governor, the mayor and the members of the municipal council continued to serve under the Greek administration.

Upon coming to Akhisar on 26 May, Çerkes Ethem, a famous militia leader of Circassian origin, shot some people who had put up Greek flags in front of their houses and reproached the district governor.[82] Meanwhile, after the Greek army crossed the Milne Line, which designated the boundaries of the Greek-controlled Smyrna zone, the Greek troops withdrew

Ethnic Cleansing in Western Anatolia

from Akhisar, and the commander of the military unit was charged with indiscipline and sentenced to twenty days' imprisonment on account of the complaints recorded on 9 June 1919.

Following the enforcement of the Treaty of Sèvres, the towns of Manisa, Kasaba and Akhisar in the Saruhan *sanjak* were officially incorporated into the Smyrna zone. Hüsnü, the former district governor, was appointed as the administrator of Manisa Province. He and the other Ottoman civil servants could keep their duties in this new province of the Smyrna zone. Thus, the Muslim civil servants in the *sanjak* of Saruhan were left untouched.

As shown in Chapter 2, subsequent to the advance of the Greek armies, Stergiades visited settlements in the Military Occupation Zone during his tour in summer 1920 in order to check on the Ottoman civil servants and encourage them to keep their positions under the Greek occupation. In a meeting with the district governor of Manisa, he asked for continued cooperation. He argued that if there were some vacant positions because of the leave of Muslim civil servants, he could demand the appointment of new ones so that the work of the administration should not be disrupted. Furthermore, as to the issue of tax collection in Manisa, he directed that the district governors collect all taxes, these being used primarily to pay the salaries of the Ottoman civil servants.[83] It was probably before the advance of the nationalist army in September 1922 that Hüsnü left Manisa and settled in Egypt, where he died in 1937.

Case 3: Fuat Bey and Abdurrahman Bey, Deputy District Governors of Aydın, in 1919

Fevzi (Toker) Bey was serving as the district governor of the Aydın *sanjak* when the Armistice of Mudros was signed. However, he was summoned to Constantinople prior to the Greek landing at Smyrna and then appointed to the district governorship of Çatalca. Fuat Bey, former head of the local correspondence office (*tahrîrât müdürü*), was then appointed deputy district governor (*mutasarrıf vekîli*) of the Aydın *sanjak*.[84]

One day after the occupation of Smyrna, a few local notables visited Colonel Şefik (Aker) Bey, Ottoman Commander of the 57th Regiment in Aydın, and discussed how they should react in the event of a Greek military attack. Şefik Bey, a Macedonia-born Ottoman officer, insisted on organising armed resistance in the west and south of Aydın[85] while the majority of the Ottoman authorities in the Aydın *sanjak*, including Fuat Bey, resolved to protest the occupation peacefully. Members of the Freedom and Accord Party, who sought permission from Fuat, played a

Officials under the Greek Administration

significant role in the organisation of this demonstration. At talks with them, Fuat said that he would not participate in the demonstration as he had been warned by the imperial government about the risk of 'violating the order', yet he would not hinder its realisation either.[86] There was a small turnout for this protest.

After the occupation of Smyrna, the Italian government coveted as compensation the south-western part of the province, including the town of Aydın, and a small Italian contingent, moving from Kuşadası, occupied the towns of Söke and Çine, not far from Aydın. Early in June 1919, while the Italians advanced on Çine, the Ottoman civil authorities in the Menteşe *sanjak* proposed to General Giuseppe Battistoni, commander of the Italian troops in Antalya, the formation of an independent administration in the *sanjak* under Italian military protection.[87]

The Freedom and Accord Party constituted a larger group among the local notables in Aydın than in Smyrna.[88] A certain increase in disorder and militia violence in Aydın prompted some notables to meet with the Italian commander in Kuşadası, a coastal town, to negotiate the Italian occupation of Aydın.[89] The lack of security was the most important dynamic that determined these conditions. The stated reason for this negotiation process was the increased raids on the towns by gangs of local bandits and a security vacuum prevailing in the rural areas.

Since the imperial government was late in appointing the new district governor (*mutasarrıf*), Fuat Bey formed a group of representatives from local Muslim and Christian notables to meet with the British intelligence officer in Aydın. He also proposed the formation of local security forces composed of Muslims and Christians. Two days later, when the attacks by nationalist militias became unbearable, the same group, including the chief of police in Aydın, negotiated with the commander of the Greek troops in Değirmendere, situated north-west of the town on the Smyrna–Aydın railroad, and asked him to send his troops and restore the peace in Aydın.[90]

Abdurrahman Bedirhan Bey,[91] the new district governor, arrived in Aydın on 25 May 1919 and immediately arranged a meeting with local notables in order to prevent the recurrence of intercommunal violence in Aydın. Abdurrahman Bey issued a decree that same day that prohibited armed conflict with Greek troops. Upon his arrival, he made one important change in the municipality of Aydın. He removed the mayor, Hacı İbrahim Eminzâde (Emin Bey), and on 1 June replaced him with Peştemalcızâde Reşat Bey. Emîn Bey, who wished to grant the Christian communities more rights in the administration of the municipality, had been elected as the mayor of Aydın by the supporters of the Freedom and Accord Party. Nonetheless, his mayoral term ended up not lasting long. The reason behind this change was that Emîn was seen as a pro-Greek figure since he was in the delegation that went out to receive the Greek troops and he also displayed the Greek flag on his house.[92]

As a consequence of the consensus between Muslim and Christian notables of the *sanjak*, Greek troops were able to enter Aydın 'without incident' on 27 May.[93] Smaragdos, metropolitan bishop of Heliopolis, Mufti Hacı Mustafa Efendi, Mayor Emîn Bey, Chief of Police Saraçoğlu Şeyh Mehmet, and a group of municipal council members consisting of Peştemalcızâde Reşat, Ioannis Iliadis and Kostas Hatziapostolos were present in the reception committee for the Greek troops entering Aydın.

The National Forces were still strong in this part of the province. The British officers who were charged with inspecting the Aydın *sanjak* noticed at the end of June that the irregular forces were concentrated in the mountainous regions. J. A. Lorimer, a British lieutenant, encountered the National Forces on 28 June:

> I left Aidin with a party of Workmen and 10 Armed Turkish Guards to repair the Railway Bridge at Clchak Chai, about a mile Aidin side of Omurlu several sleepers had been placed across the line, taking these off, we proceeded slowly, but were held up by Turkish irregulars who enquired our business and then allowed us to approach the Rly. Station where we met about 250 Turkish Regular soldiers and approx. 1000 Irregulars, the former reported that the latter were about from 5000 to 6000 strong and the officer in command of the regulars said that it was impossible for him to keep them under control, as they intended to march Aidin and oust the Unan (Greek), I told them to do his best to pacify the Irregulars as I trusted the Great Powers would make some pacific arrangements.[94]

While Ben Hodder, the British naval representative, was on his way to Smyrna on 28 June, he was attacked by some bandit leaders, who gave him an ultimatum to transmit to the district governor, the mayor and the Orthodox bishop. In this ultimatum, they gave three days' notice to the Greek troops to quit Aydın. If they did so, the nationalist bands assured them that 'the Christian population would be protected in every way.' Yet, if they did not leave Aydın, 'the consequences would be most disastrous' and 'they would burn and pillage the whole town'.

On the night of 30 June, Ben Hodder observed that a fire had started in the Greek neighbourhoods controlled by the irregular forces. He noticed that these irregulars instantly turned to loot the market square and the neighbourhoods inhabited mostly by Ottoman Greeks. Commander Şefik admitted that he had failed to hinder the looting and was unable to find a single man that would be sent out of Aydın to find help in halting

Officials under the Greek Administration

the looting.[95] The day following the fire, Hodder, who visited the local Christians, was encountered by these people in panic.[96]

After meeting with Şefik Bey about the probable disastrous consequences of this assault on the Ottoman Christians in Aydın, on 1 July, Hodder organised a train full of Christian civilians to be taken to Nazilli. The following day, he dispatched a trainload of approximately 500 civilians, both Muslims and Christians, to Dinar, and a further 500 women and children to Smyrna by train.[97]

The Greek troops, which amounted to three battalions of 800 men each, were attacked by nationalist militias with heavy guns from the south and east. At the end of the military conflict, the Greek troops were driven out of the town on 29 June.[98] The National Forces, which consisted of the remnants of the demobilised Ottoman armies as well as irregular forces, namely volunteers from Çine and Koçarlı as well as Cretan bandits under the command of Giritli Cafer Ağa, played an important role in the recapture of Aydın.[99]

When the Greek army evacuated Aydın on 29 June 1919, the town was subsequently burned, and local Christians were massacred by the paramilitaries. Ben Hodder, who had visited Aydın on 27 June, described the town 'in a state of terror' and recounted that the local Greeks had started to leave the town in the afternoon on Sunday, 29 June, as they were afraid of the excessive violence of the paramilitary formations and irregulars. Arrested by the Greek soldiers shortly before the Greek withdrawal from Aydın and taken to Smyrna, Abdurrahman Bey would be released shortly afterwards due to pressure by the British high commissioner.[100]

After the complete withdrawal of the Greek troops on 30 June, Stolzenberg, an Ottoman Catholic and the manager of the local branch of the Banque Impériale Ottomane, witnessed that

> [almost 4,000 local Greek refugees] first directed towards the Armenian Church, and then evacuated Conak of the Government. In the city the shooting continued, and the looting and murders were succeeded by the fire. At eight o'clock in the evening, on Monday, June 30, the Greek quarter was flared up from 12 different points.
>
> The next day, Tuesday, 1st of July, the most complete anarchy prevails in the city. Aidin is entirely in the hands of Zeibecks.[101]

However, the victory of the National Forces did not last long. Two days after the deportation of local Christians, the Greek troops retrieved the town. Following the collapse of the defences established by Şefik, on 9 July, the Ministry of the Interior requested a report about the situation in the town and the condition of the district governor. The next day, this telegram was answered by an officer from Nazilli, who stated that the district governor was still in custody 'due to his relations with the bands in the previous events in Aydın'.[102] Probably written by the district governor of Nazilli or the leader of the National Forces stationed there, this reply was sent to the governor-general of Aydın Province.

In August 1919, the Ministry of the Interior ordered the Aydın district governor to submit all documents and photographs concerning 'the Greek atrocities' in order to influence the report prepared by the Inter-Allied Commission of Inquiry.[103] The Ministry of the Interior sent another telegram to Aydın on 10 September and directed efforts to stop the activities of the National Forces until the outcome of the report that would be given by the Inter-Allied Commission of Inquiry was revealed, stressing that the Greek troops had stopped proceeding towards the Valley of Menderes.[104] Due to the armed conflicts between Greek troops and Turkish nationalist militias, the southern part of the Aydın *sanjak* had become a battleground and many Muslim farmers had left the region, creating labour shortages that stalled factories, workshops and farms.[105] Stolzenberg's report portrays how the town was devastated after the retreat of the Greek army:

> The tragic events in Aidin, a city whose population was mainly composed of Muslims (30,000 Turks against 5,000 Greeks and 5,000 Jews), had the most disastrous consequences for this unfortunate city, once so rich and prosperous. The fire, set on by both the Greeks and the Turks, destroyed this city in the following proportions:
>
> ⅓ of the Turkish quarters
> ½ of the Jewish quarters
> All of the Christian quarters
> ¾ of the bazaar were destroyed.
> The number of victims among the civilian population is as follows:
> 100 from the Muslim side
> 80 from the Jewish side
> 1500–2000 from the Christian side
>
> The Christian Orthodox element was particularly affected by these events. Immense stocks of oil have been plagued by flames, the oil and cotton pressing factories, the main tanneries, and soap factories have all disappeared.[106]

In the autumn of 1919, Spyros Skarpetis, the former governor of Corfu, was appointed representative (*antiprosōpos*) of the High Commission in Aydın.[107] This appointment apparently led to a series of changes in the Ottoman district governors. In mid-October 1919, Nâcî Bey, former district governor of Nazilli, was appointed deputy district governor of Aydın.[108] Nonetheless, the efforts of the Ottoman Ministry of the Interior

Officials under the Greek Administration

to assign a fully authorised district governor to the Aydın *sanjak* continued. As Abdurrahman never returned to Aydın, he was assigned to Çorum
as district governor, and Cavid Bey, former district governor of Niğde,
was named district governor of Aydın on 29 October.[109] Almost a year
later, Nâcî Bey, deputy district governor, would replace Cavid Bey.[110]

At the beginning of 1921, Georgios Vakalopoulos took Skarpetis's
place. When the Treaty of Sèvres was signed, Aydın was not included
in the Smyrna zone, which was under the jurisdiction of the High
Commission. In the representative office (*antiprosōpeia*) of the High
Commission in Aydın, Muslim clerks were employed in considerably
high numbers in accordance with the ethno-religious composition of the
region. For instance, almost half of the second-rank clerks working in
the representation office were Muslims.[111] Additionally, Hasan İbrahim
Bey held the second highest rank in the office as the secretary of the
representative whilst Mehmet Efendi was commissioned as the clerk of
the office.

In the second half of 1921, nationalist paramilitary formations began
to increase their activities in the Menderes Valley again. On the first day
of September 1922, Vakalopoulos, the representative of the high commissioner in Aydın, informed Stergiades that public order was on the verge of
collapse in the town due to attacks by the nationalist army.[112] The nationalist bands had started to organise attacks on the outer neighbourhoods of
the town and kidnapped civilians, and farmers were afraid of working on
their farms outside the town.

Case 4: The Circassian Congress of Smyrna in December 1921

At the beginning of the Greek military advance in Anatolia, the dispersed
Circassian political elites in the Ottoman capital and provinces were
divided into two factions. A large number, like Ahmet Anzavur, were still
supporting the Ottoman sultan and his policies while others, like Raûf and
Bekir Sâmî, were among the supporters of the nationalist movement.

Several Circassian associations had already been established with
the restoration of the constitutional monarchy in 1908. The Circassian
Solidarity Association (Çerkes Teâvün Cemiyeti)[113] and the Circassian
Women's Association of Solidarity (Çerkes Kadınları Teâvün Cemiyeti)
were the most important Circassian organisations in the capital and the
provinces. The basic objectives of these cultural associations were the
preservation of Circassian culture and improvement of solidarity among
the Circassians. Nonetheless, Circassian organisations did not have any
claim for autonomy until the 1920s.

183

Ethnic Cleansing in Western Anatolia

The first rupture between loyalist groups of the Circassians and the National Forces took place during the uprising of Ahmet Anzavur. Loyalist Circassian groups joined Anzavur's forces in Balıkesir, Kütahya and Bandırma. After the violent suppression of this revolt by the National Forces, anxiety among Circassian notables increased. In this tense political atmosphere, a Circassian Congress convened on 24 October 1921 in Smyrna with the participation of more than twenty Ottoman Circassians – civil servants, ex-members of the Special Organisation and former Unionists – who came from Hüdavendigâr and Aydın provinces, which were under the Greek occupation, and from the *sanjak*s of Izmit and Bolu outside of the occupation zone.

At the end of this meeting, the attendees, now calling themselves representatives of the Association for the Strengthening of Near Eastern Circassian Rights (Şark-ı Karîb Çerkesleri Temîn-i Hukuk Cemiyeti), released a manifesto entitled 'The General Statement of the Circassian Nation to the Great Powers and the Civilised World'. İbrahim Hakkı Bey, former Ottoman district governor of Izmit working as a lawyer in Smyrna, became the chairman of the association.[114] Reşit, Çerkes Ethem's brother, was another important figure who played a pivotal role in the association. The manifesto declared that nearly two million Circassians were living in Anatolia and called for recognition of the severe losses experienced by the Circassian nation after the restoration of the Ottoman constitution in 1908 due to the forceful imposition of pan-Turkism and pan-Turanism.

It seems that İbrahim Hakkı and his supporters intended to establish an autonomous Circassian political entity in the Greek occupation zone. A considerable number of Circassian notables in the occupation zone endorsed his attempt. The manifesto also declared that the Circassian participants 'decided correctly and naturally to join the Greek army, which promises to preserve them, in the occupation zone'.[115] According to its authors, the Greek government guaranteed that they would not see any difference among Circassians, Armenians, Orthodox Christians and the other elements of the population. This document would be regarded as a threat by the Grand National Assembly in Ankara.

Gingeras argues that some Circassian notables decided very soon after the Anzavur uprisings to seek some sort of autonomy.[116] Indeed, the Circassian notables revealed their desire to be politically represented in the Greek zone of occupation. It was not a coincidence that Smyrna, whose Circassian population was not large, was chosen as the centre of this congress. If the participants had chosen to organise the congress in a city or town in Hüdavendigâr Province or the Karesi *sanjak*, which hosted a large Circassian population, they could have attracted more participants.

Officials under the Greek Administration

Most probably, the organisers intended to be close to the Greek administration centred in Smyrna.

Since a negative attitude came from the nationalists in Ankara, the Circassians resolved to join the Greek Administration of Smyrna, which they believed would defend their vital interests. It is obvious that the Greek administration played a role in facilitating the Circassian Congress. After the congress, a delegation of Circassians visited Leon Tourian, the Armenian Archbishop of Smyrna, and proclaimed their participation in the Asia Minor Defence Organisation. The same delegation also approached Chrysostomos, the Greek Orthodox metropolitan.[117] This suggests that in April 1922 an important group of Circassian elites had the same interests as Greek administration, and their political aspirations intertwined with those of Ottoman Greeks and Armenians.

The local population in Aydın Province was not merely composed of so-called active collaborators and resisters. Despite the fact that a large bulk of people in the province were neutral, high-ranking Ottoman officials and other civil servants, who retained their posts under the Greek administration, even in Smyrna, were co-opted by this new administration. Many of them felt that they could function within the new political framework and that their compromise with the High Commission could guarantee the security of the Muslim population in the Greek occupation zone. Thus, regardless of the ethnicity of the individuals, the struggle for survival and opportunism were typical responses of the Ottoman high-ranking public officials to the new realities brought by the establishment of the High Commission. In other words, these civil servants adopted a wait-and-see policy, neither encouraging nor discouraging any resistance in the region. However, their choices put them at odds with the nationalist movement in Ankara. High-ranking officials, particularly governors-general and district governors who maintained close links to the imperial government in Constantinople, were regarded as unreliable by the leaders of the nationalist movement, whose connections with the regional organisations and resistance methods will be examined in the next chapter.

As stated in the previous chapter, the Greek administration did not gain legal status until the Treaty of Sèvres in the summer of 1920, despite the existence of the High Commission. It was decided in the Treaty of Sèvres that the Smyrna territory would be left under Ottoman sovereignty, yet the exercise of sovereignty rights would be given into the hands of the Greek Kingdom (Articles 69 and 70). After the interval of a five-year period, the local parliament that would be set up in Smyrna would be able to make an appeal to the Council of the League of Nations about the final status of the territory (Article 83). The provincial officials covered in this chapter

Ethnic Cleansing in Western Anatolia

continued their duties after the summer of 1920, thinking that under the Greek occupation, inhabitants of diverse ethnic religious identities would keep living together while two distinct nationalist movements (Greek and Turkish) faced off in the region. The principal characteristics of these administrators was that they formed a group that tried to keep aloof from the nationalist policies of the Ankara government and restore peace in the region based on common citizenship and tolerance towards various ethnic elements.

Among the Muslim administrators and civil servants of Aydın Province, power-sharing and collaboration transcended ethnic divisions. It encompassed Turks along with Cretans, Bosniaks, Pomaks, Kurds and Albanians. These people had divided and multiple loyalties at the same time, towards the sultan and the imperial government in Constantinople on the one hand, and towards the administrators of the Hellenic Kingdom in Western Anatolia on the other. This was because they could not simply ignore the authority of the sultan in Constantinople by relying on the patronage of the High Commission and military authorities. After all, their legitimate jurisdiction depended on relations with the imperial government in Constantinople, and the administrative and political power granted by the sultan. However, they did not have sufficient power to challenge the military authority of the nationalists in Ankara.

Notes

1. Rahmi Apak, *İstiklal Savaşında Garp Cephesi Nasıl Kuruldu* (Ankara: Türk Tarih Kurumu, 1990), 16.
2. See Gingeras, *Sorrowful Shores*, 83–6; and Doumanis, *Before the Nation*, 164.
3. Typical examples of these kinds of studies are İlhami Soysal, *Kurtuluş Savaşında İşbirlikçiler* (Istanbul: Bengi, 2008); and Türkan Çetin, 'Kurtuluş Savaşı Yıllarında İşgal Bölgesi Köy ve Köylüsü', *Çağdaş Türkiye Tarihi Araştırmaları Dergisi* 1, no. 3 (1993), 175–90.
4. Sia Anagnostopoulou, *Mikra Asia 19os ai.–1919 Oi Ellēnorthodoxes koinotēs: Apo to Millet tōn Rōmiōn sto Ellēniko Ethnos* (Athens: Hellinika Grammata, 1997), 11–14.
5. Ali Çetinkaya, *Milli Mücadele Dönemi Hatıraları* (Ankara: Atatürk Araştırma Merkezi, 1993), 11.
6. Bayar, *Ben de Yazdım*, vol. 6, 1907–9.
7. Apak, *İstiklal Savaşında*, 57.
8. Ahmet İzzet Bey was born in Istanbul in 1871. After graduating from Üsküdar Rüşdiyyesi, a secondary school in the Asiatic side of Bosporus, and from a foreign language school that he attended for two years, he served for

Officials under the Greek Administration

twenty-four years in the Translation Bureau of the Sublime Porte (Babıâli Tercüme Odası), where he had started working in 1885. Appointed as the manager of an office in the Ministry of Foreign Affairs in 1909, Ahmet İzzet later served in the Ottoman embassy in Athens. Following these posts, he was appointed governor-general of Van Province between 1912 and 1913, cf. BOA DH. SAİDd 71/119.

9. BOA DH. İ-UM. EK 66/12.

10. BOA DH. İ-UM. EK 51/98. This report in French is dated 16 August 1919. The underlying reason for the existence of this report was to present a testimony to the Inter-Allied Commission of Inquiry, which was sent to the region to check the veracity of the killings perpetrated by the Greek army after the occupation of Smyrna. İzzet presented this report to the commission on 25 August 1919.

11. Although it is alleged that İzzet was the younger brother of Kürd Sait Pasha, it is very difficult to find any definite information about this claim. Kürd Sait Pasha served as the Foreign Minister of the Empire between 1881 and 1882 during the reign of Abdülhamit II, and worked closely with Konstantinos Mousouros Pasha, the London ambassador of the Empire. During this period, Ahmet İzzet had just turned ten years old, BOA HSD. AFT 13/183. According to a document dated late October 1883, Kürd Sait Pasha was appointed as the second commissioner (*ikinci komiser*) to Aleppo, Kurdistan and Anatolia with the rank of *beylerbeyi* and was requested to follow the articles published in foreign newspapers about Midhat Pasha, a leading statesman of the late Tanzimat period who had been imprisoned in the fortress of Taif in Hejaz since 1881, BOA Y. PRK. BŞK 8/9. Despite the contraction of the non-Turkish individuals in number in the Ottoman elite, the cadres continued to remain multi-ethnic though mostly composed of the Muslim individuals. When the Ottoman Empire was collapsing, most of the Kurdish elite continued to support the sultan. Although a group of local tribal leaders supported the nationalist movement in Ankara, many Kurds who had served in the imperial capital remained attached to the Ottoman identity and loyal to the sultan–caliph, see Kemal Kirişçi, 'Minority/Majority Discourse: The Case of the Kurds in Turkey', in *Making Majorities: Constituting the Nation in Japan, Korea, China, Malaysia, Fiji, Turkey, and the United States*, ed. Dru C. Gladney (Stanford: Stanford University Press, 1998), 236. According to the memoirs of Ali Çetinkaya, Ahmet İzzet or Kambur İzzet was the son of Kürd (Kurdish) Sait Pasha, former Ottoman foreign minister, see Ali Çetinkaya, *Milli Mücadele*, 6. This information contradicts other narratives arguing that İzzet was a brother of Kürd Sait Pasha. Ali Fuat Türkgeldi states in his memoirs that İzzet was the brother-in-law of Kürd Mustafa Pasha, who presided over the Istanbul Court Martial of 1919–20, set up to judge the highest cadres of the Ottoman officials, mainly Unionists who had been involved in subversion of the constitution, war profiteering and ethnic cleansing, cf. Türkgeldi, *Görüp İşittiklerim*, 165.

Ethnic Cleansing in Western Anatolia

12. Türkgeldi, *Görüp İşittiklerim*, 164–5.
13. Erik Jan Zürcher, *Turkey: A Modern History* (London: I. B. Tauris, 2004), 134–7.
14. BOA BEO 4559/341861.
15. Serap Tabak, 'İzmir Şehrinde Mülki İdare ve İdareciler (1867–1950)', unpublished PhD thesis, Ege Üniversitesi, 1997, 108–12.
16. Bayar, *Ben de Yazdım*, vol. 5, 1642–3. Mehmed Şerif Pasha, the son of Sait Pasha, was born in 1865 in Constantinople, and graduated from the Lycée Impérial de Galatasaray (Mekteb-i Sultani). While serving as the Ottoman ambassador to Stockholm, he joined the Unionist opposition. After the restoration of the constitution in 1908, he was appointed as the CUP chief for the Pangaltı quarter. He was the leader of the Kurdish delegation sent by the Society for the Advancement of Kurdistan (Kürdistan Teâlî Cemiyeti) at the Paris Peace Conference, see Hakan Özoğlu, *Kurdish Notables and the Ottoman State: Evolving Identities, Competing Loyalties, and Shifting Boundaries* (New York: State University of New York Press, 2004), 112.
17. Ali Çetinkaya, *Milli Mücadele*, 7. Ali Nâdir Pasha was also depicted as a dark figure in the memoirs of Unionist officers, written in the early republican period. In his memoirs, Rahmi Apak talks of Ali Nâdir as the general 'who not only failed to prepare the means of defence at the time of the Greek army's landing at Smyrna, but also failed to fulfil his military and national duty (*askerlik ve vatan vazîfesini*) by facilitating this landing', Apak, *İstiklal Savaşında*, 4. Ali Nâdir Pasha tried to keep his cautious stance during the Greek landing since Admiral Calthorpe stressed that all Ottoman troops should remain in their barracks and await the instructions of the Occupation Army Commander. In vain, Ali Nâdir pleaded to Constantinople for instructions. His three telegrams remained unanswered on the day before the occupation, cf. *Rapports officiels reçus des autorités militaires Ottomanes sur l'occupation de Smyrne par les troupes Helleniques* (Constantinople: Imprimerie Osmanié, 1919), 2–5. In a telegram that he wrote to the Ministry of War in Constantinople on that day, he stated that he used all means in his power to avoid unnecessary bloodshed when the Greek soldiers entered the military barracks: 'The rate of the firing increased, which showed that its purpose was treacherous. I feel certain that the intention was to provoke our men and destroy their self-control. I thought that the best way of avoiding this was to make every endeavour to put an end to the firing. A large white flag was put on a pole and we left the gates.' For details about this telegram, see TNA FO 608/104, 20 May 1919, Ali Nadir to the Ministry of War.
18. Ali Çetinkaya, *Milli Mücadele*, 7.
19. BOA DH. İ-UM. EK 66/12.
20. BOA DH. İ-UM. EK 51/98.
21. BOA DH. İ-UM. EK 66/12. In the French report, İzzet Bey had almost the same conversation with slight differences.

Officials under the Greek Administration

22. Llewellyn Smith, *Ionian Vision*, 86. Venizelos had sent Makrakis, a Cretan politician, to win the Muslim Cretans to the prospective Greek administration in Western Anatolia.
23. BOA DH. İ-UM. EK 51/98.
24. Ibid.
25. For example, the residences in Bogiatzidika (Boyacidika) Street, where the Orthodox nuns lived, were occupied together with its furniture and goods in order to accommodate the Greek infantrymen in October 1919, cf. GAK. YAS., no. 10852, 7 October 1919 (J. C. 24 September 1919), from the [Greek] Chief of Police to the High Commission.
26. Moralı, *Mütarekede İzmir Olayları*, 9.
27. Ibid. 26–7. In his memoirs, Ragıp Nurettin says that he invented this association to make their public declaration look more serious, before sending a telegram upon the news announcing that Smyrna would soon be occupied by the Greek army, see *Babamın Emanetleri: Ragıp Nurettin Eğe'nin Birinci Cihan Harbi Günlükleri ve Harbin Sonrası Hatıratı*, ed. Güneş N. Eğe-Akter (Istanbul: Dergâh Yayınları, 2006), 331–2.
28. Kazım Özalp, *Milli Mücadele, 1919–1922*, vol. I (Ankara: Türk Tarih Kurumu, 1988), 6–7.
29. BOA DH. İ-UM. EK 66/12. British documents also verify the taciturnity of the Ottoman central government, TNA FO 608/104, 15 May 1919, Ahmed İzzet to Calthorpe. Claiming that there was no special article in the Mudros Armistice referring to the occupation of Smyrna by Greek troops, Ahmet İzzet telegraphed the matter to Damat Ferit Pasha and asked for immediate instructions. However, he did not receive any sort of instructions from the Sublime Porte.
30. At that time, Liatis was the Greek consul-general in Smyrna, cf. Victoria Solomonidis, 'Greece in Asia Minor', 57. Although Solomonidis argues that İzzet Bey was not recognised by the Greek soldiers, it seems that the Greek troops wanted to humiliate the Ottoman administrators because of their incompetence on the landing day.
31. BOA DH. İ-UM. EK 66/12. In the French report, İzzet Bey adds into this narrative that he returned to the government office with Liatis, that his office was full of Greek soldiers and that the drawers of his table were broken and his items and documents had been taken away. On the contrary, according to the report written in Ottoman Turkish, İzzet Bey and his son were directly taken aboard the *Leon*, where they would spend the whole day under arrest, before being released in the evening. The memoirs of Süleyman Vasfi also confirmed the narrative of the governor-general. 'Bir Gümrükçünün İşgal Yılları Anıları', 239.
32. BOA DH. İ-UM. EK 66/12.
33. BOA DH. İ-UM. EK 51/98.
34. Ibid.
35. GAK. EDS., tel. no. 2530, 1 June 1919 (J. C. 19 May 1919), from Stergiades to Kanellopoulos.

Ethnic Cleansing in Western Anatolia

36. TNA FO 608/104, 17 May 1919, Proclamation of the Vali.
37. Sina Akşin, *Turkey: From Empire to Revolutionary Republic* (London: Hurst, 2007), 126–7.
38. 'L'Occupation de Smyrne', *Stamboul*, 17 May 1919.
39. Sina Akşin, *İstanbul Hükümetleri ve Milli Mücadele*, vol. 1 (Istanbul: Cem Yayınevi, 1976), 273.
40. The Greek and Armenian archbishops had begun to attend the meetings of the administrative council in the spring of 1919, see TNA FO 608/103, 7 April 1919, Ian M. Smith, Area Control Officer in Smyrna, to the British High Commission in Constantinople.
41. BOA DH. ŞFR 99/239.
42. BOA DH. ŞFR 630/128.
43. BOA DH. İ-UM. EK 52/31 and BOA DH. ŞFR 631/9.
44. TNA FO 608/91, 9 July 1919, Ahmed İzzet to James Morgan.
45. TNA FO 608/91, 21 July 1919, Ahmed İzzet to James Morgan.
46. TNA FO 608/91, 29 July 1919, Ahmed İzzet to James Morgan.
47. BOA DH. İ. UM. EK 55/90.
48. TNA FO 608/91, 31 August 1919, Ahmed İzzet to James Morgan.
49. MOFA 143 doc. no. 5567, 9 December 1919, from Katekhakis to First Military Corps in Smyrna.
50. BOA DH. İ-UM 7-4/1-50.
51. TNA FO 608/271, 14 December 1919, Ahmed İzzet to General Milne.
52. BOA DH. İ-UM. EK 52/47.
53. BOA DH. İ-UM. EK 56/39.
54. BOA DH. İ-UM. EK 51/104.
55. BOA DH. ŞFR 645/87.
56. TNA FO 608/86, 19 July 1919, E. Venizelos to G. Clemenceau, president of the Peace Conference in Paris.
57. BOA DH. İ-UM. EK 55/61. Without losing time, Arthur Balfour, the British foreign minister, sent Damat Ferit Pasha a telegram saying that a Commission of Inquiry would soon be convened to probe what happened in Smyrna. Due to the pressure of the Ottoman and Greek governments, the Supreme Council approved the participation of both Greek and Ottoman representatives in the commission; however, they did not have voting rights. On 20 August, the Commission of Inquiry declared to the Greek high commissioner in Constantinople that an Ottoman officer named Kadrî Bey, head of the Secondary Office in the General Staff (*Erkân-ı Harbiye-i Umûmiye'nin İkinci Şef Müdürü*), was to be permitted to follow the work of the commission under the same conditions and privileges as the Greek officer Alexandros Mazarakis. Time preconceptions of the inquiry were determined as 'from the date of occupation to the present moment', that is, 25 July 1919. After the conduct of inquiry, a report would be submitted to the Supreme Council, cf. Victoria Solomonidis, 'Greece in Asia Minor', 78.

Officials under the Greek Administration

58. BOA DH. ŞFR 102/83.
59. BOA DH. İ-UM. EK 55/98.
60. BOA DH. KMS 52-4/20.
61. BOA DH. İ-UM. EK 56/40.
62. BOA DH. İ-UM. EK 55/95.
63. BOA DH. İ-UM. EK 55/98.
64. BOA DH. İ-UM. EK 51/98.
65. BOA DH. ŞFR 645/111.
66. BOA DH. İ-UM. EK 56/34.
67. BOA DH. İ-UM. EK 57/3.
68. TNA FO 608/86, 7 October 1919, Exposé des faits survenus depuis l'occupation qui ont été établis au cours de l'enquête, entre le 12 aout et le 6 octobre 1919.
69. BOA BEO 4610/ 345684.
70. Özalp, *Milli Mücadele*, 7–9.
71. Apak, *İstiklal Savaşında*, 23.
72. TNA FO 286/702, 31 January 1919, Resolution of the City of Magnesia and of the Neighbouring Villages; Resolution of the Educational Institutions of the Community of Muradieh, 3 February 1919; and Resolution of the City of Kasamba, 3 February 1919. Another petition, which was demanding 'the just decision of the Entente Powers who have declared and promised liberty and justice', was sent to the representatives of the Allied Powers by the elders of the Orthodox community in Kula.
73. BOA DH. İ-UM. EK 51/101.
74. TNA FO 608/111, 17 May 1919, Report of a Control Officer in Magnesia to Admiral Webb. Although he was dismissed on 10 February due to the recommendation of an inspector from the Ministry of the Interior, Hüsnü returned to his office later. It seems that he successfully survived the first wave of the Unionist attack, cf. BOA DH. ŞFR 96/133.
75. BOA BEO 4463/334701 and 'Sadrazam Paşa'nın Avdeti', *İkdâm*, 2 May 1917 (R. 2 Mayıs 1333), 2.
76. Kolodny, Des musulmans dans une île grecque, 6–9.
77. Özalp, *Milli Mücadele*, 12–13. According to Bilge Umar, Hüsnü Bey objected to the possibility of armed resistance as this could trigger clashes between the local elements in the region and, having summoned Hüseyin Vâsıf (Çınar) and his friends in Manisa to his office, he asked them to leave the *sanjak* at once, Bilge Umar, *İzmir'de Yunanlıların Son Günleri* (Ankara: Bilgi Yayınevi, 1974), 66–7.
78. TNA ADM 137/1762, 4 June 1919, A. Stergiades to Commodore Fitzmaurice.
79. Kâmil Su, *Manisa ve Yöresinde İşgal Acıları* (Ankara: Kültür ve Turizm Bakanlığı Yayınları, 1982), 43.
80. See İbrahim Ethem Akıncı, *Demirci Akıncıları* (Ankara: Türk Tarih Kurumu, 2009).

Ethnic Cleansing in Western Anatolia

81. *Bekir Sâmî Günsav'ın Kurtuluş Savaşı Anıları*, ed. Muhittin Ünal (Istanbul: Cem Yayınevi, 2002), 32.

82. For the activities of Çerkes Ethem in Akhisar, see Bülent Bilmez, 'A Nationalist Discourse of Heroism and Treason: The Construction of an 'Official' Image of Çerkes Ethem (1886–1948) in Turkish Historiography and Recent Challenges', *in Untold Histories of the Middle East: Recovering Voices from the 19th and 20th Centuries*, ed. Amy Singer et al. (London: Routledge, 2011), 106–23.

83. GAK. EDS., no. 14419, 27 July 1920 (J. C. 14 July 1920).

84. Asaf Gökbel, *Milli Mücadele'de Aydın* (Aydın: Coşkun Matbaası, 1964), 98–9.

85. Aker, *İstiklâl Harbinde 57*, vol. 2, 10–11. In his memoirs, hoping that the local Muslims would resist against the advancing Greek troops, Şefik Bey mentioned that the gates of the arms depots in Aydın were deliberately left open starting from 22 May. However, nobody attempted to loot the depots.

86. Gökbel, *Milli Mücadele'de Aydın*, 100–3.

87. Grassi, *İtalya ve Türk Sorunu*, 61.

88. Aker, *İstiklâl Harbinde 57*, vol. 1, 61.

89. Gökbel, *Milli Mücadele'de Aydın*, 114–17.

90. Apak, *İstiklal Savaşında*, 78–9.

91. Born most likely in Constantinople, Abdurrahman Bey was related to the Bedirhan family of Kurdish origin. He was educated in Lycée Impérial de Galatasaray and the School of Civil Administration (Mekteb-i Mülkiye). After working in the Ministry of Education, Abdurrahman Bey resigned from office in 1898 and moved to Switzerland. While in Geneva, he took over from his brother Mikdad Midhat the publication of the first Kurdish–Turkish bilingual newspaper, *Kurdistan*. He got close to the Young Turk opposition, which was organised against the Hamidian regime in Europe in the first decade of the twentieth century and penned some articles in Turkish for their press organ, see Murat Issı, 'Kürt Basını ve *Kürdistan* Gazetesi (1898–1902)', *Şarkiyat* 9 (2013), 130. After a certain period of exile, which he spent in Tripolitania, Abdurrahman returned to Constantinople in December 1908 and played a remarkable role in the foundation of the Society for the Spread of Kurdish Education (Kürt Neşr-i Maarif Cemiyeti). He took office as the first principal of a school named Kürt Meşrutiyet Mektebi, which was opened through the facilities provided by this society. In fact, although Abdurrahman Bey was associated with the Young Turk opposition in a certain way, in 1908 he probably dissociated himself from the Unionists and, as an individual of the Kurdish elite, which was close to the Ottoman dynasty, undertook duties in several cadres of the Empire. He served as the district governor of Hudaydah in Yemen before being appointed to district governorship of Aydın in May 1919, cf. BOA BEO 4572/342879.

92. BOA HR. SYS 2709/15.

Officials under the Greek Administration

93. TNA FO 608/89, 31 May 1919, Calthorpe to Balfour.
94. TNA T 160/50, 10 July 1919, Lieutenant J. A. Lorimer to the Commodore Commanding, British Aegean Squadron.
95. Aker, *İstiklâl Harbinde 57*, vol. 2, 121–2.
96. TNA ADM 137/1762, 10 July 1919, Ben Hodder to Lieutenant J. A. Lorimer.
97. TNA T 160/50, 10 July 1919, J. A. Lorimer to the Commodore Commanding. In his memoirs, Şefik Bey claims that he dispatched the Ottoman Greeks in Aydın to the interior towns of Nazilli, Denizli and Burdur by train in order to prevent their possible support to the Greek troops in case of their return. See Aker, *İstiklâl Harbinde 57*, vol. 2, 131. For refugees to Smyrna, see TNA ADM 137/1762, 10 July 1919, Ben Hodder to Lieutenant J. A. Lorimer.
98. TNA T 160/50, 4 July 1919, Hodder to Admiral Calthorpe.
99. Gökbel, *Milli Mücadele'de Aydın*, 237–9.
100. When Abdurrahman Bey was released, he informed the Ministry of the Interior that he awaited confirmation to return to his former office or to be appointed as a district governor for another administrative unit in the Aydın *sanjak*. In his dispatch dated 1 September, he stated that even though it was decided that he would be executed by shooting, he was released through the efforts of the Allied representatives in Smyrna, cf. BOA DH. KMS 52-4/29. Nonetheless, ten days before this dispatch, İzzet Bey had proposed to the ministry that Ahmet Şükrü Bey, who formerly occupied an important position in the provincial administration as *vilâyet mektupçusu* (chief secretary of the province), be appointed as the district governor of Aydın instead of Abdurrahman, as the latter 'never wanted to go back', cf. BOA. DH. ŞFR. 642/115. As this recommendation was rejected by the ministry, the office of the district governor remained vacant until early October 1919 when İzzet requested once again an appointment to this office, see BOA DH. ŞFR 648/33. Actually, the General Law of Provincial Administration of March 1913 authorised governors-general to nominate their staff for administrative positions and recommend the ministry on appointments, see Findley, *Bureucratic Reform*, 312–13.
101. TNA FO 680/89, 7 July 1919, Report written by Stolzenberg.
102. BOA DH. İ-UM. EK 54/29.
103. BOA DH. ŞFR 102/42.
104. BOA DH. KMS 54-3/25.
105. TNA FO 608/111, 30 September 1919, Blair Fish, a member of the British mission in Constantinople on the relief and repatriation in Aydın Province.
106. TNA FO 608/89, 7 July 1919, Report written by Stolzenberg.
107. GAK. EDS, tel. no. 12087, 20 October 1919 (J. C. 7 October 1919).
108. BOA DH. KMS 52-4/40.
109. BOA BEO 4598/344840.
110. 'Havâdis-i Vilâyet', *Âhenk*, 22 October 1920 (R. 22 Teşrîn-i Evvel 1336).

111. GAK. EDS., tel. no. 1795, 22 September 1921 (J. C. 9 September 1921), from Vakalopoulos to Stergiades.
112. GAK. EDS., tel. no. 2066, 1 September 1922 (J. C. 19 August 1922), from Vakalopoulos to Stergiades.
113. Tunaya, *Türkiye'de Siyasal Partiler*, vol. 1 (Istanbul: Hürriyet Vakfı Yayınları, 1984), 207.
114. İbrahim Hakkı and his supporters left Izmit at the end of June 1921 when the National Forces attacked the town.
115. Gingeras, *Sorrowful Shores*, 126.
116. Ibid. 132.
117. 'Vilâyet Haberleri', *Islahât*, 11 April 1922 (R. 11 Nisan 1338).

Chapter 5

Millî Hareket: The Formation of a National Resistance

In late May 1919, Dramalı Mahmut Bey, a Turkish nationalist and the director of the Tobacco Monopoly (Régie des Tabacs) in the southern Marmara city of Balıkesir, went to the government office in a hurry and reported that 'the Greek troops have just set foot in Smyrna.' Upon hearing this news, İbrahim Ethem Bey, who had worked as the administrative head of different sub-districts (*nahiye müdürü*), scampered to the government office to get this news verified. After Hurşit Bey, the commander of Gendarmerie, confirmed this news, İbrahim Ethem returned to his office. According to Ethem's memoirs, a great silence covered the room as he was explaining the course of events to Dramalı Mahmut and his close friend Süleyman Sadi Bey. While doing so, an Armenian priest passed by their office. Mahmut instantly took his gun out and said, 'Let's begin; for these are the ones who brought the Greeks here (*Yunanı buraya getiren*), those local infidels (*yerli gâvurlardır*).'[1] The others calmed him down with great difficulty as he rose to shoot the Armenian priest.

This recollection was one of the examples of how the nationalist Ottoman bureaucrats and military officers, who had a particular Unionist orientation, regarded the presence of non-Muslim Ottoman citizens in Western Anatolia immediately after the Greek landing at Smyrna. The hatred towards Ottoman Christians, who were regarded as the agents of the Greek occupation, had intensified among the Unionist civil and military officers in the unoccupied parts of the province. In turn, intercommunal relations, especially in rural areas, would be gradually affected by the nationalist agitation in the course of time.

Since local Muslim notables (*eşrâf*) had given limited support for Turkish nationalism and the bourgeoisie in the large urban centres essentially consisted of Ottoman Christians, the nationalist ideology was backed primarily by Muslim professionals. This would include a

Ethnic Cleansing in Western Anatolia

significant portion of military officers and low-level civil servants, as well as a limited number of the local notables in the province.

Following the defeat of World War I, the Unionist officers who did not comply with the instructions from the imperial government in Constantinople would try to re-organise the remnants of the demobilised Ottoman armies and local Muslim bands into small-scale resistance groups under the banner of National Forces (Kuvâ-yı Milliye), and set up fronts against the Greek armies.[2] This formation would later establish direct contact with the Turkish nationalist movement centred in Ankara and turn into the regional bastions of the nationalist movement in due course. Meanwhile, owing to its alliance with the Unionist officers in Aydın Province, a consistent hostility, directed against the Ottoman Christian populations, would arise among the members of the nationalist movement. In his speeches at the National Assembly in Ankara, Mustafa Kemal would claim that the movement was struggling for Ottoman Muslims' self-determination rights and 'against the unjust claims of Armenians and Greeks and their European supporters'.[3]

In order to comprehend the ideological conceptualisations of the National Forces, the word *millî* is likely to be the most convenient starting point. At first sight, the term *millî* appears to be identical with the Western concept of 'the national'. Nonetheless, this term brought its own restrictions originating from the recent past of the Empire. The Balkan Wars and World War I had already signalled the rise of nationalist tendencies among the prominent cadres of the CUP. Through the acknowledgement of the Greek and Armenian 'betrayal' as a solid fact during the dissolution of the Empire, Islam gained serious significance for the identification of national allegiance in the Ottoman political life. The Armenian revolts on the eastern front, the Greek occupation and the reaction of the Allies to these developments made the role of Islam crucial as an identifier of the state. The word *millî* did not underline any ethnic identity but had an inclusive character for all Muslim ethnic elements of the Empire. The eclectic structure of the nationalist movement can be explained, to some extent, by the dual nature of the word *millî*.

Accordingly, the nationalist discourse conveyed to Islam a descriptive function. The concepts used throughout the war years, such as *Mîsâk-ı Millî* (the National Pact), *ittihâd-ı millî* (national union) and *hâkimiyet-i milliye* (national sovereignty), were carefully chosen to emphasise the Islamic roots of the nationalist movement. *Mîsâk-ı Millî*, a decision made by the last Ottoman parliament convened in mid-January 1920 with no Christian deputies for the first time of its history, constituted the ground of the nationalist movement. This pact called for the protection of the

Formation of a National Resistance

Ottoman sultan–caliph and defined the acceptable borders for the Empire, the territories inhabited by an Ottoman Muslim majority within the lines of the Armistice of Mudros. Moreover, the concept of the *ittihâd-ı millî*, excluding the Ottoman Greeks and Armenians, represented the alliance of the Muslim constituents of the Empire. In a nutshell, Islam was considered to be a dominating peculiarity of the Ottoman population after the Balkan Wars, thus confined the imperial territories as a land belonging to the Ottoman Muslims.

Later, the nationalist movement in Ankara held an accommodationist attitude towards Islam as its leaders realised that the Sunni interpretation of Islam functioned as the sole bond that managed to unite the mixed populations of various Muslim ethnicities living in Western Anatolia, namely the Turks, Kurds, Caucasian migrants, Bosniaks and other Balkan Muslims. Mustafa Kemal, leader of the movement, preferred to employ the term *Türkiye milleti* (Nation of Turkey) instead of Turks during the discussions in the Ankara assembly. Although non-Turkish Muslims, such as Kurds, were included within this definition, non-Muslims, such as Greeks and Armenians, were rejected.[4]

Examples of the instrumentalisation of Islam by prominent members of the nationalist movement include: Mustafa Kemal addressing the public with religious themes emphasising *ittihâd-ı millî*, the declared intention to rescue the sultan–caliph from being the so-called prisoner of the enemy in Constantinople, and the arrangements to block non-Muslim participation in the political life.[5] At the same time, Islamic rhetoric also proved to be useful in the neutralisation of the propaganda agitated by the imperial government and the British intelligence in Constantinople.

Inasmuch as Kâzım Karabekir, the most powerful Ottoman pasha recognising the authority of the nationalist movement, had to deal with Armenian troops on the eastern borders of the Empire, the nationalist movement had to rely on regional bands for fighting against the Greek advance in the west.[6] Thus, the Greek occupation of Smyrna provided new opportunities for the bandits in the inner part of the province. These bands, which emerged as paramilitary groups in the occupation zone, embraced the methods of guerrilla warfare. The mountain ranges of the region facilitated fast strikes and easy escapes from Greek military action and provided safe havens for these paramilitary groups.

Nonetheless, relations between the nationalist movement and the paramilitary leaders became tense because of the centralisation attempts of the movement in the winter of 1920–21. The leaders of certain regional bandit groups preferred not to recognise the authority of the nationalist movement, especially after October 1920 when the National Assembly

Ethnic Cleansing in Western Anatolia

called for the creation of a regular army which would be directly controlled by the nationalist government. At the top of this conflict were the rivalling visions of the Turkish nationalist movement, supporters of the *Megali Idea*, and the ambitions of Italian imperialism. Each of these actors, somehow, established ties with militias, who had a key role in the stage of armed clashes, expulsions and mass killings in the region, in order to increase their power, thus cementing their place in Western Anatolia.

This chapter, which opens with an account of the formation of attempts of resistance in the province, focuses especially on the activities of prominent ex-Unionists. It then continues with an elaborate analysis of the National Forces and its methods of resistance on the western front. Instead of providing a virtually endless list of brutalities, exterminations and mass killings, this chapter aims to describe the motives of the various parties that participated in the Greco-Turkish War. It finally deals with the formation of the nationalist regular army under the authority of the Ankara assembly. The influence of this army over the power politics in the region, including the local militias who constituted the backbone of the National Forces, is also covered in this chapter.

Regional Networks of the Resistance

THE IZMIR ASSOCIATION FOR THE DEFENCE OF OTTOMAN RIGHTS

Although the Unionist triumvirate of Enver, Cemal and Talât Pashas left the capital after the signature of the Mudros Armistice, its cadres could still exert considerable influence in the Ottoman army, police and provincial administration.[7] Nureddin Pasha, who was commander of the 21st Corps in Aydın, was appointed governor-general of Aydın Province on 20 January 1919. Enjoying his authority over both civilian and military officers, he would play a pivotal role in the creation of an anti-Greek atmosphere in the province before the Greek landing. His short term, which ended in March of the same year, would deeply affect intercommunal relations in the province. No sooner had he come into office than he established ties with the members of the Izmir Association for the Defence of Ottoman Rights (IADOR – İzmir Müdafaa-i Hukuk-u Osmaniye Cemiyeti), founded by a group of influential Muslim notables led by two brothers, Moralızâde Halit Bey and Moralızâde Nâil Bey.[8] The other founders of this association were Menemenlizâde Muvaffak, a financial inspector (*mâliye müfettişi*), and Nâcî Bey, vice-president of the National Credit Bank (İtibâr-ı Millî Bankası). Apart from those merchants and professionals, a group of

Formation of a National Resistance

retired majors directed by Hüseyin Lûtfî and Abdurrahman Sâmî, who were most likely supported by the Fraternal Society for Reserve Officers (İhtiyât Zâbitleri Teâvün Cemiyeti), participated in the formation of the association.[9] The official objective of the IADOR was to defend Muslim interests, but it also planned to organise armed resistance in in the event of a Greek landing. This association established connections with prominent Unionists,[10] such as Celâl and Kâzım Fikrî, in the province and availed itself of the certain networks of the Unionists in the city. In the spring months of 1919, these Unionist figures had already established ties with the Muslim merchants, who feared the possible occupation of Smyrna by the Greek armies. Eczacıbaşı Süleyman Ferît, a close friend of Celâl and the member of the Renovation Party, and Doctor Hacıhasanzâde Ethem were examples of these Muslim merchants and professionals. Moralızâde Nâil recounted in his memoirs how the association came into close contact with the former Unionists in the province:

> It is a duty to record that the Izmir Association for the Defence of Ottoman Rights immensely benefited from the organisation of Union and Progress. We never forget our appreciation of and gratitude to Mahmut Celaleddin Bey, the former responsible secretary of Union and Progress in Smyrna and director of the Renovation Party in Smyrna at that time, because of his support and secret guidance.[11]

In fact, the Renovation Party was nothing other than the revival of the CUP with a new name. The centre of the party was said to be the former Union and Progress Club in Beyler Sokağı (Beyler Street). Its responsible secretary was again Mahmut Celâl Bey, the former secretary of the CUP. The other three members were again members of the Union and Progress Party. These were Giritli (Cretan) Râşit Bey, a tradesman; Sırrı Efendi, the former mufti of Foça; and Eczacıbaşı Ferît Bey.

Despite the fact that Nureddin was forced to leave the governorship in March 1919, the Unionists remained in their dominant position in the association. A British intelligence officer mentioned the Unionist control in the decision-making mechanisms of the association and the nationalist orientation of the association:

> The position of the organisation known as the Tedafai [sic] Hukuk Osmanieh (Defence of Ottoman Rights) is not at present clear. It contains many Turks who are moderate and well disposed but who joined it as having a definite programme to uphold and explain Turkish rights against the claims to the Aidin vilayet put forward by the Greeks. At the same time it contains Unionists and it is believed that they control the organisation and have provided it with funds.[12]

199

Ethnic Cleansing in Western Anatolia

In spite of their strong presence in the association, the Unionists preferred employing influential Muslim merchants, professionals and clergymen in the administrative posts of the association. The first reason behind this choice was that a certain Unionist connection might have become a handicap when pleading with the representatives of the victorious Allied Powers. Therefore, the figureheads of the association were elected among the provincial notables, merchants and professionals, as in the cases of Mustafa Necâtî, a nationalist lawyer and an active member of Turkish Hearth's Smyrna branch; Ragıp Nurettin, another member of the Turkish Hearth, who was influenced by the ideas of Yusuf Akçura and Narodnik nationalism; and Moralızâde Halit, a well-known Muslim merchant.[13]

The second reason was that the association had to follow a careful policy, especially in regard to the Ottoman statesmen who had played a significant role in the Armenian massacres. Hikmet Bey, one of the legal consultants (*hukuk müşâviri*) of the Ministry of the Interior in the province, warned Moralızâde Nâil that Şükrü (Kaya) Bey,[14] former president of the General Directorate for Refugees (Muhâcirîn Müdüriyet-i Umûmiyesi), had wired telegrams to the Ottoman governors-general about the maintenance of the deportations on behalf of the Ministry. Therefore, Şükrü Bey's arrest was expected. Accordingly, Hikmet argued that the figures whose names were mentioned among the wartime massacres, such as Şükrü, should be kept away from the association in order not to provoke the reactions of the Allied representatives.

In March 1919, 165 nationalist personalities from the neighbouring districts were invited to the congress in Smyrna organised by the IADOR. Held with the support of Nureddin Pasha, the prominent political figures from all the *sanjak*s of the province, as well as from the Karesi *sanjak* and the Menteşe *sanjak*, were in attendance. Some Turkish newspapers, supported by the Unionists, attempted to imbue nationalist sentiments among the Muslim population, generating rumours of the probable Greek annexation of the Smyrna *sanjak*. Similar to Greek intellectuals, Muslim journalists and intellectuals also launched propaganda campaigns and resorted to maps, schemes, charts and photographs to prove 'the Turkish character' of the Smyrna *sanjak*.[15]

The Unionist-dominated regional nationalist organisations, spearheaded by the IADOR members, tried to mobilise public support for the possible conflict with the Greek troops. The Rejection of Annexation Association (Redd-i İlhâk Cemiyeti) was invented as a pseudo organisation by members of the IADOR on the eve of the occupation. Thus, there was an organic connection and personnel overlap between these two associations.[16] This so-called association, which was an extension of the local branch of the

Formation of a National Resistance

Turkish Hearth, established close ties with prominent Unionists in the province. On the brink of the occupation, its members sent telegraphs to the administrative centres of the neighbouring districts and military headquarters to attract the attention of nationalist officers and mobilise the public. They also resolved to arm a group of Muslim students, unemployed people and vagrants to resist the Greek troops in downtown Smyrna.[17]

As shown in the previous chapter, the members of the IADOR, who had established an alliance with the other Unionist organisations in the province, headed the protests organised at the Jewish cemetery on the hills of Bahri Baba on the eve of the Greek landing on 15 May 1919.[18] The urban masses, which were agitated by the manifesto penned by the leaders of the association and circulated by members of the Fraternal Society for Reserve Officers and students of the Imperial School (İzmir Sultânî Mektebi),[19] started to gather in Bahri Baba in order to protest against the landing. These demonstrations turned into the looting of the ammunition stores close to the Ottoman barracks. The protestors broke into the prisons and released all the inmates. The pillage of ammunition stores that night and in the morning of the following day in the lower neighbourhoods, the seizure of guns by civilians and the release of the prisoners were the most significant reasons for the breakout of intercommunal violence after the landing.

On the day of the occupation, the members of the IADOR sent telegrams to the Unionist circles in the Ottoman capital. The violence that took place during the landing prompted reactions from nationalist intellectuals and students in the capital. A series of indignant mass rallies were organised by the Society for National Instruction and Education (Millî Talîm ve Terbiye Cemiyeti)[20] and by Karakol, both of which were Unionist organisations active in Constantinople. The first protests occurred at the Imperial University, known as Dârülfünûn-ı Şâhâne, on 18 May. A group of academics, including the president of the university, delivered speeches. The following day, a large crowd held a meeting in front of the Fatih Municipality. A large number of Muslim women were also present and carried on their breast a little shield with the words 'Izmir is in our hearts'.[21] The most crowded meeting was convened in Sultanahmet Square on 23 May. The protesters that gathered in front of the Blue Mosque, whose minarets had been draped in black as a sign of mourning due to the occupation of Smyrna, listened to the sentimental speech delivered by the nationalist author Halide Edip, who had been privately educated before being sent to the American College in Üsküdar. Despite the fact that the organising kernel of these meetings was composed of Unionists, many Turkish nationalists of different views joined the protests in the Ottoman capital. The mass mobilisation of the nationalist middle class,

Ethnic Cleansing in Western Anatolia

including women, by the Unionist-originated intellectuals against the Greek presence in Smyrna was achieved through these meetings held in Constantinople, especially those in public squares.

Following the occupation of Smyrna, the association lost its influence in the city since the Greek authorities did not tolerate open Unionist propaganda in their occupation zone. A significant number of its members had already fled to Constantinople while a small section of them joined the nationalist movement in the interior of the province.[22] Some of its members began to play an important role in arms trafficking from Constantinople to Ankara organised by the Unionist underground organisations, such as Karakol.[23] Because of the Allied control of Constantinople, the members who had settled there followed a more careful policy.

In December 1919, Câmi (Baykut) Bey, secretary-general of the association and Unionist ex-censor official, sent a dispatch to the Representative Board for the Defence of Rights in Anatolia and Rumelia (Anadolu ve Rumeli Müdâfaa-i Hukuk Heyet-i Temsiliyesi), the kernel of the nationalist movement in Ankara, mentioning the risk of the possible annexation of Smyrna by Greece.[24] This was the first official attempt of the association to establish contact with the nationalists in Ankara, which started to emerge as the main centre of the nationalist movement. Following the occupation of Constantinople in March 1920, most of its members moved to Ankara, while Moralızâde Nâil went to Rhodes and started working for the Italian intelligence.[25]

REGIONAL CONGRESSES

On the grounds that the organisation of a resistance movement was almost impossible within the Greek occupation zone, along with very limited influence from the IADOR, the Unionist officers struggled to form a fortified nationalist force along the towns bordering the occupation zone. It could easily be noticed, by having a close look at a series of congress meetings in the summer of 1919 in which the notables (*eşrâf*) of provincial towns participated, that almost all the leaders of these congresses had Unionist origins: Hacim Muhittin in Balıkesir, Mustafa Talât Efendi and Ahmet Hulûsî Efendi in Nazilli, and the same Hacim Muhittin and Paşazâde İbrahim (Tahtakılıç) Bey in Alaşehir, to name but a few. In these congresses, the creation of the National Forces (Kuvâ-yı Milliye), a militia organisation in which all Muslim band leaders were invited to participate, was discussed.[26]

As a result of the rumours that some civilian and military officers were inciting Turkish nationalist sentiments in Western Anatolia, the

Formation of a National Resistance

imperial government banned the organisation of any meetings in the provinces. Thus, the Ministry of the Interior instructed the Karesi district governorship on 28 July not to allow a Unionist-dominated convention in Balıkesir. This document stated that the people who were willing to arrange this congress were previously convicted criminals and their efforts to convene regional representatives endangered the security of the district. The Ministry asserted that these kinds of activities paved the way for the Greek occupation. Therefore, this congress had to be prevented in order to avoid these risks.[27]

With the efforts of Hacim Muhittin Bey, the former district governor (*mutasarrıf*) of Karesi and an ardent supporter of the nationalist organisation Karakol,[28] a congress was assembled in Balıkesir between 26 and 30 July 1919. From its opening, the Balıkesir Congress, whose participants included the Muslim notables and military bureaucratic elites of the Karesi *sanjak* and the northern *sanjak*s of Aydın Province, was controlled by the Unionist representatives. Nonetheless, the Unionist leadership adopted an open policy towards the non-Unionist nationalist Muslim local notables, who gathered with the intention of conducting a resistance movement vis-à-vis the Greek army. This inclusive character of the congress would be decisive for both the subsequent congresses and the nationalist movement itself. At the end of this congress, the Rejection of Annexation Committee of the National Movement (Hareket-i Milliye Redd-i İlhâk Heyeti) was founded under the presidency of Hacim Muhittin. In order to 'save the country from the enemies (*istihlâs-ı vatan*)', war mobilisation was declared in the Karesi *sanjak* and conscription of all Muslim men between twenty-four and thirty-four was decided.[29]

In the first week of August, another congress, presided by Mustafa Talât Efendi, *kaymakam* of Karacasu, was convened in Nazilli, at the southern edge of the province, in order to form the National Forces units. Representatives from the southern *sanjak*s of the province, that is, Aydın and Denizli, as well as the neighbouring Menteşe *sanjak*, attended this congress with the encouragement of Ahmet Hulûsî Efendi, Unionist mufti of Denizli.[30] At the end of the congress, they declared that the National Committee (Heyet-i Milliye) would be responsible for the recruitment of the local militia for the National Forces, restoration of security and tax collection. The places where the representatives came from prove that the sphere of influence of the conference was limited with the sparsely populated south-eastern corner of Aydın Province.

Due to the fact that these two congresses remained local meetings, the Unionists prepared to arrange a major congress, representing all of the unoccupied areas in Aydın Province and the neighbouring Karesi, Kütahya and

Ethnic Cleansing in Western Anatolia

Afyon Karahisar-ı Sahip *sanjak*s. In spite of the incessant objections of the Ministry of the Interior,[31] the Alaşehir Congress, again chaired by Hacim Muhittin Bey, commenced on 16 August 1919. Delegates from various towns in Western Anatolia participated in this congress. However, similar to the previous congress, the most significant drawback was that there was no participation from two southern *sanjak*s of Aydın Province, that is, the Aydın and Denizli *sanjak*s. In the first sessions, Hacim Muhittin, the president of the congress, propounded that it was deemed necessary to devise a special invitation for the prospective representatives of these *sanjak*s and he dispatched it via Bahri Bey, former mayor and representative of Manisa. After the arrival of the representatives from the Aydın and Denizli *sanjak*s on 21 August, the political programme of the Congress of Balıkesir, which recommended the unification of all the nationalist militias under the roof of the National Forces, was reconfirmed in the sessions of the congress. Once again, in the programme of the congress, the so-called Turkish and Muslim characteristic of Aydın Province was underlined in the last session, on 25 August. It was also decided that the Greek atrocities in Smyrna and the rest of the occupied zone be condemned.[32]

Despite the fact that the representatives reconfirmed in this series of congresses that they did not challenge the authority of the sultan and the government in Constantinople, they enjoyed a high degree of autonomy within their jurisdiction. The political bodies, which were constituted after these congresses, declared themselves responsible for the vital duties of tax-collection, recruitment to the National Forces, and the enforcement of law and order. They, however, referred to themselves with different names, such as the Central Committee (Heyet-i Merkeziye) as in the cases of the Balıkesir and Alaşehir congresses, and the National Committee (Heyet-i Milliye) in that of the Nazilli Congress.

Although the previous policies of the CUP were harshly criticised by the representatives at these congresses, most of the representatives were, in fact, either Unionists or CUP sympathisers. At the beginning, the Unionists deliberately followed a pluralist policy towards local Muslim notables of different ethnic origin so as to get their support. It would be an overstated argument to assert that all the representatives taking part in these congresses had Unionist tendencies favouring an armed resistance movement against the Allied Powers. To exemplify this, Mütevellizâde Tevfîk Bey, the most powerful figure of the notables in Alaşehir and the representative of the same town, was a supporter of the idea of the foundation of an American mandate for all territories of the Ottoman Empire.[33] Nonetheless, at the same time, he defended the formation of the National Forces against the threat of a potential Greek military advance within the province.

Formation of a National Resistance

British intelligence was of the opinion that the Society for Wilsonian Principles (Wilson Prensipleri Cemiyeti) was 'inspired by the CUP'. This society, which had members among the well-educated 'Muslim nationalists', was trying to create a public opinion for the establishment of an American mandate on the whole of the Ottoman territories. Halide Edip was one of the founders of this society and often translated and published articles in support of the establishment of an American mandate on the Empire. This society was active among the Turkish intellectuals plus 'Kurds and Circassians of the Effendi class'.[34]

The decision to carry out an armed resistance against the Greek forces would be taken after this series of congresses in the summer of 1919. Starting from December 1919, the Representative Board (Heyet-i Temsiliye) of the nationalist movement in Ankara attempted to increase its power on the western front. On 2 December, Mustafa Kemal, the leader of the board, asked the Ministry of War about the number of armed militias around Salihli and Aydın. Two days later, he ordered the establishment of direct communication between the Representative Board and Çerkes Ethem, commander of the National Forces around Salihli.[35] Together with this development, the Unionist figures, who played an important role in the organisation of these congresses, were incorporated into the movement. One of these Unionist key figures was Hacim Muhittin, who was appointed as the governor-general of Hüdavendigâr Province in April 1920 by the Ankara government.

ITALIAN SUPPORT AND ARMS SMUGGLING

As shown in Chapter 1, disagreements emerged among the Allied States concerning the clauses of the post-war settlements and redrawing of new borders in the Ottoman territories. One of the most contentious subjects at the Paris Peace Conference was the status of the Smyrna *sanjak*. Although Greek aspirations included Smyrna and its environs, these territories had already been committed to a great power, Italy, the potential rival of Greece in the Mediterranean in the post-World War I period. The Treaty of London in 1915 and the Agreement of Saint-Jean-de-Maurienne in 1917 had already guaranteed the framework of Italian interests in Western Anatolia. The latter agreement, which aimed to secure the Italian war efforts, promised a great share, including Smyrna, Antalya and Konya, in the division of the Ottoman Empire.[36] Due to these two agreements, Greek and Italian interests were in an apparent conflict over a set of issues, but the point where they most acutely clashed was over the fate of the Smyrna zone in the post-war atmosphere.

Ethnic Cleansing in Western Anatolia

When the Great War was over, the Kingdom of Italy embraced an open strategy of establishing hegemony over the Mediterranean within the framework of the *Mare Nostrum* policy. In the first quarter of the twentieth century, Italy already had flourishing economic enterprises and commercial networks in the Ottoman territories. The Italian policy-makers forged a secret policy against the Greek demands in order to protect Italian economic interests in Western Anatolia. Despite the fact that Italian Levantines were a significant group in Constantinople and Smyrna, they were not successful at competing with the Ottoman Christian merchants in Aydın Province. As rivals of the Italian enterprises in the economic realm, the Ottoman Christians' enterprises were regarded as possible obstacles for the Italian interests in Western Anatolia.[37]

Owing to the clauses of the armistice in October 1918, German and Austro-Hungarian enterprises, businessmen and merchants were forced to withdraw from the Empire. In order to fill this vacuum, Miazzi, the Italian representative in Smyrna, followed a very active policy in the commercial arena. At the beginning of 1919, he issued instructions that all Austrian subjects who possessed businesses in Smyrna could become Italian citizens by applying to his office.[38] He also started to grant Italian citizenship to Greek Catholics residing in Smyrna. It seems plausible to think that he received support from Nureddin Pasha, governor-general of the province, for his activities.

The Greek authorities in Smyrna were suspicious that Italian banks and companies were trying to dominate the financial market of Smyrna. In May 1919, the Banca Commerciale d'Italia secretly absorbed the branches of the Wiener Bankverein and La Banque Hongroise in Smyrna. By seizing the Österreichischer Lloyd, an Austrian company possessing one of the largest shipping networks in the Levant, the Italian company of Lloyd Triestino obtained a preponderating influence in local commercial maritime affairs. Nonetheless, the Italian political and economic ambitions drew the attention of the other Allied representatives in Smyrna. The extortions of the Austrian Church and the Austrian Hospital disturbed Osmin Laporte, the French representative, who claimed that all Catholic churches should be under French protection in Smyrna.[39]

Parallel to this situation, Italian agents organised propaganda among the Levantines as well as a very small part of the Muslim population who benefited from Italian protection and migrated from the Italian-controlled Dodecanese islands to Smyrna due to economic reasons.[40] To that end, an Italian propaganda bureau started its activities in the rue Parallèle in downtown Smyrna.[41]

Formation of a National Resistance

Unionist circles were not late to notice that the Italian representative in Smyrna had a very unfavourable view of the Greek territorial demands. Therefore, they tried to form an alliance with Italian political and military representatives against the territorial ambitions of Greece in the post-armistice period. As an example of those endeavours, Câmi Bey delivered a speech about Italian goodwill at the American Collegiate Institute. He stated that the Italian attitude to the Ottoman Empire was strikingly different from the British and the French. He mentioned that Carlo Sforza, the Italian high commissioner in Constantinople, assured the grand vizier of Italian opposition to the dismemberment of the Ottoman Empire and that Italian interests were purely commercial in Western Anatolia.[42] In addition to this, Ziya Bey, ex-attaché to the former Unionist governor-general Rahmî, held a secret meeting with the admiral of the Italian scout *Miévo* in the pier of Foça so as to incite the Muslim populations against the newly established High Commission.[43]

Some members of the IADOR, especially the Moralızâde family, most probably played an important role in guaranteeing Italian support for the nationalist movement. Moralızâde Nâil, who moved from Constantinople and settled on the Italian-controlled island of Rhodes, functioned as a mediator between the Italian representatives and the nationalist movement in Ankara. Nâil was involved in lengthy negotiations with Italian business circles about the supply of weapons. At that time the leaders of the nationalist movement engaged in the purchase of large amounts of arms from the Italian military command in the Dodecanese via the port of Antalya, a city situated along the Mediterranean coast. Nâil also visited Ankara a couple of times to secure this arms trafficking.[44]

In order to lay claim to a zone of influence vis-à-vis the Greek occupation, the Italian troops had already occupied some coastal towns, such as Kuşadası, Marmaris, Fethiye[45] and Antalya, which would be the bases of the Italian military and intelligence agents in the south. During the spring of 1919, the Italian military presence increased on the south-western coasts of Anatolia and reached 17,000 personnel in September[46] since the Italo-Greek confrontation in the Menderes Valley lasted throughout the autumn months. The Greek military advance in Western Anatolia triggered the rapprochement between the Turkish nationalists and Italian officers in the southern parts of the province.

Despite the fact that the Italian government hesitated to directly break the Allied embargo, Italian businessmen provided raw materials, such as oil and military equipment for the nationalist movement in Ankara. Count Carlo Sforza, who had been appointed minister of foreign affairs in June 1920, contemplated that Italian interests overlapped with those

Ethnic Cleansing in Western Anatolia

of the Turkish nationalists in Anatolia. Even while he was the Italian high commissioner in Constantinople in 1919, Sforza followed a policy backing the Unionist personalities in the province. He met Moralızâde Nâil and suggested that the IADOR send representatives to the Paris Peace Conference.[47] When he was the minister of foreign affairs, Sforza contributed to the formation of coordination and commercial links between the Italian arms brokers and the Turkish nationalists, and he allowed the Italian occupation authorities to assist the Turkish nationalist bands in their region.[48]

Nonetheless, the activities of the Italian military authorities in the region were not limited to the restoration of public order in their occupation zone. They defended the interests of the Italian irredentism through encouraging the National Forces vis-à-vis the Greek troops. Due to their proximity to the mountainous areas surrounding Ödemiş and Aydın, they could secretly provide arms for the nationalist bands. The National Forces were also allowed to establish military bases and take shelter in the Italian occupation zone.[49] In his memoirs, Celâl Bey mentioned that the Italian military authorities did not object to the efforts of the National Forces recruiting soldiers against the Greek troops in their zone.[50] For example, the Italian officers connived with the Turkish nationalists in their activities in Muğla, the centre of the Menteşe *sanjak* that turned into a supply base for the latter.[51] Even though the supply activities were sometimes interrupted, this discontinuity was the result of the displeasure of the Ottoman provincial authorities rather than the discomfort of the Italian officers.

After the Kemalist victories against the Armenians on the eastern front, the Italian authorities decided to loosen their authority in their occupation zone in south-western Anatolia. In this period, Kemalist forces started to infiltrate the Antalya region in spite of the nominal Italian administration. From the second half of 1920, the Italian decision for the rapprochement with the Turkish nationalist movement in Ankara led to the deterioration of British–Italian relations. British intelligence agents noticed in October 1920 that several oil barrels and field guns were to be delivered to the Turkish nationalists from Italian-occupied Antalya.[52] Following this tension, a British steamer, which had been wrecked in the port of Antalya, was searched by Kemalist officers. Its crew and passengers were arrested, whereas the Italian officers remained silent. In May 1921, Sforza ordered the withdrawal of the Italian troops from Antalya.[53]

Formation of a National Resistance

Kuvâ-yı Milliye: Remnants of the Ottoman Army and Local Militias

OTTOMAN TROOPS DURING THE DEMOBILISATION PROCESS

In accordance with the 5th article of the Mudros Armistice, the demobilisation of Ottoman troops was set to begin in November 1918. In the one-year period since the enforcement of the armistice, the demobilisation process was completed to a large extent. As stated in General Milne's reports, the Ottoman armies consisted of 53,000 soldiers by October 1919.[54] Two army corps, located within the borders of Aydın Province, were also affected by the demobilisation. The 21st Corps had dissolved, with its weapons and armaments dispatched to six warehouses around Smyrna on the orders of the British military mission. Except for the 21st Corps, none of the cannons possessed by the 17th Corps were turned in to the British troops. Nonetheless, an important part of its ammunition was stored in the Yenikale bastion, which was close to the port.[55]

In the spring of 1919, the 17th Corps, commanded by Ali Nâdir Pasha in Smyrna, consisted of two divisions: the 56th Division was located in Smyrna, and the 57th Division was in Aydın. The former division had three regiments, in Ayvalık (the 172nd Regiment), Urla (the 173rd Regiment) and the environs of Smyrna (the 174th Regiment),[56] while the command of the latter had been controlling three more regiments in Söke (the 135th Regiment), Aydın (the 75th Regiment) and Antalya (the 76th Regiment). As shown in the previous chapter, the command of this military force had already been persuaded not to enter into armed conflict with Greek troops in May 1919.

Since the Greek government did not allow any Ottoman troops to remain in the Smyrna zone after the occupation, Greek naval steamers evacuated the surrendered soldiers of this corps to Mudanya, a coastal town on the southern shores of the Marmara Sea. These soldiers were ordered by the Ottoman government to reunite in Bursa as a new division,[57] after Bekir Sâmî (Günsav) Bey was appointed the new commander of the 17th Corps, in place of Ali Nâdir Pasha, by proxy on 21 May. The 172nd Regiment in Ayvalık, which was under Ali (Çetinkaya) Bey's supervision, and the 57th Division in Aydın, which was under the command of Colonel Şefîk Bey, started to send weapons and armaments to Bekir Sâmî.[58]

Ethnic Cleansing in Western Anatolia

UNIONIST CONNECTIONS IN THE NATIONAL FORCES

As Erik Jan Zürcher stated, former Unionists did not only contribute to the nationalist movement, but also constituted its organisational backbone.[59] Despite the Unionist triumvirate, discredited by the defeat, leaving the capital after the armistice in October 1918, and the CUP annulling itself on 5 November, Unionist figures continued to wield remarkable power in the political arena. There was still a huge majority of Unionists in parliament, as well as officers in the army and some civil servants in the provinces. In addition, the police and gendarmerie mostly consisted of Unionists as well. The CUP aimed to organise resistance in both the capital and the provinces with the help of these connections.[60] The former CUP members were trying to mobilise the public through both underground networks, as in the case of the activities of Karakol, and its overt connections in the key political bodies, as in the case of the Ministry of War.

The Karakol, a secret society established by influential Unionists in Constantinople in the post-armistice period, was organised as cells, each of which had less than six people in it, and was labelled with a number.[61] The underground network around Karakol had two principal aims: to defend the Unionists against accusations and inquiries regarding the mass murder of Ottoman Christians during World War I, and to organise a resistance movement against the marching Greek troops. In spite of the fact that it was centred in the capital, it had strong connections in the provinces, and especially among the former members of the Special Organisation. Namely, some of Enver's former *fedâî*s, such as Ali (Çetinkaya), Yenibahçeli Şükrü (Oğuz),[62] Eşref Kuşçubaşı[63] and Çerkes Reşit, were among the first members of Karakol.

One peculiar development about Karakol was that instead of institutionalising as a separate organisation in Western Anatolia, it infiltrated the existing resistance organisations and networks. Since it was a secret organisation, its members enjoyed a kind of double positioning. They took part in the newly formed resistance organisations in the provinces with their overt identities, yet secretly continued their allegiance to Karakol. For example, Kara Vâsıf, one of the founders of the association, was elected general commander by the Alaşehir Congress for resistance against the Greek troops. He contacted the National Committee of the Law of Defence Association (Müdâfaa-i Hukuk-ı Milliye Heyeti)[64] in Uşak and managed to arrange another congress in Uşak most probably with the help of Karakol in October 1919.[65]

Mustafa Kemal had strong reservations about Karakol as control over such a clandestine organisation, whose centre was not located in Ankara,

Formation of a National Resistance

would constitute a difficulty for the centralised nationalist government. He was planning to replace it with his own intelligence networks. Bothered by Karakol's efforts to build peculiar relations with the Soviet Union, he ordered Kara Vâsıf to cease the activities of Karakol. The National Defence Committee (Millî Müdâfaa Cemiyeti), which was shortened to Mim Mim in Ottoman Turkish, replaced this group soon after. Since Mim Mim lacked an authentic programme, it became possible for Mustafa Kemal to transform this Unionist organisation into an obedient tool.[66] After the dissolution of the Ottoman parliament in March 1920, prominent members of Karakol, including Kara Vâsıf, were interned in Malta by the British.

In the summer of 1919, in a meeting with the British high commissioner in Constantinople, Ali Kemal Bey, the minister of the interior, claimed that the nationalist movement was not only directed against the Greek presence in the region, but also against the Ottoman government. He emphasised that 'it is the recrudescence of Union and Progressism'. He also added that the resistance in the northern borders of the Smyrna *sanjak* was 'inspired from the Ministry of War, and that the leading rôle was played by Djevad Pasha', a prominent Ottoman commander.[67]

Even at the time when Damat Ferit Pasha was grand vizier, a number of Unionist officers who supported the nationalist movement managed to maintain their duties in the Ministry of War.[68] Their activities within the ministry were probably condoned by the Ferit Pasha government. Apart from Karakol, these officers attempted to sabotage the demobilisation of the Ottoman army and tried to lay the groundwork for a resistance movement in Anatolia with the help of Fevzi Pasha, the minister of war in the cabinets of Ali Rıza Pasha and Salih Pasha from February to April 1920.[69]

The intelligence agents of the Allied States were well aware of the fact that the Unionists, who had a considerable influence in the Ministry of War, were plotting to absorb the leaders of local bands into the framework of the National Forces. The British intelligence had particularly been aware of the cooperation between the Ministry of War and the nationalist groups since 1919. A British agent in Smyrna stressed in one of his dispatches that the Unionists were trying to establish contacts with local band leaders, who would be supported by military equipment and money:

> Active and Reserve Officers have left for the provinces and the CUP has also sent a large number of their members. The preparations in Eudemich (Ödemiş), near Smyrna, are being organized by the Circassian Edil Bey and Major Avni Bey, ex-C.O. of the Gendarmerie Regiment. The CUP is sending a Colonel to this district. Rahmi Bey, ex-Vali of Smyrna, has contributed 80,000 liras for this cause. Unionist agents are working in Magnesia and Aidin with the object of exciting the population.[70]

Ethnic Cleansing in Western Anatolia

The structure and political orientations of the National Forces can be precisely understood once the adherents' networks of personal relations based on affinity, friendship, education and patronage become clear. In this respect, the careers of Enver's *fedâîs* exhibited the porosity between the former staff of the Special Organisation and the prominent figures of the National Forces. For example, Kel Ali Bey, one of Enver's famous *fedâîs*, became the commander of the 172nd Infantry Regiment in Ayvalık as soon as he joined the National Forces.[71] Kuşçubaşı Eşref, who played a significant role in the expulsion of the Ottoman Greek population from the coastal towns in 1914, took part in the struggle against the Greek troops after he was erroneously released from Malta in January 1920.[72] Similarly, Yenibahçeli Şükrü had a significant role in Karakol between 1918 and 1919. Raûf (Orbay), the former minister of the navy, who was a Circassian, came to Bandırma in May 1919 and contacted Çerkes Ethem, a powerful bandit, in order to organise the resistance movement in the region. Raûf, who ordered that a headquarters be founded on Kuşçubaşı Eşref's farm in Salihli, started to arm Çerkes Ethem's bandits in the region in the first half of 1920.[73]

ÇETECILIK: PARAMILITARY ACTIVITIES IN FULL BLOSSOM

Banditry was an important social phenomenon throughout the rural parts of the Empire in the nineteenth century. A security vacuum, competition over pastures and fertile lands, and re-partition of provincial wealth were the main reasons for banditry. As a parallel to this trend, the bands were usually made up of debtors, outlaws, idle townsmen, destitute peasants and adventurers. Banditry was common in Aydın Province as well. Especially in times of political crises, whole villages would get involved in the formation, maintenance and organisation of gangs that would then raid the caravans of rich merchants on the main roads to get money, steal their personal belongings or be hired to murder people.[74] The leaders of these bands, who represented a potential threat to the authority of the Empire, were known as *efe*s in the province. Despite the fact that most of the *efe*s had local origins, new bands consisting of Balkan and Caucasian migrants had started to form at the turn of the century. One of the most detailed memoranda about banditry in the province was prepared by Henry Arnold Cumberbatch, British consul-general at Smyrna, on 19 July 1906. In this memorandum, he stated that the Ottoman local authorities captured ninety-five brigands and killed forty, with twenty-four gendarmes being killed and eight wounded from July 1902 to July 1906. To this memorandum he added a list of seventy-six brigandage cases that had occurred within the

Formation of a National Resistance

previous three years and a sketch map showing the centres of brigandage marked in red in the province[75] (see Map 5.1).

Another group, military deserters, joined the bandits during the wars in the second decade of the twentieth century when the universal conscription law was enforced.[76] In August 1918, a general amnesty was declared for all military deserters and bandits.[77] This general amnesty and demobilisation led to a security vacuum in the provinces. In the post-armistice period, the ongoing disorder was aggravated in Aydın Province because of the activities of these demobilised soldiers and gendarmes, who formed a chronic security problem in the countryside. In spite of the reports asserting that provincial security could only be guaranteed through the Allied support of the Ottoman gendarmerie and liquidation of all former Unionists from the security forces, nothing was done in order to reorganise these institutions.[78]

As Gingeras remarked, paramilitarism was a provincial affair that was considered a political, economic and social institution throughout the Ottoman Empire during the Great War.[79] Paramilitary life represented

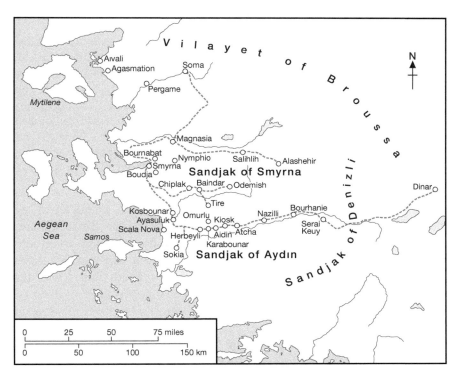

Map 5.1 Reworking of Henry Arnold Cumberbatch's sketch map of brigandage centres, July 1906. The National Archives, London.

Ethnic Cleansing in Western Anatolia

an option for those who did not want to perform military services in addition to being a means of getting by. During the post-armistice period, the number of bandits who roamed the countryside, as well as provincial towns, increased due to the participation of military deserters. A British control officer mentioned the methods of the bandits to extract money from the local notables, who distrusted the policing activities of the gendarme forces:

> Blackmail is a favourite means employed by these bands though open robbery and holding up of entire village also takes place. A letter is sent to a notable, or to the wealthier inhabitants of a village, ordering them to produce a sum of money at a certain time and place, otherwise they and their families will be murdered or the village burnt. The sum demanded is nearly always paid, the people having little confidence in the ability of the authorities to protect them, and fearing the vengeance of the band should they give information about it.[80]

The bandits in this region could be employed by landowners for the protection of their properties as the central authority weakened. In his memoirs, Rahmi (Apak) related how paramilitary actions gained popularity among deserters and their men after World War I:

> Several officers used this outfit (*bu kıyafete*) thinking that it was fashionable in those days. The citizens carrying out their obligatory military service wrapped themselves up in this outfit (*böyle kıyafetlere bürünüp*) and joined the gangs (*çetecilere*) instead of being attached to the military battalions. This also provided more interest as once one became a marauder (*çete*), his salary increased from 20 to 40 liras, food subsistence for oneself and the animals would be mostly on the shoulders of villagers ... The villagers' barley, straw, bread sheep, chicken and eggs would be lawful (*mübah*) for the marauders ... Besides, there were no strict orders (*sıkı bir zapturapt*); everyone was a landlord (*ağa*), and everyone was a commander (*komutan*).[81]

After the formation of the National Forces, the ethnic character of the bands changed rapidly. Hitherto, not only Muslims, but also Christians had been engaged in banditry. The bands were not homogenous groups in terms of ethnic identity or religious affiliation in this region.[82] After the Alaşehir Congress, an alliance of the Muslim band leaders with the Unionist officers came to be formed against the Greek troops.

In the wake of a meeting in Bandırma organised by Bekir Sâmî, Raûf (former minister of the navy) and Kâzım Fikrî in the second half of May 1919, a united front began to emerge in the northern parts of the Smyrna and Saruhan *sanjak*s. According to a plan dated 15 June, the 14th Corps, whose headquarters had been moved from Thrace to Bandırma under the command of Yusuf İzzet Pasha, would be responsible for the northern

Formation of a National Resistance

section of the front.[83] Kâzım Fikrî, who was appointed as the commander of the 61st Division in Balıkesir, along with Bekir Sâmî, would complete the establishment of the first defensive front along the line of Bergama, Akhisar, Soma and Salihli in mid-June of 1919.[84]

With the exception of Kâzım Fikrî, all those military officers had Circassian origins. Using their personal relations, they played an important role in the reconstitution of local bands in the form of paramilitary units, which constituted the backbone of the National Forces on the front. For example, the Salihli district was completely controlled by the militias of Çerkes Ethem. In Soma, again, militias constituted the majority of the armed units.[85]

The case of Çerkes Ethem provides an example of how former members of the Special Organisation were incorporated into the National Forces. He was probably the most influential Muslim bandit leader in the province when World War I ended. He was born in a Circassian village near Bandırma in the Karesi *sanjak* and had been employed by the Special Organisation since the Balkan Wars.[86] Towards the end of World War I, in the summer of 1918, he returned to his hometown of Bandırma. Using his broad range of family and personal contacts, he reformed his band in the northern parts of the province, uniting roving Muslim bandits, military deserters and fugitives of Turkish, Turcoman and Circassian origins. In a short space of time, he would be at odds with the provincial authorities – especially Rahmî Bey, the powerful governor-general of Aydın Province. Once, he attacked the farm of Aarnoud van Heemstra, a Dutch landowner in Cumaovasi, who was a personal friend of Rahmî Bey.[87] Moreover, he attempted to kill Rahmî through bombing his railway car en route to Constantinople. When Rahmî was interned in Constantinople in February 1919 due to accusations of corruption and maladministration, a band led by Çerkes Ethem and Çerkes Reşit kidnapped Rahmî's son, Alparslan, who was coming out of Miss Florence's school in Bournabat.[88] Ethem's band took the boy to a mansion in Salihli belonging to Kuşçubaşı Eşref, another prominent band leader of Circassian origin.[89]

The constituents of the National Forces were not limited to Circassian and Turcoman bands since the organisation had an all-embracing character, which aspired to encourage the participation of all Muslim populations in the armed struggle against the Greek forces. Therefore, it was centred on the local Muslim population irrespective of the ethnic identity. Around Burhaniye, Kel Ali (Çetinkaya) Bey recruited a division from the Bosniak villagers through the assistance of Hacı Tali Bey, an important merchant in this town. Thus, Bosniak gunmen under the command of local Bosniak

Ethnic Cleansing in Western Anatolia

bandits, such as *Boşnak* Hamza and *Boşnak* Kasım, sent to the frontline in the villages of Gömeç, a town near Ayvalık.[90]

While the paramilitary forces were trying to form a front in the north of the Smyrna *sanjak*, Stergiades and Zafeiriou, who underestimated Venizelos's orders, preferred extending the Greek occupation to the south of Smyrna so as to prevent an Italian advance in the Menderes Valley. The Greek troops occupied the town of Ayasuluk on 25 May. By the end of June 1919, the occupation zone had stretched from as far south as the southern stations of the Smyrna–Aydın railway to as far east as Manisa and Kasaba. As the military advance proceeded, the Greek authorities asserted that the Greek soldiers noticed 'an air of contentment' in the occupied settlements.[91]

The structure and ethnic composition of the National Forces were different in the southern section of the front, particularly around the Menderes Valley. Situated on the frontier with the Italian troops, the mountain terrain of the Aydın *sanjak*, which facilitated tactical manoeuvring and guerrilla warfare, was home to a long and proud tradition of *efe*s – a resistance group of fugitives who rebelled against any kind of central authority. By the end of World War I, public order had been shaken by the activities of these local bandits in the south-eastern towns of the Smyrna *sanjak* along the Menderes Valley, such as Tire and Ödemiş, and in the Aydın *sanjak*. Military deserters and newly demobilised soldiers had also joined these paramilitary units. Wealthy landowners in towns and villages felt obliged to join their patronage networks in order to protect their assets. These band leaders incrementally became powerful enough to raid villages and towns and even kidnap people from town centres and take them to the mountainous areas to demand ransoms.[92]

Just like the northern section of the front, no resistance took place in responce to the Greek military advance in the Menderes Valley in the spring of 1919. Having failed to encourage the local Muslim population to participate in armed resistance against the Greek troops, Şefik invited Hacı Süleyman (Bilgen) Efendi, one of the leading Unionist figures in Muğla, to Çine on 5 June 1919 to get the support of the Muslim civilians. As in the cases of the towns of Koçarlı and Çine, Unionist figures such as Hacı Süleyman, former Unionist deputy of Aydın and the professor (*müderris*) of the Muslim seminary (*medrese*) in Nazilli, contacted the Muslim notables and played a crucial role in the foundation of the national committees known as *heyet-i milliye*.[93]

Because of the relatively weak paramilitary forces in the southern section, the *efe*s and their gunmen, who were taken into the orbit of the National Forces, formed the backbone of the paramilitary forces against

216

Formation of a National Resistance

the Greek troops in the towns along the Menderes River. Celâl (Bayar), who was trying to organise the National Forces in the region under the pseudonym of Galip Hoca, was engaged in activities to encourage the local bandits in Ödemiş, Tire and Çine to confront the Greek troops. During a tour to Aydın, he organised successful meetings with the leaders of local bandits and persuaded them to fight the Greek troops.[94]

In order to keep their engagement intact, Celâl Bey charged the Ottoman military officers with supervising the activities of the band leaders. Zekâi (Kaur) Bey, a lieutenant colonel and a Muslim Cretan himself, supervised Yörük Ali Efe's band, renamed Aydın National Regiment (Aydın Millî Alayı), and started to back Şefik Bey's troops in June 1919. Yörük Ali Efe, the leader of this band, was a deserter who had started his military service in Smyrna and escaped on his way to the Caucasian front in the days of the Great War. Along with some of the deserters, he formed a band and was later engaged in negotiations with Şefik to support the National Forces.[95] There were military deserters as well as well-known brigands in his band. Demirci Mehmet Efe, another band leader who was also incorporated by Celâl[96] into the National Forces in the province, established his headquarters in Köşk, a small town in the Aydın *sanjak*, with almost 1,000 gunmen.[97] He renamed his band as the Menderes National Regiment (Menderes Millî Alayı), whose activities would be controlled by Nuri Bey, gendarmerie command in Nazilli. As seen in these cases, the military officers strived to minimise, through their regulatory positions, the competition among various band leaders.

The Greek political authorities regarded the guerrilla tactics of the National Forces as a means to justify their military operations in the towns along the Menderes Valley. The advance of the Greek troops had already been criticised by the Allied representatives since it went beyond the Smyrna *sanjak*, the predetermined occupation zone. Stergiades tried to give grounds for this advance on the alleged basis that the Greek troops were attacked by the nationalist irregulars in the Menderes Valley, who triggered a security vacuum around the Smyrna *sanjak*. He stated that Greek forces occupied Aydın because they were unable to rely on the Italian troops in the southern part of the valley.[98]

As stated above, not only the nationalist movement, but also the Greek military authorities employed Muslim bands in their forces. The reason behind the enrolment of the Muslim bands by the Greek authorities was the inadequate number of the Greek gendarmeries for the enormously difficult task of maintaining order in a hostile region. Civilian volunteers were also enrolled and armed by the Greek military authorities in many towns for the avowed purpose of 'supplementing the exiguous force of

Ethnic Cleansing in Western Anatolia

police and gendarmerie and assisting them in their task of maintaining the order'.[99] These volunteers accompanied the Greek troops in their expeditions against the villages, which were suspected to harbour nationalist bands.

The most important advantages of recruiting very considerable numbers of Muslim bandits into the Greek troops were that these paramilitary forces were familiar with local geographical features as well as the shelters of the nationalist bands in the region. Muslim bandits served in the Greek ranks essentially during the incursions of the Greek troops which took place due to the Italian withdrawal from the Menderes Valley in winter 1922. In March, a mixed detachment composed of Greek soldiers and civilian volunteers entered the village of Karatepe, consisting of some sixty houses, near Köşk in the Aydın *sanjak*. Most of its inhabitants had fled into the fields before the attack. They were, however, induced to return and assemble in the mosque on the understanding that an official communication from the authorities was to be made. The mosque was then set on fire and most of the villagers, including some children, perished in the flames. The pretext for this destruction was that the villagers had harboured a nationalist band. Indeed, a band, numbering about fifteen Muslim men of a noted brigand named Tekelioğlu İsmail, was actually in the village at the time of the attack.[100]

Whereas the numbers of Muslim militias were limited in the Greek forces, the leaders of the paramilitary organisations could exert their authority in the National Forces and challenge, in some cases, the authority of the former Ottoman officers in the period between 1919 and 1920. Since the nationalist movement, which suffered a lack of regular troops against the Greek military advance, needed those paramilitary leaders, it overlooked their excesses and centrifugal tendencies and granted them great authority in the war zone. Notwithstanding this, due to the consolidation of the nationalist movement in Ankara, these paramilitary organisations, whose control emerged as a great problem for the centralisation attempts of the nationalist movement, would be absorbed by the regular army in the winter of 1920–1.

Resistance Methods of the National Forces

ATTACKS ON LOCAL CHRISTIANS

Since the foundation of the CUP, criminals and party officers had come together to form an institution within the state apparatus. During World War I, the Ottoman intelligence service, known as the Special Organisation,

Formation of a National Resistance

was the concretised form of this alliance, effective both in the capital and at the provincial level. As exhibited above, the provincial chiefs of the CUP encouraged the attachment of the local band leaders to the remnants of the Ottoman troops under the umbrella of the National Forces in order to reverse their greatest fear, that is, the return of the expelled Ottoman Christians. As a matter of fact, most of these men who volunteered to participate in politicised gang violence (*çetecilik faaliyetleri*) were notorious figures, who had already participated in ethnic violence campaigns targeting the Christian population of the Empire during the Great War.

Parallel to the rise of the idea of the nation-state and Wilson's declaration of Fourteen Points in the post-war atmosphere, the nationalist movement yearned to form a Muslim majority in Western Anatolia. The Defence of Rights group (Müdâfaa-i Hukuk), whose members were mainly former Unionists and Turkish nationalists, formed the majority in the last Ottoman parliament in January 1920. As a reflection of this event, Christian communities were excluded from Ottoman political life. In this context, the potential for expulsions and attacks by paramilitary forces were favoured by the Turkish nationalists for the sake of transforming the heterogeneous population in Western Anatolia.

Particularly in the localities where the Greek troops occupied but retreated due to strategic reasons or attacks from the National Forces, as in the cases of Menemen in the north and Aydın in the south, nationalist violence targeted the local Christian communities as well as dissidents of the National Forces. In Menemen, on the evening of 15 June 1919, a Greek corporal was killed and several soldiers retreating from Bergama were wounded. This incident was followed by encounters and clashes in the streets between Greek soldiers and groups of Turkish and Albanian irregulars.[101] During these fights, many Ottoman officials, including the district governor (*kaymakam*), were killed on the streets. The irregulars entered the town and indiscriminately pillaged all the neighbourhoods. They terrorised the town by looting properties during a two-day rampage:

> The Turkish irregulars shot two Turks in front of the Government for having manifested sentiments of goodwill towards the Greeks. A third Turk was wounded, and it is said that one Jewish woman and an Armenian were killed. The irregulars, who were about 3000 in number, seemed to have come from Panderma, Balikesir, Soma, etc. After pillaging for two days, it was reported that Greek troops had landed at Dikili, and the irregulars went out to meet them.[102]

This paramilitary violence rendered large-scale abuse, such as mass killings and forced migrations, possible against the Ottoman Christian citizens.

219

Ethnic Cleansing in Western Anatolia

John M. Calvert, a British military officer, explained how paramilitary forces resorted to violence in June 1919 with the aim of plundering the properties of the non-Muslims after the withdrawal of the Greek troops from Nazilli in the Aydın *sanjak*. As an eyewitness, he wrote a detailed report about the escalation of violence perpetrated by the paramilitary forces:

> On Thursday 19th at approximately midnight the Greek troops occupying NAZLI evacuated the place and immediately disturbances commenced. All through the night there were signs of unrest and it was reported that several Greeks had been killed or wounded during the night. All day on Friday there was an air of suspense and hardly anyone was to be seen on the streets. At about 3 p.m. the brigands accompanied by the rougher elements of the surrounding villages, about 200 to 300 in all, raided the town and from that hour to 5 o'clock on Saturday this rabble pillaged and looted the place. The Brigands took all money, jewellery and valuables and set the villagers to pillage the Greek houses and shops. This looting was done so thoroughly that many Greeks were left with not so much as a mattress to lie on. The Greek shops were cleared of everything they contained.

On the list was attached a report by Calvert giving the names of seven Ottoman Greeks, two British workers of the Ottoman Railway Company, and one Armenian who were killed in these events, as well as the names of twenty-five Ottoman Greeks who were injured.[103]

T. B. Rees, a British naval representative, mentioned the National Forces' retaliations on the Ottoman Christians in the villages of the Saruhan *sanjak*. Besides, by mentioning the example of Yeniceköy, Rees expressed that Muslim villagers were mobilised by the band leaders through anti-Christian propaganda to join the looting:

> This morning the only 13 survivors of GIENTZE KEUY arrived here and reported to me that on the 4th inst., 10 Turkish Irregulars entered the village, which has a population of about 200 Greek and 300 Turks. These Irregulars with the help of the local Turks, for no apparent reason, proceeded to kill the Greek population who offered no resistance whatever. The killing lasted for 24 hours, the Turks looking on it as a form of sport. The Greeks were led out of their houses and allowed to run in any direction they chose while the Turks fired at them, the best shot firing last. The greater part of the young women of the village were not killed and are said to have been Islamised.[104]

Rees underlined that 'a reign of terror' prevailed outside the Greek zone and the National Forces were 'working on a definite programme, taking the destruction of [Christian] villages by turn'. He described Çerkes Reşit, Çerkes Ethem's brother, as a strong authority, formerly connected to

Formation of a National Resistance

Enver Pasha, in Salihli and explained his role in the massacres directed at Ottoman Christians.[105]

When the Greek troops started to march into the interior of Anatolia in the spring of 1920, the Ottoman Christians faced double challenges. If they were not deported from their villages and neighbourhoods yet, the Ottoman Christians were exposed to increasing attacks by the nationalist bands in the unoccupied parts of Anatolia. In the Greek occupation zone, they were anxious about what might take place if the Greek troops withdrew.

The nationalist armed bands, including criminal elements, were employed to cleanse the undesired parts of the population, that is, the Ottoman Christians. To put it briefly, the National Forces, acquiring a moral base through the arguments of fighting against the enemy, liquidated the Ottoman Christian population and looted their properties.[106] For example, İbrahim Ethem Bey, district governor of Demirci, remarked on various occasions that 'Anatolia was a land of Muslims and Turks' and that the triumph would be reached after the Ottoman Greeks and Armenians were killed.[107] İbrahim Ethem and his fellows were probably estimating that the solution to the problem lay not only in the exile of the Ottoman Greeks from Anatolia, but also in the punishment of every native Christian who might cooperate with the Greek armies in Western Anatolia.

PRESSURES ON LOCAL NOTABLES

The military conflicts between the Greek troops and the National Forces provided a cover for various crimes against the civilian populations in Western Anatolia. Whereas the Ottoman Christian populations became the victims of the carnage carried out by the nationalist bands, local Muslim notables, who dared not support the National Forces, were threatened, castigated and even murdered. As can be seen from the cases outlined below, certain groups of notables, who chose not to support the National Forces, were rather eager to help their Christian townsmen.

To begin with, exaction of tributes for the National Forces was the main reason for the conflict between the local notables and paramilitary leaders. In June 1919, the minister of the interior received unofficial news that local bands were terrorising Muslim notables in Edremit and extorting money for the nationalist movement. The local notables of this town had sent representatives to complain about the situation in their district.[108]

In some extreme cases, the military leaders of the National Forces did not hesitate to attack local notables who were unwilling to offer their financial resources and contribute to the recruitment of new gunmen for

Ethnic Cleansing in Western Anatolia

the National Forces. Bekir Sâmî Bey was one of these leaders. On 17 June, he departed from Eşme for Bursa in order to lead the 56th Division after his appointment. On his way to Kula, where he intentionally stopped by as the local notables had been indifferent to resistance, he succeeded in imprisoning the local notables of Kula on the basis of a list provided by Major Nedim Bey, the station commander. After these arrests and the rumours that these notables would be executed, an agreement with the relatives of the arrested notables was reached in regard to the formation of a resistance group of nearly 1,000 people. Right after this, the imprisoned notables were released, and a resistance force was generated. Once this force started to prevail in the town, the assaults on the Greek Orthodox community began, with its members having to take refuge in Alaşehir in late June 1919.[109]

In another case, on 5 July 1920, the provincial notables objected to the deportation of the Ottoman Greek population in Denizli to Dinar. Thereupon, Demirci Mehmet Efe sent a bandit group of forty gunmen headed by Sökeli Ali Efe to Denizli. Sökeli Ali compelled the Ottoman Greeks to get on trains he had ordered to be prepared beforehand, and insulted the Muslim notables who were trying to hide Ottoman Greeks in their houses, having them beaten. The Muslim notables of Denizli who failed to prevent this deportation and were apprehensive of Ali's threats formed a small armed group within a few days. This armed group killed sixteen members of Ali's band in an attack on the morning of 8 July and imprisoned the rest. On the same day, militias under the leadership of Demirci Mehmet Efe looted houses and shops in the town and murdered around sixty inhabitants of Denizli in retaliation. At the end of the day, Demirci Mehmet's militias started to patrol the streets of Denizli for security purposes and demanded money from members of the notable Muslim families of the city.[110]

RAILWAY SABOTAGES

Another target of the National Forces was the two different railway lines in the province which were operated by British and French companies. Despite the fact that the manager of Smyrne–Cassaba et Prolongements, the French company, did not accept the use of this railway for the transportation of Greek troops, the employment of Ottoman Christians made it susceptible to attacks from the National Forces. At the Alaşehir Congress, Hacim Muhittin called attention to the strategic importance of the railway lines for the National Forces and to the important positions of Ottoman Greeks in the administration of Smyrne–Cassaba et Prolongements,

Formation of a National Resistance

connecting Bandırma in the north and Afyonkarahisar in the east to Smyrna:

> Gentlemen! Although the railway network (*şebeke-i hadîdiye*), which cuts an important part of Aydın Province and Karesi district, is the property of a French company, its management board, which are in favor of the Ottoman Greeks (Rum *taraftarı*), makes trouble and even adopts a hostile attitude. For example, while many Muslim officers were working on this railway during the armistice period, there is none, unfortunately, today. The Ottoman Greeks and Armenians applying to the company's stations are offered facilities. On the contrary, the Muslims (İslâmlar) are exposed to difficulties. In short, they do whatever it takes to destroy the nationalist movement (Hareket-i Milliye) through espionage. In the stations, there are Ottoman Greeks, wearing French uniforms, in the company of French officers. They insult the Muslims. Unfortunately, we endure this situation, though the conquerors of this country are us. I beg you to take a decision on this question. The question is simple: four kilograms of bomb solve it (*dörder kiloluk bomba halleder*)![111]

At the end of the session, it was decided that the National Forces would not prevent the operation of the railways or attack the French officers supervising the railway. However, the Ottoman Greeks were ultimately declared unwanted elements in the settlements along this railway line.

Unlike Smyrne–Cassaba et Prolongements, the Greek army was allowed to make use of the Smyrna–Aydın Railway, operated by a British company, for transportation of its troops. Furthermore, Greek troops occupied Aydın station and the other stations in the easternmost part of the railway. As a result of this military occupation, this railway line, with its stations becoming Greek military camps, virtually transformed into the Greek front line in the spring of 1919. Due to the presence of the Greek troops, the National Forces started to target this railway and its stations. They sabotaged the operation of the railway by organising all kinds of activities, such as murdering railway employees, the robbery of ticket offices and passengers, continual cutting of railway telegraph wires, and attempts to blow up bridges.[112] As the number of local gendarmerie units had diminished, the livestock, cargo and people carried on the railroads became easy targets for the irregulars who dared to raid trains and kidnap passengers for ransom.

Kuvâ-yi Nizamiye: *Establishment of the Regular Army*

Mustafa Kemal, president of the Representative Board (Heyet-i Temsiliye), had tried to assert his influence on the Western front and exercise his authority over a group of officers from the same front at the early stages

Ethnic Cleansing in Western Anatolia

of the military conflicts. On 9 September 1919, he confirmed the decision of appointing Ömer Lûtfî (Argeşo) Bey, a former Ottoman army officer, to the National Terrain Commandership (Millî Mıntıka Kumandanlığı), including the 23rd Division in Afyon.[113] Ömer Lûtfî would wield the control of not only the 23rd Division and 159th Regiment in Afyon, but also the 68th Regiment in Uşak and the troops associated with these forces in Alaşehir. Furthermore, at the end of the Sivas Congress held in September 1919, Ali Fuât (Cebesoy) Pasha, another former Ottoman army general and a classmate of Mustafa Kemal from the Military Academy, was appointed as the General National Forces commander in Western Anatolia (Garbî Anadolu Umûm Kuvâ-yi Milliye Kumandanı). Nonetheless, at this phase the nationalist movement in Ankara needed the assistance of local paramilitary leaders as it was still too weak to enter into conflict with the Greek troops on the western front or with the Armenian forces at the north-eastern frontier of the Empire. Therefore, in return for their military support, the nationalist leaders gave paramilitary leaders carte blanche for expanding their activities, looting the urban settlements and menacing the local notables.

Although the superficial goal of the struggle for the leading cadres of the nationalist movement was the protection of the sultanate and Caliphate, they did not have any sympathy for the loyalist provincial officials who had close relations with the Greek administration. The Representative Board of the nationalist movement, therefore, decided to remove the governors-general and district governors, who were loyal to the imperial government, from their offices in November 1919.[114] The local bands, particularly Çerkes Ethem's band, also did not allow the activities of these district governors who did not support the National Forces. For instance, after forming the Mobile Troops (Kuvâ-yı Seyyâre) under his leadership, Çerkes Ethem abducted Hasan Fikret, the district governor of Salihli, and took him to Alaşehir. Hasan Fikret, who was accused of secretly inviting the Greek troops to Salihli and forming an alliance against the National Forces with the mayor and the mufti, was beaten and incarcerated in Çerkes Ethem's headquarters around Alaşehir.[115] Owing to increasing attacks by local bands on Ottoman civil servants, particularly district governors in the Saruhan *sanjak*, and 'the growing anarchy *sensu stricto (manâ-yı tammiyle bir anarşi)*', on 20 December 1919, the imperial government ordered the governor-general of Aydın to take preventive measures in order to end the attacks.[116]

There was a conflict of authority between the paramilitary leaders and military officers, usually supported by local notables, about the control of the National Forces, and this problem was generally solved through armed

Formation of a National Resistance

conflict. To illustrate, when Çerkes Ethem began to gain more power at the Salihli–Bozdağ front, the disagreement between him and Mustafa Bey, the commander of National Forces in Alaşehir, became bitter and Mustafa was obliged to orient his troops to the mountainous area around Bozdağ. The withdrawal of Mustafa's forces from Salihli put the local notables in Salihli and Alaşehir in a difficult situation. An important aspect of the local notables (*eşrâf*) in Alaşehir, including Mütevellizâde Tevfîk Bey, had been supporting Mustafa against the paramilitary forces of Ethem.[117] On 27 August, two days after the closure of the Alaşehir Congress, a skirmish occurred in Salihli between Ethem's band and the villagers of Poyrazlı, who refused to pay an annual tribute to Ethem and supported Mustafa against him. Ethem, who emerged victorious from this clash, intensified his control in Salihli. As the tension at the Salihli–Bozdağ front escalated, on 14 September the Central Committee (Heyet-i Merkeziye) in Alaşehir sent a letter to the 23rd Division Command in Afyon, inviting commander Ömer Lûtfî Bey to settle this issue. This event revealed the fact that the security concerns of the local notables would reach vital importance to the point of inviting a commander from the distant town of Afyonkarahisar.[118]

As a follow-up to these events, in the first months of 1920, Çerkes Ethem appeared as the most powerful paramilitary leader on the western front. In order to monitor his activities, the Representative Board officially ordered Ömer Lûtfî Bey, commander of the 23rd Division, to set up headquarters in Alaşehir.[119] Having been elected a member of the Ottoman parliament, Ömer Lûtfî handed his office of commandership over to Aşîr Bey on 8 January 1920. After Aşîr took over this duty, two different divisions continued to coexist in the region – one of them being the militia division under the command of Çerkes Ethem and the other the 23rd Division.[120] Ethem was too powerful to be defeated.

Two critical events, the Greek military advance and the rise of Ethem's power, stigmatised the summer of 1920 and compelled the leaders of the nationalist movement in Ankara to envisage the establishment of regular forces, which would incorporate the irregular forces, directly bound to the National Assembly. Çerkes Ethem, who successfully repressed the Çapanoğlu uprising in Yozgat in June 1920, returned to Kütahya on the western front due to the intensifying Greek attacks. In Kütahya, he released 400 prisoners with the approval of the district governor and armed them against the marching Greek troops. This group joined Ethem's band, consisting of 4,500 gunmen, including bandits as well as former military officers. Nonetheless, Ethem's increasing political and military power was disturbing the Representative Board of the nationalist movement in Ankara. While he was in Yozgat, his military power had

225

Ethnic Cleansing in Western Anatolia

irritated the nationalists. Immediately after suppressing the Çapanoğlu uprising, he attempted to punish Yahya Galip, the nationalist governor of Ankara, claiming the governor was the main person responsible for the uprising.

The establishment of a regular army on the western front was a gradual process which started in the spring of 1920 and ended at the beginning of the following year. The spring of 1920 was a very critical period for the leaders of the nationalist movement in Ankara, since they were not only faced with the Greek military advance towards Bursa and the interior of Anatolia, but also imposed a rapid centralisation policy over the National Forces, a major military and administrative undertaking. Through an order of the Executive Committee (Heyet-i Vekîle) of the nationalist movement, whose members aimed to prevent the centrifugal tendencies of the paramilitary leaders, it was announced that the National Forces would thereafter be linked to the Ministry of Defence (Millî Müdâfaa Vekâleti). Thus, starting from 16 May 1920, the expenses of the paramilitary forces acting within the National Forces were to be paid from the general budget.[121] This decision meant that all paramilitary groups and local committees had to hand over their authority and financial resources to the Ankara government. Nonetheless, some paramilitary leaders, such as Çerkes Ethem and Demirci Efe, rejected being incorporated into the regular armed forces.

The infrequent clashes between the Greek troops and the National Forces transformed into a genuine war with the advance of the former across the Milne Line in mid-June 1920. On 22 June 1920, the Greek army embarked on a major assault against the National Forces. Its troops invaded Alaşehir, Balıkesir and Bandırma within a week. On 8 July, Bursa was occupied without any resistance.[122] Bekir Sâmî (Günsav), deputy commander of the 17th Army Corps, and Kâzım Fikrî withdrew their forces from the region and agreed on the establishment of a new line of defence outside Bursa.

After the fall of Balıkesir and Bursa in spring 1920, an incriminating tone prevailed in the sessions of the Ankara assembly due to the military failures of the leaders of the local National Forces. Hamdullah Subhi (Tanrıöver), minister of national education, stated the following in the session on 13 July:

> I would like to ask the executive government (*hükümeti icraiyeye*): what has Commander Bekir Sâmî Bey, who is being reported from all sides not to have accomplished his duty in Bursa, got to do in the army? It is Governor Hacim Bey who has not done his duty. This is because he wanted to do everything. Hacim Bey has become a gang leader (*çete reisi*), a commander and a governor (*vâlî*). However, when the time for the accomplishment of his true duty (*asıl*

Formation of a National Resistance

vazife zamanı) came, I do swear (*istişhad ederim*) along with the deputies of Bursa that he was the first to escape. If I am mistaken, the fault is theirs. I am asking you.[123]

Again, at the meeting in the assembly on 14 August, Besim (Atalay), deputy of Kütahya, blamed Aşîr Bey, the commander on the front, in the following way:

Aşîr Bey indeed deserves to be handed over to the court martial (*divanı harbe*). This is because I have been unable to find answers to these three questions. First, he discharged those born in 1892, 1893 and 1894. How reasonable is it to discharge soldiers when you have a perfectly structured army fighting against you? He gave military officers permission on the occasion of the feast. He led people into excitement. Since he did not think of these things, it is necessary that this man be exposed to a great interrogation (*büyük bir suale*).[124]

In the face of these critiques in the assembly, Mustafa Kemal decided he no longer wanted to keep these commanders in their offices. Bekir Sâmî Bey was dismissed from his office on 14 July, and both Bekir Sâmî and Aşîr Bey were transferred to Antalya Regional Command (Mıntıka Kumandanlığı).[125] On 9 November, the National Assembly restructured the western front through establishing two separate command headquarters, one on the northern line and the other on the southern line of the front. While İsmet (İnönü) Bey was appointed to the northern line, Refet (Bele) Bey became the commander of the southern line.

By the autumn of 1920, the various paramilitary organisations had been incorporated into the regular troops, either voluntarily or forcefully. In January 1921, Mustafa Kemal exhorted Çerkes Ethem, one of the last remaining paramilitary leaders, to join the regular army along with his gunmen. As soon as Ethem declined this offer, a clash between his forces and the regular army troops became inevitable. Ethem's forces were taken captive, and Ethem had to take refuge in the Greek occupation zone.[126]

In July 1921, the Greek troops entered Kütahya and started advancing in the direction of Eskişehir. In this period, following the overwhelming Greek victory in Eskişehir, the number of soldiers deserting the nationalist army surpassed 45,000.[127] Greek troops reached the banks of River Sakarya and prepared to march towards Ankara, the base of the Turkish nationalists. This victory brought the Greek troops to within some 90 kilometres of Ankara. Nonetheless, while the nationalist army retreated, its soldiers dismantled the factories in Eskişehir and destroyed the local railway. This operation reduced the sense of security among the Greek troops. At the end of clashes, which lasted approximately twenty days, the eastern banks of the Sakarya were completely cleared of Greek troops on 13 September.

Ethnic Cleansing in Western Anatolia

Now the Greek troops established a new line of defence by settling in Eskişehir in the north and in Afyonkarahisar in the south.

The stalemate position, which would continue for almost a year, marked the end of the Greek military advance in Anatolia. The occurrence of more problems was nothing unexpected due to the prolongation of the military conflict. The flow of supplies and money to the Greek army had already been cut off since Allied neutrality had been declared. After the *Accord d'Angora* signalled the end of the hostilities with the French government in October 1921, it was now possible for the Ankara government to move the nationalist troops that had hitherto been kept on the southern front to the western front. Moreover, the Greek army with its 180,000 troops had to defend a very long front line starting from the south-eastern coasts of the Marmara Sea, and extending to the emplacements in Eskişehir and Afyonkarahisar in the east, and then proceeding along the River Menderes to the west, and ending in the Aegean Sea. Lord Granville, the British ambassador in Athens, reported that the Greek army had to face a serious supply crisis after the Battle of Sakarya:

> [The] figures show for the Smyrna district that a crop of 57,570 tons of wheat and 65,000 tons of barley. The district of Ushak contains 30,000 tons of wheat. These stocks are not available for the feeding of the Greek Army at Broussa or Eskishehir – in the first place because they cannot economically be brought there.[128]

Moreover, the Greek soldiers had to cope with the geographical difficulties and unfavourable weather conditions in the Anatolian plateau, parts of which were a salt desert without any water sources. The difficult weather conditions, snow in winter and the hot summer sun, had demoralised the Greek troops.[129] As the summer of 1922 drew to an end, it was obvious that the Greek troops could not stay in Anatolia for another winter.

The traditional historiography of the Turkish War of Independence regards the occupation of Smyrna as the catalyst of the National Struggle. Historians in Turkey, from Kemalist, nationalist or leftist[130] backgrounds, as well as some foreign historians,[131] agreed that the arrival of the Greek armies in Smyrna caused the emergence of a nationalist resistance movement in May 1919.

Although Turkish historians have needed such an interpretation of the war to stress the genuineness of the nationalist movement, Anglo-American scholarship's take on the events was shaped, among other things, by the restrictive use of British official documents of the period. These documents were heavily obsessed with considering the nationalist resistance as a by-product of the Greek occupation of Smyrna. The earliest examples

Formation of a National Resistance

of the British reports, which claimed there was a direct link between the occupation of Smyrna and the formation of the nationalist resistance, were written by the agents of the British General Staff in the region.[132] This perception gained currency among the offices of the British High Commission in Constantinople. Even Richard Webb, the British assistant high commissioner, in his correspondence with the Foreign Office, argued that the occupation of Smyrna stopped the disarmament and triggered the formation of the nationalist movement.[133]

However, as stated clearly by Zürcher, the starting point of the nationalist resistance movement was not the occupation of Smyrna in May 1919. The indications of the nationalist feelings were far more complicated and already existed among a group of Unionist bureaucrats and military officers. Even back in 1915, Ottoman military circles had started to discuss the prospect of setting up a nationalist guerrilla movement in the provinces in the event of a failure in the Gallipoli Campaign and a consequent occupation of the Ottoman capital by the Allied forces.[134] Nonetheless, the return of the Ottoman Christians, who had previously been intimidated and expelled from their homelands, by virtue of the occupation of Smyrna, facilitated the efforts of the Unionist leaders, who had already been organised in the Eastern provinces following the armistice, to mobilise public opinion in the western part of the Empire.

Even though the bloody events that had been directed towards the Muslim population in Smyrna on 15–16 May had torpedoed Venizelos's expansionist policy inspired by the *Megali Idea*, the occupation did not really damage relations between the Greek Orthodox and Muslim communities in the province. There were inner conflicts going on within the communities. Whereas the Venizelist–Royalist rift divided the Greek Orthodox communities, there were harsh disagreements between the Unionists and the supporters of the Freedom and Accord Party. Nonetheless, the inevitable corollary of the occupation, that is the return of Ottoman Christians to their homelands and their demands on their abandoned properties, could easily be manipulated by the Turkish nationalists, particularly the Unionists. As Hans Lukas Kieser asserted, 'the same enemy images that had operated before fall 1918 served as Kemal's popular, emotional, and ideological base for reorganizing an Anatolia-centred, post-CUP national governance (*millî teşkilat*).'[135]

The occupation led to the mobilisation of public opinion and aggravated fears that the Ottoman Christians, who had been expelled during the war years, might regain their former properties. Throughout the province, local Muslim hostility that had been instigated by the feelings of resentment and destitution due to the return of the Ottoman Christians grew harsher when

Ethnic Cleansing in Western Anatolia

the Greek soldiers landed in Smyrna. Thus, the occupation was not the starting point of the resistance, but it intensified the problems of returning and resident Ottoman Christians as well as the ownership problems of the abandoned properties.

Notes

1. Akıncı, *Demirci Akıncıları*, 2. Tobacco Monopolies were established by the OPDA, with backing from a consortium of European banks, to provide much needed income to reduce the foreign debts of the Empire. Although it was run in the major urban centres with many Levantines and Ottoman Christians in its management, its cadres were dominated by Muslim professionals in the provincial towns.
2. Zürcher, *The Unionist Factor*, 78–9.
3. Erik Jan Zürcher, 'The Importance of Being Secular: Islam in the Service of National and Pre-national State', in *Turkey's Engagement with Modernity: Conflict and Change in the Twentieth Century*, ed. Celia Kerslake et al. (Basingstoke: Palgrave Macmillan, 2010), 61.
4. Ahmet Yıldız, *'Ne Mutlu Türküm Diyebilene': Türk Ulusal Kimliğinin Etno-Seküler Sınırları* (Istanbul: İletişim Yayınları, 2001), 127–32.
5. Ibid. 100–6.
6. Erik Jan Zürcher, 'Young Turk Memoirs as a Historical Source: Kazım Karabekir's *Istiklal Harbimiz*', *Middle Eastern Studies* 22, no. 4 (1986), 564.
7. The CUP nominees still held the majority of the administrative and executive posts in the province, particularly in the administration of railways and the gendarmerie. TNA FO 608/115, 8 March 1919, Report issued by General Staff Intelligence in Constantinople on the CUP, Part I. The wealth of the committee was based on the fiscal corruptions during the war years, monopolies of rail transport and commercial restrictions. Due to these measures, a group of Unionist artisans succeeded in prospering in the provinces, see Part V of the same report.
8. Moralı, *Mütarekede İzmir Olayları*, 9–10. The guidelines of this association had already been submitted to the governor's office on 1 December 1918.
9. Ibid. 6. Tunaya mentions the names of Hâşim Enverî; Şerif Paşazâde Remzi, a famous landowner; and Câmi (Baykut) Bey, a Unionist and ex-censor official, among the founders of the association. See Tarık Zafer Tunaya, *Türkiye'de Siyasi Partiler, 1859–1952* (Istanbul: Doğan Kardeş, 1952), 481.
10. In the post-World War I period, the Unionist presence was still strong in the Ottoman security forces, including the gendarmerie and police. Nureddin Pasha, the governor-general, and also Cemil Bey, the chief of police in Smyrna, were adherents of the Unionist ideology, TNA FO 608/113, 1 March 1919, John Alexaki to Major Smith. Moreover, the Unionist officials had managed to keep their seats in the neighbouring towns in Western

Formation of a National Resistance

Anatolia. At a meeting he held with a British control officer, the district governor of Kütahya confirmed that many CUP members were still in the town, see TNA FO 608/113, 14 May 1919, Admiral Webb to Foreign Office. On 26 June, the district governor of Eskişehir demanded that thirty people be arrested on account of promoting Unionist and Bolshevik propaganda. However, three of them managed to escape with the help of the chief of police, TNA FO 608/113, 3 August 1919, Calthorpe to Foreign Office.

11. Moralı, 45.
12. TNA FO 371/ 4157, 7 April 1919, Ian M. Smith, Area Control Officer at Smyrna to General Staff Intelligence at Constantinople.
13. Moralı, *Mütarekede İzmir Olayları*, 45–51 and 62–4; and Eğe-Akter, *Babamın Emanetleri*, 17.
14. Ibid. 49–50.
15. The most prominent examples of these propaganda books were *Smyrne, ville grecque* and *Smyrne turque*. Charles Vellay, *Smyrne, ville grecque* (Paris: Librairie Chapelot, 1919); and *Smyrne turque*, ed. Société de défense des droits ottomans (Smyrne: Imprimerie Ahmed Ihsan & Compagnie, 1919). Similar to the maps compiled by the Greek intellectuals, the maps prepared by the IADOR members would be considered as 'absolutely untrustworthy' by the British authorities in Smyrna, who argued that the association was trying to influence foreign public opinion through these maps. The British Control Officer at Smyrna underlined that the association's map did not take into account the deportations taking place in the war years and asserted that even the coastal towns, such as Çeşme, were entirely populated by the Muslims. See TNA FO 371/4157, 20 April 1919, British Control Officer at Smyrna to the British High Commissioner in Constantinople.
16. Mesut Çapa, 'İzmir Müdafaa-i Hukuk Osmaniye Cemiyeti', *Atatürk Araştırma Merkezi Dergisi* 7, no. 21 (July 1991), 555.
17. Moralı, *Mütarekede İzmir Olayları*, 47–8.
18. Özalp, *Milli Mücadele*, 6–7.
19. Taçalan, *Ege'de Kurtuluş Savaşı Başlarken*, 227–32.
20. Zürcher, *The Unionist Factor*, 77.
21. TNA FO 608/104, 19 May 1919, Commandant Ceccaldi to General Fuller.
22. Câmi and Muvaffak had established relations with Hacim Muhittin, the president of the Balıkesir and Alaşehir congresses, as early as in October 1919, Hacim Muhittin Çarıklı, *Balıkesir ve Alaşehir Kongreleri ve Hacim Muhittin Çarıklı'nın Kuvayı Milliye Hatıraları* (Ankara: Ankara Üniversitesi Basımevi, 1967), 94–5.
23. Moralı, *Mütarekede İzmir Olayları*, 15–17.
24. 'İzmir Müdâfaa-i Hukuk Cemiyeti Kâtib-i Umûmîsi Câmi Bey'in Mustafa Kemal Paşa'ya Gönderdiği 31 Kânûn-i Evvel 1335 Tarihli Telgraf', document no. 406, *Harb Tarihi Vesikaları Dergisi*, no. 16 (June 1956). After the restoration in 1908, Câmi had served as the deputy of Tripolitania from 1908 to 1912 in the Ottoman parliament. In January 1920, he was elected to

Ethnic Cleansing in Western Anatolia

the last Ottoman parliament as one of the deputies for Aydın Province, see BOA DH. İ-UM. EK 112/52.

25. Moralı, *Mütarekede İzmir Olayları*, 66.

26. İlhan Tekeli and Selim İlkin, *Ege'deki Sivil Direnişten Kurtuluş Savaşı'na Geçerken* (Ankara: Türk Tarih Kurumu, 1989), 244–7.

27. BOA DH. KMS 53-2/40.

28. According to his memoirs, Hacim Muhittin Bey had regular meetings with Kara Vâsıf, one of the leaders of *Karakol*, in Constantinople in May–June 1919, see Çarıklı, *Balıkesir ve Alaşehir Kongreleri*, 16–20.

29. Ibid. 113.

30. Tekeli and İlkin, *Ege'deki Sivil Direnişten*, 181.

31. BOA DH. ŞFR 102/121.

32. Tekeli and İlkin, *Ege'deki Sivil Direnişten*, 204–8.

33. Ibid. 189.

34. TNA FO 608/115, 8 March 1919, Report on the CUP issued by General Staff Intelligence in Constantinople, Part III. Indeed, the social composition of the supporters of the establishment of an American mandate was identical to that of those supporting resistance against the territorial claims of the Greeks and Armenians. Thus, there was permeability between their social bases. Among the supporters of the American mandate were Turkish nationalists who approached the demands of the Ottoman Christians with suspicion and a part of the intelligentsia who had been acquainted with nationalist ideas at Western, especially American, schools.

35. ATASE İSH, 274/74, 8 December 1919.

36. For a detailed analysis of this agreement, see Paul C. Helmreich, 'Italy and the Anglo-French Repudiation of the 1917 St. Jean de Maurienne Agreement', *The Journal of Modern History* 48, no. 2 (June 1976), 99–139.

37. Grassi, *İtalya ve Türk Sorunu*, 25–6.

38. TNA FO 371/ 4157, 15 January 1919, Dixon, Resident Senior Naval Officer at Smyrna, to British High Commissioner. If these ex-Austrian subjects preferred Serbian citizenship, as in the cases of Nicolas Bratitch and Michel de Pezzer, they were to be deported by the Italian officers in Smyrna as a sign of their ambitious policy in Western Anatolia, cf. TNA FO 608/94, 10 May 1919, Serbian Embassy to British High Commission.

39. TNA FO 608/94, 10 May 1919, Serbian Embassy to British High Commission. When Italian officers attempted to hoist the Italian flag on these buildings in December 1918, the Austrian clerics in the city protested against them. However, these clerics were later compelled to take shelter in Constantinople, cf. BOA DH. ŞFR 609/31.

40. TNA FO 286/702, 12 August 1918, Commodore John L. Myres to British Embassy in Athens.

41. TNA FO 608/109, 14 October 1919, James Morgan to British High Commissioner.

Formation of a National Resistance

42. TNA FO 608/94, 3 March 1919, Area Control Officer in Smyrna to British High Commission.
43. TNA FO 608/94, 3 June 1919, Venizelos to Orlando, President of the Council of Ministers.
44. Moralı, *Mütarekede İzmir Olayları*, 68–73. That Nâil's brother Halit's wife was an Italian Levantine and the family had Italian passports probably helped the Moralızâdes in this smuggling operation.
45. TNA FO 371/4157, 12 May 1919, James Morgan, Representative of the British High Commissioner at Smyrna to the British High Commission in Constantinople.
46. Grassi, *İtalya ve Türk Sorunu*, 61.
47. See Moralı, *Mütarekede İzmir Olayları*, 51–2. Even though the association failed to send a representative to the conference due to the endless discussions on the election process of the representative, Câmi (Baykut) Bey, its secretary general, managed to deliver an *extrait du memoire*, describing the excesses of the Greek troops and alleging that 'ten thousand Muslims became the victims of the Greeks' blind fury' in Smyrna and Bournabat, to the conference, TNA FO 608/118, 19 June 1919, Djami Bey to Paris Peace Conference. During the convention of the Conference of London in 1921, Sforza, again, did not abstain to support the participation of the Turkish nationalists from Ankara. Thanks to his insistence, the Ankara government could send a committee consisting of Bekir Sâmî (Kunduh) and Câmi by an Italian ship from Antalya to Brindisi. After meeting with Sforza in Rome, this committee continued their journey by train.
48. Grassi, *İtalya ve Türk Sorunu*, 128–9.
49. Ibid. 62. In the northern towns bordering the Greek zone, such as Çine, the Italian authorities provided a safe haven for the withdrawing Ottoman troops, as in the case of the 57th Division.
50. Bayar, *Ben de Yazdım*, vol. 6, 1930.
51. Aker, *İstiklâl Harbinde* 57, vol. 2, 177–80.
52. TNA FO 371/5057, 23 October 1920, General Headquarters in Egypt to the British High Commissioner in Constantinople.
53. Grassi, *İtalya ve Türk Sorunu*, 141–53.
54. TNA FO 608/271, 6 January 1920, the British High Commission to Foreign Office. The gendarmerie was also affected by the demobilisation. Due to the demobilisation, the number of gendarmerie forces decreased from 25,000 to 9,000 throughout the Empire in January 1919, see *Türk İstiklâl Harbi, vol. 1: Mondros Mütarekesi ve Tatbikatı* (Ankara: Genelkurmay Basımevi, 1962), 176.
55. Apak, *İstiklal Savaşında*, 2.
56. Ibid. 1.
57. Ibid. 10.
58. Ali Çetinkaya, *Milli Mücadele*, 39.
59. Zürcher, *The Unionist Factor*, 73–7.

Ethnic Cleansing in Western Anatolia

60. Ibid. 88–93.
61. Criss, *Istanbul under Allied Occupation*, 112.
62. Zürcher, *The Unionist Factor*, 81
63. Ertürk, *İki Devrin Perde Arkası*, 180.
64. The national defence committees were regarded by the imperial govern-ment in Constantinople as one of the most distasteful nationalist bodies. According to British intelligence reports, these committees, composed of the Unionist and Bolshevik-sympathiser military officers, planned to stir up disorder in the provinces. Thus, the Ministry of War had warned officers that joining it would be 'considered as a grave breach of discipline', see TNA FO 608/115, 8 March 1919, Report issued by General Staff Intelligence in Constantinople on the CUP, Part III. These committees, which would later reassemble under an umbrella organisation – the Society for the Defence of the Rights of Anatolia and Rumelia (Anadolu ve Rumeli Müdâfaa-i Hukuk Cemiyeti) – were supported by the Fraternal Society for Reserve Officers.
65. Tekeli and İlkin, *Ege'deki Sivil Direnişten*, 224.
66. Zürcher, *The Unionist Factor*, 122–3.
67. TNA FO 608/90, 21 June 1919, the British High Commission in Constantinople to Earl Curzon.
68. For Unionist presence in the Ministry of War and their efforts to support the National Forces, a group of documents can be seen in *Türk İstiklal Harbi, vol. 7: İdarî Faaliyetler* (Ankara: Genelkurmay Basımevi, 1975). To exemplify, on a date as early as 28 December 1919, the Ministry of War announced that clothes and war equipment as well as every sort of help would be extended to the National Forces, 43.
69. Zürcher, *The Unionist Factor*, 101–2.
70. TNA FO 608/112, 26 May 1919, Captain E. D. Mackray, Intelligence Officer, to General Staff Intelligence.
71. Ali Çetinkaya, *Milli Mücadele*, 32–6.
72. TNA FO 371/ 5090, 16 May 1920, the British High Commissioner in Constantinople to Foreign Office.
73. Zürcher, *The Unionist Factor*, 86–7.
74. Yetkin, *Ege'de Eşkıyalar*, 49–52.
75. TNA FO 371/153, 19 July 1906, H. A. Cumberbatch to Sir Nicholas O'Conor, British ambassador at Constantinople.
76. At the end of World War I, it is estimated that only some 560,000 of a total 2,850,000 Ottoman mobilised soldiers remained in uniform, see Mehmet Beşikçi, *The Ottoman Mobilization of Manpower in the First World War: Between Voluntarism and Resistance* (Leiden: Brill, 2012), 113.
77. BOA DH. ŞFR 90/90 and BOA DH. ŞFR 90/104.
78. TNA FO 608/103, 7 April 1919, Admiral Calthorpe to Foreign Office.
79. Gingeras, *Sorrowful Shores*, 6.
80. TNA FO 371/4157, 20 April 1919, British Control Officer at Smyrna to the British High Commissioner in Constantinople.

Formation of a National Resistance

81. Apak, *İstiklal Savaşında*, 104–5.
82. To exemplify, a band consisting of nine Orthodox Greeks (both Ottoman subjects and Hellenes), six Muslims and two Armenians, launched a raid on the ironworks, owned by Georgios Leonidopoulos, a Hellenic national, in the Halkapınar neighbourhood in Smyrna on 14 November, 'Vilâyet Havâdisi', *Anadolu*, 29 November 1918 (R. 29 Teşrîn-i Sânî 1334). Another example was Çerkes Ethem's band that kidnapped the son of Rahmî Bey, former governor-general of the province, in collaboration with Kosmas, a fugitive, and *kolcubaşı* Atanas in February 1919.
83. Apak, *İstiklal Savaşında*, 31–2.
84. Özalp, *Milli Mücadele*, 27–31.
85. Apak, *İstiklal Savaşında*, 181.
86. Ertürk, *İki Devrin Perde Arkası*, 412.
87. *Hukuk-ı Beşer*, 13 February 1919 (13 Şubat 1335).
88. TNA FO 371/ 4157, 13 February 1919, Lewis Bailey, British Vice-Consul in Chios, to British Embassy in Athens.
89. Taçalan, *Ege'de Kurtuluş Savaşı Başlarken*, 152–4.
90. Ali Çetinkaya, *Milli Mücadele*, 71. For the assistance of the Bosniak gunmen around Edremit and Burhaniye to the National Forces, see TNA FO 608/ 90, 22 July 1919, Admiral Calthorpe to Foreign Office.
91. TNA FO 608/90, 8 July 1919, Stergiades to Fitzmaurice.
92. Apak, *İstiklal Savaşında*, 75.
93. Aker, *İstiklâl Harbinde* 57, vol. 2, 26. Süleyman Efendi regularly met with the local bandits and played an important role in the participation of Yörük Ali Efe and Demirci Mehmet Efe in the National Forces with their gunmen.
94. Bayar, *Ben de Yazdım*, vol. 7, 2086–90.
95. Apak, *İstiklal Savaşında*, 92.
96. Apart from Celâl Bey, Ahmet Hulusi Efendi, mufti of Denizli and Celâl's personal friend, played an important role in the persuasion of Demirci Mehmet Efe to join the National Forces, see Tekeli and İlkin, *Ege'deki Sivil Direnişten*, 179–80. The Ottoman archival materials reveal that the Ottoman Ministry of the Interior issued an arrest warrant for Mehmet Efe as early as 30 July 1919, and sent it to various governorships, cf. BOA DH. ŞFR 101/76.
97. Contrary to the arrest warrant by the Ministry of the Interior, as of autumn 1919, the Ministry of War began to support the expanding band of Demirci Mehmet Efe. In November 1919, Demirci Mehmet Efe requested 10,000 military cloaks and pistols from the Ministry of War, an institution dominated by the nationalists, cf. BOA HR. SYS 2554/3. It seems that the grand vizier defended the decision of the Ministry of the Interior in early December. Nonetheless, this case was one of the earliest examples of discords among the ministries in Constantinople, see BOA BEO 4603/345187.
98. TNA FO 608/91, 15 July 1919, Stergiades to Fitzmaurice.
99. TNA FO 286/790, 7 March 1922, Harry Lamb to the British High Commission.

Ethnic Cleansing in Western Anatolia

100. TNA FO 286/790, 1 March 1922, Harry Lamb to the British High Commission. However, according to a report written by the Italian high commissioner in Constantinople to his French colleague, 'the fact seems to correspond to a systematic plan of destruction of the Turkish villages and populations interior of the vilayet' and that thirteen villages in Torbalı district suffered seriously from the Greek troops and associating Muslim bandits, see CADC, 51CPCOM, P1379, 12 April 1922, Incendie des Mosquées de Karatépé.
101. TNA FO 608/90, 22 June 1919, Stergiades to Paris Peace Conference.
102. TNA FO 608/90, 27 June 1919, Representative of the British High Commissioner, Smyrna & Aydın vilayet to British High Commissioner, Constantinople.
103. TNA ADM 137/1762, 22 June 1919, Report on situation at NAZLI after evacuation of Greek troops.
104. TNA ADM 137/1762, 9 August 1919, T. B. Rees to Lieutenant J. A. Lorimer.
105. TNA ADM 137/1762, 7 August 1919, T. B. Rees to Lieutenant J. A. Lorimer.
106. The Ottoman archival documents also mention the attacks of the National Forces (Kuvâ-yı Milliye) on the local Christians, BOA DH. ŞFR 103/117 and BOA DH. ŞFR 646/51. These documents show that members of the National Forces looted the villages and raped local Greek women in the rural parts of the Saruhan *sanjak* in September 1919. The imperial government warned the district governor about these events and asked to take preventive measures. Another document reports the discontent of the Ottoman Ministry of the Interior due to the abuses (*sûistimâlât*) of the National Forces in Kırkağaç in the Saruhan *sanjak*. According to this document, the civil servants adhered to the ideas of the National Forces and banned non-Muslims from leaving the town in April 1920. However, two French passport-holders among the non-Muslims complained to the French high commissioner in Constantinople. Hence, the Ministry of the Interior asked the Saruhan district governor to investigate the civil servants, cf. BOA DH. EUM. AYŞ 40/32.
107. Akıncı, *Demirci Akıncıları*, 119.
108. TNA FO 608/90, 21 June 1919, the British High Commission in Constantinople to Earl Curzon.
109. Tekeli and İlkin, *Ege'deki Sivil Direnişten*, 132.
110. Apak, *İstiklal Savaşında*, 209.
111. Çarıklı, *Balıkesir ve Alaşehir Kongreleri*, 186–7.
112. TNA FO 608/102, 25 June 1919, James Morgan to Calthorpe.
113. Tekeli and İlkin, *Ege'deki Sivil Direnişten*, 274.
114. *Heyet-i Temsiliye Tutanakları*, ed. Uluğ İğdemir (Ankara: Türk Tarih Kurumu, 1975), 74.
115. Bezmi Nusret Kaygusuz, *Bir Roman Gibi* (Izmir: Gümüşayak Matbaası, 1955), 185.
116. BOA BEO 4606/345442.

Formation of a National Resistance

117. Tekeli and İlkin, *Ege'deki Sivil Direnişten*, 288.
118. Ibid. 288–96.
119. Kaygusuz, *Bir Roman Gibi*, 195. Ironically, the former owner of this deserted mansion was an Ottoman Greek.
120. Tekeli and İlkin, *Ege'deki Sivil Direnişten*, 299.
121. *Türk İstiklal Harbi*, vol. 7, 68.
122. Llewellyn Smith, *Ionian Vision*, 126–7.
123. Tekeli and İlkin, *Ege'deki Sivil Direnişten*, 319.
124. Ibid. 320.
125. Ibid. 318–20.
126. Zürcher, *The Unionist Factor*, 125–7.
127. Ahmet Turan Alkan, *İstiklal Mahkemeleri* (Istanbul: Ağaç Yayıncılık, 1993), 37.
128. TNA FO 286/758, Lord Granville to Greek Minister for Foreign Affairs, 31 October 1921.
129. For the difficulties faced by the Greek soldiers in Anatolia, see Akilas Millas, *Oğlunuz Er Yorgos Savaşırken Öldü* (Istanbul: Kitap Yayınevi, 2004).
130. For instance, Birtek claims that the occupation 'would change the historical scheme and pave the way for the Kemalist movement's rise to power', Faruk Birtek, 'Greek Bull in the China Shop of Ottoman "Grand Illusion": Greece in the Making of Modern Turkey', in *Citizenship and the Nation-state in Greece and Turkey*, ed. Faruk Birtek and Thalia Dragonas (London: Routledge, 2005), 31.
131. The American historian Abe Attrep claimed that the Greek occupation 'fired the hatred of the Turks, and spurred them to resist the Allies', Abe Attrep, '"A State of Wretchedness and Impotence": A British View of Istanbul and Turkey, 1919', *Journal of Middle Eastern Studies* 9 (1978), 3.
132. For an example of this kind of report, TNA FO 608/91, 21 August 1919, British General Staff report from Smyrna.
133. TNA FO 608/271, 6 January 1920, Richard Webb, Assistant High Commissioner, to Earl Curzon.
134. Zürcher, *The Unionist Factor*, 106. Zürcher's view on the roots of the Turkish nationalist movement explicitly challenges the mainstream historiography, which regarded the Greek landing at Smyrna as the catalyst for the national movement. Mainstream Turkish historians still consider the Greek landing to be the most important milestone in the beginning of the nationalist movement in order to emphasise the role of Mustafa Kemal in this movement and strengthen the argument that the Unionists played a limited role in its development.
135. Hans-Lukas Kieser, *Talaat Pasha: Father of Modern Turkey, Architect of Genocide* (Princeton: Princeton University Press, 2018), 394–5.

Chapter 6

Tartaros: Destruction of the Ottoman Coexistence

[I]t was done to treat the non-Muslim nations (*milel-i gayrimüslime*) well. Thank God, there is not such a question today … That garden of motherland must be cleaned from all pernicious thorns in order to be an excellent rose garden for the native nightingales to sing in complete liberty (*kemâl-i serbesti ile*). And thereby, the cleanings (*tathîrât*) were zealously undertaken so that thanks to God (*lehülhamd*), our homeland appears like the Kaaba today.[1]

(Osman Niyazi Bey during the meetings to alter the structure of administrative councils (*vilâyet idare meclisleri*), 20 December 1923)

As can be seen in the above excerpt from the parliamentary minutes, one of the members of the assembly of the new Republic spoke in praise of the ethnic cleansings performed during the war period between 1919 and 1922. Indeed, the victory of the Kemalist army constituted one of the most violent episodes of the disintegration of Ottoman society. Smyrna was burned down, and the Ottoman Christian communities in Western Anatolia were exposed to a series of systematic massacres and compelled to leave their hometowns at a time when the Ottoman system was in complete disarray.

Subsequent to the imposition of the population exchange and the promulgation of the Republic in the autumn of 1923, the political, social and cultural patterns of everyday life changed decisively in the former Ottoman territories. Aydın province was probably the administrative unit most affected by this transformation process. The imperial and cosmopolitan networks, in which different ethno-religious communities coexisted, could not resist the attacks of the Turkish nationalist elites. For most of the Unionist and nationalist statesmen, the idea of liberation meant the cleansing of the Ottoman Christian communities from the social and economic structure of the new nation-state. These elites would not only play an important role in the liquidation of the Ottoman Christians but

Destruction of the Ottoman Coexistence

also relegate the loyalist Ottoman civil servants in the province, who preferred keeping their ties with the Ottoman sultan. This chapter traces the nationalist dawn cast by the new elites of Turkey over the social and political structure of the imperial system in the province.

As a result, the Ottoman Christian communities witnessed a dramatic decrease in their population in the first quarter of the twentieth century. To illustrate, as late as 1914, Christians made up 20 per cent of the total population in the Empire; however, in 1927, they constituted only 2 per cent of the population of the young Republic.[2] As such, the Great Fire of Smyrna in September 1922 and the subsequent population exchange had fatal consequences for the Ottoman Christian communities. While the towns and cities in Western Anatolia were devastated because of the war, incendiarism and massacres, the presence of Ottoman Christians residing in the province, that is, Orthodox Greeks and Armenians, drew to a close by the end of the *Pax Ottomana*. Although the whole of Anatolia was overwhelmed by the population exchange, the destruction in Smyrna occurred on a far greater scale than that in other towns and cities. The Christian communities, which had formed at least 36 per cent of the population of the Aegean metropolis in the pre-war period, diminished to 1.2 per cent in 1927. In that year, only 548 Orthodox Christians and nineteen Armenians had been left in the city.[3] In short, no Ottoman city other than Smyrna, the capital of the province, experienced such a dramatic demographic shift.

Liberation: Entrance of the Nationalist Army in Smyrna

As a result of the final nationalist attack that began on 26 August 1922, the Greek troops started to flee towards the Aegean coast, and burned several Anatolian towns en route, leaving their Muslim habitants in miserable conditions. It seems that desertions from the Greek army, which started on 1 September, turned into a left-wing uprising among the troops in Afyon amid shouts of 'Long Live Lenin', and led to the plunder of the town and the execution of the officers by their soldiers within three days.[4] The troops who participated in this uprising became the main actors of the violence in the interior. On retreating, they looted and burned everything in their path (see Figure 6.1).[5]

On 5 September, the Adrianople Division of the Greek army reached Smyrna by ship in order to retain the city, yet the soldiers aboard rebelled here as well. Arguing that they were defeated in the war, many of those soldiers refused to disembark. On the afternoon of 7 September, Stergiades unexpectedly visited Osmond de Beauvoir Brock, commander-in-chief of the Mediterranean Fleet, and confided his apprehensions on board of

Ethnic Cleansing in Western Anatolia

Figure 6.1 A burned Anatolian town: Alaşehir. Les Archives de la Planète, Albert Kahn.

HMS *Iron Duke*. The British consul in the city had already advised the British colony to embark on the hospital ships anchoring in the harbour.[6] However, as testified by Brock's report, Stergiades stayed in the city until the last possible moment:

> He admitted that the Military headquarters staff and the civil officials might leave at any moment, and a very critical interregnum would occur between their departure and the arrival of Turkish regulars. He believed that his presence had a calming effect on the Greek populace and he was willing to remain as long as possible, provided he might be permitted eventually to embark in a British man-of-war.[7]

Of all the Greek officials, Stergiades was the last to depart with a diplomatic passport issued by the French consulate-general on the night of 8 September.[8] His departure from the city where he had been serving for three years meant the departure of the last administrator appointed by the Greek Kingdom.[9] To be more specific, the nationalist army entered Smyrna on 9 September, and the last Greek troops in Anatolia left Çeşme on 16 September.[10]

As soon as the Turkish nationalists entered Smyrna, Harry Lamb, the British representative in Smyrna, informed the French consul that murders and lootings had begun taking place in the city. Although he offered to 'take a collective initiative to Conak', the office of the Turkish governor Nureddin Pasha, the French consul preferred 'to postpone this process

Destruction of the Ottoman Coexistence

to the next day as it would be difficult to keep order in a city of 500,000 inhabitants'.[11] Known as the Armenian quarter (Haynots), Basmane was immediately plundered. Its market and the houses of Armenian merchants were the main targets of the irregulars.[12] Nureddin Pasha, the former governor-general of the province, was appointed military governor of the city by Mustafa Kemal. He harboured an intense animosity towards Ottoman Christian communities and had already played an important role in the deportations and mass killing of the Greek Orthodox population around Samsun and Amasya in the summer of 1920. He suppressed the Koçgiri rebellion, a Kurdish uprising in Sivas Province in February 1921. After having settled in the governor's residence, he summoned Chrysostomos, who had caused his dismissal from the city in 1919, with the intent of taking vengeance on him. He accused the metropolitan bishop of treason and threw him out of the residence. At that time a mob had already begun to convene at the Konak Square:

> The Prelate was walking slowly down the steps of the *Konak* when the General appeared on the balcony and cried out to the waiting mob, 'Treat him as he deserves!' The crowd fell upon Chrysostomos with guttural shrieks and dragged him down the street until they reached a barber's shop where Ismael, the Jewish proprietor, was peering nervously from his doorway. Someone pushed the barber aside, grabbed a white sheet, and tied it around Chrysostomos's neck, shouting, 'Give him a shave!'
>
> They tore out the Prelate's beard, gouged out his eyes with knives, cut off his ears, his nose, and his hands. A dozen French marines who had accompanied Chrysostomos to the government house were standing by, beside themselves. Several of the men jumped instinctively forward to intervene, but the officer in charge forbade them to move.[13]

It seems that Nureddin intended to cut off the city's communications with the outside world and to reduce mobility within the city. On 10 September, in a meeting with the French consul-general, he demanded the French 'withdrawal from the seafaring positions so that the British imitate them'. Stating that he 'had no other goal than the protection of the French nationals', the French consul rejected this demand. As a result, the Anglo-Eastern telegraph lines were cut off. In accordance with the martial law, a curfew was declared to be valid every evening after 7 p.m.[14]

The fire that broke out in the Basmane quarter on 13 September destroyed almost all the Christian neighbourhoods in the city as there was no attempt to stop it. Ever since, the question of who started the fire has been an issue of contention between those who argue that it was the Greek army and the Ottoman Christians who started the fire as an act of sabotage and those who claim that it was actually the nationalist officers and

Ethnic Cleansing in Western Anatolia

irregulars who deliberately set Smyrna on fire. Indeed, as for the latter, Miss Minnie Mills, the director of the American Collegiate Institute for Girls in Basmane, wrote as follows: 'Thousands were killed and looting and rape occurred on a wide scale. There is indisputable evidence that the Turks set the fires which destroyed all the Christian quarter.'[15] Mark O. Prentiss, the special representative of Near East Relief, described his impressions about the fire and attitudes of the nationalist officers to the Ottoman Christians:

> Fully a quarter of a million human being [*sic*] were doomed to death by burning, drowning or, worse still, later by starvation. Many were forced or jumped into the water ... After discussing not only this situation but all causes that produced it, it is my opinion that peace will never be restored until all Greeks and Armenians are evacuated from Turkey. All the highest Turkish officials concur in vows and urge that this to be done.[16]

Undoubtedly, the fire, which scorched and devastated Smyrna in September 1922, cannot be compared in terms of its effects to all the other fires the city had experienced for centuries. The fire reduced the economic activities in the city to a minimum level. Schools, banks, hospitals, churches and theatres were destroyed. Large stretches of the Bellavista neighbourhood and the Quay, the symbols of Ottoman modernisation in the city, were ruined. The burned area stretched along the Quay for 3,200 metres and the fire penetrated as far as five kilometres inside the city. It destroyed nearly 50,000 buildings, and more than 10,000 residential buildings were abandoned.[17] Not only did this fire destroy the commercial centre of the city, but it also annihilated the whole Ottoman social structure. Its cosmopolitan framework was completely erased in the history and space of the city.[18] *Gâvur* Smyrna, where the non-Muslim Ottoman citizens formed the majority of the population, ceased to exist (see Figure 6.2).

It is difficult to predict the number of casualties who died under these circumstances. H. W. Urquhart, the British vice-consul in Smyrna, estimated that 180,000 Ottoman Greeks fled from the shores of Smyrna up to the end of September.[19] On 18 September 1922, Nureddin Pasha, as military governor, issued a notification about the post-war treatment of the Ottoman Christians:[20]

> It is found necessary to give the following explanations in order to dispel doubts arisen upon the application of Proclamation No. 5:
>
> 1) The foreign nationalities obtained by those who were Ottoman subjects at the armistice are invalid unless the change is in conformity with the law on nationality. Such persons will be considered Ottoman subjects.

Destruction of the Ottoman Coexistence

Figure 6.2 Smyrna after the Great Fire. Les Archives de la Planète, Albert Kahn.

2) Those who, being Ottoman subjects, have received a foreign protection, will be treated as Ottomans.
3) Those of the above who are men of the ages of 18 to 45 will be sent to garrisons for prisoners of war.

In view of the necessity of preparing means of transport for those Greeks, Armenians, and Jews of Hellenic nationality, who, being inhabitants of the coast, do not leave the country before the evening of the 30th September, 1922, and remain in Smyrna or along the coast, the heads of the Greek, Armenian, and Jewish communities will inform the local military and civil authorities of the numbers of men and women who will remain and not leave by sea.

Those who hide in their houses or elsewhere arms of war and Greek soldiers or obnoxious men being searched for by the Government will at once hand them up to the military. Forty-eight hours from now searches will be made with this object, and those who have contravened this order will be executed.

The army needs all merchandise and movable property left without owner in Smyrna and district owing to fire or military operations or flight of the owners or through any other cause. It cannot be allowed that such goods and belongings should furnish an opportunity for illegitimate gain. Therefore, those who get possession of these by finding them unowned or by fictitious contracts or by other means are obliged to deliver them immediately to the commandant

Ethnic Cleansing in Western Anatolia

de la place. Those who venture to act in contravention of this order or to give themselves up to speculation or who obtain possession of abandoned things in any way whatsoever will be condemned to ten years' hard labour and to a fine from 100 l. to 5000 l.

It is forbidden to take possession without authority of houses, shops or other buildings. The vali will order the manner in which such property will be administered. Action contrary to this rule is punishable with ten years' hard labour.

Mustafa Kemal also informed the Allied representatives that the evacuations of the Ottoman Christians from Smyrna had to be completed on October 1. The American Relief Committee, Near East Relief, and various Allied agencies made every effort to carry off 300,000 Ottoman Christians, as well as some Muslims, from the port of Smyrna. After a long series of negotiations, the nationalist authorities allowed the British, American and Greek ships to carry away the local Christians and some Circassians to Greece in the last days of September.[21] Nonetheless, the display of the Greek flags on the ships and their approach to the wharfs were strictly banned. Additionally, the male population of military age, that is, those between eighteen and forty-five, were not allowed to leave Anatolia and were dispatched to forced labour camps in the interior where a great number of them died of disease, malnutrition and massacre.[22]

In October 1922, a house-to-house search was commenced to find the remaining Greek and Armenian civilians in downtown Smyrna.[23] In the interior of the province, most Christians felt obliged to desert their homes with little more than their lives because of the chaotic situation in the autumn of 1922. Following these expulsions, numerous towns and villages in the Aegean littoral were going to be depopulated.

Comparing it with its Ottoman past, Turkish Izmir would be a very different city. Due to the Great Fire of 1922, Izmir lost virtually all of its connections with its cosmopolitan past. A great number of the Ottoman Christians had already fled to Greece during the violent events and the Great Fire of Smyrna in September 1922; however, the properties of the Christian communities were a matter of concern for the local Kemalist authorities. Therefore, systematic destruction and definite defunctionalisation of the Orthodox and Armenian churches continued in the winter of 1922–3 until the signature of the convention of the population exchange between Greece and Turkey. Even the properties of the other Orthodox churches, which were not under the jurisdiction of the Ecumenical Patriarchate of Constantinople and protected by the British soldiers in the region, were also plundered or confiscated. To illustrate, the properties of the Mount Sinai Monastery in Izmir were also sequestered by the

Destruction of the Ottoman Coexistence

nationalist government. Among these properties that the monastery lost were commercial buildings, such as the Passage Sinaite, located in the rue des Verreries; a hotel in the Quay; and two depots located in the rue Parallèle and Halim Aga Market.[24]

This campaign of destruction was followed by several attacks on other Christian cemeteries and churches, mostly belonging to the Levantine populations in the city. The Dutch cemetery located in downtown Izmir was violated by local groups, and all the tombstones in the Anglican cemetery at Bornova were smashed and overthrown.[25] Even though the matter of the pillaging of the Anglican cemetery was brought to the notice of Hüseyin Aziz (Akyürek), the governor of Izmir, in October 1923, no payments for repair were made within a year despite his promises. Furthermore, the disused half of the Anglican cemetery was expropriated by the local authorities overnight in Bornova on the pretext of road building.

The silence and indifference of the elites of the new nation-state vis-à-vis the human tragedy in Western Anatolia were later to be regarded as an essential part of the history of the new Republic in that those founding elites had deliberately chosen to forget the removal of the Ottoman Christians and the violence that accompanied those events.[26] In his long speech delivered in the Ankara assembly in November 1922, Mustafa Kemal did not mention the Great Fire of Smyrna, although he did mention the fire started by the Greek army in Afyonkarahisar. Similarly, he did not refer to the Great Fire in his six-day-long speech in the Grand National Assembly in 1927.[27] Nevertheless, Fâlih Rıfkı, one of the most significant journalists of the early republican era who went on to be a member of parliament after 1923, and who was also a close friend of Mustafa Kemal, offered a much more frank account of the Great Fire in his memoirs:

> Why were we burning down Smyrna? Did we fear that we would not be able to get rid of the minorities if the villas, hotels and clubs of the Quay had remained? When the Armenians were deported in the First World War, we had burned down all the neighbourhoods and districts of Anatolia's inhabitable cities and towns with the same fear. This is nothing other than what stems from a pure sense of vandalism. It is also affected by an inferiority complex. It was as if every single corner that looked like a part of Europe, being Christian and foreign, had been destined not to be ours.[28]

İbrahim (Turhan) Bey, a deputy of Mardin, also presented a question in a secret session in the Ankara assembly on 29 November 1922 about the roles of the commanders and officers of the nationalist movement in the looting activities perpetrated in the city:

Ethnic Cleansing in Western Anatolia

We hear that a large group of officers and commanders participated in the looting activities in Izmir. Has this really happened (*Bu vâki' midir*)? Then, the Commander of the First Army [Nureddin Pasha] seized all the money and goods and handed them out to people. Is this true? How much money was handed out? Then, a friend of ours, a deputy, broke into the houses (*evlere girmiş*) and appropriated those houses. Is it true as well? I would like to pose those questions.[29]

Narrow Escape: Population Exchange

During the armistice negotiations held in October 1922 between the Allied representatives and the Turkish nationalists under the leadership of Mustafa Kemal, it became clear that the nationalists would refuse the return to Anatolia of over a million Ottoman Greeks who had been driven from their hometowns.[30] In this context, Venizelos came to favour the idea of a compulsory population exchange at the Lausanne peace talks. Onur Yıldırım argues that Venizelos deemed it a most viable and effective method to solve the problem as he also desired to Hellenise the newly acquired northern provinces of Greece.[31]

The Convention concerning the Exchange of Greek and Turkish Populations, a massive exercise in demographic engineering, stipulated the forced resettlement of Ottoman Orthodox individuals to Greece, excepting those residing in Istanbul and the two small Aegean islands of Imvros and Tenedos, and Muslims in Greece to Turkey, excluding those in Western Thrace.[32] This convention was signed on 30 January 1923 by the Greek and Turkish governments as a part of the Lausanne negotiations. According to statistics compiled by the Mixed Commission founded for the supervision of exchange and the liquidation of movable and immovable properties of the exchangees, almost 355,000 Muslims and 192,000 Orthodox Christians were involved in this displacement process after January 1923.[33] Nonetheless, most Ottoman Greeks, particularly those living near the Aegean coastline, had left their hometowns during the violent events in the autumn of 1922. Thus, it is estimated that, all in all, almost 1,200,000 Orthodox Christians were compelled to migrate to Greece in 1922–3.

By the same token, it is evident that a great number of Ottoman Christians residing in Aydın Province had already fled to Greece in September 1922 due to looting activities, physical attacks and intimidation by the irregular forces. Official records of the Mixed Commission also verified this migration. According to these data, only 2,500 of the total 190,000 Orthodox Christian exchangees left through the port of Izmir in the period between

Destruction of the Ottoman Coexistence

1923 and 1924.[34] Indeed, the Turkish nationalist authorities resolved the question of compact Christian populations on the Aegean coastline in great haste before the convention for the exchange of populations was put into effect, ultimately. This population transfer agreement both legitimised the previous migrations, particularly the flight of the Ottoman Greeks from Smyrna and other Aegean towns to Greece in the autumn of 1922, and obliged the remaining populations to leave their hometowns because of its forced and all-inclusive characteristics. In essence, the exchange mainly involved the transfer of the Ottoman Greeks in the interior of Anatolia, particularly Cappadocia, and Pontus inasmuch as the Christian populations in the Aegean coastline had already been driven out or killed by the end of September 1922.[35]

As Onur Yıldırım has argued, the property rush which began after the ethnic cleansing of the Ottoman Christian communities disturbed property configurations throughout the former Ottoman territories, particularly in Western Anatolia. Since the property problems were not easy to resolve, the nationalist government formed a new ministry, the Ministry of the Exchange, Reconstruction and Resettlement (Mübadele, İmâr ve İskân Vekâleti), in order to arrange the arrivals of the Muslim migrants from Greece and redistribute property to them. The Muslim migrants from Greece were mainly settled in the adjacent and devastated settlements, particularly along the Aegean coastline. Before the arrival of Muslim exchangees from Greece, many houses, commercial enterprises, workshops and factories left by the Ottoman Christians had been occupied by a diverse group of profiteers, mostly bureaucrats, officers and local notables, who usurped the properties through the help of their contacts in Ankara, as well as by war victims. In Izmir, three main groups constituted these war victims: the indigenous Muslim people who suffered from the Great Fire (*harîkzedeler*), the Muslim people who were living in the Greek occupation zone but migrated to Izmir due to war or poverty (*felâketzedeler*), and those who had already migrated from the eastern Anatolian provinces during the Russian military advance in 1915–16 (*vilâyât-ı şarkiye muhacirleri*).[36]

The distant approach of the provincial authorities towards the problems of the refugees emboldened the local magnates to seize abandoned properties. In Karşıyaka and Bornova, the bourgeois suburbs of Izmir that were not seriously damaged during the Great Fire, there was not even a single house left available for the resettlement of the incoming Muslim refugees from Greece. The local magnates had already sequestered these valuable properties. In most cases, they argued that their Christian clients left without paying their debts, thus seizing the abandoned properties in return for unpaid debts.[37]

Ethnic Cleansing in Western Anatolia

Republican authorities were very careful with the resettlement of those of non-Turkish descent in the coastline. They did not allow concentrations of non-Turkish-speaking Muslims in the cities, towns or villages. In accordance with the Instructions of the Population Exchange (*Ahâlî Mübadelesi Hakkında Talîmâtnâme*) dated July 1923, the proportion of refugees, whose languages and traditions were different from Turkish ones, was not allowed to exceed 20 per cent of the population in a certain city, town or village. Thus, the government hoped to make the assimilation of non-Turkish migrant groups possible in rural areas through restricting their acceptable proportion to 20 per cent.[38] In particular, the concentration of Albanian-speaking migrants was not welcomed by the administrative authorities in Izmir and created further suspicions among the nationalist deputies. Increasing numbers of Albanians triggered discussions among the republican elites and Mustafa Abdülhalik (Renda), the governor of Izmir, attracting vehement criticisms from deputies. One example was Rıza Nur, the minister of health, who accused Mustafa Abdülhalik of deliberately resettling Albanians in Izmir.[39] In March 1923, the same ministry urged the removal of some 175 Albanian households in Buca, whose total population was around 1,300 households. Another group of Albanians in Bornova were scattered to the interior provinces of Isparta and Niğde. Similarly, the properties of the Ottoman Greeks in Bornova, which were occupied by Albanian migrants, came to be earmarked for the Turkish-speaking Muslim migrants from Greece in the August of that year.[40]

Liberated Provinces: Making a Turkish Anatolia

Because of the ethnic cleansing policies employed within the previous decade, the new Republic had come to be home to a largely Turkish – but multi-ethnic – Muslim majority. Parallel to this, the republican elites established very problematic relations with the non-Muslim minorities, whose rights, albeit their shrinking numbers, were guaranteed by the Lausanne Peace Treaty in July 1923. In spite of this guarantee, the Kemalist government resorted to various methods of alienating these groups and employing legal and illegal measures to make their lives unendurable in Turkey. In this period, Kemalist elites would try to create 'a united mass without any privileges'.[41] Therefore, they would conduct a series of homogenisation policies, which affected all aspects of life, from dressing to units of measurement. The exclusion of non-Muslim minorities from commercial life, the forced assimilation of their educational institutions, arbitrary taxation of minority groups, organised attacks on

Destruction of the Ottoman Coexistence

non-Muslim communities and forced migrations were the methods used to implement these policies.

The non-Muslim individuals who were able to stay in Western Anatolia were mostly Roman Catholic Levantines and Jews.[42] Their attempts to accord themselves to the nationalist Republic would entail difficulties and disappointments. The restrictions of the new regime would be felt especially in the educational system. The ordinances which were issued in the first years of the Republic and inspired by the Unionist approach concerning the foreign and non-Muslim community schools would restrict the remaining institutions in the province in certain ways. In May 1923, the Ministry of National Education decided that history, geography and Turkish language courses had to be taught by ethnically Turkish teachers. Likewise, the elites of the new nation-state accentuated the introduction of compulsory Turkish courses by Turkish teachers in foreign and minority schools.[43] Furthermore, a Turkish deputy principal would be appointed to those schools, and foreign propaganda, which 'might harm the Turkish nation and Islamic values', would never be permitted. Due to these interventionist decisions and their arbitrary implementation, foreign and minority schools became less and less preferable for non-Muslims.

In the early republican period, at the peak of Turkish nationalism, the schools served as the key institutions where nationalism was reproduced. Foreign observers soon took notice of the new situation. In April 1923, Henry George Thursfield, the commanding officer at HMS *Concord*, informed the senior naval officer in Istanbul about the soaring anti-foreign sentiments prevailing in the economic realm of the new Republic and how the students were instigated by these feelings:

> Anti-foreign feeling is being manifested, and parties of schoolboys and rowdies parade the town, demanding the removal of all shop signs, advertisements etc. except those in Turkish characters. It is probable that if these demands are ignored, the offending sign will be torn down some night soon. Rowdyism at night is frequent during Ramadan.[44]

Undoubtedly, these campaigns affected commercial relations as well. British archival documents underline the extent to which the Ankara assembly initiated a centralisation campaign and tried to exclude foreigners from regional commerce. According to the statistics of the Izmir Chamber of Commerce, Muslim merchants of Turkish nationality started to dominate all commercial and industrial networks and markets in the region as of 1923.[45]

In brief, the presence of foreign citizens in Western Anatolia was not tolerated by the authorities of the Turkish state. On 6 February 1923,

Ethnic Cleansing in Western Anatolia

Tahsin Bey, a deputy of Izmir and former governor-general of Aydın Province, stated that the young Republic would not allow foreign entrepreneurs to play an important role in the regional commerce:

> While strolling through the Quay of Izmir (İzmir Kordonu) and touring around partially changed places, esteemed producers coming even from the interior of Anatolia will loathingly notice that those exalted buildings (*o âlî binâlar*) on the Quay were actually constructed by Ayşe's sweat and Ali's claws, and the agricultural products for which they spent their lives under the sun were seized by Georges, Hamparsons, Atanasos (Jorclar, Hamparsonlar, Atanasolar *tarafından*) instead. And then looking back on their own condition and then looking again at those owl nests, they will carry a deep grudge in their hearts against the ungrateful people (*nânkörlere*) who have sucked their blood for years. Undoubtedly, they will give thanks to God Almighty and salute infidel Smyrna as Muslim Izmir since these legations that were built upon the tears and sweat of the nation were burned and demolished, and their residents were cleared out (*def ve ref olması*).[46]

The British representatives also noticed that the nationalist authorities were inclined to create problems for non-Turkish merchants in Izmir, once a hub of foreign commerce. According to a report written by a British commanding officer, the nationalist authorities were putting every difficulty in the way of foreign citizens either while entering or leaving Izmir. As stated in the orders from the Kemalist government, any foreigners, either Europeans or Greeks, coming from Greece would not be allowed to enter the region.[47]

Despite the fact that a majority of the Levantines and European citizens were evacuated to the Aegean islands, Malta or Trieste in 1922, some of them would choose to return to Izmir after 1926 when the Kemalist government declared that it would not interfere in the return of the former European residents of the port city. Nonetheless, the returning Levantine entrepreneurs were also negatively affected by the nationalisation campaigns of the capital. To exemplify this point, the Oriental Carpet Manufacturers Ltd was forced to sell its plots located in the Quay and the rue Parallèle under pressure from the municipality, which claimed that these plots remaining in the centre of the fire zone were needed for the reconstruction of the city. Despite the fact that Edmund Giraud and Charles Molinary, the owners of the company, filed protests to the governor in November 1926 and to the municipality in May 1927, they would not receive any replies.[48]

With the re-implementation of national economy policies in the early republican period, following in the footsteps of the Unionists, Turkey did not entirely close its doors to foreign merchants and entrepreneurs, but

Destruction of the Ottoman Coexistence

imposed serious restrictions on the commercial activities of those people. Similarly, opportunities for individual enterprise were very limited, and in the early 1930s, laws were brought in to forbid foreigners and foreign passport holders from working in many professions.[49] In the 1930s, the Kemalist government nationalised the two railway lines operated by British and French companies, the port of Izmir and the telecommunications company of the region.

Aside from these nationalist–centralist concerns, the government intended to discard the irregulars and certain prominent leaders within the army, 'who had been paid with the Greek properties and old Greek furniture':

> Trade is almost standstill. The Civil Administration would be glad to be rid of the Army, they say they are hampered in every way by them.
>
> The extreme centralisation at Angora is leading to congestion and administrative chaos throughout the country.
>
> There is almost open talk of revolution, the dangerous man of the moment being NOURREDDIN PASHA, Commander of the Western Army. He is a most ambitious man, has a considerable backing in the Army, and is known to have been recently meddling in Politics. Angora is afraid of him, and are reported to be doing all they can to hold him in check.[50]

Due to a new regulation restructuring the army in the summer 1923, Nureddin Pasha had been obliged to leave without command and his power became limited within the army. He was elected as an independent deputy of Bursa in the elections held in December 1924; nonetheless, his status was rejected by the Assembly in the following year since he had a military rank and a deputy status at the same time, which was illegitimate.

The properties of non-Muslim Ottoman citizens which remained in the fire zone but were somehow rescued from destruction constituted a crucial problem in the first decade of the Republic. The new Republic not only ignored non-Muslims' property rights but also stirred up trouble for foreign representatives who tried interfering on behalf of them. For example, the property rights of S. Baliozian, an Ottoman Armenian who was forced either to leave Smyrna or be killed, were devolved on the plot of the British Consulate for the Abandoned Property Commission (Emvâl-i Metruke Komisyonu) in September 1922.[51] Despite the fact that Mustafa Abdülhalik, the governor, had assured Urquhart, the British representative, in a meeting about the unburned British property in September 1922,[52] these properties could not be saved from the nationalisation project. Thus, the British consul was obliged to move his office to the buildings of the British Seamen's Hospital for two years.[53] In addition to this, the British

Post Office, which was hardly touched by the fire, was badly damaged by the marauders who had infested the burned area. Its doors were taken away, windows smashed and the cistern dislodged.[54] An order published in *Le Levant* on 31 December 1925 announced that the value of the British and French consular properties were definitely assessed and their land would be put up to auction in line with the new urban construction plan very soon. Evidently, this order legitimised the expropriations of those properties by the Turkish state. In spite of the objections of the British ambassador in Istanbul, İhsan Lâtif (Sökmen) Pasha declared that the Commission of Evaluation considered them to be abandoned property (*emvâl-i metruke*).[55]

Republican authorities ignored the Ottoman Christians' demands concerning their properties from the very beginning. In August 1923, the Armenian refugees in Athens, led by a merchant named Essayan, sent letters to the General Assembly of the League of Nations in Geneva in order to retrieve their deposits, valuables and money kept in the foreign banks of Smyrna, such as Imperial Ottoman Bank, Credit Lyonnais, and Credit Foncier d'Algérie et de Tunisie.[56] However, the Turkish representatives had already announced in the Lausanne negotiations in July 1923 that the nationalist government, which initiated the attempts to nationalise the capital in the region, would not only regard these demands illegitimate and expropriate the sums in those banks, but also would not permit the return of the Armenians to the region.[57]

The new regime wanted to rid the Empire of non-Turkish heritage. The entire Greek occupation zone, that is, most of the territories of Aydın and Hüdavendigar provinces, was redesignated by the Assembly in Ankara as the liberated provinces (*vilâyât-ı müstahlasa*). As stated by a law which stipulated a new administrative division through the elevation of all *mutasarrıflık*s to the administrative level of a province and was ratified by the Assembly in 1924, Aydın Province was divided into four different and independent provinces, namely Izmir, Saruhan, Aydın and Denizli. Moreover, the zealous elites of the young Republic commenced a name-changing campaign for administrative units and settlements whose names were of non-Turkish stock or associated with the *ancien régime*. An example of this was seen in 1926, with the government decision declaring that the name of Saruhan Province was modified to Manisa.[58]

A new and wholly Turkish Izmir was created by republican elites on the ashes of cosmopolitan Smyrna. The Aegean metropolis which had formerly been the heart of the foreign and non-Muslim presence in Western Anatolia continued to be called Smyrna or Smyrne by the Europeans and Americans in their correspondence until 1930. Owing to the enactment of

Destruction of the Ottoman Coexistence

the Turkish Postal Service Law in March 1930, the Turkish name of Izmir was ensured as the internationally recognised name of the city. The names of its neighbourhoods were also changed by this law. While Boudjah and Bournabat, the two towns largely populated by Levantines, were turkified as Buca and Bornova, the northern centre of the city, Pounta, came to be called Alsancak (red flag), an entirely new name referring to the red colour of the Turkish flag. Another decision issued by the municipality in 1937 dictated that any street wider than twenty metres should bear a Turkish name and that numbers should be used to name streets narrower than twenty metres.[59]

Since some crucial modifications were introduced by the Grand National Assembly in 1925 to the *Ebniye Kanunu* (Building Law) of 1882, which recognised large areas where more than 150 buildings were burned down as agricultural plots (*tarla*), the municipality of Izmir could claim ownership rights of the vast areas in the fire zone, which had become a dangerous place in the early years of the Republic due to the presence of vagrants.[60] Eventually, apart from some new administrative and commercial buildings, the municipality engaged in the construction of a Republic Square and a cultural park, known as Kültürpark, which would symbolise the values of the republican period in this area in the 1930s. While the construction of the Republic Square was completed in 1932, the Kültürpark was opened to the public in 1936. In the smaller urban centres, such as Aydın and Manisa, the Christian neighbourhoods that were destroyed were transformed into recreational areas by the local authorities.

Hundred and Fifties (Yüzellilikler): Making the List of Traitors and Declaration of the List

Similar to the other post-war treaties, the Treaty of Lausanne contained a sub-heading about the declaration of a general amnesty; nonetheless, the representatives of the nationalist government revealed during the negotiations that their government had already decided to send its main Muslim opponents into exile. During the first series of the Lausanne meetings, the issue of general amnesty was negotiated in the sub-commission of minorities, led by Cesare Montagna, the Italian representative at Lausanne. Rıza Nur, representative of the Turkish nationalists, clearly underlined that the Muslims had to be kept outside the scope of the general amnesty and that the Ankara government would like to punish those Muslims who sided with its enemies. Both Rıza Nur and İsmet (İnönü) insisted that instances of high treason should be harshly punished. However, the Allied representatives kept their stance for a general amnesty without any exceptions

Ethnic Cleansing in Western Anatolia

for crimes committed from 1 August 1914 to 20 November 1922. Due to pressure from the Allied representatives, Rıza Nur and İsmet accepted the principle of general amnesty with the approval of the Ankara government on 11 January 1923.

This declaration of general amnesty stated that both Greek and Turkish governments would proclaim a reciprocal amnesty:

> No person who inhabits or has inhabited Turkey, and reciprocally no person who inhabits or has inhabited Greece, shall be disturbed or molested and reciprocally in Greece, under any pretext whatsoever, on account of any military and political action taken by him, or any assistance of any kind given by him to a foreign Power signatory of the Treaty of Peace signed this day or to the nationals of such Power, between the 1st August, 1914, and the 20th November, 1922.
>
> Similarly, no inhabitant of the territories detached from Turkey under the said Treaty of Peace shall be disturbed or molested either on account of his political or military attitude against or in favour of Turkey during the period from the 1st August, 1914, to the 20th November, 1922, or of the determination of his nationality under the said Treaty.
>
> Full and complete amnesty shall be respectively granted by the Turkish Government and by the Greek Government for all crimes and offences committed during the same period which were evidently connected with the political events which took place during that period ...[61]

Surprisingly, on 4 June 1923, at Lausanne, Rıza Nur stated that

> the Turkish government, like any other governments, reserves the right to take security measures against rioters (*karışıklık çıkarıcı unsurlara*), revolutionaries, assassins and, in general, against harmful elements ... Those who do not stir up trouble (*ortalığı karıştırmayan kimseler*) are out of the scope of this declaration.[62]

After long discussions, the Turkish representatives managed to get a concession since the Allied delegates accepted their request to exclude 150 Muslims from this general amnesty; nonetheless, determining 150 people who could not benefit from the amnesty would be a tedious task for the deputies in the National Assembly. On 4 April 1924, deputies started to discuss the issue of 'Muslim traitors' who still remained in the country. In accordance with the General Amnesty Agreement attached to the Treaty of Lausanne, the 'people who had assisted adversary parties' in Greece and Turkey during the course of World War I and the Greco-Turkish War were granted immunity from prosecution.[63]

It was then announced that a selected number of Muslim traitors to the fatherland (*vatan hâinleri*) would be deported from Turkey and deprived of their citizenship rights. Indeed, these 150 people were an eclectic group,

Destruction of the Ottoman Coexistence

composed of pro-palace public officials, members of clergy, officers, journalists and rebels against the nationalist movement in Ankara. The common ground among these people was that they had clearly sided against the nationalists. This list of 150 *personae non gratae* included, at the top, the highest officials and some former ministers of the Empire, that is, the entourage of Vahdeddin and cabinet members, including Mustafa Sabri, the former *sheikh-ul Islam* who supported the Ottoman palace against the nationalist movement, and Kiraz Hamdi, former minister of war. All of the ministers were classified under the headline of cabinet members. During the discussions for the preparation of the list, Ali Rüştü, former minister of justice, was accused by Ahmet Ferit (Tek), minister of the interior, of praising the Greek army as 'our soldier'.[64] The third and fourth headlines were the signatories of the Treaty of Sèvres and the members of the Kuvâ-yı İnzibâtiye (the Disciplinary Forces – an Ottoman military unit established against the National Forces),[65] respectively. Since the law of the Abolition of the Caliphate and the Exile of the Ottoman Dynasty outside the Republic of Turkey was passed in March 1924, members of the Ottoman dynasty were not added to this list.

A considerable number of loyalist Ottoman public officials and civil servants who were at odds with the nationalist movement were defined as traitors. Under the fifth headline of Civil Servants and Military Personnel (*Mülkiye ve Askeriye*), the names of thirty-one Ottoman civil servants and officers who had served in the occupation zones, particularly the Greek occupation zone, were listed. Most of them, who were the members of the dissolved Freedom and Accord Party, kept close ties with the Ottoman government and did not approve of the policies of the Unionists during the war years. In this part of the list, Hüsnü Bey, the former district governor of the Saruhan *sanjak*; Ahmet Asım, the legal consultant (*kadı müşaviri*) of Izmir; Küçük Ethem, the former *kaymakam* of Akhisar; and Şerif Bey, the former *kaymakam* of Kırkağaç, constituted the names who served in Aydın Province. In addition to those personalities from Aydın Province, there were other Ottoman civil servants from the Greek occupation zone listed under this title, namely Azîz Nuri Bey, former deputy governor of Bursa; Hoca Râsihzâde İbrahim, district governor of Kütahya; Hulûsî Bey, mayor of Uşak;[66] Mustafa Bey, former *kaymakam* of Adapazarı; Sabit Bey, former *kaymakam* of Afyonkarahisar; Ömer Fevzi, former mufti of Bursa; and Hafız Ahmet, former mufti of Tekirdağ in Thrace. Contrary to these high-ranking Ottoman provincial officials, Ahmet Hulûsî Bey, the counsellor of the Department of Muslim Services in the High Commission, was added to the last part of the list titled Other Persons (*Diğer Eşhas*).

Ethnic Cleansing in Western Anatolia

The sixth headline of the list, named Çerkes Ethem and His Gunmen, consisted of a group of Circassians who had participated in the Special Organisation but later came into conflict with the nationalist movement in Ankara. The participants of the Circassian Congress in Smyrna were listed under the seventh headline. The eighth headline was composed of police officers, and the following one journalists. The names of some journalists who had continued to publish their newspapers or write articles for these newspapers under the Greek administration were enclosed under the title of Journalists in the list. The names of İzmirli Hafız İsmail, owner of *Müsavat*; Ferit Bey, editor of *Köylü*; and İzmirli Mehmet Refet, owner of *Köylü*, were enumerated in this part of the list.

Eventually, those 150 so-called traitors would be allowed to return to Turkey in June 1938. When some of them requested an amnesty in 1938, the youngest member of this group had already reached the age of fifty. After a government investigation,[67] it was determined that almost half of them had died. For these reasons, they could no longer pose a serious threat to the hegemony of the Kemalist elites, so their ban was lifted.

Nonetheless, the number of Ottoman civil servants and officers who were obliged to leave the country was not limited to the list of Hundred and fifties. Some Muslim civil servants who established relations with the High Commission had already vanished or perished during the violent events following the victory of the Kemalist army. The others had to take shelter in Athens. Those civil servants who left their posts were accused by the National Assembly at Ankara of working for the enemy. For example, Hacı Hasan Pasha, the former mayor of Izmir, who already left for Athens in the autumn of 1922, was deprived of his citizenship rights by the Assembly in August 1927.[68]

The evacuation of the Ottoman civil servants from Istanbul continued during the autumn and winter in 1922–3. M. A. B. Johnston, the British military representative with the retreating Greek armies, informed the British military attaché in Athens that when the Allied troops evacuated the Ottoman capital, 144 Muslim civil servants, officers and merchants, who were 'likely to come into harm at the hands of the Kemalists', left with the Greek and Allied forces. They were dumped at Alexandroupolis, the Greek border town, since the Greek General Headquarters stated that none of these Muslims would be allowed to wander freely in the Greek territories. In this group, there were important figures who had played crucial roles in the governments, provincial administrations and political life of the Empire. Fuat Kâmil Bey, ex-director of political and commercial affairs of the Foreign Affairs Ministry; Hafız Mahmud Celâl Efendi, ex-mayor of Adana; Nuri Efendi, secretary to the war minister;

Destruction of the Ottoman Coexistence

Salih Asaf Efendi, ex-president of the Court of Appeal; Rıfkı Bey, secretary to the Freedom and Accord Party; Sâmî Bey, ex-governor of Eskişehir; Nizameddin Bey, ex-director of police at Bursa; and Evrenoszâde Sami Bey, member of the Central Office of the Freedom and Accord Party were among this group. Of these 144 people, 119 would go to Egypt, fifteen to Greece, three to Bulgaria, seven to other Balkan states and two to other British colonies.[69]

Since the nationalist movement and the Kemalist state were based on the Unionist organisations and initiatives, the presence of former Unionist leaders, considered as potential competitors, within the Kemalist structure would be regarded as a severe risk by Mustafa Kemal and his associates. This perception of risk motivated Mustafa Kemal's group to purge former Unionists from government mechanisms in 1926.[70] Following a failed assassination attempt against Mustafa Kemal in Izmir, a considerable number of prominent Unionists, including Mithat Şükrü (Bleda), Yenibahçeli Nâil and Kara Vâsıf, were arrested. The first trial was quickly carried out by the Izmir Independence Tribunal (İstiklâl Mahkemesi), with fifteen petty Unionists being condemned to death by Ali (Çetinkaya) Bey.[71] Those people were hanged in the various neighbourhoods of Izmir, while Kara Kemal, one of the fugitive Unionists, committed suicide during a police raid in his Istanbul home in July of that same year.

More than fifty Unionist defendants, including Mithat Şükrü, Hüseyin Raûf (Orbay), Mehmet Câvit, Dr Nâzım, Yenibahçeli Nâil, Rahmî Bey and Kara Vâsıf, were adjudicated during the second wave of trials, which continued in the new capital of Ankara. While Mehmet Câvit, Dr Nazım and Yenibahçeli Nâil were sentenced to capital punishment, Raûf and Rahmî were committed to prison in absentia for ten years on 26 August 1926. On the same day, Mustafa Kemal precipitately approved of these decisions.[72] Due to these purges in 1926, he achieved the creation of a power monopoly for himself and his supporters.

Both the deportations of influential Muslims connected to the Ottoman palace or government, as in the case of the Hundred and fifties list, along with the 1926 purges related to the assassination attempt against Mustafa Kemal, were complementary processes for the clearance of the remnants of the *ancien régime* and the strengthening of the Kemalists' grasp on political power. While the deportations and expatriations in 1922–3 targeted the Ottoman civil servants, local notables and journalists who came into conflict with the nationalist movement, the Kemalist faction intended in 1926 to wipe out a Unionist group within the nascent Kemalist elite, whose new loyalty towards Mustafa Kemal was dubious. Some Unionists, such as Ali (Çetinkaya), Recep (Peker) and İsmet (İnönü), who

Ethnic Cleansing in Western Anatolia

demonstrated their political constancy to Mustafa Kemal in some way, managed to sustain their places within this elite.

As in the case of Aydın Province, intimidation activities, forced migrations, expulsions and massacres affected the masses directly during the period between 1914 and 1922. The Great Fire of Smyrna, the attacks of the irregular forces and, on a more limited scale, the compulsory population exchange between Greece and Turkey, played the most crucial role in the homogenisation of the population in the Aegean littoral.

Notes

1. TBMM Z.C., Devre: 2, Cilt: 4, İçtima Senesi: 1, 20 Kânûn-ı Evvel 1339 [20 December 1923], 377, retrieved from the digital archive of the Turkish parliament. Available at <https://www5.tbmm.gov.tr/tutanaklar/TUTANAK/TBMM/d02/c004/ehttbmm02004071.pdf> (last accessed 15 December 2023).
2. *1927 Umumî Nüfus Tahriri* (Ankara: Başvekâlet İstatistik Umum Müdürlüğü, 1929), LX; and Keyder, *State and Class in Turkey*, 78–80.
3. *1927 Umumî Nüfus Tahriri*, 36. Most of them were either married to Levantine Catholics or were foreign passport holders, so they were exempted from the population exchange.
4. CADC, 51CPCOM, P1378, 4 September 1922, from Michel Graillet, French vice-consul at Smyrna, to the Affaires Etrangères.
5. For instance, while returning to Bergama via Soma on September 5, they set fire to the town, CADC, 51CPCOM, P1378, 5 September 1922, from Graillet to the Affaires Etrangères.
6. René Puaux, *La Mort de Smyrne* (Paris: Editions de la Revue des Balkans, 1922), 5.
7. TNA ADM 1/8640/114, 2 October 1922, O. De B. Brock to Admiralty. Indeed, Stergiades waited until the last moment before the arrival of the Kemalist army and left Smyrna on the evening of 8 September. On the other hand, Admiral Brock left Smyrna on 14 September, one day after the fire had broken out.
8. CADN, Izmir 643 PO/1, 97, 9 September 1922, Annexe à la dépêche Politique.
9. Stergiades did not have courage to go back to Greece. After he had left Smyrna, he went to Paris by way of Constantinople and the Romanian Black Sea port of Constanta. He stayed in Paris until early 1923 and then moved to Nice where he lived in great poverty until his death in exile in June 1949. He was made a convenient scapegoat figure who took upon himself the entire catastrophe resulting from the failure of the Greek vision in Western Anatolia. Even today, Greek public opinion considers him a person of disgrace.
10. Llewellyn Smith, *Ionian Vision*, 311.

Destruction of the Ottoman Coexistence

11. CADN, Izmir 643 PO/1, 97, 11 September 1922, Guerre Gréco-Turque, Occupation de Smyrne Suite. On the morning of 9 September, the day Turkish nationalists entered the city, Graillet urgently requested 500 passports to be dispatched, CADC, 51CPCOM, P1424, 9 September 1922, from Graillet to the Affaires Etrangères.
12. Puaux, *La Mort de Smyrne*, 6.
13. Marjorie Housepian Dobkin, *Smyrna 1922: The Destruction of a City* (Kent, OH: Kent State University Press, 1988), 132–3.
14. CADN, Izmir 643 PO/1, 97, 11 September 1922, Guerre Gréco-Turque, Occupation de Smyrne Suite.
15. Giles Milton, *Paradise Lost*, 306, quoting from 'Miss Mills Blames Turks for the Fire', *The New York Times*, 27 September 1922, p. 2.
16. Mark O. Prentiss, 'The Eyewitness Tells Story of Smyrna's Horror', *The New York Times*, 18 September 1922, p. 2.
17. Georgelin, *La fin de Smyrne*, 211–15.
18. TNA FO 141/580/1, 13 October 1922, Vice-Consul Urquhart to Sir H. Rumbold. After the fire, the Orthodox churches were systematically razed to the ground and the Christian cemeteries were desecrated and destroyed.
19. TNA FO 141/580/1, 29 September 1922, Urquhart to H. Rumbold. On 9 September, Sir Harry Lamb, British high commissioner's representative in Smyrna, had decided to get all British citizens in Smyrna evacuated. Even though the nationalist troops had not committed any atrocities immediately after they entered the city, Lamb feared that something could happen once it got dark. After a few days, he probably understood that he had made the right decision. In an interview with Harry Lamb, Mustafa Kemal uttered that his government was in a state of war with Great Britain and therefore did not recognise the high commissioner in Constantinople or his representative. He threatened the British representative that 'he would be justified in interning all British subjects he did not however want to do so', TNA ADM 1/8640/114, 13 September 1922, Harry Lamb to British High Commission.
20. In spite of all my efforts, a copy of this notification could not be found in the Ottoman Archives. Thus, I used the English copy of the same document instead. See TNA FO 141/580/1, 3 October 1922, Urquhart to Rumbold. Talat Ulusoy revealed that this document was published by local newspapers, see 'Beyanname Numero: 5', *Âhenk*, 18 September 1922 (R. 18 Eylül 1338). Three days before Nureddin's notification, in a final effort during their meeting with Mustafa Kemal in the neighbourhood of Goztepe, Admiral Dumesnil and Graillet tried to prevent the deportation of Ottoman Christian men into the interior through labour battalions. According to the report of the interview signed by Dumesnil, they emphasised that one of the reasons why panic had spread among the Ottoman Christians was the fact that the arrest of a considerable number of the male population, Greek or Armenian, terrified women. However, 'at the request of Mustapha Kemal, Ismet Pasha then explains the measures taken: the Greeks had ordered the recruitment of the

Ethnic Cleansing in Western Anatolia

population of Greek origin from the territories occupied by them. The Turks were therefore entitled to consider this population as enemies and to take measures to prevent men who could bear arms from crossing into Thrace. That's why they decided to intern men from the age of 18 to 45 in concentration camps', CADC, 51CPCOM, P1436, 16 September 1922, Entretien avec Mustapha Kemal-15 Septembre 1922.

21. Bierstadt, *The Great Betrayal*, 55–6. Some of the Muslim refugees from Western Anatolia, particularly Circassians, were housed in the refugee camps in the islands of Mytilene and Samos.

22. See *Ē Exodos: Martyries apo tis Dytikes Periferies tis Mikras Asias*, ed. G. Tenekides (Athens: Centre for Asia Minor Studies, 1980); Elias Venezis, *To Noumero 31328: Sklavoi sta Ergastika Tagmata tēs Anatolēs; Romantzo* (Mytilene and Athens: N. Theofanidis and S. Lambaridis, 1931); and Leyla Neyzi, 'Remembering Smyrna/Izmir: Shared History, Shared Trauma', *History and Memory* 20, no. 2 (Fall/Winter 2008), 106–27.

23. TNA FO 141/580/1, 10 October 1922, Urquhart to H. Rumbold.

24. TNA FO 286/908, 20 December 1923, Tewfik Rifaat, the Minister of the Foreign Affairs in Egypt, to Allenby, High Commissioner for Egypt.

25. TNA FO 141/580/1, 13 October 1922, Vice-Consul Urquhart to Sir H. Rumbold.

26. Çağlar Keyder, 'The Consequences of the Exchange of Populations for Turkey', in *Crossing the Aegean*, ed. Renée Hirschon (Oxford: Berghahn Books, 2003), 48.

27. *Atatürk'ün Söylev ve Demeçleri* (Atatürk's Speeches and Statements), ed. Sadi Borak and Utkan Kocatürk (Ankara: Atatürk Araştırma Merkezi, 1997), 274.

28. Falih Rıfkı Atay, *Çankaya* (Istanbul: Pozitif Yayınları, 2004), 351.

29. TBMM G. Z. C., 29 Teşrîn-i Sânî 1338 [29 November 1922], 1134, retrieved from the digital archive of the Turkish parliament. Available at <https://www5.tbmm.gov.tr/tutanaklar/TUTANAK/GZC/d01/CILT03/gcz01003147.pdf> (last accessed 15 December 2023).

30. Ladas, *The Exchange of Minorities*, 3.

31. Onur Yıldırım, *Diplomacy and Displacement: Reconsidering the Turco-Greek Exchange of Populations, 1922–1934* (London: Routledge, 2006), 193–5.

32. Due to the rejection of the Turkish government, the exchange of the Albanian-speaking Muslims of Chamuria was aborted in March 1926, see Dimitris Michalopoulos, 'The Moslems of Chamuria and the Exchange of Populations between Greece and Turkey', *Balkan Studies* 27, no. 2 (1986), 305. Those Albanians of Chamuria were regarded as people difficult to assimilate because of their strong ties with Albania.

33. Ladas, *The Exchange of Minorities*, 438–9.

34. Ibid. 437–9.

35. Ibid. 437–9. The statistical data collected by the Mixed Commission also confirmed this argument. According to its data, 97,951 exchangees left the

Destruction of the Ottoman Coexistence

country through the port of Istanbul, 50,124 exchangees through the port of Mersin and 38,164 exchangees through the port of Samsun between November 1923 and 1926. The numbers of exchangees who left through Izmir port and the Thracian border town of Kırkkilise (Kırklareli) were limited to 2,500 and 1,177 people, respectively.

36. Kemal Arı, '1923 Türk-Rum Mübadele Antlaşması Sonrasında İzmir'de Emval-i Metruke ve Mübadil Göçmenler', *Atatürk Araştırma Merkezi Dergisi* 6 (1990), 627–57.

37. Yıldırım, *Diplomacy and Displacement*, 94–5.

38. Erol Ülker, 'Assimilation of the Muslim Communities in the First Decade of the Turkish Republic (1923–1934)', *European Journal of Turkish Studies* 6 (2007). Available at <https://journals.openedition.org/ejts/822> (last accessed 15 December 2023), §. 26.

39. Rıza Nur, *Hayat ve Hatıratım*, vol. 3 (Istanbul: Altındağ Yayınevi, 1968), 1097–9.

40. Gingeras, *Sorrowful Shores*, 155. Later, the Memorandum of Settlement published in 1926 restricted the Albanian migration with the families of those who had already migrated. Albanians were considered along with Gypsies, Kurds and Arabs as people who had nothing common with 'Turkish culture', see 'İskana Ait Muhtıra', Tertip 63, 01/08/1926, in *Eski ve Yeni Toprak, İskân Hükümleri ve Uygulama Kılavuzu*, ed. Naci Kökdemir (Ankara: Yeni Matbaa, 1952), 192–208.

41. Ahmet Yıldız, 'Kemalist Milliyetçilik', in *Modern Türkiye'de Siyasi Düşünce, vol. 2: Kemalizm*, ed. Ahmet İnsel (Istanbul: İletişim Yayınları, 2001), 233.

42. According to the 1927 census, 18,157 Jews and 5,196 Catholic Christians were living in Izmir. The overwhelming majority of these non-Muslims had acquired Turkish citizenship, though a small group continued to hold Italian, British or French passports, see *1927 Umumî Nüfus Tahriri*, 36.

43. İsmail Kaplan, *Türkiye'de Milli Eğitim İdeolojisi* (Istanbul: İletişim Yayınları, 1999), 160.

44. TNA ADM 137/2510, 17 April 1923, H. G. Thursfield to Senior Naval Officer Afloat, Constantinople.

45. *1923 Senesi İzmir Vilâyet İstatistiği*, vol. 2, ed. Erkan Serçe (Izmir: Izmir Büyükşehir Belediyesi Kültür Yayınları, 2001), 105.

46. İzmir Mebusu Tahsin, 'İzmir İktisadî Konferansı', *Hâkimiyet-i Milliye*, 6 February 1923 (R. 6 Şubat 1339).

47. TNA ADM 116/2216, 13 June 1923, the Commanding Officer of HMS *Centaur* to the Commander-in-Chief, Mediterranean Station.

48. TNA WORK 10/ 254, 19 May 1927, Oriental Carpet Manufacturers Ltd. to Consulate-General in Smyrna.

49. Ayhan Aktar, *Varlık Vergisi ve 'Türkleştirme' Politikaları* (Istanbul: İletişim Yayınları, 2006), 121–6.

50. TNA ADM 116/2216, 19 July 1923, the Commanding Officer of HMS *Caradoc* to the Commander-in-Chief, Mediterranean Station.

Ethnic Cleansing in Western Anatolia

51. TNA WORK 10/254, 25 February 1925, H. L. Rabino, Consul-General, to R. C. Lindsay, British Representative in Constantinople.
52. TNA FO 141/580/1, 29 September 1922, Acting Vice-Consul Urquhart to Sir H. Rumbold.
53. TNA WORK 10/254, 17 November 1925, H. L. Rabino, Consul-General, to the Secretary of State for Foreign Affairs.
54. TNA WORK 10/254, 16 October 1923, W. S. Edmonds, Consul-General, to Curzon of Kedleston, Principal Secretary of State for Foreign Affairs.
55. TNA WORK 10/ 254, 17 March 1926, British Embassy, Constantinople, to Sir Austen Chamberlain.
56. TNA FO 286/853, 31 August 1923, Essayan to the General Assembly of the League of Nations.
57. *Lozan Telgrafları*, ed. Bilal Şimşir, vol. II (Ankara: Türk Tarih Kurumu, 1994), 395–6 and 410–11. Earlier, on 16 January 1923, the high commissioners of Britain, France and Italy in Constantinople had sent Adnan (Adıvar), representative of the Ministry of Foreign Affairs of the Ankara government, a diplomatic note addressing the insistence of local representatives of the nationalist government in Izmir to declare assets in the foreign banks of the city belonging to the citizens of Greece as well as to Ottoman Greeks and Armenians, see BOA HR. İM 16/106.
58. *Düstur*, 3. Tertip, vol. 7, 4248 sayılı kararname, 1681–2, 'İki İsimli Vilâyetlerimizin Yalnız Bir İsimle Yadedilmesine Dair Kararname'. Aside from Saruhan Province, the names of more than twenty provinces were changed by this decision. Most of these provinces were carrying names related with the period of Turcoman principalities or Ottoman *sanjak*s.
59. *Yeni Asır*, 11 January 1938, no. 9754, 'İzmir Sokakları Dünden İtibaren Numaralanmağa Başlandı' (Izmir Streets Have Been Started to Be Enumerated), 2. Because of this decision, names of the streets in the centre of Izmir, such as Aliotti, Petrocochino, Moelhasen, Varvara and Markela, were changed.
60. Biray Kolluoğlu Kırlı, 'Cityscapes and Modernity: Smyrna Morphing into Izmir', in *Ways to Modernity in Greece and Turkey: Encounters with Europe, 1850–1950*, ed. Çağlar Keyder and Anna Frangoudaki (London: I. B. Tauris, 2007), 226–7.
61. *Treaty of Peace with Turkey* (London: His Majesty's Stationery Office, 1923), 191–3.
62. *Lozan Barış Konferansı: Tutanaklar-Belgeler*, ed. Seha L. Meray, vol. 6 (Istanbul: Yapı Kredi Yayınları, 2001), 156–7.
63. See *Treaty of Peace with Turkey* (1923), 191–6.
64. Hakan Özoğlu, *From Caliphate to Secular State: Power Struggle in the Early Turkish Republic* (Santa Barbara: Praeger, 2011), 39–40.
65. Ali Nâdir Pasha, the Commander of the 17th Army Corps during the Greek landing, was included in the section where the members of the Caliphate Army were listed.

Destruction of the Ottoman Coexistence

66. It seems that the telegram sent by Hulûsî, a clear opponent of the National Forces, to the Greek government in October 1921, requesting the annexation of Uşak to the Smyrna zone, was not forgiven by the nationalists in Ankara, CADC, 51CPCOM, P1537, 19 November 1921, Voeu du Maire de la ville d'Ouchak. He visited Athens and the High Commission in Smyrna several times, 'Vilâyet Haberleri', *Islahât*, 30 June 1922 (R. 30 Haziran 1338), 2.

67. Around the time of the Greco-Turkish rapprochement in the 1930s, the Turkish government put pressure on its Greek counterpart to expel these people and regularly kept collecting intelligence about their activities in Greece, and the Kemalist newspapers published news about them. See CADC, 51CPCOM, P2255, 24 December 1930, Réfugies turcs anti-Kémalistes and *Cumhuriyet*, 23 September 1931, no. 2651, 'Yüz Ellilikler: Yunanistan'dakiler Öteye Beriye Dağıldılar' (Those in Greece Dispersed in Different Directions), 4. Nonetheless, it is difficult to find any archival material about these opponents of the early Kemalist regime in Greece as most of the records in both the archives of the Ministry of Foreign Affairs in Athens and the intelligence reports kept in the Republican Archives in Ankara are still inaccessible to researchers. Some memoirs narrating the early republican period reveal clues about the opponents' lives in exile. For example, in her memoirs, Gülfem İren, a native of Smyrna with notables in her family, mentions having lunch with Mehmet Refet on her way to Hamburg in the spring of 1938, when the cruise liner stopped in Athens, and also Refet's longing for his homeland, see Gülfem Kâatçılar İren, *Anılarım* (Istanbul: n.p., 2004), 59.

68. BCA Başbakanlık, Kararlar Daire Başkanlığı (1920–28), 25-46-16.

69. TNA FO 286/ 806, 27 December 1922, Major Johnston in Alexandroupolis to British Legation in Athens.

70. Zürcher, *The Unionist Factor*, 160–2.

71. Ibid. 155.

72. Erik Jan Zürcher, 'The Last Phase in the History of the Committee of Union and Progress (1923–1924)', in *Actes de la première rencontre internationale sur l'Empire Ottoman et la Turquie moderne*, ed. Edhem Eldem (Istanbul: Isis Press, 1991), 369–77.

Conclusion: Forging Catastrophe as a Solution

Today the social, economic and ethnic structure of the Aegean littoral of Turkey gives the impression of a region with a kind of unified culture and homogenous structure; however, this area was actually made up of various ethnic, religious and political groups 100 years ago. A cohesive and unified region was created through national homogenisation and a series of nation-building projects in the early twentieth century. Even during the years of the Greco-Turkish War of 1919–22, identities, interests and solidarities of the dwellers of the region had shifting boundaries.

The expulsion of the Greek Orthodox communities along the Aegean coastline at the end of the violent summer of 1914 marked the temporary end of non-Muslim presence in the province. The CUP, at this point, was able to assert its authority over the entire Aegean coastline. These policies were, of course, not peculiar to this corner of the Ottoman Empire; however, the province which suffered most from ethnic cleansing was Aydın Province on the eve of the World War I.

Despite the fact that deportations and exiles were common phenomena throughout the history of the Ottoman Empire, the nature of these events in the twentieth century was very different from the previous centuries. Until the twentieth century, Ottoman statesmen had never tried to create an ethnically homogeneous society through forced resettlements, deportations and exiles.[1]

In July 1908, the CUP restored the Ottoman constitution. This political development was the product of joint actions by Unionist officers from the Second (Thracian) and Third (Macedonian) imperial armies. Prior to 1908, these soldiers had constantly fought against Serbian, Bulgarian and Greek armed bands as well as Albanian bandits. Despite the claims of some scholars[2] that the pan-Turkic dreams of the CUP leadership played an important role in the liquidation of the non-Muslim bourgeoisie during

Forging Catastrophe as a Solution

the years of World War I, the experience of ethnic conflicts in the Balkan provinces on the part of the Unionists was more effective in undertaking an ethnic cleansing in the form of expelling the Greeks from the Aegean coastal towns in 1914.

The practices of demographic engineering in the province cannot simply be reduced to the collateral damage of the Balkan Wars and the so-called voluntary migration of the Greek Orthodox communities. These policies were gradually radicalised along the Aegean coastline with the traumatic defeat of the Ottomans in the Balkan Wars of 1912–13, as with the attempts in the summer of 1914 to force an agreement on the reciprocal voluntary exchange of populations with Greece. Despite the severity of the policies, the methods used to intimidate the Ottoman Greeks varied from location to location. Basically, the types of demographic engineering policies evolved from economic boycotts, following the declaration of a unilateral union between Greece and Crete in 1908, into the provocation of conflicts between the local Greeks and Balkan migrants after the outbreak of the Balkan Wars in 1912. Forced migrations and massacres jointly organised by the local branches of the CUP and the Special Organisation in 1914 followed afterwards.

According to Göçek, the bifurcated structure of the newly emerging Ottoman elites was the ultimate cause of the dissolution of the Empire. While the bureaucratic bourgeoisie was transforming into a Turkish national bourgeoisie, the mercantile non-Muslim bourgeoisie had forcefully been driven out and made to disappear. What I would like to add to Göçek's argument here is that, particularly in Aydın Province, those loyalist high-ranking provincial officials who did not intend to subscribe to the nationalist policies and who maintained their close ties with the sultan and the imperial government in Constantinople were eliminated by the Unionist–Kemalist cadres, that is, the founders of the new Republic. Large Christian communities consisting mostly of Ottoman Greeks and Armenians lost their chance to exist in the province after being violently deported or massacred while this group of officials was removed from the provincial administration to be replaced with nationalist officials. As a result, the non-Muslim communities which consisted mostly of Ottoman Greeks and Armenians were exposed to intensive violence and finally to deportation and massacres.

The supporters of the Ankara government were celebrated as the defenders of the nation, who were ready to die, if necessary, whereas the loyalties of the remaining provincial officials, who had not left their posts during the Greek administration, came to be demonised by the national(ist) historiography of modern Turkey. In other words, a dualist vision which

Ethnic Cleansing in Western Anatolia

portrays civil servants as either good-willed resisters or bad-intentioned collaborators has since dominated traditional scholarship, though the reality is rather more nuanced and complicated. The bitter experiences of different ethno-religious communities outlined in this study, as well as those of Muslim public officials who preserved strong ties with either the Ottoman sultan or the Greek administration, must be acknowledged as a part of the history of modern Turkey.

In spite of the sporadic periods of tension between Christians and Muslims in the pre-1919 period, the Muslim–Christian coexistence in Aydın Province continued until September 1922, thanks in part to the efforts of the High Commission under Stergiades and its policy of co-opting high-ranking Muslim provincial officials who had previously served the Ottoman government. These Ottoman officials, along with Stergiades, the high commissioner in the occupation zone, represented the last chance in the direction to preserve the coexistence of different ethno-religious communities in the region. The policy of co-opting Ottoman civil servants was a constant of the Greek policy in Western Anatolia. During the occupation, a considerable number of local civil servants adjusted themselves in different ways to the occupying authorities. An Ottoman civil servant who did not resign but adapted himself to the new administration could easily become a part of the cadres who were running the system.

Numerous Muslim officials who were involved in the military struggle in Aydın Province between 1919 and 1922 did not form or join any monolithic factions. The attitudes of Ottoman civil servants towards the Greek administration did not present the absolute pair of opposites of collaboration and resistance. Alongside the massive participation of former Ottoman civil servants in the Greek administration at higher levels, including the running of key political organisations such as the governorships (*mutasarrıflıks/valiliks*), there was also a widespread penetration by the resistance. Thus, many office holders were playing a double game.

Contrary to the nation-building process in Greece in the post-Balkan War period, in which the Muslim communities were excluded from the national community, non-Orthodox populations were included in the autonomous state-formation process in Western Anatolia in the summer of 1922. Indeed, Stergiades was well aware of the fact that he could only move within certain limitations determined by the multi-ethnic and multi-religious structure of this administrative area.

Regardless of the two-way tendency in Turkish history-making as well as public opinion to frame the war either as a war of liberation or an anti-colonial war against the colonial powers, it was in essence a very violent ethnic conflict in which the Turkish nationalists centred in Ankara

Forging Catastrophe as a Solution

managed to remove the entire Ottoman Christian population in Western Anatolia.[3] The Turkish nationalist movement, whose foundations had been laid by the Unionists at the end of World War I, brought the ethnic-cleansing policies started by the CUP on the eve of the Great War to full fruition. In the minds of the new nationalist elites, the so-called liberation of the motherland was inherently related to the cleansing of non-Muslim Ottoman communities.

The violence of the National Struggle not only tore the social fabric of intercommunal relations in Aydın Province, but also politicised the markers of identity and created new divisions among members of the Muslim community. As demonstrated in the earlier chapters, the presence of many high-ranking provincial officials who either established friendly relations with the Greek administration or remained loyal to the sultan was not tolerated by the nationalist elites of the modern Republic.

In the early republican period, the remnants of Ottoman society were replaced by the secular and nationalist norms generated by the Kemalist state through a nation-building campaign. The Ankara assembly, which nullified the six-century-old Ottoman sultanate in November 1922, obligated the members of the dynasty to leave the country. After the proclamation of the Republic in October 1923, Kemalist ideology embodied the epitome of Turkish nationalism, which had already started to spread among the elites, disallowing any ideological, ethnic and cultural pluralism in the region.

From an ideological and administrative perspective, there is a palpable continuity between the provincial administrators of the Unionist period and the governors in the early republican era. In spite of the expectations that Rahmî Bey would be appointed as the first governor of Izmir which was controlled by the nationalists,[4] Mustafa Abdülhalik (Renda) Bey, a member of the Special Organisation and the person responsible for the Armenian massacres in Bitlis Province, was appointed as the governor. Mustafa Abdülhalik's short term was followed in August 1923 by the governorship of Hüseyin Aziz (Akyürek), who also had served in the Special Organisation and enjoyed the friendship of Enver Pasha. Around the same time, the municipal council appointed Şükrü (Kaya) Bey, a former Unionist and ex-president of the General Directorate for Refugees, as mayor of Izmir. Kâzım (Dirik), another governor of Izmir, who was born in Monastir, Macedonia, and joined the CUP, was later assigned this duty between 1926 and 1935. As one of the high-ranking commanders, he had fought on the eastern front against the Armenians and replaced Kâzım Karabekir for an extended period of time. Fevzi Toker, who was charged with the duty of governing Aydın between 1930 and 1935, was one of the

Ethnic Cleansing in Western Anatolia

followers of the national economy policies and was an ardent supporter of the Kemalist regime. These administrators owed their later careers to their dedication and loyalty to the nascent Kemalist Republic.

Even though there are more Christians in the cemeteries of Izmir than on its streets today, some patterns have not undergone major changes. Different from other urban centres in the region, Izmir is still remembered as *Gâvur* İzmir and most of its citizens take pride in that designation of the past. However, this time, the main point of conflict as regards Izmir is not the constituents of the city's population, but its disloyalty to the central government and the lifestyles of its citizens. Its people's straightforwardness in developing the city's identity in a civic fashion differentiates itself from the other cities in Anatolia.

The nationalist narrative holds a one-sided view of the events leading to the Greco-Turkish War, and ignores nuances. According to this narrative, Christians and Muslims were living in peace and harmony in Western Anatolia before 1919. A large portion of the Orthodox Christians in and around Ottoman Smyrna gained extreme wealth through financing, shipping, regional and international commerce, and small-scale industrial activities. Nonetheless, the deathblow to this coexistence in the region came in May 1919 when the Greek army asserted control over Smyrna.

The main problem with this narrative is that it is blind to the sporadic tensions between Christians and Muslims in the pre-1919 period, overemphasising the role of the Greek landing in May 1919 by considering it as the ending of the coexistence among different ethno-religious communities in Western Anatolia. The boycott attempts that intensified after the end of the Balkan Wars in 1913 and the expulsions of the Orthodox population from the Aegean coastline in the summer of 1914, combined with ethnic violence which reached its apex in 1915 in the other parts of the Empire, are never taken into consideration by the followers of this approach. In my opinion, the coexistence in the region, which continued despite difficulties in a relatively effective way, ended completely with the entrance of the nationalist forces into Smyrna in September 1922. In this sense, the ethnic violence and the massacres which ravaged the settlements in Western Anatolia in September 1922 and led to the mass migration of non-Muslim Ottoman citizens without return formed the most crucial discontinuity in the history of this region.

In the autumn of 1922, Christian–Muslim coexistence vanished from the face of Aydın Province and Ottoman cosmopolitanism, which prevailed for three centuries in Smyrna, the main port and later capital of the province, was buried in the ashes of this city. By all means, my intention is not to idealise the Ottoman heritage in the pluralistic port city of Smyrna.

Forging Catastrophe as a Solution

Indeed, Ottoman–Levantine cosmopolitanism and the lifestyle it produced faded in all major ports of the Eastern Mediterranean, that is, Smyrna, Alexandria, Beirut and Constantinople, one after the other in the early twentieth century, due to the political, social and cultural changes imposed by the emerging nation-states. However, the most important particularity of Smyrna, which distinguished it from the other port cities, is that the transformation of Smyrna to Turkish Izmir was realised within the span of one month, that is, in September 1922, by an intense wave of mass violence and a series of massacres, whereas the nationalisation of the other port cities took place over several years.

Notes

1. See Ömer Lütfi Barkan, 'Osmanlı İmparatorluğu'nda Bir İskân ve Kolonizasyon Metodu Olarak Sürgünler', *İstanbul Üniversitesi İktisat Fakültesi Mecmuası*, no. 11 (1949–50), 524–69. As Barkan points out, the exile (*sürgün*) method was employed in order to secure the mountain passes (*derbent*) and military routes that were of utmost importance in the classical period of the Empire. However, nineteenth-century settlement policies, for example, of the Circassians, were also made with the aim of creating loyal zones in strategic regions, but they did not aim to create an ethnic homogeneity based on the Turkish-speaking Sunni element. To that end, the settlement policies during the reign of Abdülhamit II can be best explained within the framework of Benedict Anderson's concept of official nationalism, see Benedict Anderson, *Imagined Communities: Reflections on the Origin and Spread of Nationalism* (London: Verso, 1991), 83–113. As can be grasped from the cases of Hamidiye regiments, tribal schools, and the resettlement of Caucasian and Balkan migrants after the Russo-Ottoman War of 1877–8, official nationalism took a new turn and began to set a pro-Islamic re-orientation of politics, reflecting the autocratic centralisation trends popular during the reign of Abdülhamit II. The resettlement of Caucasian and Balkan migrants was a self-protective policy linked to the preservation of imperial interests. Official nationalism emanating from the state served the interests of the state. Anderson borrowed this term from Hugh Seton-Watson's work *Nations and States: An Enquiry into the Origins of Nations and the Politics of Nationalism*, see Benedict Anderson, *Imagined Communities*, 86–7.
2. Robert Melson, *Revolution and Genocide: On the Origins of the Armenian Genocide and the Holocaust* (Chicago: University of Chicago Press, 1996), 138–9.
3. Keyder, 'A History and Geography of Turkish Nationalism', 11–12.
4. TNA ADM 116/2216, 12 December 1922, the Commanding Officer at HMS *Cambrian* to the Commander-in-Chief in Mediterranean.

Bibliography

Primary Sources

ARCHIVAL MATERIALS

Başbakanlık Cumhuriyet Arşivleri (BCA), Ankara
Başbakanlık (30-0-0-0)
Kararlar Daire Başkanlığı (1920–28) (30-18-1-1)

Başbakanlık Osmanlı Arşivleri (BOA), Istanbul
Bâb-ı Âlî Evrak Odası (BEO)
Dâhiliye Nezâreti
Emniyet-i Umumiye Asayiş Kalemi (DH. EUM. AYŞ)
Emniyet-i Umumiye Üçüncü Şube (DH. EUM. 3ŞB)
Emniyet-i Umumiye Beşinci Şube (DH. EUM. 5ŞB)
Hukuk (DH. H)
İdare-i Umumiyye (DH. İ-UM)
İdare-i Umumiyye Ekleri (DH. İ-UM. EK)
Kalem-i Mahsûs (DH. KMS)
Sicil Defterleri (SAİDd.)
Şifre Kalemi (DH. ŞFR)
Muamelat (DH. TMIK. M)
Hâriciye Nezâreti
Mektubî Kalemi (HR. MKT)
Siyasî (HR. SYS)
Satın Alınan Evrâk
Ali Fuat Türkgeldi Evrâkı (HSD. AFT)
Yıldız
Başkitabet Dâiresi Marûzâtı (Y. PRK. BŞK)

Bibliography

Centre des Archives Diplomatiques (CADC), La Courneuve
51CPCOM (Correspondance politique et commerciale)
P1378
P1379
P1424
P1436
P1533
P1537
P2255

Centre des Archives Diplomatiques (CADN), Nantes
Izmir (643, PO/1)
Collection de dépêches; rapport les événements de 1919–23 (26)
Expropriation du cimetière catholique d'Izmir (75)
Questions grecques (97)

Genelkurmay Askerî Tarih ve Stratejik Etüd Arşivi (ATASE), Ankara
İstiklâl Harbi Katalogu (İSH)

Genika Archeia tou Kratous (GAK), Athens
Ypati Armosteia tis Smyrnis (YAS)
Elliniki Dioikisi tis Smyrnis (EDS)

Ministry of Foreign Affairs (MOFA), Athens

TBMM [G.] Z.C., TBMM Kütüphanesi, Ankara
Gizli Celse Zabıtları, 29 Teşrîn-i Sânî 1338 [29 November 1922].
Devre: 2, Cilt: 4, İçtima Senesi: 1, 20 Kânûn-ı Evvel 1339 [20 December
  1923].

The National Archives (TNA), London
Admiralty (ADM)
Foreign Office (FO)
Treasury (T)
War Office (WO)
Ministry of Works (WORK)

NEWSPAPERS

American Newspapers
The New York Times (New York)

British Newspapers
The Manchester Guardian (Manchester)

Ethnic Cleansing in Western Anatolia

French Newspapers
La Réforme (Smyrna)
Stamboul (Constantinople)

Greek Newspapers
Kosmos (Smyrna)

Turkish Newspapers
Âhenk (Smyrna)
Anadolu (Smyrna)
Cumhuriyet (Constantinople/ Istanbul)
Hâkimiyet-i Milliye (Ankara)
Hukuk-ı Beşer (Smyrna)
Islahât (Smyrna)
İkdâm (Constantinople/Istanbul)
Köylü (Smyrna)
Müsavat (Smyrna)
Şark (Smyrna)
Yeni Asır (Smyrna/ Izmir)

PAMPHLETS, BOOKLETS AND BROCHURES

A Survey of Some Social Conditions in Smyrna, Asia Minor – May 1921. Edited by Rıfat N. Bali. Istanbul: Libra Kitap, 2009.
Akçura, Yusuf. *Üç Tarz-ı Siyaset* [Three Types of Policy]. Ankara: Lotus, 2005.
Appels des femmes de Thrace et d'Asie Mineure. Athens: Conseil National de Femmes Hellènes, 1922.
Dragoumis, Ion. *Osoi Zōntanoi.* Athens: Nea Zoi, 1926.
Ormanian, Malachia. *The Church of Armenia: Her History, Doctrine, Rule, Discipline, Liturgy, Literature, and Existing Condition.* Translated by Marcar Gregory. London: A. R. Mowbray, 1912.
Rigas Velestinlis. *Revolutionary Scripts.* Translated by Vassilis K. Zervoulakos. Athens: Scientific Society of Studies Pheres-Velestino-Rhigas, 2008.
Smyrne turque. Edited by Société de défense des droits ottomans. Smyrne: Imprimerie Ahmed Ihsan & Compagnie, 1919.
Türk Tarihin Ana Hatları. Istanbul: Devlet Matbaası, 1930.
Vellay, Charles. *Smyrne, ville grecque.* Paris: Librairie Chapelot, 1919.

MINUTES, REPORTS, REGISTERS AND TREATIES

Düstur. 2. Tertib. vol. 1. Dersaadet: Matbaa-i Osmaniye, H. 1329.
Düstur, 3. Tertip, vol. 7, Ankara: Devlet Matbaası, 1944.
Heyet-i Temsiliye Tutanakları [Registers of the Representative Board]. Edited by Uluğ İğdemir. Ankara: Türk Tarih Kurumu, 1975.

Bibliography

Iōakeimoglou, Geōrgios. *Praktika tēs Akadimias Athēnōn* [Minutes of Athens Academy], vol. 25. Athens: University of Athens, 1952.

Janin, Raymond. 'L'Eglise Arménienne'. In *Echos d'Orient* 18, no. 110–11, January–April 1916, 5–32.

Kökdemir, Naci (ed.). *Eski ve Yeni Toprak, İskân Hükümleri ve Uygulama Kılavuzu* [Guide to the Application of Old and New Land and Resettlement Decisions]. Ankara: Yeni Matbaa, 1952.

Lacombe, J. 'Chronique des Eglises Orientales'. In *Echos d'Orient* 21, no. 125, January–March 1922, 98–118.

Lacombe, J. 'Chronique des Eglises Orientales'. In *Echos d'Orient* 24, no. 137, January–March 1925, 86–116.

Lozan Barış Konferansı: Tutanaklar-Belgeler [Lausanne Peace Conference: Proceedings–Documents]. Edited by Seha L. Meray, vol. 6. Istanbul: Yapı Kredi Yayınları, 2001.

Lozan Telgrafları [Lausanne Telegrams]. Edited by Bilal Şimşir, vol. II. Ankara: Türk Tarih Kurumu, 1994.

Meclis-i Mebusan Zabıt Ceridesi [Parliamentary Minutes]. Devre: III, İçtima: V, v. 1. Ankara: TBMM Basımevi, 1992.

Rapports officials reçus des autorités militaries Ottomanes sur l'occupation de Smyrne par les troupes Helleniques. Constantinople: Imprimerie Osmanié, 1919.

Treaty of Peace with Turkey. London: His Majesty's Stationery Office, 1920.

Treaty of Peace with Turkey. London: His Majesty's Stationery Office, 1923.

Türk İstiklâl Harbi [Turkish War of Independence], vol. 1: *Mondros Mütarekesi ve Tatbikatı* [Armistice of Mudros and Its Implementations]. Ankara: Genelkurmay Basımevi, 1962.

Türk İstiklâl Harbi [Turkish War of Independence], vol. 7: *İdarî Faaliyetler* [Administrative Activities]. Ankara: Genelkurmay Basımevi, 1975.

CATALAOGUES AND STATISTICS

1333 Senesi Tevellüdat ve Vefeyat İstatistiği: İzmir ve Çevresi Nüfus İstatistiği, by Aydın Vilayeti İstatistik Müdüriyeti [Population Statistics of Smyrna and Its Environs]. Edited by Erkan Serçe. Izmir: Akademi Kitabevi, 1998.

1921 Annuaire Oriental: Oriental Directory. Edited by Alfred Rizzo. Constantinople: Imprimerie de l'Annuaire Oriental, 1921.

1923 Senesi İzmir Vilâyet İstatistiği [1923 Statistics of İzmir Province], vols 1–2. Edited by Erkan Serçe. Izmir: Izmir Büyükşehir Belediyesi Kültür Yayınları, 2001.

1927 Umumî Nüfus Tahriri. Ankara: Başvekâlet İstatistik Umum Müdürlüğü, 1929.

İslâm Tüccâr ve Esnâflarına Mahsûs Rehber [The Guide Pertaining to Muslim Merchants and Artisans]. Izmir: Donanma-yi Osmaniye, 1914.

Ethnic Cleansing in Western Anatolia

TRAVELLERS' ACCOUNTS

Bierstadt, Edward Hale. *The Great Betrayal: A Survey of the Near East Problem.* London: Hutchinson, 1924.

Cochran, William. *Pen and Pencil in Asia Minor; or Notes from the Levant.* London: Law, Marston, Searle and Rivington, 1887.

Cuinet, Vital. *La Turquie d'Asie, géographie administrative, statistique descriptive et raisonnée de chaque province de l'Asie Mineure.* Paris: E. Leroux, 1894.

Eudel, Paul. *Constantinople, Smyrne et Athènes, Journal de Voyage.* Paris: E. Dentu, 1885.

Pernot, Maurice. *Rapport sur un voyage d'étude.* Paris: Firmin-Didot, 1913.

Somerville, Alexander Neil. *The Churches in Asia: Extracts from the Home Letters of A. N. Somerville (1885).* Whitefish, MT: Kessinger Publishing, 2010.

Tchihatcheff, Petr Aleksandrovitch de. *Asie Mineure: Description physique, climatologie, zoologie, botanique, géologie, statistique et archéologie de cette contrée,* 8 vols. Paris: Gide et J. Baudry, 1853–69.

Upward, Allen. *The East End of Europe: The Report of an Unofficial Mission to the Provinces of Turkey on the Eve of the Revolution.* London: John Murray, 1908.

Warner, Charles Dudley. *In the Levant.* Boston: Charles Osgood, 1877.

MEMOIRS, INTERVIEWS AND NOVELS

Aker, M. Şefik. *İstiklâl Harbinde 57. Tümen ve Aydın Milli Cidali* [The 57th Division and Aydın National Fighting in the Independence War], vols 1–2. Istanbul: Askeri Matbaa, 1937.

Akıncı, İbrahim Ethem. *Demirci Akıncıları* [Demirci Raiders]. Ankara: Türk Tarih Kurumu, 2009.

Aksoy, Yaşar. *Bir Kent, Bir İnsan: İzmir'in Son Yüzyılı, S. Ferit Eczacıbaşı'nın Yaşamı ve Anıları* [The Last Century of Smyrna, Life and Memories of S. Ferit Eczacıbaşı]. Istanbul: Eczacıbaşı Vakfı Yayınları, 1986.

Apak, Rahmi. *İstiklal Savaşında Garp Cephesi Nasıl Kuruldu* [How the Western Front Was Formed in the War of Independence]. Ankara: Türk Tarih Kurumu, 1990.

Atatürk'ün Söylev ve Demeçleri [Atatürk's Speeches and Statements]. Edited by Sadi Borak and Utkan Kocatürk. Ankara: Atatürk Araştırma Merkezi, 1997.

Bayar, Celal. *Ben de Yazdım* [And so I Wrote], vols 5–7. Istanbul: Baha Matbaası, 1967–9.

Bekir Sâmî Günsav'ın Kurtuluş Savaşı Anıları [Bekir Sâmî Günsav's War of Independence War]. Edited by Muhittin Ünal. Istanbul: Cem Yayınevi, 2002.

Çarıklı, Hacim Muhittin. *Balıkesir ve Alaşehir Kongreleri ve Hacim Muhittin Çarıklı'nın Kuvayı Milliye Hatıraları* [The Balıkesir and Alaşehir Congresses and Hacim Muhittin Çarıklı's Memoirs about the National Forces]. Ankara: Ankara Üniversitesi Basımevi, 1967.

Bibliography

Cemal Paşa. *Hatıralar* [Memoirs]. Istanbul: Türkiye İş Bankası Yayınları, 2006.

Çetinkaya, Ali. *Milli Mücadele Dönemi Hatıraları* [Memoirs of the National Struggle Period]. Ankara: Atatürk Araştırma Merkezi, 1993.

The Cretan Drama: The Life and Memoirs of Prince George, High Commissioner in Crete. Edited by A. A. Pallis. New York: Robert Speller & Sons, 1959.

Ē Exodos: Martyries apo tis Dytikes Periferies tis Mikras Asias [The Exodus: Testimonies from Asia Minor]. Edited by G. Tenekides. Athens: Centre for Asia Minor Studies, 1980.

Eğe-Akter, Güneş N. (ed.). *Babamın Emanetleri: Ragıp Nurettin Eğe'nin Birinci Cihan Harbi Günlükleri ve Harbin Sonrası Hatıratı* [Reminiscences of My Father: Ragıp Nurettin Eğe's World War I Diaries and Post-War Memoirs]. Istanbul: Dergâh Yayınları, 2006.

Ertürk, Hüsamettin. *İki Devrin Perde Arkası* [Two Eras behind the Scenes]. Edited by Samih Nafiz Tansu. Istanbul: Sebil Yayınevi, 1996.

Gökbel, Asaf. *Milli Mücadele'de Aydın* [Aydın in the National Struggle]. Aydın: Coşkun Matbaası, 1964.

Kâatçılar İren, Gülfem. *Anılarım*. Istanbul: n.p., 2004.

Kararas, Nikos. *O Bournovas* [Bournabat]. Athens: n.p., 1955.

Kaygusuz, Bezmi Nusret. *Bir Roman Gibi* [Like a Novel]. Izmir: Gümüşayak Matbaası, 1955.

Loverdos, Spyridon. *O Mētropolitēs Smyrnēs: Chrysostomos* [The Metropolitan Bishop of Smyrna: Chrysostomos]. Athens: P. D. Sakellarios, 1929.

Moralı, Nail. *Mütarekede İzmir Olayları* [Izmir Incidents during the Armistice]. Ankara: Türk Tarih Kurumu Basımevi, 1973.

Öktem, Haydar Rüştü. *Mütareke ve İşgal Anıları* [Memories of Armistice and Occupation]. Edited by Zeki Arıkan. Ankara: Türk Tarih Kurumu Basımevi, 1991.

Özalp, Kazım. *Milli Mücadele, 1919–1922* [National Struggle (1919–1922)], vol. I. Ankara: Türk Tarih Kurumu, 1988.

Pallis, Alexandros Anastasios. *Greece's Anatolian Venture: A Survey of the Diplomatic and Political Aspects of the Greek Expedition to Asia Minor, 1915–1922*. London: Methuen, 1937.

Politis, Kosmas. *Stou Chatzēfrangou* [In the Hadjifrangos Neighbourhood]. Athens: Estias, 2001.

Puaux, René. *La Mort de Smyrne*. Paris: Edition de la Revue des Balkans, 1922.

Rıza Nur. *Hayat ve Hatıratım* [My Life and My Memories], vol. 3. Istanbul: Altındağ Yayınevi, 1968).

Rodas, Mihail L. *Ē Ellada stēn Mikran Asia (1918–1922): Ē Mikrasiatikē Katastrofē* [Greece in Asia Minor (1918–1922): Asia Minor Disaster]. Athens: Kleisiouni, 1950 [Reprinted Lavyrinthos, 2019].

Şahingiray, Mehmet Reşit. *Hayatı ve Hatıraları: İttihad ve Terakki Dönemi ve Ermeni Meselesi* [His Life and Memoirs: The Union and Progress Period and the Armenian Question]. Edited by Nejdet Bilgi. Izmir: Akademi Kitabevi, 1997.

Ethnic Cleansing in Western Anatolia

Sartiaux, Félix. *Le sac de Phocée et l'expulsion des Grecs Ottomans d'Asie Mineure en juin 1914*. Paris: Typographie Philippe Renouard, 1914.

Simpson, Donald H. *Anglican Church Life in Smyrna and Its Neighbourhood 1636–1952*, manuscript. Diocese of Gibraltar, 1952, held by Guildhall Library.

Solomōnidēs, Chrēstos. *Ē Dēmosiografia stē Smyrnē (1821–1922)* [Journalism in Smyrna (1821–1922)]. Athens: Ar. Mauridē, 1959.

Solomōnidēs, Chrēstos. *Ē Paideia stē Smyrnē* [Education in Smyrna]. Athens: n.p., 1961.

Solomōnidēs, Chrēstos. *O Smyrnēs Chrysostomos* [Chrysostomos of Smyrna], 2 vols. Athens: Ethnikis Mnimosynis, 1971.

Türkgeldi, Ali Fuat. *Görüp İşittiklerim* [Those I Saw and Heard]. Ankara: Türk Tarih Kurumu, 2010.

Uran, Himi. *Hatıralarım* [My Memoirs] Ankara: Ayyıldız Matbaası, 1959.

Venezis, Elias. *To Noumero 31328: Sklavoi sta Ergastika Tagmata tēs Anatolēs; Romantzo* [The Number 31328: Slaves in the Labour Brigades of Anatolia; A Novel]. Mytilene and Athens: N. Theofanidis and S. Lambaridis, 1931.

Yalçın, Hüseyin Cahit. *Siyasal Anılar* [Political Memoirs]. Istanbul: Türkiye İş Bankası Yayınları, 1979.

Zavitzianos, Kōnstantinos G. *Ai anamnēseis tou ek tis Istorikis Diafōnias Vasieleōs Kōnstantinou kai Eleutheriou Venizelou opōs tēn ezēse (1914–1922)* [Memories about the Historical Conflict between King Constantine and Eleftherios Venizelos], vol. II. Athens: Rodis, 1947.

Secondary Sources

BOOKS

Aksakal, Mustafa. *The Ottoman Road to War in 1914: The Ottoman Empire and the First World War*. Cambridge: Cambridge University Press, 2010.

Akşin, Sina. *İstanbul Hükümetleri ve Milli Mücadele* [The Istanbul Governments and the National Struggle], vol. 1. Istanbul: Cem Yayınevi, 1976.

Akşin, Sina. *Turkey: From Empire to Revolutionary Republic*. London: Hurst, 2007.

Aktar, Ayhan. *Varlık Vergisi ve 'Türkleştirme' Politikaları* [Capital Tax and 'Turkification' Policies]. Istanbul: İletişim Yayınları, 2006.

Alkan, Ahmet Turan. *İstiklal Mahkemeleri* [Independence Tribunals]. Istanbul: Ağaç Yayıncılık, 1993.

Anagnostopoulou, Sia. *Mikra Asia 19os ai.–1919 Oi Ellēnorthodoxes koinotēs: Apo to Millet tōn Rōmiōn sto Ellēniko Ethnos* [Asia Minor, 19th century–1919: The Greek Orthodox Communities: From *Rum Millet* to the Hellenic Nation]. Athens: Hellinika Grammata, 1997.

Anderson, Benedict. *Imagined Communities: Reflections on the Origin and Spread of Nationalism*. London: Verso, 1991.

Anscombe, Frederick F. *State, Faith, and Nation in Ottoman and Post-Ottoman Lands*. New York: Cambridge University Press, 2014.

Bibliography

Atay, Falih Rıfkı. *Çankaya*. Istanbul: Pozitif Yayınları, 2004.

Augé, Marc. *Les forms de l'oubli*. Paris: Editions Payot & Rivages, 2001.

Augustinos, Gerasimos. *Consciousness and History: Nationalist Critics of Greek Society, 1897–1914*. New York: Columbia University Press/East European Quarterly, 1977.

Augustinos, Gerasimos. *The Greeks of Asia Minor: Confession, Community, and Ethnicity in the Nineteenth Century*. Kent, OH: Kent State University Press, 1992.

Berber, Engin. *Sancılı Yıllar: İzmir, 1918–22: Mütareke ve İşgal Döneminde İzmir Sancağı* [The Sorrowful Years: İzmir, 1918–22: İzmir Sanjak in the Armistice and Occupation Periods]. Ankara: Ayraç Yayınevi, 1997.

Berkes, Niyazi. *Turkish Nationalism and Western Civilization: Selected Essays of Ziya Gökalp*. New York: Columbia University Press, 1959.

Beşikçi, Mehmet. *The Ottoman Mobilization of Manpower in the First World War: Between Voluntarism and Resistance*. Leiden: Brill, 2012.

Bora, Siren. *İzmir Yahudileri Tarihi, 1908–1923* [History of İzmir Jews, 1908–1923]. Istanbul: Gözlem Basın ve Yayın, 1995.

Bruinessen, Martin van. *Agha, Sheikh, and the State*. London: Zed Books, 1992.

Çetinkaya, Y. Doğan. *1908 Osmanlı Boykotu: Bir Toplumsal Hareketin Analizi* [The 1908 Ottoman Boycott: Analysis of a Social Movement]. Istanbul: İletişim Yayınları, 2004.

Çetinkaya, Y. Doğan. *The Young Turks and the Boycott Movement*. London: I. B. Tauris, 2014.

Clark, Bruce. *Twice a Stranger: Greece, Turkey, and the Minorities They Expelled*. London: Granta Books, 2006.

Criss, Nur Bilge. *Istanbul under Allied Occupation, 1918–1923*. Leiden: Brill, 1999.

Daskalakēs, Apostolos V. *To politeuma tou Rēga Velestinlē* [The Polity of Rigas Velestinlis]. Athens: Vagionakēs, 1976.

Davison, Roderic. *Reform in the Ottoman Empire, 1856–76*. New York: Gordion Press, 1973.

Dobkin, Marjorie Housepian. *Smyrna 1922: The Destruction of a City*. Kent, OH: Kent State University Press, 1988.

Doumanis, Nicholas. *Before the Nation: Muslim–Christian Coexistence and Its Destruction in Late-Ottoman Anatolia*. Oxford: Oxford University Press, 2012.

Dündar, Fuat. *İttihat ve Terakkinin Müslümanları İskân Politikası (1913–1918)* [The Committee of Union and Progress and Its Resettlement Policy for Muslims]. Istanbul: İletişim Yayınları, 2001.

Dündar, Fuat. *Modern Türkiye'nin Şifresi: İttihat ve Terakki'nin Etnisite Mühendisliği (1913–1918)* [The Code to Modern Turkey: Ethnicity Engineering of the Committee of Union and Progress (1913–1918)]. Istanbul: İletişim Yayınları, 2008.

Ethnic Cleansing in Western Anatolia

Eksertzoglou, Haris. *Nostaljinin Ötesinde Kaybedilmiş Memleketler: Osmanlı İmparatorluğu'ndaki Rumların Toplumsal ve Kültürel Bir* Tarihi [Lost Homelands beyond Nostalgia: A Social and Cultural History of Greeks in the Ottoman Empire]. Istanbul: Tarih Vakfı Yurt Yayınları, 2015.

Erhan, Çağrı. *Greek Occupation of Izmir and Adjoining Territories.* Ankara: Stratejik Araştırmalar Merkezi, 1999.

Ersanlı Behar, Büşra. *İktidar ve Tarih: Türkiye'de 'Resmi Tarih' Tezinin Oluşumu, 1929–37* [Power and History: The Formation of the 'Official History' Thesis in Turkey, 1929–37]. Istanbul: Afa Yayınları, 1992.

Falmpos, Filippos K. *Smyrnaïka Meletēmata* [Studies on Smyrna]. Athens: n.p., 1980.

Findley, Carter Vaughn. *Bureaucratic Reform in the Ottoman Empire: The Sublime Porte, 1789–1922.* Princeton: Princeton University Press, 1980.

Findley, Carter Vaughn. *Ottoman Civil Officialdom: A Social History.* Princeton: Princeton University Press, 1989.

Fortna, Benjamin C. *Imperial Classroom: Islam, the State, and Education in the Late Ottoman Empire.* New York: Oxford University Press, 2002.

Fortna, Benjamin C. *Learning to Read in the Late Ottoman Empire and the Early Turkish Republic.* Basingstoke: Palgrave Macmillan, 2011.

Fortna, Benjamin C. *The Circassian: A Life of Eşref Bey, Late Ottoman Insurgent and Special Agent.* London: Hurst, 2016.

Foucault, Michel. *The History of Sexuality, vol. I: An Introduction.* New York: Pantheon Books, 1978.

Georgelin, Hervé. *La fin de Smyrne: Du cosmpolitisme aux nationalismes.* Paris: CNRS, 2005.

Georgeon, François. *Aux origines du nationalisme turc: Yusuf Akçura, 1876–1935.* Paris: ADPF, 1980.

Georgiadou, Maria. *Constantin Carathéodory: Mathematics and Politics in Turbulent Times.* Berlin: Springer, 2004.

Gingeras, Ryan. *Sorrowful Shores: Violence, Ethnicity, and the End of the Ottoman Empire, 1912–23.* Oxford: Oxford University Press, 2009.

Gingeras, Ryan. *Fall of the Sultanate: The Great War and the End of the Ottoman Empire, 1908–1922.* Oxford: Oxford University Press, 2016.

Göçek, Fatma Müge. *Rise of the Bourgeoisie, Demise of the Empire: Ottoman Westernisation and Social Change.* New York: Oxford University Press, 1996.

Gökbilgin, Tayyip. *Milli Mücadele Başlarken* [At the Beginning of the National Struggle], 2 vols. Ankara: Türkiye İş Bankası Yayınları, 1959–65.

Gologlu, Mahmut. *Türkiye Cumhuriyeti Tarihi: Birinci Kitap: Devrimler ve Tepkiler, 1924–1930* [History of the Republic of Turkey: Book 1: Revolutions and Reactions, 1924–1930]. Ankara: Başnur Matbaası, 1972.

Grassi, Fabio L. *İtalya ve Türk Sorunu, 1919–1923* [Italy and the Turkish Question, 1919–1923]. Istanbul: Yapı Kredi Yayınları, 2003.

Bibliography

Gratien, Chris. *The Unsettled Plain: An Environmental History of the Late Ottoman Frontier*. Stanford: Stanford University Press, 2022.

Grigoriadis, Ioannis N. *Instilling Religion in Greek and Turkish Nationalism: A 'Sacred Synthesis'*. New York: Palgrave Macmillan, 2013.

Hanioğlu, M. Şükrü. *Preparation for a Revolution: The Young Turks, 1902–1908*. Oxford: Oxford University Press, 2001.

Helmreich, Paul C. *From Paris to Sèvres: The Partition of the Ottoman Empire at the Peace Conference of 1919–1920*. Columbus, OH: Ohio State University Press, 1974.

Hirschon, Renée (ed.). *Crossing the Aegean: An Appraisal of the 1923 Compulsory Population Exchange*. Oxford: Berghahn Books, 2003.

Kalyviōtēs, Aristomenēs. *Smyrnē, Ē Mousikē Zōē*. Athens: Music Corner & Tinella, 2002.

Kan, Paul Rexton. *The Global Challenge of Militias and Paramilitary Violence*. Cham: Palgrave Macmillan, 2019.

Kaplan, İsmail. *Türkiye'de Milli Eğitim İdeolojisi* [The Ideology of National Education in Turkey]. Istanbul: İletişim Yayınları, 1999.

Karabıçak, Yusuf Ziya. *The Development of Ottoman Policies towards Greek Associations (1861–1912)*. Istanbul: Libra Kitap, 2014.

Karal, Enver Ziya. *Modern Türkiye ve Atatürk* [Modern Turkey and Atatürk]. Ankara: Türk Tarih Kurumu, 1980.

Karatheodōrē-Rodopoulou, Despoina, and Despoina Vlachostergiou-Vasvatekē. *Kōnstantinos Karatheodōrē: O Sofos Ellēn tou Monachou* [Constantine Caratheodory: The Greek Scholar of Munich]. Athens: Kaktos, 2001.

Karpat, Kemal. *Ottoman Population, 1830–1914: Demographic and Social Characteristics*. Madison: University of Wisconsin Press, 1985.

Kasaba, Reşat. *The Ottoman Empire and the World Economy: The Nineteenth Century*. Albany: State University of New York Press, 1988.

Kasaba, Reşat. *A Moveable Empire: Ottoman Nomads, Migrants and Refugees*. Seattle: University of Washington Press, 2009.

Kayalı, Hasan. *Imperial Resilience: The Great War's End, Ottoman Longevity, and Incidental Nations*. Oakland, CA: University of California Press, 2021.

Keskin, Mehmet Ali. *İzmir Valileri, 1300–1989* [The Governors of Izmir, 1300–1989]. Izmir: Karınca Matbaacılık, 1989.

Keyder, Çağlar. *State and Class in Turkey: A Study in Capitalist Development*. London: Verso, 1987.

Kieser, Hans-Lukas. *Iskalanmış Barış: Doğu Vilayetleri'nde Misyonerlik, Etnik Kimlik ve Devlet, 1839–1938* [The Missed Peace: Mission, Ethnicity, and State in the Eastern Provinces of Turkey, 1839–1938]. Translated by Atilla Dirim. Istanbul: İletişim Yayınları, 2005.

Kieser, Hans-Lukas. *Talaat Pasha: Father of Modern Turkey, Architect of Genocide*. Princeton: Princeton University Press, 2018.

Kili, Suna. *Türk Devrim Tarihi* [Turkish Revolution History]. Istanbul: Tekin Yayınevi, 1982.

Ethnic Cleansing in Western Anatolia

Kiminas, Demetrius. *The Ecumenical Patriarchate: A History of Its Metropolitanates with Annotated Hierarch Catalogs*. San Bernardino, CA: The Borgo Press, 2009.

Kramer, Alan. *Dynamic of Destruction: Culture and Mass Killing in the First World War*. Oxford: Oxford University Press, 2009.

Ladas, Stephen Pericles. *The Exchange of Minorities: Bulgaria, Greece, and Turkey*. New York: Macmillan, 1932.

Llewellyn Smith, Michael. *Ionian Vision: Greece in Asia Minor, 1919–22*. New York: Columbia University Press, 1998.

Lowenthal, David. *The Past is a Foreign Country*. Cambridge: Cambridge University Press, 1985.

Mansel, Philip. *Levant: Splendour and Catastrophe on the Mediterranean*. New Haven, CT: Yale University Press, 2011.

Masters, Bruce. *Christians and Jews in the Ottoman Arab World: The Roots of Secterianism*. Cambridge: Cambridge University Press, 2001.

Mazower, Mark. *Greece and the Inter-war Economic Crisis*. Oxford: Oxford University Press, 1991.

Mazower, Mark. *Salonica, City of Ghosts: Christians, Muslims, and Jews, 1430–1950*. New York: Alfred A. Knopf, 2005.

Melson, Robert. *Revolution and Genocide: On the Origins of the Armenian Genocide and the Holocaust*. Chicago: University of Chicago Press, 1996.

Millas, Akilas. *Oğlunuz Er Yorgos Savaşırken Öldü* [Your Son Private Yorgos Died while Fighting]. Istanbul: Kitap Yayınevi, 2004.

Milton, Giles. *Paradise Lost: Smyrna 1922, The Destruction of Islam's City of Tolerance*. New York: Basic Books, 2008.

Mitchell, Timothy. *Colonising Egypt*. New York: Cambridge University Press, 1988.

Mylonas, Harris. *The Politics of Nation-building: Making Co-nationals, Refugees, and Minorities*. Cambridge: Cambridge University Press, 2012.

Nahum, Henri. *Juifs de Smyrne, XIXe–XXe siècle*. Paris: Aubier, 1997.

Ozil, Ayşe. *Orthodox Christians in the Late Ottoman Empire: A Study of Relations in Anatolia*. London: SOAS/Routledge Studies on the Middle East, 2012.

Özoğlu, Hakan. *Kurdish Notables and the Ottoman State: Evolving Identities, Competing Loyalties, and Shifting Boundaries*. New York: State University of New York Press, 2004.

Özoğlu, Hakan. *From Caliphate to Secular State: Power Struggle in the Early Turkish Republic*. Santa Barbara: Praeger, 2011.

Pekin, Müfide (ed.). *Yeniden Kurulan Yaşamlar: 80. Yılında Türk-Yunan Nüfus Mübadelesi* [Lives Reconsidered: Eighty Years after the Greek–Turkish Compulsory Population Exchange]. Istanbul: Istanbul Bilgi Universitesi, 2005.

Philliou, Christine M. *Turkey: A Past against History*. Oakland, CA: University of California Press, 2021.

Quataert, Donald. *Social Disintegration and Popular Resistance in the Ottoman Empire, 1881–1908: Reactions to European Economic Penetration*. New York: New York University Press, 1983.

Bibliography

Schmitt, Oliver Jens. *Les Levantines: Cadres de vie et identités d'un groupe ethno-confessionnel de l'Empire Ottoman au 'Long' 19e siècle.* Istanbul: Isis Press, 2007.

Soysal, İlhami. *Kurtuluş Savaşında İşbirlikçiler* [The Collaborators during the War of Independence]. Istanbul: Bengi, 2008.

Su, Kâmil. *Sevr Antlaşması ve Aydın (İzmir) Vilayeti* [The Treaty of Sèvres and Aydın Province]. Ankara: Kültür Bakanlığı Yayınları, 1981.

Su, Kâmil. *Manisa ve Yöresinde İşgal Acıları* [The Grief of Occupation in Manisa and Its Environs]. Ankara: Kültür ve Turizm Bakanlığı Yayınları, 1982.

Suny, Ronald Grigor. *'They Can Live in the Desert but Nowhere Else': A History of the Armenian Genocide.* Princeton: Princeton University Press, 2015.

Taçalan, Nurdoğan. *Ege'de Kurtuluş Savaşı Başlarken* [While the Independence War was Starting in the Aegean]. Istanbul: Milliyet Yayınları, 1970.

Tekeli, İlhan and Selim İlkin. *Ege'deki Sivil Direnişten Kurtuluş Savaşı'na Geçerken* [Civil Resistance to the War of Independence in the Aegean]. Ankara: Türk Tarih Kurumu, 1989.

Toprak, Zafer. *Türkiye'de Milli İktisat, 1908–1918* [The National Economy in Turkey]. Istanbul: Doğan Kitap, 2012.

Toumarkine, Alexandre. *Les Migrations des Populations Musulmanes Balkanique en Anatolie (1876–1913).* Istanbul: Isis, 1995.

Toynbee, Arnold J. *The Western Question in Greece and Turkey.* London: Constable, 1922.

Tunaya, Tarık Zafer. *Türkiye'de Siyasî Partiler, 1859–1952* [Political Parties in Turkey, 1859–1952]. Istanbul: Doğan Kardeş, 1952.

Tunaya, Tarık Zafer. *Türkiye'de Siyasal Partiler, vol. 1: İkinci Meşrutiyet Dönemi* [Political Parties in Turkey, vol 1: The Second Constitutional Era]. Istanbul: Hürriyet Vakfı Yayınları, 1984.

Tunçay, Mete. *Türkiye Cumhuriyeti'nde Tek-Parti Yönetimin Kurulması (1923–1931)* [The Establishment of the Single-party Regime in the Republic of Turkey (1923–1931)]. Istanbul: Yurt Yayınları, 1981.

Turan, Şerafettin. *Türk Devrim Tarihi 2: Ulusal Direnişten Türkiye Cumhuriyeti'ne* [Turkish Revolution History 2: From National Resistance to the Republic of Turkey]. Istanbul: Bilgi Yayınevi, 1995.

Umar, Bilge. *İzmir'de Yunanlıların Son Günleri* [The Last Days of the Greeks in Smyrna]. Ankara: Bilgi Yayınevi, 1974.

Üstel, Füsun. *İmparatorluktan Ulus-Devlete Türk Milliyetçiliği: Türk Ocakları, 1912–1931* [Turkish Nationalism from Empire to Nation-state: The Turkish Hearths, 1912–1931]. Istanbul: İletişim Yayınları, 1997.

Vassiadis, George A. *The Syllogos Movement of Constantinople and Ottoman Greek Education, 1861–1923.* Athens: Centre for Asia Minor Studies, 2007.

Weiner, Myron, and Michael Teitelbaum. *Political Demography, Demographic Engineering.* New York: Berghahn Books, 2001.

Woodhouse, C. M. *Rhigas Velestinlis: The Proto-martyr of the Greek Revolution.* Limni: Denise Harvey, 1995.

Ethnic Cleansing in Western Anatolia

Wyers, Mark David. *'Wicked' Istanbul: The Regulation of Prostitution in the Early Turkish Republic*. Istanbul: Libra Kitap, 2012.

Yetkin, Sabri. *Ege'de Eşkıyalar* [Bandits in the Aegean]. Istanbul: Tarih Vakfı Yurt Yayınları, 1997.

Yıldırım, Onur. *Diplomacy and Displacement: Reconsidering the Turco-Greek Exchange of Populations, 1922–1934*. London: Routledge, 2006.

Yıldız, Ahmet. *'Ne Mutlu Türküm Diyebilene': Türk Ulusal Kimliğinin Etno-Seküler Sınırları (1919–1938)* [How Happy is the One Who Can Say He Is a Turk: Ethno-Secular Boundaries of Turkish National Identity (1919–1938)]. Istanbul: İletişim Yayınları, 2001.

Zarkovic Bookman, Milica. *The Demographic Struggle for Power: The Political Economy of Demographic Engineering in the Modern World*. London: Routledge, 1997.

Zürcher, Erik Jan. *The Unionist Factor: The Role of the Committee of Union and Progress in the Turkish National Movement (1905–1926)*. Leiden: Brill, 1984.

Zürcher, Erik Jan. *Turkey: A Modern History*. London: I. B. Tauris, 2004.

ARTICLES

Achladi, Evangelia. 'De la guerre à l'administration grecque: la fin de la Smyrne cosmopolite'. In *Smyrne, la ville oubliée?*, edited by Marie-Carmen Smyrnelis, 180–95. Paris: Editions Autrement, 2006.

Adanır, Fikret. 'Bulgaristan, Yunanistan ve Türkiye Üçgeninde Ulus İnşası ve Nüfus Değişimi'. [Nation-building and Population Exchange in the Triangle of Bulgaria, Greece and Turkey] In *Türkiye'de Etnik Çatışma*, edited by Erik Jan Zürcher, 19–26. Istanbul: İletişim Yayınları, 2005.

Adanır, Fikret. 'Non-Muslims in the Ottoman Army and the Ottoman Defeat in the Balkan War of 1912–1913'. In *A Question of Genocide: Armenians and Turks at the End of the Ottoman Empire*, edited by Ronald Grigor Suny, Norman Naimark and Fatma Müge Göçek, 111–25. Oxford: Oxford University Press, 2011.

Agelopoulos, Georgios. 'Contested Territories and the Quest for Ethnology: People and Places in İzmir 1919–22'. In *Spatial Conceptions of the Nation: Modernizing Geographies in Greece and Turkey*, edited by Nikiforos Diamandouros, Çağlar Keyder and Thalia Dragonas, 181–92. London: I. B. Tauris, 2010.

Ahmad, Feroz. 'Vanguard of a Nascent Bourgeoisie: The Social and Economic Policy of the Young Turks, 1908–1918'. In *Social and Economic History of Turkey (1071–1920)*, edited by Osman Okyar and Halil İnalcık, 329–50. Ankara: Meteksan Limited Şirketi, 1980.

Akder, Halis. 'Forgotten Campaigns: A History of Disease in Turkey'. In *Turkey's Engagement with Modernity: Conflict and Change in the Twentieth Century*, edited by Celia J. Kerslake, Kerem Öktem and Philip Robins, 210–35. Basingstoke: Palgrave Macmillan, 2010.

Bibliography

Aktar, Ayhan. 'Osmanlı Meclisi Ermeni Meselesini Tartışıyor: Kasım-Aralık 1918'. [The Ottoman Parliament is Discussing the Armenian Question: November–December 1918] In *İmparatorluğun Çöküş Döneminde Osmanlı Ermenileri: Bilimsel Sorumluluk ve Demokrasi Sorunları*, edited by Fahri Aral, 353–82. Istanbul: Bilgi University Press, 2011.

Alexandris, Alexis. 'The Constantinopolitan Greek Factor during the Greco-Turkish Confrontation of 1919–1922'. *Byzantine and Modern Greek Studies* 8 (1982): 137–69.

Alexandris, Alexis. 'The Greek Census of Anatolia and Thrace (1910–1912): A Contribution to Ottoman Historical Demography'. In *Ottoman Greeks in the Age of Nationalism*, edited by Dimitri Gondicas and Charles Issawi, 46–69. Princeton: The Darwin Press, 1999.

Allamanē, Efē and Krista Panagiōtopoulou. 'O ellēnismos tēs Mikras Asias se diōgmo'. [The Hellenism of Asia Minor in Persecution] In *Istoria tou Ellēnikou Ethnous, vol. 15: Neōteros Ellēnismos apo to 1913 ōs to 1941*, 98–103. Athens: Ekdotikē Athēnōn, 1978.

Anagnostopoulou, Sia. 'The Process of Defining Izmir's "Historical National Mission" in the 19th C.–1919'. In *The Passages from the Ottoman Empire to the Nation-states: A Long and Difficult Process: The Greek Case*, 75–101. Istanbul: The Isis Press, 2004.

Anestides, Stavros Th. 'The Church of Smyrna'. In *Smyrna: Metropolis of the Asia Minor Greeks*, edited by Nikos Hatzigeorgiou, 115–36. Athens: Ephesus Publishing, 2004.

Anestides, Stavros Th. 'Education and Culture'. In *Smyrna: Metropolis of the Asia Minor Greeks*, edited by Nikos Hatzigeorgiou, 137–60. Athens: Ephesus Publishing, 2004.

Arai, Masami. 'Between State and Nation: A New Light on the Journal *Türk Yurdu*'. *Turcica* 24 (1992): 277–95.

Arı, Kemal. '1923 Türk-Rum Mübadele Antlaşması Sonrasında İzmir'de Emval-i Metruke ve Mübadil Göçmenler'. [Abandoned Properties and Migrants after 1923 Turkish–Greek Population Exchange] *Atatürk Araştırma Merkezi Dergisi* 6 (1990): 627–57.

Arıkan, Zeki. 'İşgal Sırasında İzmir'de Kurulan Bir Dernek'. [An Association Established in Smyrna during the Occupation] *Atatürk Yolu* 3 (1989): 355–71.

Attrep, Abe. '"A State of Wretchedness and Impotence": A British View of Istanbul and Turkey, 1919'. *Journal of Middle Eastern Studies* 9, no. 1 (1978): 1–9.

Avdela, Efi. 'Between Duties and Rights: Gender and Citizenship in Greece, 1864–1952'. In *Citizenship and Nation-state in Greece and Turkey*, edited by Faruk Birtek and Thalia Dragonas, 117–43. London: Routledge, 2005.

Barkan, Ömer Lütfi. 'Osmanlı İmparatorluğu'nda Bir İskân ve Kolonizasyon Metodu Olarak Sürgünler'. [Exiles as a Method of Resettlement and Colonisation in the Ottoman Empire] *İstanbul Üniversitesi İktisat Fakültesi Mecmuası* 11 (1949–50): 524–69.

Ethnic Cleansing in Western Anatolia

Beşikçi, Mehmet. 'Militarizm, Topyekun Savaş ve Gençliğin Seferber Edilmesi: Birinci Dünya Savaşı'nda Osmanlı İmparatorluğu'nda Paramiliter Dernekler'. [Militarism, Total War and Mobilisation of the Youth: Paramilitary Associations in the Ottoman Empire in World War I] *Tarih ve Toplum: Yeni Yaklaşımlar* 8 (Spring 2009): 49–92.

Bilmez, Bülent. 'A Nationalist Discourse of Heroism and Treason: The Construction of an "Official" Image of Çerkes Ethem (1886–1948) in Turkish Historiography and Recent Challenges'. In *Untold Histories of the Middle East: Recovering Voices from the 19th and 20th Centuries*, edited by Amy Singer, Selçuk Akşin Somel and Christoph K. Neumann, 106–23. London: Routledge, 2011.

'Bir Gümrükçünün İşgal Yılları Anıları: İzmir Gümrükleri Başmüdürlük Tahrirat Başkatibi Süleyman Vasfi Bey'in Anılarından'. [Memoirs of a Customs Agent during the Occupation Years: From the Memoirs of Süleyman Vasfi Bey, Chief Registrar of Izmir Customs General Directorate]. In *Üç İzmir*, edited by Enis Batur, 237–63. Istanbul: Yapı Kredi Yayınları, 1992.

Birtek, Faruk. 'Greek Bull in the China Shop of Ottoman "Grand Illusion": Greece in the Making of Modern Turkey'. In *Citizenship and the Nation-state in Greece and Turkey*, edited by Faruk Birtek and Thalia Dragonas, 37–48. London: Routledge, 2005.

Bjornlund, Matthias. 'The 1914 Cleansing of Aegean Greeks as a Case of Violent Turkification'. In *Late Ottoman Genocides: The Dissolution of the Ottoman Empire and Young Turk Population and Extermination Policies*, edited by Dominik Schaller and Jürgen Zimmerer, 34–50. London: Routledge, 2009.

Boura, Catherine. 'The Greek Millet in Turkish Politics: Greeks in the Ottoman Parliament (1908–1918)'. In *Ottoman Greeks in the Age of Nationalism*, edited by Dimitri Gondicas and Charles Issawi, 193–206. Princeton: The Darwin Press, 1999.

Çapa, Mesut. 'İzmir Müdafaa-i Hukuk Osmaniye Cemiyeti'. [Izmir Association for the Defence of Ottoman Rights] *Atatürk Araştırma Merkezi Dergisi* 7, no. 21 (July 1991): 553–66.

Carras, Costa. 'Greek Identity: A Long View'. In *Balkan Identities: Nation and Memory*, edited by Maria Todorova, 294–326. New York: New York University Press, 2004.

Çetin, Türkan. 'Kurtuluş Savaşı Yıllarında İşgal Bölgesi Köy ve Köylüsü'. [The Village and Villagers in the Occupation Zone during the War of Independence Years] *Çağdaş Türkiye Tarihi Araştırmaları Dergisi* 1, no. 3 (1993): 175–90.

Clogg, Richard. 'The Greek *Millet* in the Ottoman Empire'. In *Christians and Jews in the Ottoman Empire: The Functioning of a Plural Society*, edited by Benjamin Braude and Bernard Lewis, vol. I, 185–207. London: Holmes & Meier, 1982.

Clogg, Richard. 'The Byzantine Legacy in the Modern Greek World: The Megali Idea'. In *The Byzantine Legacy in Eastern Europe*, edited by Lowell Clucas, 253–81. New York: Columbia University Press/East European Monographs, 1988.

Bibliography

Deringil, Selim. '"They Live in a State of Nomadism and Savagery": The Late Ottoman Empire and the Post-colonial Debate'. *Comparative Studies in Society and History* 45 (2003): 311–42.

Ditchev, Ivaylo. 'The Eros of Identity'. In *Balkan as Metaphor: Between Globalization and Fragmentation*, edited by Dušan Bjelić and Obrad Savić, 235–50. Cambridge, MA: Massachusetts Institute of Technology Press, 2005.

Findley, Carter Vaughn. 'The Tanzimat'. In *The Cambridge History of Turkey, vol. 4: Turkey in the Modern World*, edited by Reşat Kasaba, 11–37. Cambridge: Cambridge University Press, 2008.

Finefrock, Michael M. 'Atatürk, Lloyd George and the *Megali Idea:* Cause and Consequence of the Greek Plan to Seize Constantinople from the Allies, June–August 1922'. *The Journal of Modern History* 52, no. 1 (March 1980): 1047–66.

Gawrych, George. 'The Culture and Politics of Violence in Turkish Society, 1903–14'. *Middle Eastern Studies* 22, no. 3 (1986): 307–30.

Georgelin, Hervé. 'Armenian Inter-community Relations in Late Ottoman Smyrna'. In *Armenian Smyrna/Izmir*, edited by Richard G. Hovannisian, 177–90. Costa Mesa, CA: Mazda Publishers, 2012.

Glavinas, Ioannis. 'In Search of a New Balance: The Symbiosis between Christian and Muslim Inhabitants of the Greek State, 1912–1923'. In *Balkan Nationalism(s) and the Ottoman Empire, vol. I: National Movements and Representations*, edited by Dimitris Stamatopoulos, 159–78. Istanbul: Isis Press, 2015.

Goffman, Daniel. 'Izmir: From Village to Colonial Port City'. In *The Ottoman City between East and West: Aleppo, Izmir, and Istanbul*, edited by Edhem Eldem, Daniel Goffman and Bruce Masters, 79–134. Cambridge: Cambridge University Press, 2001.

Gould, Andrew. 'The Burning of the Tents: The Forcible Settlements of Nomads in Southern Anatolia'. In *Essays in Honor of Andreas Tietze*, edited by Heath Lowry and Donald Quataert, 71–86. Istanbul: Isis, 1993.

Güneş, Günver. 'İzmir Türk Ocağı (1912–1918)'. *Kebikeç* 4 (1996): 149–58.

Helmreich, Paul C. 'Italy and the Anglo-French Repudiation of the 1917 St. Jean de Maurienne Agreement'. *The Journal of Modern History* 48, no. 2 (June 1976): 99–139.

Henze, Paul. 'Circassian Resistance to Russia'. In *The North Caucasus Barrier: The Russian Advance towards the Muslim World*, edited by Marie Bennigsen Broxup, 62–111. London: Hurst, 1992.

Huyugüzel, Ö. Faruk. 'İzmir'in Uzun Süre Yayımlanmış İstikrarlı Bir Gazetesi: Ahenk'. [A Consistent Newspaper of Smyrna: *Ahenk*] *Yeni Türk Edebiyatı* 3 (March 2011): 23–35.

Ilbert, Robert. 'Alexandrie, cosmopolite?' In *Villes ottomanes à la fin de l'empire*, edited by Paul Dumont and François Georgeon, 171–185. Paris: Editions l'Harmattan, 1992.

Ethnic Cleansing in Western Anatolia

Issı, Murat. 'Kürt Basını ve *Kürdistan* Gazetesi (1898–1902)'. *Şarkiyat*, no. 9, 2013: 127–147.

'İzmir Müdâfaa-i Cemiyeti Kâtib-i Umûmîsi Câmi Bey'in Mustafa Kemal Paşa'ya Gönderdiği 31 Kânûn-i Evvel 1335 Tarihli Telgraf'. [TheTelegraph sent by Câmi Bey, the Secretary-general of the Izmir Association for the Defence of the Rights, to Mustafa Kemal Pasha] Document no: 406. *Harb Tarihi Vesikaları Dergisi*, no. 16 (June 1956).

Jensen, Peter Kincaid. 'The Greco-Turkish War, 1920–1922'. *International Journal of Middle East Studies* 10, no. 4 (November 1979): 553–65.

Jersild, Austin Lee. 'From Savagery to Citizenship: Caucasian Mountaineers and Muslims in the Russian Empire'. In *Russia's Orient: Imperial Borderlands and Peoples, 1700–1917*, edited by Daniel Brower and Edward Lazzerini, 101–14. Bloomington: Indiana University Press, 1997.

Karpat, Kemal. 'The People's Houses in Turkey, Establishment and Growth'. *The Middle East Journal* 17 (1963): 55–67.

Kasaba, Reşat. 'İzmir'. In *Doğu Akdeniz'de Liman Kentleri, 1800–1914*, edited by Eyüp Özveren, Çağlar Keyder and Donald Quataert, 1–22. Istanbul: Tarih Vakfı Yurt Yayınları, 1994.

Kasaba, Reşat. 'Economic Foundations of a Civil Society: Greeks in the Trade of Western Anatolia, 1840–1876'. In *Ottoman Greeks in the Age of Nationalism*, edited by Dimitris Gondicas and Charles Issawi, 77–88. Princeton: Darwin Press, 1999.

Kasaba, Reşat. 'Izmir 1922: A Port City Unravels'. In *Modernity and Culture: From the Mediterranean to the Indian Ocean*, edited by Leila Tarazi Fawaz and C. A. Bayly, 204–229. New York: Columbia University Press, 2002.

Katsikas, Stefanos. '*Millet* Legacies in a National Environment: Political Elites and Muslim Communities in Greece (1830s–1923)'. In *State-nationalisms in the Ottoman Empire, Greece, and Turkey: Orthodox and Muslims, 1830–1945*, edited by Benjamin C. Fortna, Stefanos Katsikas, Dimitris Kamouzis and Paraskevas Konortas, 47–72. London: Routledge, 2013.

Kechriotis, Vangelis. 'Greek Orthodox, Ottoman Greeks or just Greeks? Theories of Coexistence in the Aftermath of the Young Turk Revolution'. *Etudes Balkaniques* 1 (2005): 51–72.

Kechriotis, Vangelis. 'La Smyrne grecque: des communautés au pantheon de l'histoire'. In *Smyrne, la ville oubliée?*, edited by Marie-Carmen Smyrnelis, 63–79. Paris: Editions Autrement, 2006.

Keyder, Çağlar. 'The Consequences of the Exchange of Populations for Turkey'. In *Crossing the Aegean*, edited by Renée Hirschon, 39–52. Oxford: Berghahn Books, 2003.

Keyder, Çağlar. 'A History and Geography of Turkish Nationalism'. In *Citizenship and the Nation-state in Greece and Turkey*, edited by Thalia Dragonas and Faruk Birtek, 3–17. London: Routledge, 2005.

Kiossev, Alexander. 'The Dark Intimacy: Maps, Identities, and Acts of Identifications'. In *Balkan as Metaphor: Between Globalization and*

Bibliography

Fragmentation, edited by Dušan Bjelić and Obrad Savić, 165–91. Cambridge, MA: Massachusetts Institute of Technology Press, 2005.

Kirişçi, Kemal. 'Minority/Majority Discourse: The Case of the Kurds in Turkey'. In *Making Majorities: Constituting the Nation in Japan, Korea, China, Malaysia, Fiji, Turkey, and the United States*, edited by Dru C. Gladney, 227–45. Stanford: Stanford University Press, 1998.

Kitromilides, Paschalis, and Alexis Alexandris. 'Ethnic Survival, Nationalism, and Forced Migration: The Historical Demography of the Greek Community of Asia Minor at the Close of the Ottoman Era'. *Deltio Kentrou Mikrasiatikon Spoudon* 5 (1984–5): 9–44.

Kitromilides, Paschalis. '"Imagined Communities" and the Origins of National Question in the Balkans'. *European History Quarterly* 19 (1989): 149–92.

Kitromilides, Paschalis. 'Greek Irredentism in Asia Minor and Cyprus'. *Middle Eastern Studies* 26 (1990): 3–17.

Köker, Osman. 'Tehcir Öncesinde Osmanlı Devleti'nde Ermeni Varlığı'. [Armenian Presence in the Ottoman State before the Deportation] In *İmparatorluğun Çöküş Döneminde Osmanlı Ermenileri: Bilimsel Sorumluluk ve Demokrasi Sorunları*, edited by Fahri Aral, 21–30. Istanbul: Istanbul Bilgi University Press, 2011.

Kolluoğlu Kırlı, Biray. 'Cityscapes and Modernity: Smyrna Morphing into Izmir'. In *Ways to Modernity in Greece and Turkey: Encounters with Europe, 1850–1950*, edited by Çağlar Keyder and Anna Frangoudaki, 217–37. London: I. B. Tauris, 2007.

Kolodny, Emile. 'Des musulmans dans une île grecque: Les "Turcocrétois"'. *Mediterranean World* 14 (1995): 1–15.

Macar, Elçin. 'The Muslim Emigration in Western Anatolia'. *Cahiers balkaniques* 40 (2012): 227–34.

Michalopoulos, Dimitris. 'The Moslems of Chamuria and the Exchange of Populations between Greece and Turkey'. *Balkan Studies* 27, no. 2 (1986): 303–13.

Minassian, Anahide Ter. 'Les Arméniens: Le dynamisme d'une petite communauté'. In *Smyrne, la ville oubliée?*, edited by Marie-Carmen Smyrnelis, 70–91. Paris: Editions Autrement, 2006.

Nanakis, Andreas. 'Venizelos and Church–State Relations'. In *Eleftherios Venizelos: The Trials of Statesmanship*, edited by Paschalis M. Kitromilides, 346–73. Edinburgh: Edinburgh University Press, 2006.

Neyzi, Leyla. 'Remembering Smyrna/Izmir: Shared History, Shared Trauma'. *History and Memory* 20, no. 2 (Fall/Winter 2008): 106–27.

Noutsos, Panagiotis. 'The Role of the Greek Community in the Genesis and Development of the Socialist Movement in the Ottoman Empire, 1876–1923'. In *Socialism and Nationalism in the Ottoman Empire*, edited by Mete Tunçay and Erik Jan Zürcher, 77–88. London: I. B. Tauris, 1994.

Özbek, Nadir. 'Defining the Public Sphere during the Late Ottoman Empire: War, Mass Mobilization, and the Young Turk Regime (1908–18)'. *Middle Eastern Studies* 43, no. 5 (September 2007): 795–809.

Peckham, Robert Shannan. 'Internal Colonialism: Nation and Region in Nineteenth Century Greece'. In *Balkan Identities: Nation and Memory*, edited by Maria Todorova, 41–59. New York: New York University Press, 2004.

Rappas, Alexis. 'Memorial Soliloquies in Post-colonial Rhodes and the Ghost of Mediterranean Cosmopolitanism'. *Mediterranean Historical Review* 33, no. 1 (2018): 89–110.

Renan, Ernst. 'What is a Nation?' In *Becoming National: A Reader*, edited by Geoff Eley and Ronald Grigor Suny, 42–55. New York: Oxford University Press, 1996.

Said, Edward W. 'Representing the Colonized: Anthropology's Interlocutors'. *Critical Inquiry* 15, no. 2 (Winter 1989): 205–25.

Schmitt, Oliver Jens. 'Les Levantines, les Européens et le jeu d'identités'. In *Smyrne, la ville oubliée?*, edited by Marie-Carmen Smyrnelis, 106–19. Paris: Editions Autrement, 2006.

Şeker, Nesim. 'Osmanlı İmparatorluğunun Son Döneminde "Demografi Mühendisliği" ve Ermeniler'. ['Demographic Engineering' and the Armenians in the Last Period of the Ottoman Empire] In *İmparatorluğun Çöküş Döneminde Osmanlı Ermenileri: Bilimsel Sorumluluk ve Demokrasi Sorunları*, edited by Fahri Aral, 165–74. Istanbul: Bilgi University Press, 2011.

Shaw, Stanford J. 'Resettlement of Refugees in Anatolia, 1918–1923'. *The Turkish Studies Association Bulletin* 22, no. 1 (1998): 58–90.

Stoianovich, Traian. 'The Conquering Balkan Orthodox Merchant'. *The Journal of Economic History* 20, no. 2 (June 1960): 234–313.

Stouraiti, Anastasia, and Alexander Kazamias. 'The Imaginary Topographies of the *Megali Idea*: National Terrory as Utopia'. In *Spatial Conceptions of the Nation: Modernizing Geographies in Greece and Turkey*, edited by Nikiforos Diamandouros, Thalia Dragonas and Çağlar Keyder, 11–34. London: I. B. Tauris, 2010.

Themopoulou, Emilia. 'The Urbanisation of an Asia Minor City: The Example of Smyrna'. In *Smyrna: Metropolis of the Asia Minor Greeks*, edited by Nikos Hatzigeorgiou, 77–114. Athens: Ephesus Publishing, 2004.

Tınal, Melih. 'Yunan İşgali Döneminde İzmir Mekteb-i Sultanisi'. [İzmir Sultânî Lycée during the Greek Occupation] *Tarih ve Toplum* 188 (August 1999): 4–10.

Toprak, Zafer. 'Osmanlı Donanması, Averof Zırhlısı ve Ulusal Kimlik'. [Ottoman Navy, *Averof* Battleship and the National Identity] *Toplumsal Tarih* 113 (2003): 10–19.

Ülker, Erol. 'Assimilation of the Muslim Communities in the First Decade of the Turkish Republic (1923–1934)'. *European Journal of Turkish Studies* 6 (2007), <https://journals.openedition.org/ejts/822> (last accessed 15 December 2023).

Vranousēs, Leandros. 'Ē sēmaia, to ethnosēmo kai ē sfragida tēs 'Ellēnikēs Dēmokratias' tou Rēga'. [The Flag, the Colours and the Shield of the 'Greek Democracy' by Rigas] *Deltion Eraldikēs kai Genealogikēs Etaireias Ellados* 8

Bibliography

(1992): 347–88. Xanalatos, Diogenis. 'The Greeks and the Turks on the Eve of the Balkan Wars: A Frustrated Plan'. *Balkan Studies* 3 (1962): 277–96.

Xydis, Stephen G. 'Modern Greek Nationalism'. In *Nationalism in Eastern Europe*, edited by Peter F. Sugar and Ivo J. Lederer, 207–58. Seattle: University of Washington Press, 1969.

Yıldız, Ahmet. 'Kemalist Milliyetçilik'. [Kemalist Nationalism] In *Modern Türkiye'de Siyasal Düşünceler, vol. 2: Kemalizm*, edited by Ahmet İnsel, 210–34. Istanbul: İletişim Yayınları, 2001.

Zürcher, Erik Jan. 'Young Turk Memoirs as a Historical Source: Kazım Karabekir's *Istiklal Harbimiz*'. *Middle Eastern Studies* 22, no. 4 (1986): 561–70.

Zürcher, Erik Jan. 'The Last Phase in the History of the Committee of Union and Progress (1923–1924)'. In *Actes de la première rencontre internationale sur l'Empire Ottoman et la Turquie moderne*, edited by Edhem Eldem, 369–77. Istanbul: Isis Press, 1991.

Zürcher, Erik Jan. 'The Vocabulary of Muslim Nationalism'. *International Journal of the Sociology of Language* 137 (1999): 81–92.

Zürcher, Erik Jan. 'Ottoman Labour Battalions in World War I'. In *Der Völkermold an den Armeniern und die Shoah*, edited by Hans-Lukas Kieser and Dominik J. Schaller, 187–96. Zurich: Chronos, 2002.

Zürcher, Erik Jan. 'The Young Turks – Children of the Borderlands?' *International Journal of Turkish Studies* 9 (2003): 275–86.

Zürcher, Erik Jan. 'The Late Ottoman Empire as a Laboratory of Social Engineering'. *Il Mestiere di Storico* 10, no. 1 (2009): 7–18.

Zürcher, Erik Jan. 'The Importance of Being Secular: Islam in the Service of National and Pre-national State'. In *Turkey's Engagement with Modernity: Conflict and Change in the Twentieth Century*, edited by Celia Kerslake, Kerem Öktem and Philip Robins, 55–68. Basingstoke: Palgrave Macmillan, 2010.

Zürcher, Erik J. 'The Young Turk Mindset'. In *The Young Turk Legacy and Nation Building: From the Ottoman Empire to Atatürk's Turkey*, 110–23. London: I. B. Tauris, 2010.

PhD Theses

Katsikas, Michalis. 'Dragoumis, Macedonia, and the Ottoman Empire (1903–1913): The Great Idea, Nationalism, and Greek Ottomanism'. Unpublished PhD thesis, Centre for Byzantine, Ottoman and Modern Greek Studies, University of Birmingham, 2008.

Solomonidis, Victoria. 'Greece in Asia Minor: The Greek Administration of the Vilayet of Aidin, 1919–1922'. Unpublished PhD thesis, King's College, University of London, 1984.

Tabak, Serap. 'İzmir Şehrinde Mülki İdare ve İdareciler (1867–1950)'. [The Civilian Administration and Administrators in the City of Smyrna (1867–1950)]. Unpublished PhD thesis, Ege Üniversitesi, 1997.

Index

Abandoned Property Commission, 60, 251
Abdülmecid, Prince, 66
Abdürrahim, Prince, 68
Abdurrahman Bedirhan Bey, 179, 181, 183, 192
Adrianople, 23, 27, 45, 54, 84, 239
Afyonkarahisar, 36, 99, 204, 223–5, 228, 239, 245, 255
Agreement of Saint-Jean-de-Maurienne, 205
Ahmed Besim Bey, 65, 175
Ahmet Asım, 255
Ahmet İzzet Bey, 8, 65–7, 79, 82, 100, 121, 159, 161–75, 176, 186–7, 188, 189, 190, 193
Ahmet İzzet Pasha, 62, 63
Ahmet Şükrü, 112–13, 193
Ahmet Tevfik Pasha, 161–2
Akhisar, 54, 133, 172, 177–8, 192, 215, 255
Alaiyelizade Mahmut Bey, 57
Alaşehir, 26, 98–9, 105, 117, 177, 202, 204, 210, 214, 222, 224–6, 231–2, 236, 240
Alaşehir Congress, 204, 210, 214, 222, 225, 231
Albanians, 23, 43, 84, 186, 248, 260–1
Alexandria, 21, 75, 269

Ali Bey (Çetinkaya), 159, 163, 187, 209–10, 212, 215, 257
Ali Nâdir Pasha, 163–4, 188, 209, 262
American Collegiate Institute, 142, 155, 207, 242
American Relief Committee, 244
Anadolu, 147, 166, 202, 224, 234–5
Ankara government (nationalists in Ankara) 5–6, 8–9, 19, 88, 113, 185–6, 202, 205, 208, 226, 228, 233, 253–4, 262–3, 265
Anzavur, Ahmet, 183–4
Apak, Rahmi, 160, 188, 214
Apollon, 131
Armenian, 1, 5, 10, 14, 21–2, 26–32, 35–7, 39, 42, 44–5, 47, 50, 57–8, 61–4, 67, 69, 86, 93, 100, 106, 109, 112–13, 119, 126, 131–3, 142–3, 145–6, 148–9, 155, 158, 163, 165, 170, 177, 181, 184–5, 190, 195–7, 200, 208, 219–21, 223–4, 232, 235, 239, 241–5, 251–2, 259, 262, 265, 267, 269
Armistice of Mudros, 12, 62, 161, 174, 178, 189, 197–8, 209
Asia Minor Defence Organisation, 185
Aşîr Bey, 225, 227

Balıkesir, 99, 184, 195, 202–4, 215, 219, 226, 231

Index

Balıkesir Congress, 203
Baliozian, S., 251
Balkan Wars, 2, 4, 14, 23, 43, 45, 49–50, 52, 70, 74–5, 77, 82, 85–6, 117, 196–7, 215, 265, 268
Basmane, 26, 122, 126, 133, 142, 241–2
Battistoni, Giuseppe, 179
Beirut, 3, 65, 269
Bekir Sâmî (Günsav), 177, 183, 209, 214–15, 222, 226–7
Bekir Sâmî (Kunduh), 233
Bergama, 25, 46, 51, 59, 96, 105, 119, 139, 215, 219, 258
Berlin Congress, 44
Berlin–Baghdad Railway, 55
Besim (Atalay), 227
Bezmi Nusret, 177
Bosniaks, 23, 45, 109, 186, 197
Bournabat, 26–7, 57, 78, 82, 140, 213, 215, 233, 245, 247–8, 253
Boycottage Association (Boykotaj Cemiyeti), 48–9
Boys' School of Bournabat Orthodox Community, 140
Britain, 3, 48, 62, 73, 84, 113, 172, 259, 262
British High Commission, 32, 69, 79–80, 100, 104, 115, 118–24, 157, 169, 181, 190, 229, 231–6, 259
Brunetti, Enia, 148–50
Bulgaria, 45, 257
Bunoust, Georges Hippolyte, 172–3
Bursa, 8–9, 27, 68, 99, 105, 209, 222, 226–7, 251, 255, 257

Calthorpe, Somerset, 62, 69, 115, 123, 164–7, 170, 188–9, 193, 231, 234–6
Calvert, John M., 220
Câmi (Baykut) Bey, 202, 207, 230–1, 233
Cappadocia, 2, 145, 247

Carathéodory, Constantin, 143–4, 146, 155–6
Catholic Greeks, 49, 126
Cavid Bey, 183
Cemal Pasha, 52, 55, 71–3, 198
Central Committee of the CUP, 18, 42
Central School for Girls (*Kentrikon Parthenagogeion*), 139
Çerkes Ethem, 6, 46, 79, 177, 184, 192, 205, 212, 215, 220, 224–7, 235, 256
Çerkes Reşit, 79, 184, 210, 215, 220
Çeşme, 24–5, 36, 51, 53–4, 69, 71, 96, 106–7, 109, 139, 231, 240
Cevat Bey, 64
Chamber of Deputies, 86
Chania, 176
Chios, 25, 28, 59, 76, 235
Chiotika (neighbourhood), 134, 153
Chrysostomos (Kalafatis), 59, 64, 66, 90, 118, 146, 159, 163, 185, 241
Çine, 179, 181, 216–17, 233
Circassian, 2, 6, 9, 15, 29, 39, 43, 46, 74, 113, 160–1, 177, 183–5, 211–12, 215, 256
Circassian Congress, 160–1, 183–5, 256
Committee of Union and Progress (CUP), 2, 4–5, 8, 10, 13, 18, 39–50, 52, 55–8, 60–4, 67, 70, 72–4, 77, 79, 93, 117, 147, 157, 159, 161–3, 175, 188, 196, 199, 204–5, 210–11, 218–19, 229–32, 234, 264–5, 267
Comte, Auguste, 40
Conference of London, 83, 110, 233
constitution, 39–40, 44, 48, 85, 111, 118, 162, 184, 187–8, 264
Cordelio, 26, 112–13, 126, 146, 155, 247
Council of State (*Şura-yı Devlet*), 162
Credit Lyonnais, 252
Cretan Muslims, 15, 35, 46–7, 69, 165, 176

Cretan question, 48, 75
Cretans, 15, 23, 35, 45–8, 69, 75, 85,
   91, 116, 161, 165, 176, 181, 186,
   189, 199, 217
Crete, 3–4, 48–9, 70, 85–6, 88, 98,
   117–18, 176, 265
Çukurova, 16, 32
Cumberbatch, Henry Arnold, 212, 234

Dall'olio, Alfredo, 172
Dardanelles, 13, 49, 59, 62
Denizli, 20–2, 29, 117, 176, 193,
   203–4, 222, 235, 252
Department of Muslim Affairs, 65,
   91–3, 97, 102, 137–8, 171
Dinar, 181, 213, 222
Directorate for Settlement of Tribes
   and Refugees, 50, 60
Dragoumis, Ion, 4, 82, 85–6, 116
Dramalı Mahmut Bey, 195

Eastern Mediterranean, 36, 269
Edremit, 59, 99, 109, 123, 141, 155,
   221, 235
Emin Süreyyâ (Sabitzâde), 29, 148
Enver Pasha, 45–6, 52, 55, 77, 198,
   210, 212, 221, 267
Ergatis, 47
Estia, 146
Ethniki Amyna (National Defence
   League), 110, 124
Evangeliki Scholi, 139, 150, 156
Extraordinary Court Martial, 89,
   99–102, 122, 149

Ferit Bey, 256
Fevzi (Toker) Bey, 178, 267
Fraternal Society for Reserve
   Officers,166–7, 199, 201, 234
Free Nationalist Party, 169

Gallipoli campaign, 56, 59, 229
General Directorate for Refugees, 67,
   75, 200, 267

George, Prince of Greece and
   Denmark, 85
Giraud, Edmund, 250
Gökalp, Mehmet Ziya, 41–3
Gooding, Lt, 70, 80
Göztepe, 126, 155, 259
Greco-Ottomanism, 84
Greece, 4, 6, 17, 19, 23, 48–9,
   53, 59–60, 70, 77, 82–8, 90,
   92–3, 95, 98–9, 106, 111–12,
   114–17,122, 128, 135, 143,
   145, 150, 165, 174, 176, 202,
   205, 207, 244, 246–8, 250, 254,
   257–8, 262–3, 265–6
Greek, 1–2, 4–13, 15–30, 33–6,
   38–39, 42, 44–53, 57–64, 66–71,
   73, 75, 77–161, 163, 165–93,
   195–212, 214–33, 235–7,
   239–48, 250–2, 254–6, 258–60,
   262–8
Greek Administration of Smyrna, 4,
   10, 88, 94, 96–7, 117, 137–8,
   147–8, 150–1, 185
Greek Orthodox, 2, 24–6, 33, 35, 38,
   44, 47–8, 50, 52–3, 59–61, 66,
   68–70, 79, 83, 86, 89–90, 110,
   113, 115, 118, 126, 130, 133,
   139–42, 152, 154–5, 175–7, 185,
   222, 229, 241, 264–5
Greek Red Cross, 128–9, 133, 135

Hacı Mustafa Efendi, 180
Hacim Muhittin, 202–5, 222, 226,
   231–2
Hadji Davud Farkoh, 57, 74
Hafız İsmail, 256
Halide Edip, 201, 205
Halil Zeki, 109, 149
Hamdullah Subhi (Tanrıöver), 79, 226
Hare, Robert Hugh, 172
Harlow, Samuel Ralph, 94
Hasan Fikret, 177, 224
Hasan Pasha, Hacı, 109, 112–13, 119,
   256

Index

Hasan Tahsin, 63, 157
Haydar Rüştü Öktem, 63, 147, 156
Hellenes (Greek nationals), 47–8, 84, 86, 100, 171, 235
High Commission of Smyrna, 8, 10, 33, 65, 71, 82, 87–99, 101–7, 109–11, 113–15, 118–23, 128, 131, 133–50, 153, 163, 170–1, 175, 182–3, 185–6, 189, 207, 255–6, 263, 266
   Department of Education, 97, 137, 141, 143, 154–5
   Administration of Muslim Schools, 137–8
   Department of Finances, 97, 105, 121, 123
   Department of the Interior, 97
   Department of Muslim Affairs, 65, 93, 97, 102, 137–8, 171
   Department of Public Health, 92, 97, 128, 133, 135
   Department of Repatriation and Rehabilitation, 92, 106, 109, 123
   General Secretariat, 92, 97, 102, 123
Hodder, Ben, 70, 80, 180–1, 193
Hüseyin Aziz (Akyürek), 245, 267
Hüsnü Bey, 5, 8, 175–8, 191, 255

İbrahim (Turhan) Bey, 245
İbrahim Ethem Bey, 177, 195, 221
İhsan Lâtif (Sökmen) Pasha, 252
Ilinden Uprising, 44
Imperial Ottoman Bank, 93, 105 252
İnönü, İsmet, 227, 253–4, 257, 259
Inter-Allied boards, 91, 114
   Inter Allied Board of Censors (IBC), 146–8 Inter-Allied Commission of Exports, 104
   Inter-Allied Commission of Inquiry, 172–3, 182, 187
   Inter-Allied Commission of the Railways, 109
Internal Macedonian Revolutionary Organisation (IMRO), 44

Ioachim/Yovakim (Vafiedis), 176–7
Ioakeimoglou, Georgios, 143–4, 156
Ionian University of Smyrna, 124, 128, 143–4, 146, 156
İsmail Hakkı, 8, 113
Italy, 4, 40, 48, 54, 73, 87, 147, 172, 205–6, 262
İzmir Association of Defence of Ottoman Rights, 163, 174, 198–202, 207–8, 231

Jewish, 5, 21, 27, 37, 101, 112–13, 119, 124, 126, 133, 142–3, 165, 167, 182, 201, 219, 241, 243
Johnston, Capt M. A. B., 108, 256, 263

Kalkandelenli Tahsin, 164
Kara Vâsıf, 210–11, 232, 257
Karaburun, 24, 51, 53, 69, 96, 106
Kasaba, 27, 96, 112, 119, 124, 130, 176–8, 216
Kâzım Fikrî (Özalp), 175–6, 199, 214–15, 226
Kâzım Karabekir, 197, 267
Kesisoglou, Theologos, 145
Kilizman, 60
Koçarlı, 181, 216
Koçgiri rebellion, 241
Kolettis, Ioannis, 83
Konak (neighbourhood), 81, 95, 101, 126, 133, 152, 241
Kosmos, 146
Kritika, 161, 176
Kritikos, Nikolaos, 145
Kula, 98–9, 156, 191, 222
Kurdish, 14, 32, 39, 41, 161, 187–8, 192, 241
Kurds, 42–3, 106, 109, 145, 186–7, 197, 205, 261

Labour battalions, 60, 78, 259
Lamb, Harry, 102, 121–2, 124, 235–6, 240, 259

Ethnic Cleansing in Western Anatolia

Laporte, Osmin, 157, 206
Lausanne Peace Treaty, 11, 248, 253–4
Le Bon, Charles-Marie Gustave, 40, 71
League of Nations, 87, 94–5, 185, 252, 262
Leghorn, 21
Levantines, 26–8, 37, 56, 122, 131–2, 206, 230, 249–50, 253
List, Friedrich, 4
Lloyd George, David, 17, 110, 113
local correspondence office (tahrîrât müdürü), 178
Lowther, Gerald Augustus, 49, 74–5

Macedonia, 47, 51, 64, 86, 109, 117, 178, 267
Mahmut Celâl (Bayar) Bey, 46, 55, 67, 79, 159, 163, 199, 208, 217, 235
Mahmut Şevket Pasha, 44 Makronisi, 56
Manisa, 5, 8, 20, 22, 25–7, 57, 67, 71, 77, 92, 96, 119, 133, 136, 175–8, 191, 204, 216, 252–3
Manisa Bank of Grape Farmers, 57
Marseille, 21, 28
Megali Idea, 4, 83–7, 116, 198, 229
Mehmet Ali (Gerede) Bey, 169–70
Mehmet Cavit, 42, 49, 72, 257
Mehmet Fuat (Köprülü), 42
Mehmet Refet, 256, 263
Mehmet VI Vahdeddin, Sultan, 30, 66, 161–2, 255
Menderes (River), 25, 172, 217, 228
Menemen, 14, 25–6, 51, 54, 91, 96, 119, 130, 175, 219
Menemen Incident, 14
Menemenlizâde Muvaffak, 198, 231
Military Occupation Zone, 88–9, 97–9, 105, 123, 178
Millet, 8, 26–7, 39, 84, 118
millî, 42–3, 58, 158, 195–7
Mills, Minnie, 242

Milne Line, 177, 226
Ministry of Foreign Affairs (Greek), 4, 237, 263
Ministry of Foreign Affairs (Ottoman), 101, 161–2, 187, 256, 262
Ministry of Justice (Greek), 84
Ministry of Justice (Ottoman), 101, 255
Ministry of Pious Endowments (Evkaf Nâzırı), 93, 161
Ministry of the Exchange, Reconstruction and Resettlement, 247
Ministry of the Interior (Greek), 113
Ministry of the Interior (Ottoman), 52, 54–5, 66, 68, 70, 79, 92, 94, 101, 117–19, 161, 169–74, 181–2, 191, 193, 200, 203–4, 211, 221, 235–6, 255
Mitakos, Konstantinos, 102
Mithat Şükrü (Bleda), 257
Molinary, Charles, 250
Moralızâde Halit Bey, 166, 198, 200
Moralızâde Nâil Bey, 198–200, 202, 207–8
Morgan, James, 79–80, 115, 118–19, 121–2, 124, 164–8, 170–1, 190, 232–3, 236
Mount Sinai Monastery, 244
Mufti Abdürrahim, 8
Müsavat, 5, 63, 78, 147, 256
Mustafa Abdülhalik (Renda), 65, 248, 251, 267
Mustafa Kemal, 12–13, 30–1, 125, 158, 196–7, 205, 210–11, 223–4, 227, 237, 241, 244–6, 257–9
Mustafa Necâtî (Uğurel), 166, 200
Mustafa Talât Efendi, 202–3
Mütevellizâde Tevfîk Bey, 204, 225

Nâcî Bey, 182–3, 198
Nâîbzâde Ali, 65, 91, 112, 171
narodnik, 41, 71, 200
National Bank of Aydın, 57, 77

Index

National Defence Committee, 58, 77, 211

National Forces (*Kuvâ-yı Milliye*), 93, 101, 106, 119, 160, 172, 174–5, 180–2, 184, 194, 196, 198, 202–5, 208–12, 214–26, 234–6, 255, 263

National Pact (*Mîsâk-ı Millî*), 196

National Schism (*Dichasmos*), 87

National Struggle, 5, 13, 15, 18, 158, 228, 267

Nazilli, 26, 173, 181–2, 193, 202–4, 213, 216–17, 220

Near East Relief, 242, 244

Nider, Konstantinos, 147, 172

Nureddin İbrahim Pasha, 30, 64–7, 70, 162, 175, 198–200, 206, 230, 240–2, 246, 251

Nutuk, 12, 30

Ödemiş, 26, 70, 96, 119, 171, 208, 211, 213, 216–17

Odessa, 21, 25

Ömer Lûtfî (Argeşo), 224–5

Omerion School for Girls, 139

Oriental Carpet Manufacturers Ltd, 250, 261

Ottoman Empire, 1, 10, 14–15, 17, 20, 25–7, 29, 31–2, 35, 38, 40–3, 45, 47, 52, 54–7, 62, 64, 72, 84–5, 87, 94, 106, 110, 112–13, 126, 131, 135, 150, 153, 156, 158, 169, 172, 174, 187, 204–5, 207, 213, 264

Ottoman Greeks, 4, 25, 42, 44, 46, 48, 52, 58, 60, 64, 68–71, 73, 77, 85, 89–90, 98, 106–9, 130–2, 139, 141, 151, 158, 160, 163, 166, 168, 170–1, 180, 185, 193, 197, 212, 220–3, 237, 242, 246–8, 262, 265

Ottoman lira, 103

Ottoman Peace and Welfare Party, 79, 169

Ottoman Public Debt Administration (OPDA), 69, 105, 123, 138, 230

Ottoman Railway Company, 55, 76, 123, 220

Ottomanism, 16, 39, 41, 50, 84

Palamidas, Kostas, 48

Panionios, 131

Paparrigopoulos, Konstantinos, 84

Paradiso, 82, 142

Paris Peace Conference, 87, 106, 143, 162–3, 165, 169, 172, 188, 190, 205, 208, 233, 236

Parvus Efendi, 42

Patriarchate of Constantinople, 59, 70, 90, 118, 244

population exchange, 11, 45, 156, 238–9, 244, 246–8, 258, 260, 265

Prefects (*eparchoi*), 92

Prentiss, Mark O., 242, 259

Progressive Republican Party (Terakkiperver Cumhuriyet Fırkası), 14

Protopapadakis, Petros, 112

Punta, 133, 153

Ragıp Nurettin (Ege), 166, 189, 200, 214

Rahmetullah Efendi (Çelebioğlu), 59, 97, 109–10, 137–8

Rahmi (Apak), 160, 188, 214

Rahmî Bey (Arslan), 32, 46–7, 56–9, 61, 63–5, 67, 74–9, 124, 144, 207, 211, 215, 235, 257, 267

Rauf (Orbay), 62, 183, 212, 214, 257

Refik Halit (Karay), 17

Regional governors (*nomarchoi*), 92

Renovation Party, 63, 199

Rigas Velestinlis, 82–4, 116

Rıza Nur, 248, 253–4

Rodas, Mihail, 146–50

Royalists, 91, 98

Russia, 23, 32, 41, 48, 55, 59, 73, 84

295

Russo-Ottoman War (of 1877–8), 23–4, 43, 269

Sabri Hoca, 113
Salihli, 98–9, 102, 120–1, 177, 205, 212, 215, 221, 224–5
Salonica, 20, 23, 27, 36, 40–2, 47, 65, 70, 74, 77, 124, 146
Samos, 25, 51, 59, 69, 213, 260
Sapancalı Hakkı, 46
Sazonov, Sergey, 54
Şefik (Aker), 80, 178, 180–1, 192–3, 209, 216–17
Sephardic Jews, 27
Seudikeuy (Sevdikoy), 53
Sèvres Peace Treaty, 65, 87–8, 94–9, 102, 110, 112–14, 120, 150, 175, 178, 183, 185, 255
Sforza, Carlo, 207–8, 233
sharia courts, 86, 97, 100, 102, 120
Sheikh Said Rebellion, 14
Simonyan, Mesrob, 57
Sivas Congress, 224
Skarpetis, Spyros, 182–3
Smaragdos (metropolitan bishop), 180
Smith, Col Ian M., 79–89, 157, 164–6, 190, 231
Smith, Heathcote, 47, 74–5, 106, 123
Smyrna, 2, 4–5, 10–11, 13–14, 17–28, 32–7, 46–9, 51–61, 63–9, 71, 73–6, 79–83, 87–98, 100–7, 109–15, 117–22, 124, 126–8, 130–44, 146–61, 163–7, 169–175, 177–81, 183–5, 187–90, 193, 195, 197–202, 204–7, 209, 211–14, 216–17, 223, 228–40, 242–3, 255–63, 267–9
Smyrna Quay, 25, 68, 81, 113, 158, 242, 245, 250
Smyrna Sultânî Lycée (İzmir Sultânî Mektebi), 137–8, 166, 173, 201
Smyrna Women's Association League, 130

Smyrne-Cassaba et Prolongements, 122, 222–3
Söke, 24, 70, 80, 133, 179, 209, 213
Soma, 98–9, 213, 215, 219, 258
Souliotis-Nikolaïdis, Athanasios, 4, 85–6
Special Organisation (*Teşkîlât-ı Mahsûsa*), 18, 45–6, 70, 73, 184, 210, 212, 215, 218, 256, 265, 267
Spitalia (neighbourhood), 133
Sporting Club, The, 131
Stergiades, Aristides, 10, 18, 82, 88–95, 98, 100, 102, 104–5, 110–12, 118–19, 122–4, 139, 143–4, 148–50, 157, 170–2, 177–8, 183, 189, 191, 194, 216–17, 235–6, 239–40, 258, 266
Subhî Efendi, 65, 118, 175
Sublime Porte, 15, 86, 159, 175, 187, 189
Supreme Military Command, 103, 113
Synadelfos, 146

Tamiolakis, Haralambos, 149
Tatars, 23–4, 41, 145
Theodoridis, Frixos, 145
Thessaly, 83, 86
Thursfield, Henry George, 249, 261
Tire, 27, 96, 119, 213, 216–17
Tobacco Monopoly (Régie des Tabacs), 105, 195, 230
Tourian, Leon, 185
Translation Bureau, 159, 187
Treaty of Adrianople, 84
Treaty of Bucharest, 46
Trieste, 21, 250
Turcoman nomads, 24, 32
    Manavs, 24
    Tahtacıs, 24
Turkey, 1, 5, 7, 9–14, 16, 18–20, 30, 47, 159, 197, 228, 230, 239, 242, 244, 246, 248, 250, 254–6, 258, 264–6

Index

Turkish Hearth (*Türk Ocağı*), 41, 58, 77, 147, 166–7, 200–1
Turkish History Thesis, 11
Türk Yurdu, 41–2

Ulucak, 53–4
Urla, 24–5, 49, 69, 71, 96, 101, 106–7, 139, 171, 209

Vakalopoulos, Georgios, 183, 194
Venizelists, 91, 98
Venizelos, Eleftherios Kyriakou, 86–8, 90, 93, 98, 106, 110, 115–18, 121, 143, 166, 168, 189–90, 216, 229, 233, 246
Vodena, 86

Wangenheim, Hans Freiherr von, 55
Webb, Richard, 191, 229, 231, 237

Whittall, Donald, 82
Wiener Bankverein, 206
Wilson, Woodrow, 87, 176, 205, 219

Xenopoulos, Petros, 49

Yenibahçeli Şükrü (Oğuz), 210, 212
Yeniceköy, 220
Yorgakis, Anastasios, 48
Yörük Ali, 174, 217, 235
Yusuf Akçura, 41, 200
Yusuf İzzet Pasha, 214

Zafeiriou, Nikolaos, 147, 159, 169, 216
Zavitzianos, Konstantinos, 115, 125
Zeki Bey, 94, 120
Ziya Bey, 207